For Karen
"indefinitely"

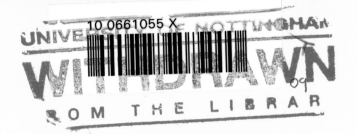

Twentieth-Century Multiplicity

AMERICAN THOUGHT AND CULTURE
Lewis Perry and Howard Brick, Series Editors

Twentieth-Century Multiplicity

American Thought and Culture, 1900–1920

Daniel H. Borus

ROWMAN & LITTLEFIELD PUBLISHERS, INC.
Lanham • Boulder • New York • Toronto • Plymouth, UK

ROWMAN & LITTLEFIELD PUBLISHERS, INC.

Published in the United States of America
by Rowman & Littlefield Publishers, Inc.
A wholly owned subsidiary of The Rowman & Littlefield Publishing Group, Inc.
4501 Forbes Boulevard, Suite 200, Lanham, Maryland 20706
www.rowmanlittlefield.com

Estover Road
Plymouth PL6 7PY
United Kingdom

British Library Cataloguing in Publication Information Available

Library of Congress Cataloging-in-Publication Data:

The hardback edition of this book was previously cataloged by the Library of Congress
as follows:

Borus, Daniel H.
  Twentieth-century multiplicity : American thought and culture, 1900–1920 / Daniel
H. Borus.
      p. cm. — (American thought and culture)
  Includes bibliographical references and index.
  1. Philosophy, American—20th century. 2. United States—Civilization—20th
century 3. Pluralism. I. Title.   *100661055X*
  B936.B67 2009
  191—dc22
                                                                        2008027290

ISBN: 978-0-7425-1506-2 (cloth : alk. paper)
ISBN: 978-0-7425-1507-9 (pbk. : alk. paper)
ISBN: 978-0-7425-6458-9 (electronic)

Printed in the United States of America

∞™ The paper used in this publication meets the minimum requirements of
American National Standard for Information Sciences—Permanence of Paper
for Printed Library Materials, ANSI/NISO Z39.48-1992.

~

Contents

~

Foreword

Twenty years ago, this series in the History of American Thought and Culture began with the aim of offering concise, provocative volumes that, taken together, would survey the long span of American intellectual and cultural life from the 16th century to the present. Since then, the output of richly documented monographs in the field has continued to grow, sustaining the demand for inventive historical syntheses. The goal of the series has always been to bring together books that are readable and well informed and that stand on their own as introductions to significant periods in American thought and culture. There is no attempt to establish a single interpretation of all of America's past, for the diversity, conflict, and change that are features of the American experience would frustrate any such attempt. All the authors in the series, innovative practitioners in the field in their own right, bring their own independent research to bear as they strive for a broad reach in interpretation. They aim to explore issues that are of critical importance to the particular period under discussion and, on that basis, to cast new light on the whole of American experience as it shaped that time and was transformed by it.

The series now nears completion with the publication of this and three other forthcoming volumes treating discrete periods of the twentieth century. The culture and intellectual life of the United States remain subjects of heated debate. Scholars of the mid-twentieth century often assumed that the country bore a common culture that could be summed up in a few basic themes or characteristic dilemmas. By the 1980s, historians were more likely to recognize a plurality of thoughts and traditions in the American past.

Diversity and conflict among the multiple strands of American consciousness made it difficult to achieve a synthetic view of the culture in times past. Nonetheless, tension between the many and the one continues to preoccupy historical observers. Few historians today are likely to challenge a strong emphasis on diversity among subcultures in American life. At the same time, the international primacy this country has attained—for example, as a purveyor of mass culture or the vanguard of a "war on terror"—again poses the question of what collective identity or cultural wholeness Americans share. As the U.S. looks out on the world at large, and the world looks back, who are "we"?

Daniel Borus's book examines a formative moment in the American ability to face these questions. The principle of "multiplicity" he sees giving a special cast to the first two decades of the twentieth century went well beyond the idea of accepting and celebrating American demographic variety—not an utterly new idea by itself. Rather, Borus finds a growing sense that singular, self-evident definitions of truth, beauty, and good could no longer provide a secure, meaningful orientation in the world. This sensibility struck some as a breath of fresh air permitting inquiry, experiment, and change; for others, it represented a vertiginous unmooring of existence. Henry Adams was only one of the more extreme worriers who sensed that change and variety, indeed the accelerating speed of experience uncontained by familiar limits, would ultimately (and perhaps not too far in the future) dissipate the energy that the nation and its people could muster to face a challenging reality. Others such as Gertrude Stein suggested on the contrary that a new vitality arose precisely from the encounters and interactions of different persons, groups, and perspectives, all of which made up a "world" wider than familiar American custom. The onset of modernist arts, the playfulness of newspaper comic strips, the agony of the social relations and politics bound up with "race" in the United States: all these indicated that existence was profoundly unsettled and unsettling, for better or worse. War in 1917 served to suppress the appreciation of multiplicity and "transnational" ideals, to demand cultural unity once again. To be sure, the renewed politics of national purpose could hardly straighten all the crooked paths in the multiple reality of American life. The historian faces the challenge, nonetheless, not to simplify things but still to make sense of them. In his bold account of multiplicity at the start of the twentieth century, Borus brings remarkable clarity to a scene as tumultuous as any in the experience of the United States.

Howard Brick and Lewis Perry, Series Editor

~

Introduction:
Twentieth-Century Multiplicity

Historians often maintain that change marks every period of the past, but Americans on the eve of the Great War had reason to note that the transformations since Appomattox had been especially intense and far-reaching. Most visible were changes in material life. Such objects as automobiles, electric lighting, skyscrapers, telephones, and movies—none of which had existed half a century earlier—dominated the American landscape by the second decade of the twentieth century. Striking too was the degree to which the country had developed institutions of mass production and consumption. Instead of shops, factories made the bulk of goods. An increasing number of the burgeoning new goods and services were available in department stores, a phenomenon most Americans living in 1860 did not know. Accompanying such economic and cultural changes were transformations in long-standing work routines and traditional notions of property. Change extended to the nature of the American population itself. The migration from country to city, and the "second wave" of immigration from Southern and Eastern Europe, Mexico, and Asia, reconfigured the United States as more urban and ethnically and religiously diverse than it had been. Also prominent in the post–Civil War alterations was the emergence of a more interventionist federal government that asserted greater regulatory powers at home and advanced imperial claims in the Philippines and in the Caribbean Basin abroad. Nor were gender relations static. The erosion of the idea of separate spheres for the sexes and of received understanding of femininity struck at relations many Americans had believed natural and permanent. Even harder to measure with any precision but nonetheless noted by Americans was a changing cultural constellation that placed new value on individual pleasure, expression, and experimentation rather than on work, duty, and conformity. Taken as a whole, these changes were signposts of a larger transformation that historians have designated as modernity.[1]

Not all Americans found modernity congenial. Discomfort, however, did not negate the necessity of apprehending the new modes of life, and intellectual discourses and cultural practices responded accordingly. Although some Americans believed that the established understandings remained viable, a significant number of men and women who came to prominence in the early twentieth century regarded the presuppositions of much nineteenth-century thought and culture as ill suited for the new reality. In varying ways, the pragmatism of William James and John Dewey, the cinematic art of Charlie Chaplin and D. W. Griffith, the dancing of Isadora Duncan, the cultural anthropology of Franz Boas and Elsie Clews Parsons, the political pluralism of Arthur Bentley, the aesthetic and political rebellion of the Young Intellectuals of Greenwich Village, the forthright declaration of racial justice by W. E. B. Du Bois and Ida B. Wells, Catholic modernism, Alfred Stieglitz's photography, John Commons's institutional economics, and George Mead's social psychology—all aimed at refurbishing the intellectual and cultural tools with which Americans made sense of their world. The extent to which change was on the agenda may be gauged by the number of endeavors that practitioners championed as "new." There were movements for a new poetry, physics, women, Negroes, socialism, morality, theology, and history, among others.[2]

The new presented a distinct challenge to those who subscribed to the unique mixture of practical idealism, progress, and Arnoldian notions of culture as the best that was thought and said in the world. In the developments of the early twentieth century, the men and women whom the historian Henry May has labeled "cultural custodians" detected the discarding of basic truths and morals, the endorsement of the less attractive aspects of the self, the jettisoning and the destruction of accepted canons of beauty. Established critics and analysts feared that impulse would replace bodily restraint and rationality as a cultural lodestone. Such efforts to remake cultural and intellectual life, they charged, demonstrated a disregard for the clear distinctions between the acceptable and right, on the one hand, and the unacceptable and wrong on the other. In their more excitable moments, genteel commentators saw in the new discourses and practices a coordinated endeavor to overturn long-standing principles of civilization that affected even former presidents. Writing in the midst of the hotly contested election campaign of

1912, the *Nation* wondered if there was a connection between the emotional and unseemly nature of Roosevelt's third-party campaign and outbreaks of irrationality in philosophy and art.[3]

The *Nation* prided itself on its "sane conservatism," but others in the cultural and intellectual elite were worried less about change as such than about the kind of change that they discerned in the new developments. Dominant opinion had long regarded the United States as a vehicle of progress, developing according to well-established overarching principles that resulted not only in material and moral betterment, but also in unity and harmony.[4] Civilization rested on such harmony, yet much of the "new" avoided and even shunned formulations that offered singular explanations. Many of the discourses made no pretense that they aimed to resolve complications and contradictions or that they provided ultimate answers. Instead, they offered temporary, contingent, or provisional understandings. The historian Henry Adams termed the condition in which the piecemeal dominated "multiplicity." Adams had originally attached the subtitle *A Study in Twentieth-Century Multiplicity* to his famous *Education*, indicating that he regarded his own life as a prime example of the phenomenon.[5] Well aware that his famous lineage, which included two presidents, set him apart, Adams nonetheless reckoned that his struggles to understand the world were a specific instance of a more general condition. It was, in part, for this reason that he wrote of "Adams," rather than of "I" or "me," observing himself from the outside and abjuring in-depth explorations of "Adams's" emotional life. The story that Adams tells is the story of how the promise of the eighteenth-century principles of unity and order crashed and burned by the twentieth. Enlightenment discourses took for granted that the world was harmonious and balanced, operating under the rule of comprehensive law. Few schooled in eighteenth-century precepts doubted that the disparate observations about the world would eventuate in general unifying principles and all-encompassing syntheses. The Enlightenment world was one governed by overarching truths, unqualified morals, and universal standards of beauty. As such, it could be reliably measured and ultimately known in all its aspects.

Ironically, improved modes of measurement in many fields of inquiry did little to reduce uncertainties. In matters ranging from number theory to dispersion of energy, expected results failed to materialize. At times, observers wondered if the act of measurement itself introduced disturbances into systems or obscured other phenomena, a point that would be explored more fully in investigation of subatomic particles as well as sociological forays into uncharted urban neighborhoods.[6] As a result, Adams thought it unlikely that there was a unity to the world. We lived, he concluded, in a probabilistic world, one that did not develop in an orderly fashion but was instead engulfed in flux. That flux was a direct consequence of the laws of thermodynamics. Opting for the wisdom of physics rather than a melioristic and optimistic reading of biology, Adams was particularly impressed with the tendency of systems toward energy dispersion in the long run. He concluded that the theory of degradation was written into the fabric of existence. Rather than a *universe* in which things held together, the law of degeneration stipulated a *multiverse* in which particular things seemed unconnected and ungrounded. Adams conjectured that the loss of energy made less of it available to enforce order. Efforts to stem multiplicity would, he feared, only increase illusion and exacerbate alienation from truth. He foresaw an impending entropic heat death in which the world achieved the negative unity of steady state dissipation of energy, placing the date of this disaster in 1921. In the meantime, his reading of the meaning of the new science led him to insist that humans could not comprehend the increasing fragmentation and disunity of things. Humanity's condition was one of "endless displacement," Adams declared. "Chaos," he opined, "was the law of nature; Order was the dream of man" (451, 455). Under such circumstances, the goal of writing a scientific history, which Adams had long entertained, seemed fruitless.

Whether Adams fully understood the implications for physical phenomena of the laws he cited is a matter of some dispute. Critics have observed that the second law of thermodynamics results in the steady state that Adams feared only if unobstructed. Adams generalized too quickly from the closed systems of physics to the real world, where in fact forces that centralize and replenish energy limit diffusion. Entropy is a tendency rather than an inevitability. Even more controversial, of course, is his equation of human systems with physical ones. Here, challengers to Adams point to the entirely different quality of energy, the absence of closed systems for which the second law was derived, and the ability of humans, as opposed to atoms, to reason, as limited a faculty as it may in fact be.[7]

We need not accept Adams's physics or his pessimism to grant validity to his contention that a culture of unity was a prominent feature of nineteenth-century life. For many cultured Americans, finding harmony among disparate phenomena was something of a reflex. No matter how confusing, anomalous, or even horrendous an event or condition, the accepted protocol was to search out the general law at work. Underneath complexity, there was order. Thus, Herbert Spencer, the English polymath who was highly influential in the United States in the late nineteenth century, could declare that the direction of change was toward increasing heterogeneity but be assured that this unfolding would lead to increased rather than decreased social cohesion.

What historian Theodore Porter has termed "statistical thinking" relied upon similar assumptions. In compiling records of the incidence of what were ostensibly independent acts of autonomous individuals, statisticians discovered regularities in the aggregate. Such behavior as suicides and marriages occurred at standard rates. Variation and error there indeed were, but they occurred in predictable and knowable patterns, as the famous bell curve attests. The discovery of standard deviations allowed statistical thinkers to bracket particulars, assured of rule-bound behavior as a whole.[8]

Statisticians were not the only ones in the nineteenth century who regarded contingencies as secondary to the generation of knowledge and the production of beauty. The major discourses of aesthetics and morals assumed an integrated field. The pursuit of culture under the terms set down by the English critic Matthew Arnold, the ethics that derived from the work of the German philosopher Immanuel Kant, and the laws of classical political economy all asserted that particular states or processes were but components of central, universal laws or principles. The applicability of such principles did not depend on conditions or circumstances. Unexpected outcomes that varied with circumstances were often excluded from discourse and treated as exogenous. Treating contingency as friction ensured that the particular did not interfere with the ultimate unity. Arnoldians, for instance, wanted perfect form that evoked a spirituality beyond time and place. The purpose of culture, they held, was to see things steadily and see them whole. Kantian ethics, for its part, treated morality as acts beyond interest. Indeed, Kantians and neo-Kantians conceived moral law as universal, structured so as to guide moral agents to the right action in every possible situation. Classical and neoclassical political economics assumed something of an orthodoxy by insisting that markets operated in accordance with natural laws that produced their optimal outcomes when allowed to operate without interference. Because mainstream models did not anticipate the permanent existence of depressions, monopoly pricing, and labor unions, the leading economists regarded them as abnormal irregularities, best bracketed or dismissed as unnatural.

The unity proposition complemented other prominent philosophical positions in the nineteenth century. Many who believed in an integrated world saw a justification for their universalism, the position that laws and principles applied to all members of a class. Likewise, unity undergirded much absolutism and objectivism in nineteenth-century American life. That phenomena were independent and valid regardless of the perception of observers was a proposition that enabled many thinkers to talk of general principles and laws. This complex of positions bequeathed to a segment of American thought and culture an air of certainty. It was the certainty of the culture of unity that a growing number of Americans found unwarranted in the early twentieth century. Their efforts to understand the extent to which unity truly characterized the world ushered in the moment of multiplicity.[9]

By using Adams's subtitle, I mean to argue the admittedly ironic contention that multiplicity gave coherence and meaning to the development of thought and culture in the years between 1900 and 1920. In many branches of knowledge, the significant trend was away from a single standard of evaluation or unified truth. The new cultural orientation tilted toward pluralism, retreating from the position that the world hung together with the same perfect cohesion that beautiful objects were said to possess. For some inquiries and practices, multiplicity meant loosening the hold of determinism. For others, it entailed a rejection of the possibility of universalism. For still others, it meant denying the possibility that phenomena could be unconditioned or that perspective did not matter. The result for the culture as a whole was a proliferation of truths, goods, and beauties. This proliferation prompted a signature attitude that life in all its fullness was not explicable by any single theory. Life was messy, and theory, however useful, did not fully comprehend it. The writer and critic Walter Lippmann insinuated as much when he contended that life bore a "fantastic resemblance to a cubist painting." For Lippmann, as for a significant number of men and women for whom multiplicity formed their basic outlook on the world, abstract theorizing meant being confined by the "stiff and solid frames of thought" that obscured the "subtlety of life." In pinpointing subtlety, Lippmann in effect contrasted the tendency of older discourses and practices to culminate in generalization with the newer emphasis on greater recognition of distinction and difference.[10]

Multiplicity held no monopoly over the intellectual and cultural life of the early twentieth century. Rather than constituting a transformation once and for all from a culture permeated with unity to one infused with multiplicity, the first two decades of the twentieth century were ones in which the momentum and impetus fell to positions that resisted singularity of evaluation. Even at its most pronounced, the notion of plural standards rarely swept the field. Its targets were never fully routed, retaining the allegiances of broad swathes of the American people. Classical and neoclassical economics, the absolutist philosophy of Josiah Royce, and the "one best way" approach of scientific management under Frederick Winslow Taylor were and continued to be prominent mainstays of American thought and culture. Those who promulgated positions of multiplicity always had to contend not only with old and established absolutist and unity perspectives, but also with ones developed during the period. As we shall see, racial thought dedicated to solitary explanations was particularly vibrant during the first two decades of the twentieth century. In addition, the dominance of multiplicity proved to be no more permanent than that of unity had been. Many who undertook forays into multiplicity did so temporarily or provisionally, exploring with an eye toward new syntheses.

Emphasis on the many rather than the one did not suddenly appear full-blown in the first decades of the twentieth century. Multiplicity had long contended with unity as an approach to knowledge. A number of pre-Socratic Greek philosophers had seen flux and numbers as more indicative of the world than was unity. Cratylus, for instance, maintained that diversity was so dominant that reason could not grasp it. Even the fabled unity of nineteenth-century thought was much less monolithic than some accounts would have it. The growing current of atheism and the constant reportage of anomalies to general principles in the sciences were significant instances of multiplicity in the nineteenth century. So too was the persistence of philosophical nominalism, which held that only particular things existed, and the view of John Stuart Mill and Wilhelm Dilthey that different kinds of knowledge existed, each with its own validity and mode of apprehension. By the last decade of the century, the United States even had a decadent movement and a group of professional cynics appearing in the public prints.[11] Not until the early twentieth century, however, did multiplicity garner culture-wide significance. Where once it had been the position of small coteries, on the eve of the Great War the idea of many truths, goods, and beauties was a commonplace in nearly every discourse and practice, even if it was never completely accepted.

Multiplicity owed its prominence in the early twentieth century to the widely shared effort to account for contingency. Rather than downplay or dismiss conditions and circumstances as incomplete or "disturbing" factors, the new discourses of multiplicity explored them. Context mattered in physics, the social sciences, and the arts in ways that it had not before. Even fields of inquiry that retained elements of unitary and universal principles accepted the import of specific conditions. Freudian analysis, for instance, insisted on the universality of drives and desires, yet interpretation and treatment depended on the discovery of the ways in which circumstances and fortuitous events shaped the nature of the self.[12] Likewise, another development that did not accept "the cubist view of life," progressivism, for all the commitment of most practitioners to a belief in a uniform direction of history, drew coherence from its recognition that the economy did not function harmoniously when left unattended but required attention to contingent conditions.

We might get a sense of the scope of the new explorations by attending to the manifold meanings of the word *contingency*. Depending on usage, the word indicates something liable but not certain to occur, a result that depends on a specific condition or conditions (as in "the contract is contingent on her agreement"), a fortuitous occurrence, or a proposition not universally true. If some of the new discourses and practices emphasized dependency on condition, others stressed chance. Some, such as the new depth psychology or institutional economics, came to a sense of multicausal explanations or conditional truths as a consequence of a resolve to sharpen understanding of specific determinants of phenomena. Others, such as the vitalist currents in the arts and certain portions of the pragmatism of William James, adopted multiplicity in order to embrace open-ended possibilities that proponents thought had been denied by the restrictive and determinative character of discourses and practices that sought abstract, general truths. The emphasis on fortuitousness and the stress on dependency on condition were not necessarily incompatible. One could as easily maintain that multiple outcomes resulted from the action of many determinants as one could assert that meaningful or necessary determination was nonexistent. Attending to contingency made for diffuse developments.

Not surprisingly, perhaps, twentieth-century multiplicity was a multifaceted affair. At times, it was as blooming and buzzing as vitalists maintained all of existence was. Readers should not expect to find unanimity among its major participants. There was no multiplicity party, no multiplicity manifesto. Emphasis on contingency did not guarantee agreement on political, social, and philosophical issues. Not all whose work contributed to an understanding of the world as a multiverse gleaned liberation or promise in multiplicity. Some still devoted themselves (blithely and unjustifiably in Adams's pessimistic view) to reconstruction, albeit on less absolute foundations. The differences among the agents of multiplicity could be stark. Aesthetic modernists and those biblical critics who stressed the context of the writing of the text rather than its transcendent universality had little common ground. Few philosophical pragmatists appreciated jazz or cubism before the war, if they even knew of either. Despite efforts of Greenwich Village bohemians to link radical art and radical politics, artistic endeavors of twentieth-century multiplicity rarely fit comfortably with the politics. As historians have documented, the alliance scuttled on differing views of science, collective action, and the purposes of art. If the journalist Hutchins Hapgood could discern the photographer Alfred Stieglitz and the Wobbly "Big Bill" Haywood as part of a common program to "dynamite the baked and hardened earth so that fresh flowers can grow," the two themselves found little on which to agree.[13]

Introduction ~ 9

Some of the challenges to the culture of unity began rather modestly as efforts to fill in gaps in knowledge, settle nagging questions, and explain deviations from the norm. As investigators in geology, biology, the physics of gases, and mathematics encountered difficulties and anomalies, and exceptions continued to pile up, many scientists began to question the basic assumptions of their fields. As William Everdell has pointed out, the new hypothesis emphasized discontinuity and distinctiveness rather than continuity and the ability of phenomena to be subsumed under general principles.[14]

Such challenges to paradigms took place in the context of political and social uncertainties. Whether internal problems would have forced shifts by themselves remains hotly contested in the history of science, but in the early twentieth century, "internalist" doubts coexisted with political and social conditions that made certainty about progress and harmony of the existing setup more difficult to sustain. Few observers doubted the material advances that had been at the core of notions of the seamless progress of history, but a number grew increasingly concerned about the persistence of conflict, which much theory had predicted would dissipate. A roller-coaster economy of booms and busts, and fierce class and ethnic clashes that intensified rather than dissipated over time, all contributed to the sense that something was out of kilter. For no less a figure than Herbert Spencer, the social violence in the form of imperialism caused consternation, precisely because his notion of evolutionary unity had regarded such use of force as outmoded. Many could take recourse in regarding such problems as temporary or as caused by the famed exogenous or disturbing factors. Others, however, doubted the viability of the culture of unity and turned to multiplicity because it seemed a better approximation of the climate in which they lived.

Some challenges to prevailing unities were overt, deliberate efforts to change history and reality as well as to apprehend it. For women and African Americans, nineteenth-century syntheses of social life tended to work against their exercise of full citizenship rights. Much prevailing social thought equated white and male with human, treating female and black interests as somehow particular, partial, and incomplete. Much of the collective agitation from feminist and civil rights groups aimed simultaneously at the recognition of difference and at the inclusion of previously marginalized and degraded groups, embracing pluralism and hoping for a new unity in which they too would be included. Although legal segregation and social custom mediated against full-blown success in our period, the conscious efforts of women and blacks to dismantle understandings that assigned them firm and inferior places was yet another reason that multiplicity was the keynote of early-twentieth-century cultural and intellectual life.

We would be remiss if we regarded early-twentieth-century multiplicity as a version of late-twentieth-century postmodernism. If early-twentieth-century thinkers regarded truth as partial and particular, they drew the line at seeing it as arbitrary. The antifoundationalism of early-twentieth-century multiplicity was an effort to find modest truths, not to expose the interested power behind any warranted assertion. That truth could prevail in one situation but not in another framework did not invalidate the concept of truth—just its claim to ultimate foundation. Few of the early-twentieth-century writers and thinkers who form the basis of this study thought that by abandoning Truth with a capital "T" they were putting quotation marks around the entire word. By the same token, the indeterminism of early-twentieth-century multiplicity tended more often than not to be a matter of allowing for numerous outcomes rather than viewing chance as so prevalent that all guidelines were blind stabs at order. Few of the thinkers and artists who fostered twentieth-century multiplicity went as far as Henry Adams did in his bleaker moments and treated multiplicity as the equivalent of chaos that went all the way down. Nor was twentieth-century multiplicity so intent on the manifold nature of the world that it saw only particulars that were incapable of synthesis. If truths did not unite into one, it did not follow that they did not unite at all. Veblenian social science, to take one example, was hardly timid about generalization, even as it made adaptation to circumstances in production and distribution its cardinal point of departure.

Taken on its own terms and placed in its own context, a focus on the fortunes of multiplicity in American thought and culture offers the prospect of viewing the much-studied early twentieth century from another angle. Multiplicity is not an all-purpose explanation for the new discourses and practices of the early twentieth century. It does not necessarily settle once and for all old debates. Investigating how Americans handled contingency does, however, provide important ways to understand how Americans conceptualized their world. In putting heterogeneity and pluralism at the center of our exploration, we will get a better handle on the issues that defined the moment. Looking for the uses of multiplicity will enable us to see old phenomena in new ways. We might come to understand progressive ideology as something more than about perfecting social bonds or patching things up. We will even be able to glean resemblances that we might not have otherwise fully recognized. A position on multiplicity, for instance, does not necessarily divide Victorians from moderns. If in other respects, the two were distinctly separate types, a commitment to multiplicity was not characteristic of all modernists or unknown among those regarded (and who regarded themselves) as Victorians.

Multiplicity can be an amorphous concept, but understanding it is immensely aided by recalling Isaiah Berlin's distinction between the hedgehogs,
those who knew one thing, and the foxes, thinkers who knew many things
without trying to fit them into an all-embracing unitary vision. The early
twentieth century was the moment of the foxes, even if there were quite a
few hedgehogs. It is salutary to recall that Berlin saw the value of and need
for both.[15] These days, hedgehogs are out of favor, at least in many circles.
Hedgehogs are associated with universalist propositions and are inclined to
envision things like clashes of civilizations and see political struggles as existential ones. Their opponents have roundly criticized them for ignoring or reducing all particulars to their chosen universal theme and for needlessly worrying that any recognition of multiplicity leads to a debilitating relativism.
Yet, for all their propensity toward single, encompassing narratives and explanations, hedgehogs call our attention to the connections between seemingly unlike things. Where foxes remind us of the dangers of overgeneraliza-
tion and homogenization, hedgehogs remind us how helpful and at times
necessary significant and meaningful generalizations are. Put another way, I
am not arguing here that multiplicity is necessarily any more descriptive of
reality or always more right than unity.

As significant a change as twentieth-century multiplicity was from the
culture of unity that was dominant in many quarters in the nineteenth century, I am reluctant to label the years of early-twentieth-century multiplicity
as crisis-filled. To be sure, the clashes between the new multiplicity and established notions of a universe were remarkable for their intensity and their
breadth throughout the culture. Defenders of unity, like the editors of the
Nation, did claim that multiplicity would make human endeavor pointless.[16]
Nonetheless, it is not clear that the tensions in American life and the worries and fears that they occasioned among many stalwarts constitute a moment of profound uncertainty that made a way of life no longer viable. Plenty
of Americans, perhaps even blithely, traversed the first two decades of the
century with their identities intact and their sense of the way the world
worked secure. Life, as pragmatism suggests, is a series of disturbances that
force us to decide which course of action will restore equilibrium. To qualify
as a crisis of culture, it seems to me, a historical period must be one in which
achieving equilibrium requires wholesale jettisoning of cultural presumptions. Such wholesale jettisoning did not, to my judgment, happen, despite
the significant and meaningful changes that did occur. I concur with Gail Bederman's dissent from the notion that there was a "crisis" of masculinity at
the turn of the century. Bederman argues that most turn-of-the-century men
never lost confidence that people with male bodies possessed "both a man's

identity and a man's right to wield power," even if they were not certain how bodies, identities, and powers all fit together.[17] Likewise, most Americans never doubted their ideals, even if they were not quite certain how to define and defend them.

Because multiplicity is a matter of our concepts, a matter of how well we think general ideas explain fully the world in which we live, *Twentieth-Century Multiplicity* is an old-fashioned, but I hope still valuable, history of ideas. I aim to explore how principles that had bequeathed a unity to things underwent revision and how Americans responded to the new multiplicity. To that end, I have concentrated on developed thought and culture, with ventures into some of the more innovative popular culture of the period. I have curtailed some of the biographical details of the cast of characters and make little pretense to chart their careers. This is not a survey in the usual sense. It is far from exhaustive, and it makes little pretense that all developments can be explained by reference to the multiplicity/unity contest. In writing a history of ideas, I have concentrated on the discourses that furthered multiplicity rather than on explicating how widespread was its adherence. Therefore, I have accorded Greenwich Village and bohemians less prominence than they have received in other accounts. I have done so not because I think the activities of the circle around the Liberal Club and the *Masses* were insignificant; such folk undertook the absolutely crucial step of attempting to realize others' ideas and to facilitate the production of multiplicity in salons, magazines, and books. Few bohemians, however, originated new understandings. Readers will, however, find the greatest hits here. Pragmatism, that much-studied phenomenon, gets its treatment. So too do relativity theories, the Armory Show, feminism, and Du Bois's *Souls of Black Folk*. They will also find lesser-known but worthy toilers in thought and culture: Winsor McCay, the artist of *Little Nemo's Adventures in Dreamland*; James Branch Cabell, the author of *Jürgen*; Henry Poels, the Catholic theologian; and Elsie Clews Parsons, the feminist anthropologist.

Chapter 1, "Foundations," details how a number of building blocks of nineteenth-century unity fragmented in the early twentieth century. The seemingly stable physical world, the notion of a rock-solid truth, and the existence of unchanging moral precepts were all less settled as a consequence of the new physics, pragmatism, biblical criticism, and vitalism. Chapter 2, "Beauties," addresses the new senses of beauty that accompanied the emergence of the consumer culture of the twentieth century. Where the cultural elite had maintained the beautiful as spiritual, universal, and moral, many artists and critics rejected the old precepts, forging new versions of beauty that were at times plebeian, particular, and even amoral. A consequence of a culture-wide reevaluation of pleasure and new technologies that could deliver it, the aesthetic multiverse made beauty a many-splendored thing and made the reconstruction of aesthetic unity a daunting proposition. Chapter 3, "Selves," maps the alternatives to the conception of the sovereign individual, which was the dominant position of the nineteenth century. The chapter demonstrates how the notion of the social self challenged the self-determining individual, how Freudianism took on notions of individual integration, and how feminism set its sights on the notion that the self was ethereal and disembodied by insisting upon the centrality of gender in the constitution of the self. Chapter 4, "Collectivities," focuses on the changing notions of human association. At issue are the dissent from natural law in economic and social behavior and the centrality of race in determining human groupings. Chapter 5, "War," charts the fate of multiplicity as a cultural logic in the run-up to the Great War and in its aftermath.

A word on terminology. Naming the cast of characters is no easy matter. In one sense, "multiplicitists" describes their project, but it also implies a cohesiveness that was not present; it is ugly, besides. "Advocates of multiplicity" is an awkward phrase but will make an appearance or two. "Rebels" assigns an intention not always there and overestimates the nature of the challenge. "Moderns" has two implications—one useful, one not for my purposes. On the one hand, it connotes the fragmenting, decentralizing aspect of modern industrial life. On the other, those who note that modern industrial life also engendered the countervailing tendency toward centralization and uniformity have a perfectly valid point. Multiplicity does not dominate a modern life that combines the centripetal and the centrifugal. I have used "pluralists" at times, although it does not quite capture the qualities of the innovations. For those for whom multiplicity was an anathema, I have used the term "cultural conservative." It suffers from evoking two qualities that are not always involved: excessive gentility and political conservatism. I mean simply a person who adheres to the dominant evolutionary progressivism that provided a foundation for intellectual and cultural activity. Not all who believed in such foundations were prudish or friends of the political and cultural status quo.

• • •

I owe an enormous debt to the writers who have broken this ground before me. In light of the intellectual and cultural ferment, the early twentieth century has attracted some of the more talented historians and writers. Few other periods can boast of surveys of such depth and perception as Henry May's *End of American Innocence*, David Noble's *Progressive Mind*, James Kloppenberg's *Uncertain Victory*, James Livingston's *Pragmatism and the Political*

Economy of Cultural Revolution, or T. J. Jackson Lears's *No Place of Grace* or such extraordinary treatments of more circumscribed portions of cultural and intellectual life as Dorothy Ross's *Origins of American Social Science*, Robert Westbrook's *John Dewey and American Democracy*, and Casey Blake's *Beloved Community*. It is a measure of the wealth of resources available to a historian working in this period that the historical novels that cover the moment are such treasures of insight. John Dos Passos's *USA*, E. L. Doctorow's *Ragtime*, and Thomas Pynchon's *Against the Day* have been particularly rewarding, since they take as their great subjects, in one form or another, multiplicity. I have long thought of *Twentieth-Century Multiplicity* as an interpretation of this literature, rather than as a challenge to it. Had I put the above works in every note in which they were relevant, the reference section would grow exponentially.

My debts to the editor of the series, Howard Brick, are both professional and personal. For the thirty-plus years of our friendship, he has been the source of enormous intellectual stimulation. What has been true in general has been even more true in the writing of this book. A comment of his in passing about Henry Adams many years ago started me on this path, and his commentary on the manuscript has been penetrating, prompting me to refine the argument, consider opposite viewpoints, and attend to the implications of what I was writing. His support is the epitome of intellectual, as well as personal, friendship, and I am forever in his debt.

It has been my privilege to teach at the University of Rochester. It has allowed me to encounter the work of Jeffrey Brown, John Wenzler, Lisa Szefel, and Karen McCally, authors of four extraordinary dissertations on early-twentieth-century vitalism, political economy, poetry, and reform, respectively. Theirs are clearly cases where the students teach the professor. My colleague Ted Brown explained physics to someone who conspicuously failed to master the subject in high school. My colleague Robert Westbrook has generously offered me countless insights over the years, has patiently aided my understandings in matters ranging from pragmatism to politics, and generally exemplified scholarship at its highest, not to mention possessing the slyest sense of humor in the metropolitan area.

The usual caveats about responsibility apply to the readers of this manuscript. I am grateful for the efforts of Casey Blake, Howard Brick, Lynn Dumenil, Lewis Perry, Dorothy Ross, John Wenzler, and Robert Westbrook, all of whom made the book richer, more precise, and more enjoyable to write than it would have been without their wise counsel.

Rowman and Littlefield has provided truly wonderful help. I have benefitted from the aid of editors Michael McGandy, Asa Johnson, Michelle Cassidy, and Niels Abadoe, the production assistance of Doug English, and the sharp-eyed copyediting of Lisa Williams. I have other debts as well. Stephanie Frontz and Brian Conlon were enormously helpful in tracking down illustrations. Michael Brick did yeoman's service in securing the photograph of the Filipino exhibit at the St. Louis World's Fair. Emily Morry was indispensible in helping to index the book. By continually providing tape and glue, Sean Donohue considerably eased what could have been a "miserable" couple of years.

My family has borne much of the costs of this book. My children, Benjamin and Sarah, have never known a moment when I was not writing it. Although this has at times been hard on them, they have contributed immeasurably to its completion. Every day they have reminded me of two cardinal tenets of multiplicity: there are indeed many truths in this world, and there is no guarantee that there is an inherent order to things.

Finally, to Karen, whose support and encouragement have been intangibles that can never be fully capitalized, I dedicate this book

Notes

1. The story of the transformations of the early twentieth century may be found in John Whiteclay Chambers, *The Tyranny of Change: America in the Progressive Era, 1900–1917*, ed. Vincent P. Carosso (New York: St. Martin's Press, 1980); Steven J. Diner, *A Very Different Age: Americans of the Progressive Era* (New York: Hill and Wang, 1998); Michael E. McGerr, *A Fierce Discontent: The Rise and Fall of the Progressive Movement in America, 1870–1920* (New York: Free Press, 2003); Nell Painter, *Standing at Armageddon: The United States, 1877–1919* (New York: W. W. Norton, 1987); Mark Sullivan, *Our Times: America at the Birth of the Twentieth Century*, edited and abridged (New York: Scribner's, [1926] 1996); and David Traxel, *Crusader Nation: The United States in Peace and the Great War, 1898–1920* (New York: Alfred A. Knopf, 2006). Two diametrically different but superlative efforts to link culture to political economy are T. J. Jackson Lears, *No Place of Grace: Antimodernism and the Transformation of American Culture, 1880–1920* (New York: Pantheon, 1981); and James Livingston, *Pragmatism and the Political Economy of Cultural Revolution, 1850–1940* (Chapel Hill: University of North Carolina Press, 1994).

2. The classic and in many ways still unsurpassed account of the early twentieth-century cultural and intellectual transformation is Henry May, *The End of American Innocence* (New York: Oxford University Press, [1959] 1970). Other noteworthy discussions are Casey Blake, *Beloved Community: The Cultural Criticism of Randolph Bourne, Van Wyck Brooks, Waldo Frank & Lewis Mumford* (Chapel Hill: University of North Carolina Press, 1990); Peter Conn, *The Divided Mind: Ideology and Imagination in America, 1898–1917* (New York: Cambridge University Press, 1983); Martin Green, *New York 1913: The Armory Show and the Paterson Strike Pageant* (New York: Charles Scribner's Sons, 1988); James Kloppenberg, *Uncertain Victory: Social Democracy and Progressivism in European and American Thought, 1870–1920* (New York:

Oxford University Press, 1986); Daniel Joseph Singal, ed., *Modernist Culture in America* (Belmont, CA: Wadsworth, 1991); Christine Stansell, *American Moderns: Bohemian New York and the Creation of a New Century* (New York: Metropolitan, 2000); and Morton Gabriel White, *Social Thought in America: The Revolt against Formalism* (Boston, MA: Beacon Press, 1957). Stephen Kern, *The Culture of Time and Space, 1880–1918* (Cambridge, MA: Harvard University Press, 1983) and William R. Everdell, *The First Moderns: Profiles in the Origins of Twentieth-Century Thought* (Chicago: University of Chicago Press, 1997) expertly put cultural transformation in trans-Atlantic perspective.

3. The dissection of what he labeled "cultural custodians" may be found in May, *Innocence*, 1–117.

4. J. B. Bury, *The Idea of Progress: An Inquiry into Its Origin and Growth* (New York: Dover, [1921] 1932); Christopher Lasch, *The True and Only Heaven: Progress and Its Critics* (New York: W. W. Norton, 1991); and Robert A. Nisbet, *History of the Idea of Progress* (New York: Basic Books, 1980), explore the concept of progress.

5. Originally completed in 1905, the book was published posthumously in 1918. All subsequent references are from Henry Adams, *The Education of Henry Adams: An Autobiography* (Boston, MA: Houghton Mifflin, 1961).

6. See, for instance, Everdell, 30–62.

7. One suggestive discussion that retains a sympathy to Adams's criticism of progressives while noting his limitations is David Marcell, *Progress and Pragmatism: James, Dewey, Beard, and the American Idea of Progress* (Westport, CT: Greenwood, 1972), 1–25, 330–34.

8. Theodore M. Porter, *The Rise of Statistical Thinking, 1820–1900* (Princeton, NJ: Princeton University Press, 1986).

9. Arnold's definite statement on culture is Matthew Arnold, *Culture and Anarchy* (New Haven, CT: Yale University Press, [1869] 1994). The Yale edition contains a number of essays from critics that suggest how contested his legacy remains. Nineteenth-century ethical theory is handled in, among other places, Rene Welleck, *Confrontations: Studies in the Intellectual and Literary Relations between Germany, England, and the United States During the Nineteenth Century* (Princeton, NJ: Princeton University Press, 1965); and Bruce Kuklick, *A History of Philosophy in America, 1720–2000* (Oxford and New York: Clarendon Press, Oxford University Press, 2001). Veblen's essay was "Why Economics Is Not an Evolutionary Science," *Quarterly Journal of Economics* 12, no. 4 (July 1898): 373–97.

10. Walter Lippmann, *Drift and Mastery* (Madison: University of Wisconsin Press, [1913] 1985), 159.

11. The significance of nineteenth-century agnosticism is handled in James Turner, *Without God, without Creed: The Origins of Unbelief in America* (Baltimore: Johns Hopkins University Press, 1985). John Wenzler, "Transcendental Economics: The Quest to Harmonize Economic and Moral Law in Nineteenth-Century American Social Thought" (PhD diss., University of Rochester, 1998), is an extraordinar-

ily original and compelling argument about the unique nature of American political economy.

12. Eli Zaretsky, *Secrets of the Soul: A Social and Cultural History of Psychoanalysis* (New York: Alfred A. Knopf, 2004), contends that psychoanalysis was especially attuned to contingency.

13. In addition to Green, May, and Stansell, bohemian efforts to link politics and culture are explored in Edward Abrahams, *The Lyrical Left: Randolph Bourne, Alfred Stieglitz, and the Origins of Cultural Radicalism in America* (Charlottesville: University Press of Virginia, 1986); Leslie Fishbein, *Rebels in Bohemia: The Radicals of the* Masses (Chapel Hill: University of North Carolina Press, 1982); and Steven Watson, *Strange Bedfellows* (New York: Abbeville Press, 1991). The Hapgood quotation is from Abrahams, 165–66.

14. See, for instance, Everdell's discussion, 1–62, 159–76. This internal-problems argument owes much to Thomas Kuhn's work (Thomas S. Kuhn, *The Structure of Scientific Revolutions* [Chicago: University of Chicago Press, 1996]). The commentary on Kuhn is extensive, with charges ranging from irrationality to insufficient contextualization. See Steve Fuller, *Kuhn vs. Popper: The Struggle for the Soul of Science* (New York: Columbia University Press, 2004), and James A. Marcum, *Thomas Kuhn's Revolution: An Historical Philosophy of Science* (New York: Continuum, 2005), for recent rundowns of the state of the debate.

15. Isaiah Berlin, *The Hedgehog and the Fox: An Essay on Tolstoy's View of History* (New York: Simon and Schuster, 1986).

16. The adequacy of such contingent projects was one thing that Adams and his friend William James disputed throughout their years, with the temperature particularly rising in the years just prior to James's death in 1910. See, for instance, Marcell, *Progress and Pragmatism,* 1–22.

17. Gail Bederman, *Manliness & Civilization: A Cultural History of Gender and Race in the United States, 1880–1917* (Chicago: University of Chicago Press, 1995), 10–16.

CHAPTER ONE

~

Foundations

For all the disagreement among various philosophical schools and religious denominations that sprouted throughout the nineteenth century, few of the nation's intellectual and cultural elite doubted that American culture was built on a sturdy foundation. Those who wrote for the leading journals of opinion, held professorships at the nation's prestigious colleges, or occupied its distinguished pulpits throughout the nineteenth century by and large concurred that the universe was a fairly integrated place, knit together by a set of overarching laws and truths that made sense of the particulars of the world. A rough consensus in the mid-nineteenth century held that such grand laws emanated from the Creator or Nature and therefore formed an unimpeachable cornerstone. The rules that governed both spiritual and material reality existed time out of mind and were absolute in the sense that they operated without regard to context. The task of human thought, then, was to reaffirm their manifestation. James McCosh, who served as president of Princeton University from 1868 to 1888, relied on the assumption of unified truth to justify a prescribed curriculum. "Having seen that there are a priori truths in mathematics, the mind will be better prepared to admit that there are eternal and unchangeable principles lying at the basis of morality and religion, and guaranteeing to us the immutable character of law and of the justice of God."[1] Belief in the eternal and unchanging principles confirmed for many Americans the propriety of dividing their world into a series of mutually exclusive categories: true and false, good and bad, human and animal, culture and savagery, man and woman, self and society. There were dissenters to such a schema, but not until the early twentieth century did objections and challenges achieve prominence in the intellectual life of the nation.

McCosh's linking mathematics to God's rule points to another aspect of the culture of unity in the nineteenth century: the two principal roads to knowledge—religion and science—were considered complementary rather than antagonistic. Presuming integration, many Americans regarded the empiricism of science to be working in tandem with the transcendent truths of faith. Observation reaffirmed the presence of things unseen. In the dominant view of the American middle class, there was fit to the things of the world, an exquisite interlocking of time and space, a poetry in the mechanical precision of energy creation and use. Working from such a premise, it was not hard for Americans to treat daily demonstrations of unity as proof of the unity of the universe. The assumption of fit survived the growing secularization of American higher education. Although many Protestants protested efforts of such educational pioneers as Daniel Coit Gilman of Johns Hopkins and Charles Eliot of Harvard to deny pride of place to religion, few thought the answer was to abandon science. For his part, Eliot could justify the systematic study of the material world as having moral, if not necessarily religious, consequences. Scientific knowledge, he asserted, "ennobles and purifies the mind."[2]

Even Darwinian evolution did not end the sense of a rock-bottom order. Faced with the threat to order posed by random variation and environmental change, many American thinkers devoted their energies in the late nineteenth century to reconciling natural selection with their general sense of direction and purpose in the universe. Only a minority of American intellectuals argued that evolution properly understood disrupted general principles, overturned fundamentals, or placed the universe up for grabs. The English writer Herbert Spencer, in a passage that expressed the orderliness of the changing universe, asserted a cosmic covering to the process. "Evolution is an integration of matter and concomitant dissipation of motion, during which the matter passes from an indefinite, incoherent homogeneity to a definite, coherent heterogeneity; and during which the retained motion undergoes a parallel transformation."[3] Coherent heterogeneity confirmed progress, not the existence of a multiverse. Few Americans imagined that a world without universal laws could be anything other than chaotic and nihilistic.

Asserting the principle of coherence was one thing; confirming it, quite another. Over time, foundational assumptions failed to integrate phenomena fully. In some inquiries, especially in the physical sciences, the mounting anomalies raised questions about the viability of reigning paradigms. In the social sciences, political and social events seemed to mock the very idea of equilibrium and harmony that guided the major schools of thought. For such late-nineteenth-century writers as Edgar Saltus and Ambrose Bierce (and Mark Twain in his more pessimistic moods), the response was akin to sophisticated despair, convinced as they were that humankind faced an abyss of meaninglessness. All their lampooning of middle-class morality and belief in progress did not prevent American nihilists, however, from sharing with the confident middle class an expectation that order and control should be given in the world. Their anger and distance from human affairs owed much to their sense that the failure of universal and absolute foundations to sustain themselves meant there were no foundations whatsoever.[4]

More prevalent and influential were efforts to divorce meaning from the notion of unity. Chauncey Wright, Charles Sanders Peirce, and William James had begun in the nineteenth century to build a set of arguments that aimed at putting American thought and culture on a new footing, one that relied less on the presumption of a single truth and a unified set of goods. It was indicative of the strength of twentieth-century multiplicity that by 1920 every basic and central premise about physical, intellectual, and spiritual existence had undergone critique. A sizable contingent of philosophers, moralists, scientists, and artists raised meaningful challenges to the unified postulates that had looked so obvious to most Americans a half century earlier. What constituted truth and morality—the very building blocks of American cultural life—underwent considerable reworking, as pluralists disputed the existence and necessity of unifying laws. Perhaps surprisingly, it was ideas about the materiality of the world that showed the greatest tendency toward multiplicity. Where once space, time, and matter were taken for granted as solid and stable entities, the work of the early twentieth century undid such assured perception.[5]

Flux and the Physical World

The orderly unity of the physical world was a central component of assumptions of wholeness in the nineteenth century. However changing the terrain or in flux the built environment, consensus held that the basic laws that governed mattered were universal, absolute, and whole. The Newtonian world of stable equations regulated motion, revealed the components of energy, and established parameters of space and time. The laws of thermodynamics only reinforced the sense that the world was regulated and understandable. That energy was neither created nor destroyed and that it spontaneously tended to flow from states of high concentration to ones of low concentration, and not the other way around ("heat of itself cannot pass from a colder to a hotter body"), described a world that humans could understand and master. In due course, worries about the disorder that resulted from diffusion (entropy) would dominate thinking about energy. Throughout much of the nineteenth century, however, the second law was dubbed "time's arrow," because it allowed people to know that a diver would not come shooting up out of the water to the diving board or that rocks in a valley would not suddenly roll up a mountain. However erratic humans might be, observed nature was the ultimately law-bound entity, manifesting phenomena that were, in the words of historian Daniel Kevles, "continuous, describable in space and time, causally predictable, and, as such, mathematically expressible in differential equations."[6]

The trust in the unity of the physical world was not just that of the general public; professional physicists insisted upon it as well. When the talented lay writer John Stallo wrote in *Concepts and Theories of Modern Physics* (1882) that "neither mass nor motion is substantially real" and that all concepts were no more than "symbolical representations" of the real world, academicians dismissed him as a mistaken amateur. Although Henry Adams found Stallo's contention that the science of physics rested on convention a justification for his own argument about multiplicity, professionals regarded knowledge of the physical world as both secure and nearly complete.[7] During much of the 1880s, John Trowbridge, the department head at Harvard, warned bright graduate students away from physics on the grounds that the essential problems had been solved. All that remained, he believed, was to fill in the few remaining details, a task more routine than creative. In 1894, future Nobel Prize winner Albert Michelson of the University of Chicago told an audience that "it seems probable that most of the grand underlying principles have been firmly established and that further advances are to be sought chiefly in the rigorous application of these principles to all phenomena which come under our notice. . . . The future truths of physics are to be looked for in the sixth place of decimals."[8]

Michelson was premature in his judgment. Within a decade, the underlying principles that he judged to be firmly established would all undergo thorough revision. One year after Michelson's authoritative declaration, Wilhelm Roentgen had discovered the amazing properties of what he called X-rays, which resulted from the impact of cathode rays on a material object. X-rays, as patients the world over know, pass through solid objects like bodies and produce images of interior features such as teeth and bones. Only later would these mysterious rays be shown to be of the same electromagnetic nature as light, although vibrating at much higher frequencies. The effort to understand these rays led to further discoveries. The French scientist Antoine Henri Becquerel discovered that uranium could emit energy without an external source of energy such as the sun. This spontaneous emission of radiation could be deflected by a magnetic field, which meant it must consist of charged particles. Further, as Ernest Rutherford showed, some elements

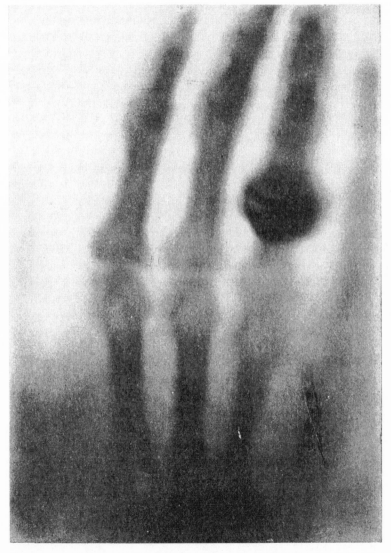

Figure 1.1. Roentgen's X-ray of his wife's, Anna Bertha's, hand. **Passing through solid objects to reveal interior structure, the rays challenged a prevailing sense of solidity of things. Mrs. Roentgen regarded the image with dread, envisioning in it her own demise.**

such as uranium and radium could decay, transmuting, in a way akin to alchemy, into something else. As scientists tried to understand radiating particles, they turned their attention to the architecture of the atom, where they encountered new surprises. A number of researchers postulated that much of the atom was empty space, a consequence of Rutherford's 1910 proposal of a nucleus made of positively charged particles orbited by negatively charged electrons. In one and a half decades, matter had become less substantial, less permanent, and less predictable.

Light, another staple of the study of the physical world, proved equally hard to understand. Conventional wisdom held that light was a wave. Because waves were disturbances in a medium, the task before physicists was to locate that substance. They settled upon something they labeled ether. Ether was mystifying because it seemed to be indiscernible. All efforts to measure its effect, such as Michelson's 1881 experiments to register its drag on the earth, yielded no results. Yet physicists still insisted that this apparently weightless and motionless substance must exist, for without it the propelling of electromagnetic waves was inconceivable. The British physicist Lord Kelvin firmly asserted in his 1884 lectures in Philadelphia that he and other scientists had no doubt of the "reality and substantiality" of "luminiferous ether." That certainty vanished in the first decade of the twentieth century with the advent of Albert Einstein's special relativity theory. By the end of the Great War, physics would dismantle much of the Newtonian edifice and, with it, conventional understandings of space and time. No longer would time and space designate absolutely distinct categories; instead, they would assume relative form, presenting physicists with the challenge of unifying again the physical world.[9]

Einstein was not the first to propose a relativity theory; Galileo had formulated one in response to the discoveries of Copernicus. Since the earth was no longer the stationary center of the universe but was, in fact, in motion, it could not serve as an absolute frame of reference against which to measure the motion of matter. In Galileo's system, everything was in motion relative to everything else. Everything, that is, but ether. Building from the equations of James Clerk Maxwell, which had set down the basic laws of electricity and magnetism, Einstein set out to explain why it had not been possible to discover the motion of earth relative to the "light medium." Part of Einstein's explanation was his contention that, contrary to older belief, the speed of light was constant, not infinite, relative to observers. Rejecting the need for "absolute rest," Einstein rendered ether "superfluous." What Einstein concluded from these two postulates was remarkable. Because the velocity of the electromagnetic waves bringing images to observers was a constant ratio of distance and time, time would differ for observers in different systems moving at different velocities. It was as if each moving body had its own clock. Likewise, the size of an object would vary according to the speed of a system. For an observer in a relative state of rest, the measurement of the length of a rod aboard a moving object such as a ship would have to shorten in the direction of motion and would grow shorter the faster the ship moved relative to the nearly stationary observer. Things would look the reverse from the vantage point of the moving system. Time and space had become relative fields, contingent on the context of the observer.[10]

The special theory of relativity dealt with systems moving at uniform speeds. The general theory of 1915 dealt with bodies in motion that were accelerating. Here, Einstein's target was the Newtonian theory of gravity, which had failed to explain how the phenomenon worked or why gravitational acceleration is independent of the mass or composition of an object. Einstein's theory countered that space was influenced by the matter and energy in the world, which told space how to curve. Space in return told matter how to move. Nor did Einstein stop with melding space and time. Matter and energy seemed to be equivalent, as well. That famous equation $E=mc^2$, which appeared in his September 1905 paper "Does the Inertia of a Body Depend upon Its Energy Content?" posited an enormous amount of rest energy, a position that was to have enormous consequences in the decades to come.

Einstein's rejection of absolute entities and categories was not a rejection of integration, however. He personally saw his work as forwarding unity, rather than dissolving it. Space-time and matter-energy were, to his mind, new ways to understand how contingencies could be explained, providing syntheses for space and time, gravitation and geometry, and light, matter, and energy. "The supreme objective of any physicist is to arrive at elementary laws with which the cosmos can be reconstructed by pure deduction," he wrote in 1918.[11]

Einstein's discoveries did not result in the unity that he envisioned. Although much of the debate took place after the war, there were those in the first one and a half decades of the century who saw the new physics as justifying multiplicity. Such sentiments were particularly pronounced among those who studied the dynamics of the atom and the behavior of subatomic particles. Atoms, it turns out, act in ways that the classical synthesis could not explain. Investigators struggled to account for their stability, the mechanism by which they emit light, and the behavior of negatively charged particles, electrons, which circle the atomic nuclei but do not do so in well-defined orbits. One clue came from the discoveries of the German physicist Max Planck, who had solved the "black body" problem. "Black bodies"—objects that absorb but do not reflect energy—emit radiation not in accord with the expected continuous relation between the intensity of radiation and wavelength, but rather clumped together around unexpected peaks. Planck proposed that energy, rather than being emitted in a continuous, infinitely divisible fashion, was actually emitted in discrete, indivisible units ("quanta") mathematically equal to the frequency times a constant.[12] Einstein himself had contributed to quantum theory, demonstrating that radiation behaved as though it consisted of discrete particles, rather than in ways that the wave theory of light predicted.[13] Particles follow a trajectory along which both their position and velocity are specified at a given time; waves are not localized at all but have a continuous character. Radiation did both, at least in different situations. When investigators tested for wave properties, they found them. When they tested for those of particles, they found them too. Some physicists proposed a solution to the problem of the nature of radiation in the principle of complementarity, in which neither wave nor particle was sufficient but both were necessary. The Danish physicist Neils Bohr and his student Werner Heisenberg would eventually make quantum mechanics a theory of probability (a move that Einstein himself did not fully accept, as indicated by his famous remark that God did not play dice with the universe). The heart of the Bohr-Heisenberg position was that total certain knowledge could not be ascertained, because the act of measurement of atomic- and subatomic-level processes invariably alters some aspect of what is being measured. Copenhagen physics, as the position came to be known, contends that concepts like waves and particles are operational tools, and our knowledge of radiation can be defined only contextually. In stressing the multiplicity of quantum mechanics, physicists tabled the quest for unity in favor of explanations that were true contingently. Or, as Bohr once put it, if one does not believe the results of quantum physics to be weird, one has not understood it.[14]

Americans were not the primary movers of the new physics. They did, however, make contributions. In addition to Michelson's experiments, Europeans deemed Willard Gibbs's mathematics indispensable, but they were published in less widely circulated journals and were "difficult to read," even for the mathematician Henri Poincaré. Robert Millikan's 1909 oil-drop experiment was hailed for its demonstration that electric charges were quanta, not continuous. Their work, however, did not always resonate with their colleagues in the first decade of the twentieth century. Trowbridge's survey of the state of the field for the *Atlantic Monthly* in 1909 did indeed announce the new interest in electrons, radium, and radioactivity, but did not mention either Planck or Einstein. Still committed to the ether, Trowbridge warned his readers that science needed to avoid plunging into the "unfathomable abyss" of philosophical speculation about the nonexistence of matter.[15] Americans could, however, get wind of changes from other sources. Coverage of the World Congresses at the 1904 St. Louis World's Fair mentioned the talks of Rutherford and Poincaré, among others. In 1906, the *Nation* published a rundown of the state of the discipline that showed an awareness of the changes afoot. "Physics has outgrown the old formulas of gravity, magnetism, and pressure; has discarded the molecule and atom for the ion, and may in its recent generalization be followed only by an expert in higher, not to say the transcendental, mathematics. . . . In short, one may not say that the average cultivated man has given up science, but that science has deserted him."[16] By the second decade of the twentieth century, Einstein was a well-known figure to readers of journals of opinion. When he toured the United States in 1921 to raise funds for Zionist causes, he was feted as a celebrity, due in large measure to observations of a British team of the 1919 eclipse of the sun, which provided confirming evidence for his argument about curvature of space.

Since the new physics addressed phenomena at the atomic and cosmic levels, few experienced relativity and quantum physics directly. With the significant exception of problems of frames of reference that came into play by the new kinds of speeds that people experienced, much of the new multiplicity was imagined rather than perceived. At the middle level of experience, the physical world followed its Newtonian and thermodynamical course. Yet the impact of the erosion of the absolute could be profound. Writing of the poor quality of science education in the 1880, journalist-turned-historian Mark Sullivan pointed to an upheaval, in his famed discussion of American life, *Our Times* (1926):

> Had the schoolchildren of the 1880s been taught what science then thought it knew, they would have learned the principle of immutability of the chemical elements—and would have lived to see it overturned by the discovery of radioactivity. They would have learned the principle of the conservation of mass—and would have lived to see that principle vanish with the experimental discovery of the increase in mass of the electron with speed as the velocity of light is approached. They would have learned the principle of the conservation of energy—and would have lived to see that principle suffer a material change "when both experimental and theoretical evidence came forward that energy and mass are interconvertible terms related by the Einstein equation $mc^2 = E$, since in that discovery the ideas of energy and of mass became completely scrambled. They would have learned the principle of conservation of momentum—and would have seen it denied universality by the subsequent formulation of the quantum theory."[17]

As Paul Vitz and Arnold Glimcher have demonstrated, visual science also gravitated toward multiplicity in the late nineteenth and early twentieth centuries. Rather than synthesizing and integrating, visual scientists emphasized components, fragments, and parts as crucial to perception of space and color. Nowhere was the importance of contingency more important than in the understanding of Euclidian space as a limited model. Euclidian concepts posited a constant world, unaffected by the objects placed within it. The new understanding of space, in contrast, jettisoned a spatial world in which universal law prevailed, for ones that were contingent, dependent upon the particular fields under investigation. Some fields were filled with surprises for those who believed in universal geometric laws, as was the case in those geometries where it was entirely possible that parallel lines could intersect. Vitz and Glimcher note that the reworking of space was also a reworking of hierarchy. Where the conventional notions of spatial perception rested on assumptions that some elements, such as the foreground, had a higher meaning than others, such as background, the new visual science held that such a scheme was just one arbitrary system among many possible ones.[18]

The shifts in the ways the arts handled space and time were probably more attributable to reworking the new experiences of radio, automobile, elevator, and cinema than to conscious efforts to apply the precepts of the new physics and visual sciences. The results, nonetheless, bore a family resemblance to the multiplicity of time and space that the more explicitly scientific discourses derived. Manipulating time and space has a long and honorable history in the arts, but the first twenty years of the twentieth century witnessed a spate of aesthetic ventures that made relativity a central, if not *the* central, facet of the artwork, rather than a trick or playful element. If previous work hinted at contingent truths depending upon time and place, a growing number of artworks highlighted multiplicity. In both the high precincts of the avant-garde and the low ones of mass culture, Americans took pleasure in cultural expression that explored the multiplicity of the physical world. From the new comic strips and movies to new forms of narration in the novel and abstraction in painting, the arts generated a panoply of artifacts in which universal and absolute vantage points gave way to particularist ones. Those new techniques enabled the arts to mirror the new physics in suggesting that time and space were conventions, true only with respect to limited frames of reference.

In the hands of Winsor McCay and George Herriman, the comic strip could produce some startling aesthetic effects. The first modern comic strip with continuing characters was James Swinnerton's *California Bears*, drawn for the San Francisco *Examiner* in 1892. Swinnerton's was a rather undeveloped attempt. It lacked dialogue and individualized character development. An immediate circulation booster, however, the idea soon spread east, where the form took hold. The most famous strips of the early years deliberately courted working-class readers. The title character of Richard Outcault's famous *Yellow Kid* was clearly of the slum, having originated in *Gasoline Alley*. Bald, with protruding ears, and wearing only a long nightshirt, he first appeared in single panels depicting multiple actions, and instead of being contained within speech balloons, conversation, usually with liberal doses of slang, appeared as lettering on his shirt. Mayhem and violence were the hallmark of two other favorites: Rudolf Dirks's *Katzenjammer Kids* and Bud Fisher's *Mutt and Jeff*. The latter, begun in 1907, became the first successful daily strip, largely because it brought vaudeville and burlesque slapstick to the page. The hapless Jeff served a twenty-five-year sentence as the punching bag of the racetrack swell Mutt. In addition to the violence, Fisher's humor depended upon his dressing his plebeian characters in incongruous clothes designed to puncture their pretension and point out their bad taste.[19] The success of anti-genteel comic strips prompted genteel alternatives, of which Richard Outcault's full-page *Buster Brown* was the most well known. Brown was an exceedingly moralistic middle-class young man, whose mischievousness was always innocent and whose strip always ended with a panel devoted to what lessons he drew from his experience.[20]

None of these strips emphasized the mutability of space and time as thoroughly as McCay's *Little Nemo in Slumberland* and Herriman's *Krazy Kat*. *Nemo* was in one sense a formula. Nemo falls asleep, has a series of dreams—some appealing, others terrifying—and wakes up in the last panel. Nemo himself had little personality; he was simply a dreamer to whom things happened. Many of the dreams themselves were rather unexceptional. What did strike readers as beautiful was McCay's imagination in presenting them. He broke his page into forms and shapes that varied from strip to strip, ranging from as few as five to as many as twenty panels. At times he would devote half a page to a single picture, or put a circular drawing smack dab in the middle and place other pictures around it. He would tell stories with cinematic techniques, shifting vantage points and propelling the reader into the panel itself. McCay's manipulation of perspective, his attention to the pleasures of the decorative, and his ability to endow things with life gave his strip an enchanted quality of near infinite possibility.[21]

George Herriman continually denied he had artistic inclinations, claiming in a 1902 article in the *Bookman* that he, like all cartoonists, lacked inspiration. He had lost "that delicate sense of the poetic and artistic" and was interested only in worrying out "idioticies [sic] for the edification of an inartistic majority."[22] Herriman was born in New Orleans in 1880. His birth certificate designates him "colored," a judgment that Herriman himself often ratified on the grounds that his hair was kinky. His father moved the family to California three years later, but Herriman's strips contain a good deal of the Creole patois impulse. Working on a number of strips in the first decade of the twentieth century, Herriman hit upon his masterwork almost by accident. He placed at the bottom of his strip *The Dingbats*, the saga of a family besieged by upstairs neighbors, a mouse throwing a brick at the family cat. Originally a way to fill space, the maneuver struck a chord with readers, who enjoyed the role reversal. Soon complications set in. It turned out that the cat, sex entirely indeterminate, adored the beanings for reasons having to do with racial memories that extended back to ancient Egypt. The Dingbat and the cat–mouse storylines ran concurrently in the same space, separated by a border until October 28, 1913, when *Krazy Kat* made its debut.

The strip was, as Herriman's biographers have noted, at heart about obsession. Ignatz, the mouse, is driven by his hatred of cats to throw the brick at Krazy, not knowing that s/he reacts with joy at this sign of his abiding love for her/him. Likewise, Kat, whom Herriman described as a sprite, never knew that s/he was the object of affection of Offissa Pupp, who saw it as his duty to protect the Kat from the "sin's most sinister symbol," Ignatz's brick. Set in the Arizona desert of Coconino County, the strip was particularly inventive in the Sunday page. Free to exercise his spatial imagination and verbal play, Herriman filled his space kinetically. His use of variations in shades of dark allowed him to achieve effects from opaque to translucent. Particularly popular were his shifting backgrounds. Herriman often had the mouse and cat standing perfectly still while the background moved from mountain to sea as the panels progressed. Nor was he above making the desert suddenly bloom or dotting his landscape with symbols. Herriman delighted in such jokes as placing a caricature of Mount Fujiyama as "intermission" or putting a hole in the middle through which a minor character breaks out and directly addresses the reader with a commentary on the action of Kat and Ignatz. Matching his pictorial experimentation was a hybrid language that emphasized the texture and sounds of words, varying their rhythm and pace, mixing Spanish, French, Yiddish, and his own concoctions. Herriman's great success was that he could make the repetition of brick throwing break through the shackles of time and become something fresh.[23]

Multiplicity in time and space was the major attraction of the cinema, which by 1920 was the premier popular art form in the nation. Although the dream of a moving art was an old one, Americans took awhile to regard film as an aesthetic medium. During the 1890s, the various inventors of cameras

Figure 1.2. Krazy Kat. **In a strip from 1918, Kat awaits Ig-natz's brick, which s/he regards as a sign of undying love. In his use of patois, variation of translucent effects, and disregard for conventions of time and space, Kat's creator, George Herriman created a landmark comic that superbly demonstrated the pro-visionality of both physical and mental worlds. (Source: Library of Congress)**

and film stock (contrary to popular opinion, the motion-picture camera was not solely, or even mainly, the work of Thomas Edison, as numerous antitrust cases revealed) regarded their handiwork as best dedicated to documenting intricacies of movement and to revealing places that people had not seen or events that they could not witness. Hailed as a marvel, the early exhibited films were primarily single shots, lasting no longer than a minute, of sneezes, kisses, and dances. Edison specialized in kinetography, as it was known, for individual peep machines, until showings at variety houses as filler or inter-mission material indicated the appeal of the new medium. As advances in filming and projection made large showings feasible, camera operators and producers experimented throughout the first decade of the twentieth century with techniques that could dramatically convey temporal and spatial relationships. The process of cutting between one action and another enabled filmmakers to show parallel developments and establish connections without relying on lengthy exposition. Likewise, the closeup allowed clear sight of characters' faces and the emotions that their features signified. Arrangement of characters and objects within a frame could make relationships palpable. What would take a novelist pages to describe and explain, a filmmaker could accomplish economically. Through dissolves and gradual transitions from one image to another, filmmakers could liberate their stories from the constraints of real-life time. A five-minute movie could tell a story that took place in a day or in a year. As a consequence, the movies created their own world, but, as it turned out, one that bore a striking resemblance to the one in which people lived.[24]

Although it is hard to credit any particular discovery in film technique as original, on the grounds that experimentation in the new medium was a global phenomenon, Edwin S. Porter has received special recognition for two 1903 films, *The Life of an American Fireman*, released in the spring, and *The Great Train Robbery*, which was a Christmas sensation. Porter had worked as a projectionist, a job that required he arrange the short single-shot films in an entertaining order. Impressed by the storylines that English cinematographers were assembling, Porter put that training to use when he assembled from disparate shots the story of a fireman who rescues a woman and her child from a burning building. Porter's editing (splicing different film rolls together with acetone) gave viewers something that was not possible to put on the stage. He showed the same act—the fireman's rescue—from exterior and interior views, so that spectators saw the man climbing the ladder (a spectacular effect in and of itself), followed immediately by the interior shot.

The Great Train Robbery consisted of fourteen shots (not counting the "realism" shot in which the actor who played the lead bandit, Justus Barnes, stands against a dark background and fires his revolver at the camera, which could be shown at the beginning or the end of the film, as exhibitors wished). Taken from positions ranging from the back of a coal tender of the besieged train to a vantage point beside the tracks, and demonstrating a moving camera that gave a panoramic shot of the fleeing robbers, the shots told two stories. The first was of the robbery of the train itself. The second was of the telegraph operators' capture and release. The two storylines meet up again as the posse catches up with the thieves. The exhibited time and space of the film bore little relationship to the shooting time and space, which allowed Porter to tell a continuous story.

Experimental literature, aesthetic-oriented photography, and painting were especially attuned to the possibilities for multiplicity contained in the new understanding of the physical world. In the imagist poetry of Amy Lowell, the work of Alfred Stieglitz and his comrades at *Camera Work* and his small gallery space, "291," and the postimpressionism that came to prominence during the famed 1913 Armory Show, Americans had an array of cultural expression that deliberately and provocatively aimed at fracturing time and bending space. Artists felt no need to rely upon conventions that presented space as objective or time as universal. For those unschooled in the new aesthetics, the work looked strange and deformed. The inability to fix time and space in the painting was one reason that numerous observers thought Matisse (with his startling and nontraditional color and physical oddities (four toes in *Blue Nude*) and the nonrepresentationalists insane. The critic Royal Cortissoz, who saw himself as guardian of tradition, excoriated the modernists for their inability to master established conventions of time and space. Wrote Cortissoz: "He [the cubist] paints you his riddle of line and color, and then, as in the case of M. Marcel Duchamp, calls it 'Nude Descending a Staircase.' In other words, he has the effrontery to assert that his picture bears some relation to human life." Joel Spingarn, who was more favorable to experiment than Cortissoz, called the painting—a brown blur of descending force lines—"an explosion in a shingle factory."[25]

The new art embodied, and in some cases directly drew upon, a new version of the philosophy of vitalism that flamed brightly throughout the period. Strictly speaking a position in biology that rejects the notion that life can be explained by non-life (i.e., physical or chemical) factors, vitalism was a broad-ranging orientation that spurned determinism, a priori conceptual grids, and abstract principles in favor of an acceptance of the contingent, fluctuating, never-quite-capturable nature of experience. Vitalism came to the United States through the work of the French philosopher Henri Bergson.[26] Such a celebrity in his day that his 1913 visit to New York caused traffic jams on Broadway, Bergson capped a current of thought that influenced bohemians and reformers alike. He contended that scientific time—an objective, regular measurement—missed the subjective nature of experience, in which every instant contained the fullness of the past within it and was therefore unique. Time, he argued, did not unfold along a line. Science erred in treating internal phenomena as if they could be measured externally. Rather than static and homogeneous, time is actually dynamic and heterogeneous. He labeled this flux duration and proclaimed it was there that life was lived. Flux had a similar geometric component. In place of the abstract space that science postulated, Bergson, like the visual scientists, noted the subjective aspect of motion.

Bergson accepted that some abstraction was necessary for humans to make their way in the world. But, Bergson and his admirers contended, this came at a cost: the detachment from the mental province in which resided the rich and creative flow that was both the fountainhead and the very totality of the real. In his later work, Bergson took aim at subject–object dualism, which he held incorrectly rested on the notions of absolute time and space to forge an unbridgeable chasm between internal and external worlds. Real duration, he contended in *Introduction to Metaphysics*, was an active component of the natural world out there, however dependent it seemed on private feelings and memories. "The consciousness we have of our own self in its continual flux introduces us to the interior of a reality, on the model of which we must represent other realities," Bergson declared.[27] Breaking down spatial differences required finding some way out of the stalemate between realists, who insisted that the mind seized knowledge from things in themselves, and idealists, who claimed perception began with intrinsic ideas of the mind. Bergson's solution was to treat the individual as a locus of relationships, within and part of the flow of primordial experience. Worried about the fatal division between intellect and emotion, Bergson placed special emphasis on the ability of the intuition to place individuals into reality and penetrate to authentic duration. Bergson accorded art a special status, arguing that it had the unique capacity to dismantle abstract time and space to allow experience of duration and motion.

Bergson's work appeared in a number of avant-garde art publications, most notably Alfred Stieglitz's influential *Camera Work*. Stieglitz, a notable photographer in his own right, discerned in Bergson warrant for personal understanding of time and place. In the New York paintings of John Marin, a member of Stieglitz's circle, Bergsonian ideas that movement and duration are essential to life at its fullest come to the forefront. In an effort to realize Bergsonian intuition, in which the artist moves sympathetically into objects, Marin drew a city in constant motion. In Marin's New York, space, rather than being distinctly bound, is kinetic, fluid, and decentering. His technique of broad brushstrokes, melting forms, and splashes of color, which, despite his explicit denials of influence, resembles that of the Fauves, conveys the blooming and buzzing that the vitalists understood to be at the heart of "life." That blooming and buzzing drew no distinction between inanimate and animate. "Shall we consider," asked Marin,

> the life of a great city as confined simply to the people and animals on its streets and in its buildings? Are the buildings themselves dead? . . . If these buildings move me, they too must have life. Thus the whole city is alive; build-

ings, people, all are alive; and the more they move me the more I feel them to be alive. I see great forces at work; great movement; the large buildings and the small buildings; the warring of the great and the small; influences of one mass on another greater or smaller mass. Feelings are aroused which give the desire to express the reaction of these "pull forces," those influences which play with one another; great masses pulling smaller masses, each subject in some degree to the other's power. In life all things come under the magnetic influence of other things; the bigger assert themselves strongly, the smaller not so much, but still they assert themselves, and though hidden they strive to be seen and in so doing change their bent and direction. . . . I try to express graphically what a great city is doing.[28]

Elements of Bergsonian time were also essential building blocks of the fiction of Gertrude Stein. Born in Pittsburgh and educated at Radcliffe, where she studied with William James, and at Johns Hopkins, Stein applied Cubist principles to the written word. Abjuring the hierarchy of space, she wrote pieces in which neither ground nor figure received any special emphasis. Her greatest verbal experiments were in the use of repetition, of which "A rose is a rose is a rose" has become so famous that it is fodder for parody. In *Three Lives* (1909), *The Making of Americans* (written 1906–1908, but published 1925), and *Tender Buttons* (1914), Stein used the technique, along with "-ing" verbs to portray a continuous present. In the first, in which she daringly chose two immigrant servants and a young black woman as protagonists, her touch was ultimately ironic. Her delight in flux stood in marked contrast to the difficulties that her characters had in negotiating and adjusting to it, as critic David Minter has pointed out.[29] Although an expatriate, she retained her fascination with her homeland as the country most dedicated to rejecting the bonds of history. Like Stephen Dedalus in James Joyce's *Ulysses*, Stein tended to think of history as a prison house to escape. As she herself said of her goals, "When I began writing I was always writing about beginning again and again. In *The Making of Americans* I was making a continuous present a continuous beginning again and again, the way they do in making automobiles or anything, each one has to be begun, but now everything having been begun nothing had to be begun again." In *Tender Buttons*, Stein includes only fleeting references to represented things. Her associations of the sound and looks of words with food and objects were playful juxtapositions that aimed at Bergsonian duration. Stein was a writer for a coterie of like-minded modernists. Yet her reputation and staying power throughout the century testified to how deep-seated multiplicity of time and space was to become.[30]

Unfinished Truths

The new physics did more than alter the understanding of the physical world. It also challenged the conception of scientific truth that had held sway in the United States for more than a century. According to conventional understanding, the methods of science revealed a truth that existed independent of human knowledge of it. Science differed from intuition in its protocols, and those protocols enabled human beings to treat its truths as certain. Each new discovery filled in the picture of how things were in the world, augmenting a growing and more nearly complete stock of knowledge. The new sciences not only suggested that what humans had known of the world had not been progressing toward completeness, but that the very model of truth on which science was rested was mistaken. In place of a notion of truth as a firmed and fixed relation, the new science offered probabilistic statements and warranted assertions. Truth was both provisional and often inconsistent with other truths. In challenging absolute space and time, the new science implied that even the basic categories and concepts by which humans organized their knowledge lacked ultimate foundation. This in turn raised the possibility that truth was as much made by human activity as discovered lying out there in the world. It was a new version of what constituted truth that underwrote twentieth-century multiplicity.

Science was not the only discourse in the early twentieth century in which the nature of truth was at issue. Doubts about prevailing conceptions of truth were at the heart of intensifying debates among philosophers as well. Probably a majority held to a correspondence or realist position. As James Pratt of Williams College put it, truth was "merely this simple thing, that *the object of which one is thinking is as one thinks it*."[31] Challengers, however, did not regard Pratt's "simple thing" as so simple. At heart, they charged, it was a metaphysical position masquerading as common sense. That was because, critics pointed out in an argument that resembled that of Bergson, it depended upon the assumption that there was an unbridgeable divide between subject and object. Correspondence theory treated the world out there (including our own bodies, as well as the thoughts and minds of other people) as of an entirely different order than our own mental activity. If our mental activity conformed to reality, then our thoughts were true. That maneuver gave truth an absolute foundation, but it also made the way of the world independent of human emotion and orientations. Judging this correspondence would require an Olympian point of view that few challengers believed was possible, since it meant getting outside ourselves and securing the foundations of truths independently of our practices in the world. Although the challengers were far from agreement as to what truth was, much less the different but related question of the nature of reality, they nonetheless rejected notions of a deep foundation for truth. In so doing, they accepted that the goal of certainty was not possible, at least in its nineteenth-century form.

Given its insistence that the natural science version of truth was unassailable, the approach known as positivism would on first glance seem an unlikely candidate to foster a new understanding of what constituted truth. Positivism emphasized the truth of the observable and the provable, rejecting as untrue the metaphysical and the emotional. This rigorous insistence on the empirical kicked over the traces of many foundations on which Americans constructed their notions of unity in the nineteenth century. Particularly influential in the United States were German physicist and philosopher Ernst Mach's *Analysis of Sensations* (1886) and the British biometric statistician Karl Pearson's *Grammar of Science* (1892). Both men shared a hostility to metaphysics and to the search for the ultimate cause. Mach argued forcefully that all sciences regardless of formal subject matter dealt with sensations, not forces or things. He insisted that such sensations did not betoken a reality beyond them. As such, he held that scientific laws were not statements about the way things were, but rather correlations of experience. In Mach's system, hypotheses functioned as predictors of future sensation perception. His positivism led Mach to challenge the existence of entities ranging from atoms and egos to absolute space and absolute time. All these, he held, were fictions that may or may not be useful, adopted by necessity but discardable in the face of new experience and needs. The sum of all sensations, Mach implied, was chaos, which humans shaped to achieve meaning.[32] As the Austrian modernist novelist Robert Musil noted in his PhD dissertation on Mach's work, Mach aimed for a "presuppositionless science" in which concepts needed to be purged of their unverifiable, emotional content. In a similar vein, Pearson concluded that "cause and effect" were "only statements of phenomenal sequence"—their recurrence a matter only of probability. Rejecting introspection as unverifiably subjective, Pearson turned to statistics as a "supra-personal standard of judgment." Homogeneity, Pearson maintained, was a metaphysical conceit, an effort to skirt multiplicity. Like other positivists, he had no given principle by which to integrate his truths.[33]

If positivists held that science was the only acceptable path to knowledge, their carefully circumscribed limits of what science could investigate ironically allied them with Bergsonian vitalists, who found science too constricting in their suspicions of an absolute truth that subsumed all particulars to overarching claims. American social scientists drew upon both to formulate challenges to singular and reductive explanations. The circle of anthropologists around Franz Boas drew upon both Mach and Bergson in their challenges to the evolutionary progressivism of previous anthropologies. Robert Lowie, for one, seized upon Mach's insistence on the supremacy of experience to challenge the authority of both biology and history that previous anthropologists had treated as necessary to provide meaning. Unfurling the banner of reason, Lowie saw much of what passed as science as the "folklore of philosophic and scientific system-mongers."[34] The sociologist Franklin Giddings drew upon Mach's denial that scientific laws posited a reality behind the phenomena to argue that social science needed to abandon its Baconian legacy of searching for true causes. In its stead, Giddings proposed a sociology of multiplicity in which the mix of human wishes and actions was subject to multiple causes. Social science under such conditions was itself a selection of relevant factors rather than an impartial rendering of truth.[35]

The impetus for a definition of truth that supported multiplicity was more likely in the early twentieth century to take the form of pragmatism than of positivism. More a philosophical orientation than a systematic body of substantive principles as such, pragmatism in the first twenty years of the twentieth century was an attempt to cut through metaphysical conundrums and paralyzing puzzles by arguing their irrelevance. Although the philosopher Arthur Lovejoy, himself a realist opponent of pragmatism, claimed in 1908 that there were thirteen varieties (a number that has grown exponentially in the last century), nearly all varieties shared an antifoundational sense that a claim was true if it was verified in practice rather than if it mirrored reality. Pragmatists linked truth to human thought and practices, rather than envisioning it as something pristine and transcendent. Judging truth by the consequences of a belief, the pragmatist conception of truth differed from those versions that made truth a matter of conforming to preexisting realities or a priori strictures. The new understanding of the truth emphasized the concrete instead of the universal and absolute, opening the way for multiplicity.[36] As John Dewey noted, absolutes were rather vague and meaningless. Humans, he insisted, do not live "in general." They seek health, wealth, learning, justice, or kindness in specific ways. "Action," he maintained, is "always specific, concrete, individualized, unique. And consequently judgments as to acts to be performed must be similarly specific."[37] For his part, William James took direct aim at all thought that convinced people to believe in a "block universe" that blinded them to different possibilities of action. Pragmatists reached no accord over a slew of issues ranging from what counted as verification to how the world hung together. Yet by turning to the methods of science as the best ways to fix belief provisionally, pragmatists made their major contribution to American thought and culture, an understanding that truth was not fundamentally grounded but was contingent.

Pragmatism owed much to the theory of meaning that Charles Sanders Peirce (1839–1914) advanced in the 1870s and 1880s. Beliefs, Peirce contended, were plans of action, not intuitions or replicas of reality. It was impossible, Peirce averred, for beliefs to have meaning without envisioning the practical bearings that the objects of conceptions have. They were, in effect, hypotheses that needed to be tested. Take, for instance, the claim that an object is hard. For a pragmatist, the meaning of hard can only be determined through experimental test, practice. So if our object can scratch other objects without being scratched itself, it meets our test. Hardness, then, means the quality of not being scratched by many other substances. Our belief that an object is hard is fallible, based on past experience. Peirce's notions of belief extended even to those mathematical and logical beliefs most writers took as givens. They too were hypotheses that had gone through practical tests at one time, Peirce maintained. They may well be so deep-seated that we believe we see their truths immediately, but a prioris were simply what we are inclined to believe and were not on that account necessarily true.[38]

Peirce cleared brush for some other paths that pragmatism was to tread. He regarded inquiry as a social endeavor, undertaken by a community of inquirers who converged on a consensus, which in his first iteration of a theory of truth he regarded as reality. He further postulated a mechanism for inquiry in which habit becomes disrupted and humanity works to integrate its beliefs so as to end dissonance and confusion. He found untenable arguments that logically implied the ability to chart outcomes precisely. Fastening on the absence of teleology in Darwinism, Peirce postulated a probabilistic universe in which chance accounted for much in the world, from natural laws to human faculties. The iconoclastic, irascible Peirce only flirted with multiplicity, often turning back once he started down the path. His pragmatic theory of meaning did not eventuate in a full rejection of the realist theory of truth. By the first decade of the new century, Peirce was working on theories of truth that resembled the correspondence theory. Although he accepted that any given proposition was in doubt at any moment, he held that ultimately science would converge on and reveal the truth. In the end, his quest was metaphysical, wanting to "understand God's mind," as he put it in 1903. At points, his logic led him to impose a priori categories on reality, a considerably less fluid position than his earlier work had staked out.[39]

With Harvard psychologist and philosopher William James (1842–1910), pragmatism exhibited a far more thorough multiplicity. James extended Peirce's theory of meaning into a full-blown antifoundational theory of truth. In due course, he ventured propositions about the pluralistic nature of the world. Writing in an expansive and accessible style, James put a public face on pragmatism, introducing his version through well-known work on consciousness (*Principles of Psychology*), religion (*Varieties of Religious Experience*), and truth (*Pragmatism*), interventions against American imperialism, and meditations on social responsibility ("The Moral Equivalent of War") and class relations ("On a Certain Blindness"). This disparate output was as important for its sensibility of tolerance as for its precise articulation of arguments. Convinced that philosophies of a lockstep universe inhibited action, James set himself the task of developing ones that could encourage it by demonstrating how much of the world was as yet unformed. As James summed up his fighting creed in *Pragmatism* (1907), a pragmatist "turns his back resolutely and once for all upon a lot of inveterate habits dear to professional philosophers. He turns away from abstraction and insufficiency, from verbal solutions, from bad a priori reasons, from fixed principles, closed systems, and pretended absolutes and origins. He turns toward concreteness and adequacy, towards facts, towards action, and towards power."[40]

James identified the correspondence theory of truth as the pivot on which "fixed principles, closed systems, and pretended absolutes and origins" hinge. In contrast, James championed an understanding of truth that made verification its cornerstone. We make our way in the world, James contended, through verification rather than correspondence, and we actually live in environments of multiplicity. James predicated his notion of truth on an argument gathered from Peirce that beliefs were plans for action. If so, James continued, truth was a matter of judging a belief by whether it worked. A belief was true if it yielded the proposed results when acted upon. Unlike those theories that made truth a matter of conforming to an antecedent reality, James's pragmatic truth was one that had a future orientation. "Truth," James famously declared in *Pragmatism*, "*happens* to an idea. It *becomes* true, is *made* true by events" (97). Truth, then, was in a state of not-yetness, of not being fully complete and open to change. Because it relied upon a notion of truth as provisional, Jamesian pragmatism was less likely to underwrite efforts to treat phenomena as part of an integrated order of things. Rather than taking the order as somehow true, pragmatism asked what were the effects of holding the belief of such order. In many cases, James concluded, there were none and the question was meaningless. The number of such meaningless questions with which philosophy wrestled led James to focus on the concrete, prompting him to speak of truths rather than of truth. For other discourses, words such as "God" or "Reason" were solutions to problems and ended investigation, James maintained. Pragmatism did not let such words close its search but had to use them, putting them into action and letting them form experience. By calling "God" or "Reason," a "program for more work" (21–22) rather than a solution, James was urging a concentration on the consequences of acting in specified ways. Overarching truths were therefore not so much false as bracketed, not foundational but in a state of constant provisionality.

Holding a proposition as provisional required an active mind, something that pragmatists found missing in the correspondence theory. That theory had a "kodak fixation," Dewey charged, and it made the mind a passive reflector of reality. However "commonsensical" such a definition of truth was, pragmatists charged it with failing to take account of the evolutionary significance of human thinking. Thinking, they averred, arose as a way to solve problems; it was instrumental to the survival of the species. Truth was made rather than found, pragmatists argued, because, as Darwin maintained, the relations between humans and their environment was constantly disrupted. Since truths were plans of action, thinking helped humans regain equilibrium by aiding them to respond successfully to disturbances. For his part James emphasized the utility of truth. "You can say . . . either that 'it is useful because it is true' or that 'it is true because it is useful.' Both these phrases mean exactly the same thing, namely that here is an idea that gets fulfilled and can be verified. True is the name for whatever idea starts the verification process, useful is the name for its completed function in experience" (98). So Dewey: "*If* ideas, meanings, conceptions, notions, theories, systems are instrumental to an active reorganization of the given environment, to a removal of some specific trouble and perplexity, then the test of their validity and value lies in accomplishing this work. If they succeed in their office, they are reliable, sound, valid, good, true. If they fail to clear up confusion, to eliminate defects, if they increase confusion, uncertainty and evil when they are acted upon, then are they false."[41] In eliminating an absolute foundation, the "if" prompted opponents to accuse Dewey and the pragmatists of an incoherent relativism.

James was the first popularizer of pragmatism. Dewey was its mature spokesman, refining Jamesian formulations and teasing out the implications of pragmatism for a whole host of public concerns. Born in Burlington, Vermont, on the eve of the Civil War, Dewey had begun his career in philosophy as an idealist, an orientation that his most perceptive biographer, Robert Westbrook, notes he never completely discarded in the prewar years. While at the University of Chicago, Dewey experienced firsthand the social problems and abuses of power of the industrial age. His work with Hull House and University Lab School, where he worked out his famous ideas in progressive education, were important influences on the philosophical position he was to develop. During the course of a career that spanned half the twentieth century, Dewey essayed responses to a wide swath of problems, bringing his philosophy to bear on subjects ranging from ethics to aesthetics, from war and peace to education.

Dewey's effort to fashion a philosophy rooted in public problems and concerns of practice rested on his understanding that philosophy had not been an impartial discourse, surveying the universe from ethereal heights. In his *Reconstruction in Philosophy* (1920), written in a moment characterized by the recrudescence of primitivism, political violence, and antidemocratic concentration of power, Dewey argued that philosophy had through much of its history served to secure the rule of the few, who had a vested interest in controlling or halting change. Philosophy had functioned as a support by valorizing the abstract and ideal at the expense of experience. In separating pure thought from lesser action, philosophy legitimated those who would rule change out of court. In Dewey's rendition, classical philosophy was committed to the stasis of ideal forms, and it treated change as a falling-away from the higher reality of perfect form. Since change often entailed conflict and division, it constituted a threat to the unity that classical philosophers located in the ideal. Like all claims to truth, philosophy had emerged in good pragmatic fashion to meet a need. That need was to replace custom as "the source and guarantor of higher moral and social values." Metaphysics had "arrogated to itself the office of demonstrating the existence of a transcendent, absolute or inner reality and of revealing to man the nature and features of this ultimate and higher reality. It has therefore claimed that it was in possession of a higher organ of knowledge than is employed by positive science and ordinary practical experience, and that it is marked by a superior dignity and importance." By separating high theory from low practice, philosophy had established grounds for elite rule (since the elite were presumably the ones who had the mastery of higher reality) and complicated the process of knowing and truth telling to distance it from the experience and verification procedures that were more homely.[42]

Dewey's own politics of philosophy were considerably different. Challenging the political implications of high and low, Dewey celebrated the virtues of everyday tools and condemned those received norms that obfuscated their value. Dewey maintained that the import of experience was that it fostered intelligence. As opposed to the much more heavily lauded Reason, which was rationality in the abstract, intelligence entailed manipulation of materials to desired ends. Dewey championed intelligence because it broke with the view of previous philosophies that ideal forms needed to be preserved, emphasizing instead the world as a resource with which to respond to change. "Since changes are going on anyway, the great thing is to learn enough about them so that we be able to lay hold of them and turn them in the direction of our desires," he maintained in a passage that revealed yet again his activist bent. Holding philosophies that invoke natural law to be fundamentally elitist, Dewey pointed to the way that they made humans objects rather than subjects. By Dewey's lights, men and women needed to be makers rather than recipients of history. "Conditions and events are neither to be fled from nor passively acquiesced in; they are to be utilized and directed. They are either obstacles to our ends or else means for their accomplishment. In a profound sense knowing ceases to be contemplative and becomes practical."[43] Reconstruction of philosophy, then, required an emphasis on the making of truth by people with tools that belonged to the species as a whole.

As suggested in Dewey's contention that the contemplative became the practical, part of his pragmatism consisted of erasing dualisms. Where other philosophers, especially of the analytic persuasion, located knowledge in the creation of distinctions, Dewey aimed at dismantling the boundaries between terms that others considered mutually exclusive. In part a remnant of his original Hegelian impulse to find unity, his efforts to integrate thought and action, however, were less a matter of seeking a single overarching truth than an effort to expand the understanding of experience. His initial foray in this regard was an intervention in a problem of psychology. In contrast to the convention of regarding stimulus and response as analytically and chronologically distinct, Dewey maintained that the whole of the experience made the parts. Actions that were labeled reflexes contained in fact their goals. A young child drawn to a flame, Dewey argued, did so not because the flame stimulated the touching, but rather because the child saw in order to touch.[44] Deweyan pragmatism prompted other unifying moves in a wide array of discourses to dismantle such long-standing distinctions as self and society, and facts and values. In the burgeoning field of social psychology, for instance, pragmatists argued that selves were not distinct from society but rather embedded within it, so that relations were transactions that were interplays of similarity and difference. By the same token, pragmatist knowledge was not somehow value-free, but linked to value, if only because values determined why humans might want to know anything in the first place.

Erasure of boundaries did not make the pragmatist version of truth any more prone toward unity. Committed to the fallibility and provisionality of propositions, pragmatists were more likely to see truth as piecemeal and contingent, rather than as integrated. Pragmatism did not rule out of court the possibilities that truths could combine, perhaps even in syntheses. However, its tilt toward antifoundational positions was more conducive to sponsoring many truths. It was that absence of any foundation that made pragmatism a well-used target for academic philosophers. Idealists such as Josiah Royce,

James's Harvard colleague, found pragmatism too willing to abandon the Absolute. Royce himself had a good deal in common with pragmatism, going so far at one point as to label himself an Absolute pragmatist. Pragmatist theories on thinking and verification met his approval, but he balked at the multiplicity at the heart of pragmatism. Like Peirce, Royce did not accept that truth had no foundations other than consensus, holding that eventually some other reality coerces that consensus. Royce found that reality in the Absolute, an Omniscient Mind. It was the Absolute, Royce held, that in fact thought both the thinker and her ideas. In so doing, the Absolute guaranteed that our ideas captured the real, since they were both of the same substance. The Absolute afforded Royce what he could not find in pragmatism: perfect harmony and absence of conflict, which he held was the basis of perfect freedom. "For the unity of things is never, for us mortals, anything that we find given in our experience. You cannot see the unity of knowledge; you cannot

Figure 1.3. The University of Chicago Philosophy Club, 1896. **Pictured here is one of the seedbeds of pragmatism, which emphasized the provisional nature of truth and the need for its verification. Judging truth on the basis of the consequences of a belief, pragmatism took direct aim at notions of truth as conformity to a preexisting reality. Stressing particularity rather than universality, the thought of George Herbert Mead (fifth from the left, second row) and John Dewey (to Mead's left) made a mark in social psychology, epistemology, aesthetics, and ethics. (Source: University of Chicago. Reprinted with Permission from the Special Collections Research Center, the University of Chicago)**

describe it as a phenomenon. It is for us now, an ideal. And precisely so, the meaning of things, the relation of knowledge to life, the significance of our ideals, their bearing upon one another—these are never, for us men, phenomenally present data."[45] James dismissed the argument as equivalent to arguing that a cat cannot look at a king unless some other being looks at them both. Dewey rejected Royce's position as flawed, because it severed an individual's life from organic life at large.

Perhaps the most common complaint about pragmatism was that it was cold to the point of denying some basic humanity. Critics lambasted it as a philosophy of manipulation rather than one of justice or goodness, the philosophy of the imperial ego rather than one of restraint, and one, because of its emphasis on what works, that legitimated the competitiveness and amorality of the marketplace. Here the target was less James, whose effort to sanction belief had elements of tenderheartedness, than Dewey, who explicitly linked science and thought on political grounds. The British writer G. K. Chesterton claimed that pragmatism was clearly insufficient as a philosophy, since it failed to meet the needs of humans for something substantial and meaningful. Echoing Royce's complaint about pragmatism's reluctance to confront ultimate essences, Chesterton complained that its trust in verification through experience meant it skated blithely along the surface of things, providing only thin gruel for the undernourished who hankered for reassurance.[46] Bertrand Russell, while applauding the scientific bent of pragmatism, also concluded that "for those who feel that life on this planet would be a life in prison if it were not for the windows into a greater world beyond; for those to whom a belief in man's omnipotence seems arrogant, who desire rather that Stoic freedom that comes of mastery over the passions than the Napoleonic domination that sees the kingdoms of this world at its feet—in a word, to men who do not find Man an adequate object of their worship, the pragmatist's world will seem narrow and petty, robbing life of all that gives it value."[47] As Dewey wryly noted, the notion that pragmatism lacked the ability to nourish humans was a tacit admission that pragmatism was correct when it argued truth had to take into account human needs.

Realists such as Pratt and Lovejoy disputed the status that pragmatists accorded verification in the determination of truth. Pratt held that pragmatism reversed the relationship between verification and truth. Verification, he insisted, did not make an idea truth; rather, verification was possible because an idea was true. Because pragmatism rejected this correspondence between an idea and reality, it was in Pratt's view repackaged idealism, dependent upon the manipulation of the subject making claims. In putting so much emphasis on experience, Pratt contended, pragmatism was unable to credit the truth of past events, because no one living actually observed them. Lovejoy centered his objections on the protocols that James accepted to judge a proposition successful. In his view, James applied impermissibly loose standards to the verification problem. At times, he seemed to count the emotional satisfaction to the holder of a belief as counting as whether or not a belief worked, especially in matters of religion and health. Such procedures, Lovejoy maintained, had a great potential for mischief. That a belief in the existence of unicorns helped us walk confidently in dark woods does nothing to establish the reality of the beasts, he maintained. Such notions of verification, argued realists, were a relativism in which a claim that one had reasons to believe a proposition to be true was resistant to refutation by others' experience.[48]

James's expansiveness did not always result in precision. Even his fellow pragmatists noted that his early discussions often moved from determining the meaning of a claim to assessing its meaningfulness. At times, he treated the true as if it were the good. As Dewey noted in a number of essays in the first decade of the twentieth century in which he laid out his own circumspect formulations, James often construed consequences in ways that committed pragmatism to take positions on issues that could not be validated empirically. On such matters, pragmatism could not be brought to bear. In his response to Pratt, Dewey pointed out how Pratt had misconstrued the nature of pragmatism's claims. Pratt used experience to denote mental events, but pragmatists used the term not as a synonym for *subjective*, but to indicate the entire organism–environment interchange. Thus, verification was not a matter of feeling or validating what one wanted but of measurable and verifiable change. Likewise, Pratt misunderstood what pragmatists meant by consequences, since he confused occurrence (which was true of past events) with judgments about the occurrence (which could have consequences as long as those occurrences left effects that could give rise to testable propositions). In short, Dewey concluded, "intellectualists" like Pratt treated verification as something rather mystical in which "we first look a long while at the facts and then a long time at the idea until by some magical process the degree and kind of their agreement become visible."[49]

The controversy that pragmatism provoked pointed not only to the attachment that many Americans had to foundations for knowledge but also to their concern for unity. Realists had built constraint into their ontology by separating subjects from objects by an unbridgeable gulf. Pragmatists argued that the gulf did not exist, which led many to worry that the continuous fashioning of truth devalued it and that without stability in truth, standards for judgment in all fields would consequently break. Critics discerned in the prospect of many truths the specter of competing truths, of uncontrolled change, and other forms of instability. Yet the multiplicity that pragmatism sanctioned was, despite the worries of its critics, hardly an embrace of anything-goes. James, for one, never thought pragmatism repealed reality and iterated on numerous occasions that those who ignored it were bound to experience ill effects.[50] Nor did pragmatism court chaos. In large measure, pragmatism was an equilibrium theory, noting ways in which disturbance set change in motion. In the absence of disturbance, pragmatists accepted that the world ran by the great flywheel of habit. When change did occur, equilibrium was, by most pragmatist accounts, the goal of action and its end result. If James did not see unity in the nature of things, he did see changes as interconnected and truths as linked and combinable. New verification, he maintained, "preserves the older stock of truths with a minimum of modification, stretching them just enough to make them admit the novelty, but conceiving that in ways as familiar as the case leaves possible. An *outrée* explanation, violating all our preconceptions, would never pass for a true account of a novelty. . . . The most violent revolutions in an individual's beliefs leave most of his old order standing. Time and space, cause and effect, nature and history, and one's own biography remain untouched. New truth is always a go-between, a smoother-over of transitions. . . . We hold a theory true just in proportion to its success in solving this 'problem of maxima and minima.'"[51] Such equanimity was one reason that James's friendly antagonist Henry Adams found James's pragmatism another species of nineteenth-century progressive optimism blithely dreaming of a nonexistent order.[52]

Dewey hardly fit the part of particularist without portfolio. Generalized patterns and abstractions, he held, were both necessary and beneficial. If experience was not generalizable, there would be little point in caring about it, he maintained. "More definitely, abstraction is indispensable if one experience is to be applicable in other experiences. Every concrete experience in its totality is unique; it is itself, nonreduplicable. Taken in its full concreteness, it yields no instruction, it throws no light. What is called abstraction means that some phase of it is selected for the sake of the aid it gives in grasping something else. Taken by itself, it is a mangled fragment, a poor substitute for the living whole from which it is extracted. But viewed teleologically or practically, it represents the only way in which one experience can be made of any value for another—the only way in which something enlightening can be secured," Dewey claimed, hinting that there was even something liberating in abstraction. "The more theoretical, the more abstract, an abstraction, or the farther away it is from anything experienced in its concreteness, the better fitted it is to deal with any one of the indefinite variety of things that may later present themselves."[53] Categories may have been on probation until they proved their usefulness, but once they did, they pointed to the persistence of patterns that made pragmatism something other than a carnival of uncertainty.

Provisionality enabled pragmatists to criticize all propositions that relied on totalizing claims or that regarded events and conditions as the inevitable consequence of natural law. In their wariness over abstraction, pragmatists were concerned to meld means to ends—in large part because they regarded as a kind of abstraction arguments that reduced people to means for some overarching or ultimate end. They took pains to advocate understanding all human beings as active participants in truth making. That commitment gave much early twentieth-century pragmatism rudimentary political commitments. On the premise that the wider the participation in decision making, the better the chance for a more fruitful solution, pragmatists opened new possibilities for multiplicity in public discourse. Their tilt toward the particular has, however, also led pragmatists to refuse the kinds of generalizations that might aid human endeavor. Dewey and Deweyan style social analysis have often resisted talking about society as a whole, holding that "society . . . is many associations not a single organization. Society means association; coming together in joint intercourse and action for the better realization of any form of experience which is augmented and confirmed by being shared."[54] This multiplicity made Deweyan pragmatists less inclined to characterize human interaction as dependent upon general laws that operated beyond and behind everyday human awareness. In concentrating on the immediate rather than the persistent and obdurate, pragmatists have generally opted for piecemeal reform and a general meliorism. Critics, especially of pragmatists' support for American entrance into the Great War, have charged that in downplaying the depth of obstacles to reform, pragmatists have misconstrued the steps necessary to achieve meaningful change.

Often dismissed in its day as the American philosophy, in part to convey the crass practicality of a business civilization that it supposedly justified, pragmatism moved easily out of the academy into the wider intellectual and cultural arena in the early twentieth century. Its success was due less to desires to justify all behaviors by whether they worked than to its imprimatur on the validation of experience for its own sake. Pragmatism appealed to those who were suspicious of the pigeonholing of grand theory and of the concomitant limitations placed on human agency. It bolstered those who opposed both hidebound traditionalists and conventional socialists as clinging to reductionist doctrines that wrongly proclaimed overarching truths. Both were far too certain about how the world held together for a new generation of independent leftists. Among those who drew upon one variant or another of pragmatism before the First World War were Walter Weyl, an editor of the *New Republic*, Randolph Bourne, Max Eastman, the editor of the *Masses*, and Walter Lippmann. Many progressive reformers too saw in pragmatism a flexible philosophy of change and engagement. Like pragmatism, progressivism was a complicated entity, one which has bedeviled analysts ever since it announced its presence in the early twentieth century. Some strains of progressivism, imbued with moral certainty and the desire to uplift, probably owed little to pragmatism. But other strains, especially that of Jane Addams, owed at least as much to pragmatism as pragmatism owed to her. Her willingness to confront first principles, to examine her own orientation, her interest in what made life more satisfactory, all demonstrate the family resemblance. It is no surprise that the Chicago pragmatists had affiliation with Hull House.[55]

Pragmatism was less directly implicated in the new arts. With the exception of Gertrude Stein, who did point to her study under William James as an important influence, few of the new artists proclaimed an overriding debt to pragmatism. This lack of direct acknowledgment may well have to do with pragmatists' preference for reason over sensibility and for science, rather than intuition, as a way of knowing. Their respectable tone too may well have played a part. Dewey, for one, was not always a fan of postimpressionism, seeing in it studied disorganization and lack of control.[56] Much of the revolution in arts and mores depended as well on a subjectivism that pragmatism with its emphasis on community determination generally avoided. One can find family resemblances in both parties' wariness of absolutist, universalizing propositions and experimental attitudes toward the world. Bohemians, to be sure, were more certain about the liberating aspect of a world without foundations. But both bohemians and pragmatists were more comfortable with perspectival truth and incomplete perceptions than a whole host of Americans, especially when the topic at hand was a moral order.

Contingent Moralities

The most profound and disquieting confrontation that most Americans had with multiplicity was more often than not in their spiritual lives. Here the lure of unity remained strongest. Few could conceive of many moralities, much less many divinities. At issue in the major denominations was less a full-fledged multiplicity than the challenge to the bedrock belief in the transcendent character of Christianity. Part of the challenge was the quiet but steady growth in agnosticism and atheism.[57] Even more bracing were the developments within Christianity itself. To a people accustomed to accepting the Word of God as universal, efforts to place religion within the sweep of history rather than above it were at times disorienting. Those who rethought Christianity in this way imagined that they were doing little more than bringing it into accord with the teleological sweep of secular history. Few doubted that history was progressive or that Christianity was the pinnacle of moral truth. Yet by pruning away elements that did not conform with science, the religious reformers of the early twentieth century fostered a multiplicity in which religion and science did not always easily mesh. Even as they tried to call some truths figurative rather than literal in order to achieve unity, the leading lights of liberalizing currents (as reformers were known) opened space for fissure and unraveling of an integrated Christianity.

Although the struggle over evolution would capture attention in the 1920s, the most significant issue of the early twentieth century was biblical inerrancy. Throughout the nineteenth century, most mainline Protestant denominations held that the Bible was the Word of God and as such contained no errors. Wrote Benjamin Warfield of Princeton Theological Seminary in 1889,

> God speaks to us now, in Scripture, not only mediately through his representatives, but directly through the Scriptures themselves as his inspired word. The Scriptures thus become the crystallization of God's authoritative will. . . . But God has caused his grace to abound to us in that he not only published redemption through Christ in the world, but gave this preachment authoritative expression through the apostles, and fixed it with infallible trustworthiness in his inspired word. Thus in every age God speaks directly to every Christian heart, and gives us abounding safety to our feet and divine security to our souls. And thus, instead of a mere record of a revelation given in the past, we have the ever-living word of God; instead of a mere tradition however guarded, we have what we have all learned to call in a unique sense "the Scriptures."[58]

Warfield's target was the growing number of scholars who stressed the historicity of the scriptures. Throughout the nineteenth century, analysts had applied the tools of literary analysis to biblical texts. Judging style, vocabulary, and sentence construction, they concluded that the radical difference in style in various books and testaments meant that the Bible was the product of multiple (and presumably fallible human) authors. German scholars had pioneered this form of biblical criticism in the 1830s and 1840s, and their findings gradually worked their way across the Atlantic. In time, other biblical scholars amplified this view of the Bible as deeply steeped in the time and place of its writing rather than transcending it. They pointed to biblical accounts that seemed to be anachronistic or that transposed geographical features. Others regarded the miracles as violations of the laws of nature, and thus not literal truth. As historian Mark Noll has put it, "by 1900, Christians contended with each other as to *how* the Bible was the Word of God and the academic world at large had asked *if* it was."[59]

American higher criticism (the effort to establish the historical origins of the Bible, as opposed to lower criticism, which aspired to reproduce and authenticate the original version of the biblical text) owed much to the interventions of Washington Gladden. A Presbyterian minister who served in North Adams, Massachusetts, and Columbus, Ohio, Gladden is best known for his advocacy of the Social Gospel, the current of thought that the gospel required social involvement and responsibility for the welfare of the entire community. Yet Gladden's more controversial stance was his 1880s and 1890s contention that the school of biblical inerrancy was decidedly unscientific. Biblical inerrancy, Gladden charged, underwrote the literal truth of the myths and legends of Genesis and insisted upon the unsustainable notion that Moses wrote the Pentateuch. Gladden's original forays were directed at the Old Testament, but queries as to the perfect veracity of the New Testament were not long in coming. Higher criticism raised a knotty problem for theologians who accepted the possibility that different human beings had contributed to the biblical text. They had to confront how to resolve the conflict between the sacredness of the Bible and the acts of humans who had clearly been inspired in different ways and to different degrees of Truth. Christians had faced similar problems in trying to reconcile Darwinian evolution and religion. Downplaying the challenges to teleology and the randomness of Darwinian change, many liberal Christians had argued that evolution was the method by which God worked his way in the world. In the matter of biblical inerrancy, liberals accepted the verdict of science but argued that nondivine parts were elevated by the association with the divine ones. What mattered, they contended, was the symbolic truth, the ineffable spiritual certainties that remained behind the words. If the Bible was a matter of many truths or more precisely truths from many writers, it was united by the central truth at its core. Complexity, however, could shake foundations. As president of Cornell Jacob Gould Schurman wrote in *Cosmopolitan* in 1909, "history and criticism have made the Bible a new book, or rather a new collection of books, written, for the most part, we know not by what authors or at what dates, and put together, as a Bible, we know not on what principle. All the landmarks, Moses, Solomon, Job, are gone; and a restless sea of criticism threatens to engulf religion with the records it adored."[60]

Many American churches were reluctant to accept arguments that removed the divine foundation from the Bible. Between 1890 and 1910,

American Protestantism witnessed a number of heresy trials in which a number of ministers stood accused of denying the unitary nature of religious truth. The most famous and sensational were those of Charles A. Briggs, professor of theology at Union Seminary, who was charged with violating Presbyterian doctrine in 1893, and Algernon Crapsey, rector of St. Andrew's Church in Rochester, New York, who was accused of heresy by the Episcopalian Church because of controversial teachings about the humanity of Jesus Christ in 1906. Briggs's interest in higher criticism grew steadily throughout the 1870s and 1880s. As the editor of the *Presbyterian Review* during the 1880s, he opened its pages to discussions of German theories of biblical authorship. In *Whither* (1879), Briggs maintained that inerrancy was in fact a modern view and not explicitly authorized by the Westminster Confession, the 1646 declaration of faith rooted in Calvinist principles that formed the basis of the Church of England, Presbyterians, and Congregationalists, among others. Briggs maintained that the Bible was the only infallible rule of faith and practice but had no authority beyond the moral and religious sphere. His address at his inauguration for a chair in Biblical Theology at Union Theological Seminary angered his opponents, resulting in heresy charges against him. At the end of a bitter two-year struggle, Briggs was excommunicated. His excommunication did not, however, end his effort to find a middle ground between inspiration and science. Like many of his fellow high critics, Briggs was concerned about a priori claims that inspiration or any divine process must have certain characteristics. The certainty with which orthodox theologians delivered judgments about divine mind and activity struck him as lacking humility, as irreverent and presumptuous, concerned more with what God should do than with what God had done. Yet these efforts were unavailing in a polarizing environment. Noll notes that by 1915 higher critics found Briggs as conservative as they did Warfield.[61]

A half decade after the Briggs trial, Union was again the site of conflict, when A. C. McGiffert argued in his *History of Christianity in the Apostolic Age* (1897) that historical change trumped religious teaching and that one could conclude that there was no continuing "essence" of Christian history. McGiffert avoided a heresy trial by leaving the Presbyterian Church and becoming a Congregationalist. Even more destabilizing was the theology of Algernon Crapsey. In a series of lectures in 1905, Crapsey directly challenged the divine foundations of religion. "Religion and history," he maintained, "are so closely associated that it is impossible to treat of the one without reference to the other." Higher critics had generally retained possibilities for the divine. Crapsey, on the other hand, steadfastly moved to dissolve that basis, holding that fixing one's belief in that which could not be demonstrated made religion a superstition. Since religion had no absolute foundation, Crapsey turned to the multiple truths of the scientific method as a substitute. His moral teachings made right conduct a matter of trial and error rather than following received truth. Much to the anger of the Episcopal governing body, Crapsey denied the existence of miracles. His Jesus was not a divine savior, but a historical figure. "The Founder of Christianity no longer stands apart from the common destiny of man in life and death, but He is in all things physical like as we are." For Crapsey, the historical Jesus was more inspiring than the divine one. "When we come to know Jesus in His historical relations, we see that miracle is not a help, it is a hindrance, to an intelligent comprehension of His person, His character, and His mission. We are not alarmed, we are relieved when scientific history proves to us that the fact of His miraculous birth was unknown to Himself, unknown to his mother, and unknown to the whole Christian community of the first generation."[62] Crapsey's commitment to many truths expanded over the years after his removal, eventuating in a form of pantheism.

The tides of multiplicity beat against another stronghold of absolutism, the Catholic Church. In practice, as Jay Dolan has demonstrated, American Catholicism was not as unified and hierarchical an institution as its Protestant detractors took it to be. American Catholicism had a number of significant ethnic variations. Its Mexican variant differed from its Italian, which in turn differed from the Irish version. Despite efforts of the hierarchy to wipe out different emphases in worship, these remained. Many historians have argued that private devotions to saints and spiritual heroes played a larger part in the religious life of nineteenth-century Catholicism than did the mass and the sacraments. Likewise, Dolan contends, during the nineteenth century a significant number of Catholics rejected the culture of sin and authority. Catholicism was "a curious blend of official and folk beliefs and practices."[63]

At the level of doctrine too, American Catholicism generated new, more flexible approaches to faith. One such approach was Americanism. Led by such figures as John Ireland, the archbishop of St. Paul, John Keane of Richmond, Virginia, and Dennis O'Connell, rector of the North American College in Rome, Americanists campaigned for English liturgy, cooperation with Protestants on a number of issues, and a church independent of foreign interference. Americanism was both a strategic and an intellectual development. On the strategic level, it aimed at neutralizing the diverse ethnic differences within the church and removing the taint of foreignness at a time when American Protestants intensified their concern about ethnic and religious purity. Aware of the precarious state of Catholics in the United States, Americanists accepted the separation of church and state as the guarantee of

Figure 1.4. Religious multiplicity. **Algernon Crapsey, an Episcopal minister, whose Social Gospel and belief that religion was historically contingent rather than received, led to his conviction for heresy in 1905. (Source: University of Rochester)**

religious liberty. Although, as Dolan indicates, this toleration did not extend
to archdiocesan politics, the formal acknowledgment of religious pluralism
constituted an unprecedented step toward multiplicity in the church. While
not denying the divinity of the church (they regarded it as God's chosen instrument for progress), Americanists hoped to unite it with the age, to allow
it to become more meaningful in meeting the spiritual needs of its parishioners in the modern world. As Ireland put it, the Americanists believed that
the church "must herself be new, adapting herself in manner of life and in
method of action to the new conditions of the new order, thus proving herself, while ever ancient, to be ever new, as truth from heaven it is and ever
must be."[64]

Americanism ran into opposition from a number of quarters. Much of the
laity resisted the homogenizing efforts as untoward intervention in their religious practices. In Chicago, for example, Cardinal George Mundelein
squared off with Polish Catholics over the existence of Polish-language
parishes. Mundelein, one of the architects of Americanism, saw language-
based parishes as an impediment to Catholic unity and, at times, a source of
superstition. He was, however, unable to convince the Poles, who sent a
steady stream of petitions to Rome accusing him of being bent on the destruction of their nationality. At issue in many of the Americanization struggles between the church and its parishioners were the problems of how to
worship and how to educate children. Also at stake was whether identity
would be singular or multiple—homogeneous or heterogeneous. Others accused Americanizers of compromising the church's transcendence and autonomy. Rather than plunging the church into history, the opponents of
Americanism wanted the church to maintain its position as immune to the
secular fashions and the transitory influences of human history. They also
condemned concessions to Protestantism and pluralism as granting rights to
error, something that the Holy Church could not accept. Especially worrying
was the emphasis on the Holy Spirit rather than on the institution of the
church, the one perfect visible society. That emphasis, they charged, cleared
the way for American individualism. Rather than uniting church and age,
such opponents wanted to keep them separate and hostile.[65]

Eventually, Pope Leo, in *Testem Benevolentiae* in 1899, excoriated all currents that insisted that the universal church needed to adapt to parochial situations rather than the other way around. By his lights, Americanism and related movements among Catholics violated a central tenet of the faith by
putting natural virtues ahead of supernatural ones. A similar fate befell a second current known as modernism, which overlapped and was often confused
with Americanism but which had different origins and emphases. Modernism

was a self-conscious attempt to examine traditional Catholic teachings on the nature of revelation, biblical inspiration, and religious knowledge in light of modern natural and social science. Accepting that modern science had demonstrated the impossibility of various points of dogma, modernists spurned efforts to make phenomena integrate into dogma. They rejected ingrained neo-scholasticism as falsely asserting the primacy of inspiration over history and science. Modernist understanding of science was firmly rooted in nineteenth-century conceptions of the discourse as an unambiguous source of truth and of history as a narrative of progress. Modernist goals in both the United States and in Europe, where if anything it was stronger, entailed creating a new synthesis of faith and science. For Protestants, that goal was old hat. For Catholics, that enterprise meant acknowledging new forms of knowing.[66]

Catholic modernism shared with its Protestant counterparts efforts to reexamine both the status of the Bible and the nature of Christ. The leading Catholic higher critic, Henry Poels, of Catholic University in Washington, D. C., argued in a vein similar to that of Charles Briggs that based on literary analysis, biblical authorship was clearly multiple. Casting this conclusion as rooted in science, Poels argued that the church did damage to faith and its faithful by continuing to advance teaching that science could easily overturn. Poels's views spread to a number of seminaries, with St. Joseph's in Yonkers run by the Sulpician Fathers taking the lead role in expounding modernism. Hoping to effect a renewal of Catholic theology, the leading lights of St. Joseph's, James Driscoll, Francis Gigot, and philosophers Francis Duffy and John Brady, founded the New York Review in 1905. The Review struck a blow for a Catholic version of multiplicity by arguing that inquiry rather than propagating dogma or protecting the faith was the essence of intellectual activity. Perhaps its most controversial line of inquiry was the debate over Christ's human nature. Suggesting that there were limitations on Jesus's knowledge, Review authors demonstrated that early church doctrine had admitted that Christ was not omniscient. Although the Bible has held a lesser place in the Catholic tradition than in the Protestant one, in large measure because Catholic teaching emphasizes the church as the embodiment of the Spirit, Rome was far from nonchalant about Poels's work. When the American hierarchy removed him from his duties, the Vatican assented, denying his appeal. The Review was even more vulnerable, especially when the seminary invited Protestant scholars to lecture. In 1907, Pius X issued his wide-ranging encyclical against modernism, Pascendi Dominici Gregis. The encyclical not only detailed the errors of modernism but mandated each diocese establish councils to monitor compliance with doctrine. Journals were closed down, libraries pruned, and, according to Jay Dolan, "brain rot set in."[67]

The hold of orthodoxy in the first two decades of the twentieth century was as strong in conceptions of morality as it was in theology. For most Americans right and wrong were unchanging and obvious, rooted in values that existed time out of mind. Context and situation mattered for naught in evaluating whether acts were moral. As long as individuals acted in their personal lives in accord with this code, best enunciated in the Ten Commandments, virtue prevailed. By increasing the scope and pace of interactions and creating novel situations, industrial life upset the equilibrium of goal and act that the code had set. Or at least a significant number of Americans thought so. Those who felt the need for readjustment in what constituted right conduct pointed less to redefinition of ethics than to an expansion of the venue in which honest and honorable dealing took place. The most prominent development in this regard was the Social Gospel. With few exceptions, Social Gospelers assumed a common set of Christian values, which they hoped would infuse social life and result in a homogeneous and unified society. Having become dismayed by the disjunction between private virtues and public behavior, Social Gospelers tried to make reality square with values, rather than questioning values at all. Many of the virtues that advocates of the Social Gospel commended were those that historians have labeled traditional ones—thrift, self-restraint and self-control, honesty, and selflessness. The desire to realize those values propelled Social Gospelers to public crusades against prostitution and drinking, and into campaigns against rapacious, monopolistic behavior (especially on the municipal level) and "selfish" corporate bargaining with labor. The Social Gospel question, "What would Jesus do?" echoed throughout the period in an effort to call men and women to apply moral principles throughout the whole of their lives.

Policing public behavior, of course, had a long history in the United States. What separated the Social Gospel from previous incarnations of public morality was its emphasis on society rather than the individual as the locus of judgment. Social Gospelers concerned themselves, at least in rhetoric, with how just social life was and how organized action fulfilled the public good. Washington Gladden, for instance, maintained that his reform politics were the consequence of his rejection of biblical inerrancy. Locating the spiritual truth of the Bible in a version of the Golden Rule, Gladden envisioned his advocacy of social responsibility, fair wages, and progressive reform as part of his duty to act like Christ. Externalizing salvation, Gladden trusted a history that he believed humans could and should make better. Theological liberalism did not preordain interventionist politics. Many who shared Gladden's biblical analysis were politically conservative. Likewise, prewar theological conservatives could and did engage in collective social action.

Charles Gardiner's *Ethics of Jesus and Social Progress* (1914) documents how strong liberal political views could emerge from an insistence on orthodoxy among Southern Baptists.[68] Although the Social Gospel was a Protestant phenomenon, Catholic churchmen pushed beyond alms to a comprehensive program of social reconstruction. With a fundamentally working-class constituency, Catholic priests invariably confronted the "social question" in the course of their duties. Like their Protestant counterparts, they were aware of erosion in attendance and moved to combat it. Most prominent was John Ryan, who penned the famous *A Living Wage* (1912) and who was instrumental in the postwar plans for the Bishops' Program for Social Reconstruction. That program included the unfettered right of labor to organize, old age insurance, health insurance, and unemployment insurance, regulation of public utility rates, public control of monopolies, and the establishment of cooperative enterprises.[69]

As historians have rightly argued, the Social Gospel promised individuals therapeutic benefits, redefining salvation as the glow that followed contributions to social improvement instead of the task of spiritually preparing individuals to accept an unseen power or the discomfort of examining one's soul.[70] At times, historians have suggested that efforts to find inner peace and ease self-doubts drove even the two most articulate proponents of the social morality, Walter Rauschenbusch, the Baptist scholar and minister in Rochester, New York, and Jane Addams. They point to his efforts to negotiate his life with his authoritarian and demanding father, and to her famous "Subjective Necessity of Settlement Houses," in which she proposes settlement house work as the solution to the vacuum in which middle-class women lived, as key pieces of evidence. Whatever personal motives spurred Rauschenbusch and Addams, however, complemented their efforts to derive a code of conduct that achieved good on a collective scale. In their hands, the task of establishing a social morality was something more than an attempt to squash diversity and tame difference.[71] Few thought as seriously about how to define and achieve a meaningful collective good that committed men and women to the well-being of others. Addams's less-cited but equally important "Objective Necessity of Settlement Houses" was just the first articulation of their career-long efforts to redefine morality as social justice. Few Social Gospelers were as willing to commit their lives so fully to help others collaborate on achieving social goods. Addams's famous Hull House work and her selflessness earned her the title of "Saint Jane." For his part, Rauschenbusch damaged his health early in the century during his extensive work on the Lower East Side of New York before coming to Rochester. Particularly noteworthy in their new morality was their wariness of charity, which they regarded as a misplaced compassion that depended upon pity for the "less fortunate," and their embrace of action to dismantle social hierarchy and invidious distinction. If Addams and Rauschenbusch did not completely fulfill the goals they set for themselves or did not always provide meaningful analyses of the social problems they deplored, they nonetheless offered a version of the good that went beyond both individual well-being and bromides of social harmony.

Like Gladden and Algernon Crapsey, Rauschenbusch found the inerrancy of the Bible difficult to accept. Nor was he certain that a divine justice operated in the world. If it did, it did not obviate the need for human justice. Too often, he argued, the quest for individual salvation that theological conservatives saw as the full compass of moral action meant a lack of concern with the temporal fate of one's fellows. Denying that salvation could constitute the full measure of right conduct, Rauschenbusch proposed a morality rooted in love. He had in mind by the term less a warm, fuzzy feeling that gushed sentimental and overlooked faults and problems, but "the equalizing and society-making impulse." In his version, Christ lived and died to bring love into the world. It was the duty of Christians to fulfill the potential that Christ had made possible. Rauschenbusch explicitly recognized Christ was not "a social reformer of the modern type," by which he meant his activities were less systematic and scientific than the activists of the twentieth century. Nor, he hinted, was Christ's morality as dogmatic as those of professional do-gooders who launched schemes for social perfection. In Rauschenbusch's version of Jesus, he was less a teacher of morality than one who discovered how to live a religious life, one less certain and more open to the world than traditionalist moralists made him out to be. Knowing the love of God, the Father, Jesus set out to share it as a matter of social duty. That led him to sympathy for the poor and an opposition to ceremony in place of ethics, but not necessarily to an implacable hatred of the rich. Rauschenbusch's Christ was a thus a more complicated figure than that of many early-twentieth-century radicals who deployed Jesus to justify their politics or, perhaps, to provide an example of what their political schemes would create. The editors of the left-wing journal the *Masses* were particularly enamored of the notion of Christ as labor organizer and rebel. So too was Frank Tannenbaum, an IWW organizer who led the unemployed in occupation of wealthy congregations in a demand for reparations.[72]

Rauschenbusch's social morality had elements of multiplicity to the degree that he did not specify precisely what constituted social goods, preferring to allow collective determination to arrive at the particulars. Favoring at a minimum provisioning for all and equal voice in decision making,

Rauschenbusch generally avoided outright prescription. Rauschenbusch's social morality did, however, eventuate in unity. He held that self and society melded and that suppression of individualism was a necessary goal. What he envisioned, as he wrote in *Christianity and the Social Crisis* (1907), was a state in which "the swift instincts of self-preservation" made it incumbent on us to "divine what we owe to our neighbor. Anything incompatible with love would stand indicted. . . . Self development is desirable because it helps us to serve the better."[73] That selves were so inextricably connected to others that conflict was a misunderstanding characterized Addams's orientation as well. Less interested in a "purified nation," shorn of individual sins, than in "a regenerated and reorganized society," she insisted that mutual participation was not only the core of democracy but also the measure of the good. "We have learned to say that the good must be extended to all of society before it can be held secure by any one person or any one class; but we have not yet learned to add to that statement, that unless all men and all classes contribute to a good, we cannot even be sure that it is worth having."[74] Addams's commitment to collective determination led her, as it did Rauschenbusch, to view clashes of interests as only surface manifestations covering a deeper connection. She laid out the position in the cauldron of the Pullman Strike (when the end of rail traffic prevented her from reaching her ill sister in southern Illinois). In a paper published some years after the event, she criticized Pullman's false paternalism and haughty treatment of workers' concerns but also workers' sense that social problems could not be solved without the angry action of the aggrieved. Her sense of true comity across class lines was at the heart of why she could never join the Socialist Party, despite her attractions to many socialist positions. It was this commitment that led the critic Randolph Bourne to write his friend Alyse Gregory that Addams never challenged the social and cultural substructure, and to complain of the prim unity of her position. "Causes have only finally triumphed when the rational 'gradual progress' men have been overwhelmed. Better crude irrationality than the rationality that checks hope and stifles faith."[75]

Not all of the redefinition of right conduct in the early twentieth century involved the new concern for social goods. Bourne's evocation of the virtues of crude irrationality was a distinguishing feature of the famed revolt against Victorianism. The rebellion of the young against nineteenth-century middle-class morals, which Bourne had chronicled in major journals in the early 1910s, was predicated on a sense that the prescriptive morality that divided the world into mutually exclusive categories was ill suited to take account of the flux of modern life. By the lights of such critics as Bourne and Floyd Dell, the old morality cut off humans from experience and their own powers by regarding a portion of life as unacceptable. Previous generations had drawn the boundary between the rational and the irrational in such a way as to condemn the latter as impulsive emotion that originated in drives that moral humans should control. The new moralists recognized the security that such a moral map conferred but criticized its costs. One result was a chilling atmosphere of smugness and conformity. Bourne spoke for his generation when he wrote that wherever "you come across that combination of selfless devotion with self-righteousness, you have the essence of the puritan."[76] The animosity directed at "Puritans" (actually an invention of the new moralists rather than the historic Puritans) demonstrated the bohemian understanding that a truly human morality did not depend on separating mind from body. Rejecting the uplift and improvement on which the old morality insisted, the bohemians of the early twentieth century staked their sense of good on pleasure, which the old morality at best constrained but more often than not actually suppressed.[77]

Accused of simply inverting moral life and justifying mindless pleasure, the dissenters saw themselves as constructing an ethics that would generate meaningful ideals rather than unrealistic ones. In taking the truly human to be the intermingling of what nineteenth-century moralists tried to segregate, moderns put a new spin on the romantic ideal of "authenticity." Romantics had envisioned the true self an entity that society suppressed. When the essential self freely expressed itself, the result would be a natural morality in the manner of Rousseau. Moderns, at least as they articulated the matter, saw the vital component that needed expression as in the process of formation. As such, their emphasis was less freeing drives for their own sake than accepting complexity and learning from the trials of experience. This preference for vitalism is one reason that Jung rather than Freud was the psychoanalyst of choice in the Village. The emphasis on experience rather than natural qualities underlines why the feminism of the 1910s rejected the nurturing service and moral uplift of the nineteenth-century woman movement. And why many regarded socialism, with its central planning and its trust in the progressive unfolding of history, as "dull-as-dishwater" when compared with its lively rival anarchism, which many regarded as the embodiment of Max Stirner's vision of life as "naked freedom."[78]

Because the new morality did not rest on obligation to fulfill a preexisting code, proponents contended that they made good rather than conformed to it. Such a human-centered ethics opened the way, they maintained, for creativity in conceptions of justice and responsibility. Its ad hoc, unfinished quality made it the beginning of multiplicity in morals. Rebels against Victorianism proudly championed their ethos for its freedom of association, its

promotion of self-expression and discovery, its refusal to make a priori judgments, and its acceptance of a more rounded picture of what was truly human. For all their talk of rebellion and even amorality, the Greenwich Villagers and like-minded souls in bohemian enclaves scattered around the
country shared with their erstwhile opponents more than they acknowledged. As Henry May has noted, both the new morals and the old culture
possessed a cheerful optimism that Europeans have long found an irritating
part of American life.[79] The stray pessimist on the order of an Ambrose
Bierce notwithstanding, the new moralists had their own version of progress.

In the most hotly contested part of the new morality, relations between
the sexes, the stark rhetorical differences between the old and the new often
obscured resemblances. In any event, the liberation often proved to be less
sweeping than advertised. Free love and other assorted nonmarital relations,
for all their differences from bourgeois marriages, all too often led to disor-
ganized unhappiness. As a number of historians have documented, bohemian
relationships were often cases of the return of the repressed, reproducing prevailing notions of gender in which male freedom exploited female duty. In
some spheres, the new morality was less tolerant than the old. The old rigidly
separated public and private, allowing in private what it scorned in public.
The new did not. As a consequence, gays and lesbians fared poorly among
the insistent heterosexuals of Greenwich Village.[80]

The most thoroughly articulated (and considerably more measured) articulation of multiplicity in morals during the period was John Dewey's. Ethical
behavior, he maintained, was not a matter of consulting "a table of commandments in a catechism" and obeying without deviation. In line with his
inclination to treat things specifically, Dewey saw the answers provided by
general principles as never as definitive as the questions they purported to
solve. General principles, Dewey noted, aided in personal choice but were
hardly sufficient in matters of "moral perplexity."[81] Dewey attributed the misapprehension of the nature of the good to philosophies (and here he had
Kant in mind) that rigidly separated means from ends. Kantian ethics, ori-
ented as they were toward decisions based on principles regardless of interest,
envisioned means as somehow pedestrian and ends as elevated and pure. This
emphasis, Dewey charged, resulted in separating judgment from behavior.
Kantian trust in universal reason, locked within moral agents who divorced
themselves from actual life, misapprehended how moral decisions were made.
Just as nonpragmatist versions of truth required a God's-eye view of events,
so too did moral dualism. In contrast, Dewey offered a theory of ethics that
might be called particularistic.

Dewey's ethical arguments turned on his understanding of a moral situation. Explicitly exempting those situations in which goods were generally understood and accepted, Dewey turned his attention to those moments in which judgment and choice were required before overt action. Moral situations admitted to no ready-made conclusions because they usually involved "conflicting desires and alternative apparent goods." Since these were situations in which there was no consensus on the "one supreme end," human beings had to weigh means and ends. In Dewey's scheme, moral action was more akin to intelligent choice, a formulation that he claimed did not abandon responsibility, only located it. Moral action entailed inquiry about the particulars of a situation, of seeing more than the vivid traits, tracing likely consequences of various forms of action, and regarding the decision as hypothetical until supposed consequences were squared with actual ones. Dewey's version of moral excellence included wide sympathy, keen sensitivity, and persistence in the face of the disagreeable, because it was they that would enable intelligent choice.[82]

Thus, Kantian moral universals were spectacularly irrelevant. Treating judgments on acts as specific and concrete because actions were specific, Dewey fashioned an ethical theory that accepted that morality meant not placing oneself in harmony with preexisting principles but undertaking acts that directed intercourse among people into "the modes of greatest fruitfulness," as he put it in Reconstruction. Deweyan fruitfulness was not a fixed goal, for that would yield "unworthy selfishness or insipid tedium." There is, therefore, something unspecified in Deweyan ethics, an emphasis on process, growth, change, and expansion through intelligence rather than a guidebook for right conduct. This multiplicity stemmed from the emphasis on experience, again understood as interaction between thinking agent and adaptable world. Such experience was "messy," not easily classifiable, and in true pragmatist fashion involved a problem, often that of weighing incompatible interests. It was also one in which judgments were considerably less blanket. Mistakes, Dewey contended, should be regarded as something other than "mere unavoidable accidents" or "moral sins to be expiated and forgiven." They are lessons in the wrong methods of using intelligence and should be regarded as indications of the need for development and readjustment.[83]

Many critics, then and now, had strong reservations about Dewey's moral multiplicity. His failure to specify overriding principles left some thinking his ethics were extremely vague and useless. Others interpreted Dewey's notion of interest as equivalent to self-interest, leading to charges that Dewey sanctioned selfishness. Given Dewey's insistence that action was social, that individualism in ethics only increased conflict, and that intelligent inquiry required shared experience to achieve justice, the charge is less persuasive than it seemed to contemporaries who were shocked by Dewey's multiplicity. More have worried about its usefulness, professing to see a loss of moorings, a dangerous permissiveness, and a promiscuous relativism in Dewey's notions of ethics without absolute foundation. Recently, the historian John Diggins has resurrected the charge, holding that pragmatism fails to provide either a check on the imperial ego or resources to limit power. Diggins is especially troubled by Dewey's contention that mistakes are lessons and by his position that morality, properly conceived, is "flexible, vital, growing." Sentiments like these, Diggins concludes, are a refusal to label evil by its name. In opting instead to label acts mistakes or failure, pragmatism in Diggins's view cannot effectively oppose totalitarianism.[84]

Diggins's analysis is the classic objection to multiplicity. Without a unifying principle, critics of multiplicity worried, there was no independent source of authority and no way to launch a critique or to establish value. A culture of multiplicity is too easily swayed by prevailing fashion that could be resisted were a foundation acknowledged. In some ways, Diggins's criticisms mirror the more famous ones of Randolph Bourne during the debate over the First World War. Reacting strongly to pragmatists' support for the a war that he regarded as decidedly unfruitful, Bourne scathingly charged that pragmatists loved technique and worshipped power. Having no independent principles by which to guide their conduct, they found themselves surrendering to prevailing ones.[85] Yet, viewed from another angle, Bourne's argument is that Dewey and his fellow war supporters were not pragmatic enough, in that they did not sufficiently gauge the forces at work or the chances of achieving meaningful outcomes, or take account of obdurate facts and determinations. In any event, those who asserted the need for firm foundations gave little indication during this period how they might be recouped, saved for faith or fiat.

The fight over multiplicity in morals had another, less apparent side during the first two decades of the twentieth century. It touched upon matters of beauty and entertainment, as well. If the United States had not yet become a full-fledged leisure or consumer society at the turn of the century, culture and pleasure did assume a new importance in American life. As aesthetic questions invariably came to the fore, so too did moral ones. As how to experience pleasure became less obvious, Americans faced in another way the ramifications of multiplicity.

Notes

1. McCosh, quoted in John O'Donnell, *The Origins of Behaviorism: American Psychology, 1870–1920* (New York: New York University Press, 1985), 56.

2. Eliot, quoted in Daniel Kevles, *The Physicists: The History of a Scientific Community in Modern America* (New York: Vintage, 1977), 24.

3. Herbert Spencer, *First Principles* (New York: Appleton, 1864), 145.

4. Fin-de-siècle nihilism is covered in Larzer Ziff, *The American 1890s: Life and Times of a Lost Generation* (New York: Viking Press, 1966), 120–45, 166–74; and Melinda Knight, "Cultural Radicalism in the American Fin de Siècle: The Emergence of an Oppositional Literary Culture" (PhD diss., New York University, 1992).

5. Wright's and Peirce's encounters with multiplicity have been extensively chronicled. Although they shared many positions—particularly on the scientific method and the role of chance, they differed on ultimate ends and the shape knowledge would assume. See, among others, David Marcell, *Progress and Pragmatism: James, Dewey, Beard and the American Idea of Progress* (Westport, CT: Greenwood Press, 1972); and Louis Menand, *The Metaphysical Club: A Story of Ideas in America* (New York: Farrar, Straus, and Giroux, 2001).

6. Kevles, *The Physicists*, 162.

7. Ibid., 30.

8. R. P. Crease and C. C. Mann, *The Second Creation: Makers of the Revolution in Twentieth-Century Physics* (New York: Macmillan, 1986), 10.

9. Kelvin, quoted in Richard Panek, *The Invisible Century: Einstein, Freud, and the Search for Hidden Universes* (New York: Viking, 2004), 14–15. My account of relativity has been drawn from Panek, Kelves, Etienne Klein and Marc Lachièze-Rey, *The Quest for Unity: The Adventure of Physics* (New York: Oxford University Press, 1999); Jeremy Bernstein, *Secrets of the Old One: Einstein, 1905* (New York: Springer, 2006); David Bodanis and Simon Singh, eds., *E=mc²: A Biography of the World's Most Famous Equation* (New York: Walker, 2000); Ronald William Clark, *Einstein: The Life and Times* (New York: H. N. Abrams, 1984); and John S. Rigden, *Einstein 1905: The Standard of Greatness* (Cambridge, MA: Harvard University Press, 2005).

10. Einstein's paper, the third in the *annus mirabilis* year of 1905, was entitled, "On the Electrodynamics of Moving Bodies."

11. Einstein, quoted in Klein and Lachièze-Rey, *Unity*, 105.

12. Discussion of the revolution in physics is drawn from Kevles, *The Physicists;* George Gamow, *Thirty Years That Shook Physics: The Story of Quantum Theory* (New York: Dover 1985 [1966]); Hans Riechenbach, *The Philosophy of Space and Time* (New York: Dover, 1957); and John Rigden, *Einstein 1905: The Standard of Greatness* (Cambridge, MA: Harvard University Press, 2005).

13. Kevles, *The Physicists*, 85–86.

14. William R. Everdell, *The First Moderns: Profiles in the Origins of Twentieth-Century Thought* (Chicago: University of Chicago Press, 1997), 166–76, 220–40,

331–60; Stephen Kern, *The Culture of Time and Space, 1880–1918* (Cambridge, MA: Harvard University Press, 1983), 18–21; Kevles, *The Physicists*.

15. John Trowbridge, "Physical Science To-day," *Atlantic Monthly* (August 1909), 318–24.

16. "Exit the Amateur Scientist," *Nation* 83 (August 23, 1906), 106.

17. Mark Sullivan, *Our Times: America at the Birth of the Twentieth Century* (New York: Scribner, [1926] 1996), 132.

18. Paul Vitz and Arnold Glimcher, *Modern Art and Modern Science: The Parallel Analysis of Vision* (New York: Praeger, 1984), 20–36, 70–75.

19. Edward Wagenknecht, *American Profile, 1900–1909* (Amherst: University of Massachusetts Press, 1982), 200–208.

20. Ian Gordon, *Comic Strips and Consumer Culture, 1890–1945* (Washington, DC: Smithsonian Institution Press, 1998), discusses middle-class appropriation of comic strips.

21. Wagenknecht, *Profile*, 205–8; Heinz Politzer, "From Little Nemo to Li'l Abner," in *The Funnies, an American Idiom*, ed. David Manning White and Robert H. Abel (New York: Free Press of Glencoe, 1963), 40–45.

22. La Touche Hancock, "The American Comic and Caricature Art," *Bookman* (November 1902), 263–74.

23. Patrick McDonnell, Karen O'Connell, and Georgia Riley de Havenon, *Krazy Kat: The Comic Art of George Herriman* (New York: Harry N. Abrams, 1986) is the definitive source, and has wonderful reproductions to boot. For a fascinating argument of the way in which Herriman anticipated modern physics, see "Zip! Pow! Ah-a-a . . ." Scientific Musings by Chet Raymo, January 29, 2006, http://www.science-musings.com/musingsarchive/2006_01_29_musings.html (accessed July 18, 2008).

24. For the early history of the movies, see Robert Sklar, *Movie-Made America: A Cultural History of American Movies* (New York: Vintage, 1975); Charles Musser, *The Emergence of Cinema: The American Screen to 1907*, vol. 1 of *History of the American Cinema* (New York: Charles Scribner's Sons, 1990); Eileen Bowser, *The Transformation of Cinema, 1907–1915*, vol. 2 of *History of the American Cinema* (New York: Charles Scribner's Sons, 1990); and Kevin Brownlow, *The Parade's Gone By* (Berkeley and Los Angeles: University of California Press, 1976).

25. Cortissoz, quoted in Milton Brown, *The Story of the Armory Show* (New York: Abbeville Press, 1988), 141, 174.

26. Vitalism as an international and historical phenomenon is surveyed in George Rousseau *Organic Form: the Life of an Idea* (London: Routledge and Keegan Paul, 1972). Bergson's influence on U.S. thought and culture remains terribly understudied, despite the general acknowledgment of his significance. Two places to start: Thomas Quirk, "Bergson in America," *Prospects* 11 (1987): 453–90; and Jeffrey Scott Brown, "Vitalism and the Modernist Search for Meaning: Subjectivity, Social Order, and the Philosophy of Life in the Progressive Era" (PhD diss., University of Rochester, 2001).

27. Henri Bergson, *Introduction to Metaphysics* (New York and London: G. P. Putnam's Sons, 1912), 189.

28. Marin, quoted in William Innes Homer, *Alfred Stieglitz and the Photo-Secession* (Boston, MA: Little, Brown, 1982), 105.

29. David Minter, *A Cultural History of the American Novel: Henry James to William Faulkner* (New York: Cambridge University Press, 1994), 60–63.

30. Margot Norris, "Modernist Eruptions," in Emory Eliott, *Columbia History of the American Novel* (New York: Columbia University Press, 1991), 311–30, puts Stein in context of other modernist writings.

31. James Pratt, *What Is Pragmatism?* (Bristol, UK: Thoemmes Press, [1909] 2001), 67.

32. Desley Deacon, *Elsie Clews Parsons: Inventing Modern Life* (Chicago: University of Chicago Press, 1997), 100–128; Everdell, *First Moderns*, 28–29, 223, 230, 234; Robert C. Bannister, *Sociology and Scientism: The American Quest for Objectivity, 1880–1940* (Chapel Hill: University of North Carolina Press, 1987), 71–75; David S. Luft, *Robert Musil and the Crisis of European Culture, 1880–1942* (Berkeley and Los Angeles: University of California Press, 1980), 81–89.

33. Dorothy Ross, *The Origins of American Social Science* (New York and Cambridge: Cambridge University Press, 1991), 327. For Pearson's influence on American social scientists, see Bannister, *Sociology and Scientism*. Pearson's contribution to statistical thinking is covered in Theodore M. Porter, *The Rise of Statistical Thinking, 1820 –1900* (Princeton, NJ: Princeton University Press, 1986), 296–314.

34. Deacon, *Parsons*, 100–103.

35. Bannister, *Sociology and Scientism*, 70–79. Henry Adams was particularly affected by Pearson's *Grammar of Science* (1892), holding that it brought home to him how limited science was to make sense of chaos. See Henry Adams, *The Education of Henry Adams: An Autobiography* (Boston, MA: Houghton Mifflin, [1918] 1961), 449–60. For Pearson's racial views, see Ivan Hannaford, *Race: The History of an Idea in the West* (Baltimore: Johns Hopkins University Press, 1996), 290, 330–32.

36. Now that pragmatism has been revived the literature it has generated has been absolutely enormous. The account of pragmatism that follow draws heavily on the diverse presentations of Tom Burke, *Dewey's New Logic: A Reply to Russell* (Chicago: University of Chicago Press, 1994); Andrew Feffer, *The Chicago Pragmatists and American Progressivism* (Ithaca, NY: Cornell University Press, 1993); James Kloppenberg, *Uncertain Victory: Social Democracy and Progressivism in European and American Thought, 1870–1920* (New York: Oxford University Press, 1986); James Livingston, *Pragmatism and the Political Economy of Cultural Revolution, 1850–1940* (Chapel Hill: University of North Carolina Press, 1994); Brian Lloyd, *Left Out: Pragmatism, Exceptionalism, and the Poverty of American Marxism, 1890–1922* (Baltimore: Johns Hopkins University Press, 1997); Marcell, *Progress and Pragmatism*; Robert B. Westbrook, *John Dewey and American Democracy* (Ithaca, NY: Cornell University Press, 1991); and Westbrook's *Democratic Hope: Pragmatism and the Politics of Truth* (Ithaca, NY: Cornell University Press, 2005), in addition to the writings of the pragmatists themselves.

37. John Dewey, *Reconstruction in Philosophy* (Boston, MA: Beacon Press, [1920] 1948), 166–87.

38. Charles Sanders Peirce, "How to Make Our Ideas Clear," *Popular Science Monthly* (January 1878), 286–302; and "Fixation of Belief," *Popular Science Monthly* (November 1878), 1–15, are the best known and most succinct expressions of Peirce's proto-pragmatism.

39. See Paul Conkin, *Puritans and Pragmatists* (Bloomington: Indiana University Press, 1968), 193–265.

40. William James, *Pragmatism, a New Name for Some Old Ways of Thinking; The Meaning of Truth, a Sequel to Pragmatism* (Cambridge, MA: Harvard University Press, 1978), 20. Subsequent references are in the text.

41. Dewey, *Reconstruction in Philosophy*, 156.

42. Ibid., 16–17, 23.

43. Ibid., 116.

44. John Dewey, "The Reflex Arc Concept in Psychology," *Psychological Review* 3 (1896): 357–70. See also Burke, *Dewey's New Logic*, esp. 120–28; Ian Burkitt, *Social Selves: Theories of the Social Formation of Personality* (London: Sage, 1991); John Burnham, "The Mind–Body Problem in the Early Twentieth Century," in *Paths into American Culture: Psychology, Medicine, and Morals* (Philadelphia: Temple University Press, 1988), 25–40; Marcell, *Progress and Pragmatism*, 220–28; Menand, *The Metaphysical Club: A Story of Ideas in America*, 327–30; Westbrook, *John Dewey and American Democracy*, 67–70.

45. Josiah Royce, "The Sciences of the Ideal," in *International Congress of Arts and Science: Universal Exposition, St. Louis, 1904*, ed. Howard J. Rogers (Boston, MA: Houghton Mifflin, 1905), 1:155.

46. Menand, *Metaphysical Club*, 362.

47. Bertrand Russell, "Pragmatism" (1909), in Russell, *Philosophical Essays* (New York: Simon and Schuster, 1966), 110–11.

48. Pratt makes his case in Pratt, *What Is Pragmatism?* Much of Lovejoy's engagement with pragmatism can be found in Arthur O. Lovejoy, *The Thirteen Pragmatisms, and Other Essays* (Baltimore: Johns Hopkins Press, 1963). See especially "Pragmatism and Realism," 30–39.

49. John Dewey, "Control of Ideas by Facts" (1907), in John Dewey, *Middle Works*, 4:85. Other crucial refinements include "A Short Catechism on Truth" (1909), "What Pragmatism Means by Practical," and "Valid Knowledge and the 'Subjectivity of Experience'" (1910).

50. James, *Pragmatism*, 95–113.

51. Ibid., 35.

52. Marcell, *Progress and Pragmatism*, 3–51, 322–34.

53. Dewey, *Reconstruction in Philosophy*, 149–50.

54. Ibid., 205.

55. For a discussion of the relations between pragmatism and Chicago in general, and Hull House in particular, see Mary Jo Deegan, *Jane Addams and the Men of the Chicago School, 1892–1918* (New Brunswick, NJ: Transaction Books, 1986); Feffer, *Chicago Pragmatists and American Progressivism*.

56. Dewey's particular judgments can be found in *Art as Experience* (New York: Minton, Balch, 1934).

57. James Turner, *Without God, without Creed: The Origins of Unbelief in America* (Baltimore: Johns Hopkins University Press, 1985) is the definitive treatment.

58. Benjamin Warfield, "The Authority & Inspiration of the Scriptures," *Westminster Teacher* (September 1889), cited in http://www.ondoctrine.com/2war0801 .htm.

59. Mark Noll, *Between Faith and Criticism: Evangelicals, Scholarship, and the Bible in America* (San Francisco: Harper and Row, San Francisco, 1986), 11.

60. Schurman, quoted in Ferenc Morton Szasz, *The Divided Mind of Protestant America, 1880–1930* (Tuscaloosa: University of Alabama Press, 1982), 33.

61. Noll, *Between Faith and Criticism*, 15–37.

62. Algernon Crapsey, *Religion and Politics* (New York: Thomas Whittaker, 1905), 3–5, 288–96.

63. Jay P. Dolan, *The American Catholic Experience: A History from Colonial Times to the Present* (Notre Dame, IN: University of Notre Dame Press, 1992), 225–35.

64. Ibid., 295–305.

65. Ibid., 306–11.

66. Ibid., 294–320.

67. Gerald P. Fogarty, S.J., *American Catholic Biblical Scholarship: A History from the Early Republic to Vatican II* (San Francisco: Harper and Row, 1989), 98–170; Dolan, *American Catholic Experience*, 318–20.

68. Noll, *Between Faith and Criticism*, 35–40; Szasz, *The Divided Mind of Protestant America, 1880–1930*, 35–95. Szasz argues convincingly that it was the postwar years in which the link between political and theological conservatism hardened as opposed to the fluidity of the prewar years.

69. Dolan, *American Catholic Experience*, 340–41, 346.

70. Discussions of the Social Gospel include Susan Curtis, *A Consuming Faith: The Social Gospel and Modern American Culture* (Baltimore: Johns Hopkins University Press, 1991); David Danbom, *The World of Hope: Progressives and the Struggle for an Ethical Public Life* (Philadelphia: Temple University Press, 1987); Szasz, *The Divided Mind of Protestant America, 1880–1930*.

71. This argument is made most succinctly in Rivkah Shpak-Lisak, *Pluralism & Progressives: Hull House and the New Immigrants, 1890–1919* (Chicago: University of Chicago Press, 1989).

72. In addition to Curtis, Danbom, and Szasz, other works on Rauschenbusch include Christopher Hodge Evans, *The Kingdom Is Always But Coming: A Life of Walter Rauschenbusch* (Grand Rapids, MI: Eerdmans, 2004). Rebecca Zurier, *Art for the Masses: A Radical Magazine and Its Graphics, 1911–1917* (Philadelphia: Temple University Press, 1988), contains a number of examples of the radical use of Jesus.

73. Walter Rauschenbusch, *Christianity and the Social Crisis* (New York: Macmillan, 1907), 308–9. David W. Noble, *The Progressive Mind, 1890–1917* (New York:

Rand McNally, 1970), 71, provocatively argues that for all his talk about plunging into history, Rauschenbusch preferred a state of nature in which harmony and cooperation reigned. Rauschenbusch, like all progressives according to Noble, saw history as complication, interruption, and uncertainty.

74. Jane Addams, *Democracy and Social Ethics* (New York: Macmillan, 1913), 219–20.

75. Addams's position on Pullman was published as "A Modern Lear," in *Survey* (1912), from a talk delivered in 1896. Bourne's letter, cited in Edward Abrahams, *The Lyrical Left: Randolph Bourne, Alfred Stieglitz and the Origins of Cultural Radicalism in America* (Charlottesville: University Press of Virginia, 1986), 65.

76. Randolph Bourne, "The Puritan's Will to Power," in *War and the Intellectuals: Essays by Randolph S. Bourne, 1915–1919*, edited by Carl Resek (New York: Harper Torchbooks, 1964), 158–59.

77. Among the treatments of the new morality are Henry May, *The End of American Innocence* (New York: Oxford University Press, [1959] 1970); Singal, *Modernist Culture in America*, especially Singal's introduction; Christine Stansell, *American Moderns: Bohemian New York and the Creation of a New Century* (New York: Metropolitan, 2000); and Leslie Vaughan, *Randolph Bourne and the Politics of Cultural Radicalism* (Lawrence: University Press of Kansas, 1997).

78. On vitalism, see Brown, "Vitalism." On the contrast between feminism and the woman movement, see Nancy Cott, *The Grounding of Modern Feminism* (New Haven, CT: Yale University Press, 1987), 1–50. Floyd Dell, *Intellectual Vagabondage* (New York: George H. Doran, 1926), 152.

79. May, *Innocence*, 216.

80. Discussions of the first counterculture of the twentieth century include Rick Beard and Leslie Cohen Berlowitz, eds., *Greenwich Village: Culture and Counterculture* (New Brunswick, NJ: Rutgers University Press, 1993); Christopher Lasch, *The New Radicalism in America, 1889–1963* (New York: Alfred A. Knopf, 1965); Vaughan, *Randolph Bourne and the Politics of Cultural Radicalism;* Singal, *Modernist Culture in America;* Leslie Fishbein, *Rebels in Bohemia: The Radicals of* the Masses (Chapel Hill: University of North Carolina Press, 1982); May, *Innocence;* Zurier, *Art for the Masses;* Casey Blake, *Beloved Community: The Cultural Criticism of Randolph Bourne, Van Wyck Brooks, Waldo Frank & Lewis Mumford* (Chapel Hill: University of North Carolina Press, 1990); Stansell, *American Moderns: Bohemian New York and the Creation of a New Century.* For a history of gay life in Manhattan, see George Chauncey, *Gay New York: Gender, Urban Culture, and the Making of the Gay Male World, 1890–1940* (New York: Basic Books, 1994).

81. John Dewey and James H. Tufts, *Ethics*, rev. ed. (New York: Henry Holt, 1932), 175–76.

82. Dewey, *Reconstruction in Philosophy*, 166–67.

83. Ibid., 175, 181, 206.

84. John Diggins, *The Promise of Pragmatism: Modernism and the Crisis of Knowledge and Authority* (Chicago: University of Chicago Press, 1994); Dewey, *Reconstruction in Philosophy*, 175.

85. Randolph Bourne, "War and the Intellectuals," in *War and the Intellectuals: Essays by Randolph S. Bourne*, 1915–1919, edited with an introduction by Carl Resek (New York: Harper Torchbooks, 1964). The Dewey–Bourne debate will be discussed in greater detail in chapter 5.

CHAPTER TWO

~

Beauties

Nineteenth-century criticism that they were a philistine people who favored practical action over contemplation or sensual enjoyment notwithstanding, Americans demonstrated a remarkable interest in the beautiful. Europeans may have disdained American taste as vulgar, but such scorn did not deter the middle classes from a dedicated pursuit of aesthetic pleasures. The English novelist Arnold Bennett, for one, maintained that Americans outdid their English counterparts in depth and breadth of reading. The impressionists' major dealer, Durand-Ruel, staged an 1886 show of their work in the United States because he was convinced that both sales and reviews would be better than in France.[1] No doubt some accumulation of European art was undertaken to earn the social distinction of sophisticated taste, but the degree to which middle-class Americans attributed aesthetic qualities to such quotidian artifacts as vases, bowls, fabrics, curtains, boxes, and chairs suggests a commitment to aesthetic stimulation. If critics bemoaned the ornate ornamentation and the constant profusion of objets d'art as an unacceptable mélange that substituted quantity over quality, many Victorians embraced their aesthetic for its enhancement of perception. Despite the well-circulated dismissal among the American business class of art as both a waste of time and feminizing pursuit—succinctly captured in Christopher Newman's first word in the Louvre in Henry James's *The American*, "Combien?"—a significant counterculture existed that celebrated art as a release from the incessant impulse to produce and as a means to disregard the norms of everyday deportment.[2]

Most middle-class Americans tempered their sensuality with uplift. Prevailing aesthetic thought understood beauty as ultimately spiritual in nature. Beautiful objects stimulated sensual pleasure and refined it by perfectly blending form and content. Evoking perfection on account of its supposed universality, beauty was also an agent of morality. Although many nineteenth-century critics did indeed judge artwork by the lessons it explicitly taught, most writers on aesthetics were more prone to celebrate the ability of beauty to compel personal transformation by training exquisite perception and fine discrimination. Because the beautiful was so precious, it required protection from less pure influences. That concern prompted the construction of the great museums and symphony halls of the nineteenth century and the establishment of institutions of criticism and education intended to cast and enforce judgment. A burgeoning critical establishment relegated art that failed to evoke the proper attitude or demonstrate moral probity to the category of low or trash and labeled it immoral. Critics were hardly omnipotent. More than once, an aesthetic approach consigned to the category of nonart nonetheless demonstrated considerable appeal. In such cases (literary realism being the most prominent example in the nineteenth century), critics responded by re-interpreting such artwork as "really" universal and moral. Cultural custodians even made the aestheticism of Oscar Wilde and Walter Pater part of the consensus, at least until its amoralism could no longer be ignored.[3]

By 1920, however, the neat aesthetic package had unraveled. Within the space of twenty years, philosophers, critics, and practicing artists successfully challenged the understanding of beauty as ethereal elevation. Questioning the requirements for universal, celestial, and moral art, challengers offered in both theory and practice a wide array of alternatives to the accepted understanding of the pleasure of beauty. In opening up questions of appropriate subject matter and form, the new aesthetics raised the possibility of many beauties rather than a singular one. Some came to multiplicity by making beauty a direct expression of particular needs and desires, whether of groups or of individuals, rather than the articulation of the universal. Others objected to the canon of propriety that dictated only a certain subject matter, arguing that what nineteenth-century critics had dismissed as crude and coarse had its beauty in its very being. Still others disputed the very conception of moral art at all, claiming that any prescription for uplift clamped on beauty a deadening hand that obliterated aesthetic enjoyment altogether. Contributing to the upheaval in conceptions of beauty were the claims of many new forms of expression to the once-privileged status of art. Some, such as photography, sound recordings, and movies, were direct products of machines, supposedly the antithesis of art. Although the new aestheticians disagreed among themselves over each of these principles, with some keeping morality and others ethereality, the upshot was an aesthetic landscape in which beauty was clearly understood in the plural.

The new, of course, did not fully sweep out the old. Impressionism, realism, and the sonnet more than held their ground. Similarly, moral criticism continued in vogue. Efforts to demystify art, to undercut its cultural capital, proved in many respects to be counterproductive. Dada experiments in which everyday objects were paraded as art did not have the desired effect of demonstrating the arbitrary nature of the distinction between art and nonart; rather by exciting outrage and confusion, they often increased the aura of art objects. Moderns loved to imagine themselves without antecedents and in complete revolt against their predecessors, whom they represented as having no meaningful thoughts or desirable values. Despite the defenses of the pleasures of subjectivity, vulgarity, and amorality, however, much in the new aesthetic climate was a reconstitution rather than an obliteration of aesthetic transcendence. Yet enough changed so that the old ceased to enjoy the unparalleled status it once had.

The tenuous hold of the nineteenth-century ideals of beauty is evident in the bold declarations of the new architecture, new dance, new drama, and new poetry that characterized the period. Not only did an impressive number of path-breaking artists begin their careers or produce their most important work in the early twentieth century, but an equally number of significant critics and commentators who championed them did so as well. Such lists are admittedly arbitrary, but a survey of those whose aesthetic commentary or practice during the period launched new directions would include the novelist and short-story writer Sherwood Anderson; the New Humanist critic Irving Babbitt; the composer Irving Berlin; the Young American essayist Van Wyck Brooks; the novelist Willa Cather; the film star Charles Chaplin; the leading proponent of post-impressionism, Charles Caffin; the literary critic and managing editor of the *Masses*, Floyd Dell; the naturalist Theodore Dreiser; the modern dancer Isadora Duncan; the film director D. W. Griffith; the feminist playwright and founding member of the Provincetown Players Susan Glaspell; the creator of *Krazy Kat*, George Herriman; the photographer Lewis Hine; the Nietzschean chronicler of the arts James Huneker; the sui generis composer Charles Ives; the master of ragtime Scott Joplin; the modernist painter of urban America John Marin; the critic and gadfly H. L. Mencken; the jazz pianist Jelly Roll Morton; the dramatist Eugene O'Neill; the modernist poet Ezra Pound; professor of literature and antimoralist aesthetician Joel Spingarn; the experimental novelist Gertrude Stein; the photographer and impresario Alfred Stieglitz; the torch singer Sophie Tucker; the novelist Edith Wharton; and the architect Frank Lloyd Wright. Absent from the roster, yet vital to understanding the proliferation of beauty in the first twenty years of the twentieth century, are such Europeans as James Joyce, Marcel Duchamp, Richard Strauss, and Gustav Mahler, who either worked in the United States or mixed easily with American practitioners. Together with the Americans who watched, listened, and read their work, these practitioners created the aesthetic multiverse.

The Genteel Tradition and Its Discontents

Writing of the power of beauty in 1896, the influential critic of the progressive and genteel journal the *Outlook*, Hamilton Wright Mabie, informed his readers that culture gave men and women the ability to see "behind the material phenomena" to the "force which moves it, the laws which govern it, and the spiritual fact which it symbolizes."[4] Mabie's religious language was not idiosyncratic. Middle-class Americans of the late nineteenth century attributed sacred overtones to beauty. The English critic Matthew Arnold frankly acknowledged the religious impulse. Culture, which he famously defined as the best that has been thought and said in the world, had as its goal "harmonious perfection." Like the sacred, Arnoldian-inflected beauty was its own end, worthy of attention in and of itself, and not on account of its utility. Transcending its own materiality, gesturing to the infinite, and prompting an awed contemplation, beauty was a sign of the good.[5] That relationship led cultural custodian and literary gatekeeper at Scribner's William Crary Brownell to remark that taste was the guardian of morality.

Genteel custodians did not regard taste as solely a private matter. Proper taste did work in the world, suffusing and transforming souls. Such work seemed especially necessary in an industrial age, a marked contrast to the moral and physical ugliness that many discerned in polluting factories and grasping capitalists. Often accused by later generations as humorless, Gilded Age advocates revered beauty as part of the play spirit, a deliberate contrast to legal regulation—Hellenism rather than Hebraism, in Arnold's formulation. American Arnoldians did not shun sensual delight. Their favored art catered to it. It was a sensual delight, however, that was ultimately upright and refining. It acquainted men and women with the ethereal. As such, beautiful art was well suited to combat class conflict, greed, and antisocial individualism. Beauty reminded people of their social obligations, of their connection not only to the living but also to the past. Mastery of culture dictated personal control and restraint, repose, and self-discipline. As the

New York Times asserted, "art is needed to embellish life, and now that wealth is accumulating in masses, this great civilizing agent should assert its power, so as to prevent opulence from falling into extravagant display or vulgar ostentation, far removed from true dignity, and by bad example [be] a corruptor of public morality. . . . We shall have less brutality, cruelty and vulgarity when people are brought up to a standard of life that is not wholly sordid and sensuous."[6]

Such was the theory. Embedded in the conception was a set of distinctions that militated against beauty becoming the unifying force that the *Times* envisioned. Rather than creating a community beyond conflict, cultural arbiters' insistence that beauty was perfection created a clear line between the elevated and the mundane. Artifacts that appealed primarily to sensation or simply entertained may have been pleasurable, but few academics, critics, or analysts placed them in the more prestigious category of art. The alleged sensuality and pandering of the popular arts and its status as a commodity disqualified serious consideration of the emerging mass culture as beautiful. It was a short step from distinguishing among artifacts to ranking people on the basis of the aesthetic pleasures they preferred. Those who favored the easily accessible, immediately gratifying, and purely sensual artifacts revealed themselves to lack the discipline to make distinctions. Not surprisingly, in fact, the distribution of taste correlated with social standing. Much ink was spilled bemoaning the inability of workers and immigrants to exercise aesthetic judgment or to develop the rudiments of aesthetic knowledge. Likewise the middle class came in for criticism for its unrefined tastes. Critics seemed blind to the ways in which the aura of sanctioned art intimidated outsiders or how pleasures of a commercial culture were not always uncontrolled sensuality. Nor did they realize that they invariably located aesthetic perfection in the past and dismissed contemporary work as somehow failing to meet the standards of great beauty.[7]

Cultural hierarchy, in and of itself, need not lead to social discrimination. Judgments that one thing is better or more worthy than another, after all, are a fairly widespread component of human behavior. What matters, as Jane Addams and W. E. B. Du Bois both realized, was who makes the judgment and under what conditions. Both subscribed to the nineteenth-century ideal of beauty as perfection, but each constructed a more participatory and inclusive notion of aesthetic life, one in which more people were involved in the determination of beauty and in which beauty was bent toward democratic purposes. Realizing that the universal standards cultural custodians proclaimed were limited, they hoped that aesthetics could be made to approximate more closely actual universality.

Born in Great Barrington, Massachusetts, in 1868, Du Bois was educated at Fisk and Harvard, where in 1895 he became the first person of African descent to earn a PhD, for his dissertation on the suppression of the slave trade. Du Bois's specialization in economics and history did not foreclose his concern with aesthetics. At Harvard, Du Bois imbibed the cultural ideals of professor of English Barrett Wendell. Du Bois's justly celebrated *Souls of Black Folk* (1903) is as much a meditation on beauty as a political and social indictment. One can without much trouble identify the characteristic nineteenth-century notions of beauty: Du Bois's classical allusions, his use of the balanced prose taught in Adams Sherman Hill's *Principles of Rhetoric* (1878), his equation of culture and moral duty, his emphasis on spiritual strivings, and his advocacy of his version of the "saving remnant," the Talented Tenth. In one famous passage, Du Bois imagines himself mingling with the spirits of Balzac and Shakespeare, who do not wince and do not shun him. This embrace of high "white" culture has long prompted charges of Du Boisian elitist disregard for the needs and expressions of the field hand. For many biographers, *Souls* foreshadowed Du Bois's career-long failure to appreciate such black popular forms as blues and jazz as anything other than mere commercial artifacts.[8]

Yet Du Bois's aesthetics were a protest against the pervasive denial of cultural citizenship to black people. He daringly associated black folk life with aspirations to beauty, rejecting the conventional link between race and culture. Du Bois placed at the head of each chapter a specimen of poetry— which Arnoldians held was the art form most capable of representing beauty—and bars from the Sorrow Songs, signifying each was aesthetically valuable. Proclaiming the Songs "not simply as the sole American music, but as the most beautiful expression of human experience born this side of the seas," Du Bois maintained the beauty lay in their longing, their expression of the human heart, and faith in redemption and ultimate justice.[9] Not passive, but full of striving, they stood in contrast to the hymns of Atlanta, the cold, money-grubbing Philistine desert of dollars and smartness.

Using this genteel critique against those who claimed to have a monopoly on culture, Du Bois charged that the failure of whites to let blacks participate in the culture had wounded both black folk and America. Black folk suffered from an inability to express fully their love of beauty. Losing the joy in this world, they seized upon the possibilities of the next. Yet to live in the margins, to see a modern nation all around them but not to be able to participate led to a "painful self-consciousness" and a "moral hesitancy" among blacks. Divided between being a Negro and an American, but free to be neither fully, black men and women lived alienated, doubled lives. Survival often meant denial of a balanced self. Or as Du Bois put it in a well-known line, "the price of culture is a Lie" (224). For white America, the cost of denying blacks was a world of Atlantas. "Will America be poorer if she replace her brutal dyspeptic blundering with light-hearted but determined Negro humility? or her coarse and cruel wit with loving jovial good-humor? or her vulgar music with the soul of the Sorrow Songs?" (52).

Du Bois's desire to "be a coworker in the kingdom of culture" was in part, as critics charged, a personal lament built from a sense of personal injustice. Yet Du Bois's insight that black folk had aesthetic gifts separated him and the Talented Tenth from the paternalism of white genteel uplifters. Unlike numerous other improvement programs that arose at the turn of the century, Du Bois's plans for the education of black men were not predicated on the complete denial of the legitimacy and authenticity of the aspirations of the remaining 90 percent of the population. Like others schooled in the genteel tradition, Du Bois valued and wanted to extend the knowledge of the best that was thought and said in the world. Where Charles Dudley Warner, author of an 1872 essay, "What Is Your Culture to Me?" that bemoaned the crude tastes of laborers and the petty bourgeoisie, imagined the downward diffusion of culture as remaking the working class, Du Bois conceived it as more akin to allowing the unfolding of what was inherent but unexpressed due to racial and class prejudice. To leave blacks as "an ignorant, turbulent proletariat" was to court disaster; for "they are not fools, they have tasted of the Tree of Life, and they will not cease to think, will not cease to read the riddle of the world" (135). Such sentiments arguably tempered the potential elitism of his notion that "progress in human affairs is more often a pull than a push, a surging forward of the exceptional man, and the lifting of his duller brethren slowly and painfully to his vantage-ground" (127). The sum of his views was to make the mastery of culture a human responsibility rather than a privilege of birth lorded over those easily dismissed as irretrievably uncultured.

Du Bois's insistence that blacks and whites must be coworkers in the kingdom of culture hints at his resistance to aesthetic multiplicity. The culture of which he dreamed was clearly a common one. So that the price of culture not be a lie, Du Bois challenged all positions that would concede blacks were incapable of combining meaningful work and meaningful expression. It was this point on which Du Bois staked his opposition to Booker T. Washington. Du Bois was not just exasperated with what he regarded as Washington's accommodation to white racism and violence; he also set himself against Washington's vision of black possibilities, which seemed to Du Bois to be decidedly constricted and soul-killing. He found especially troubling Washington's materialism and narrow utilitarianism. Particularly galling was

Washington's dismissal of the educated man as a species of confidence man. The genteel tradition had a name for such attitudes: Philistinism.

Du Bois remained suspicious of commercial culture, opting for the romantic authenticity of folk culture. That genteel sentiment was that of settlement-house pioneer Jane Addams as well. Born in Cedarville, Illinois, in 1860, Addams imbibed many of her aesthetic principles from John Ruskin, a stance reinforced by the views of her companion Ellen Gates Starr. Addams's *Spirit of Youth and the City Streets* (1910) can read like a good number of genteel criticisms of popular culture.[10] The book condemns "vice disguised as pleasure," frets about the baleful social effects on the young of sex and violence in darkened movie theaters, and a play impulse not sufficiently organized. Like others who shared her conception of beauty, Addams envisioned aesthetic experience as the transcendence of sensuality or, at the very least, its management. "It is neither a short nor an easy undertaking to substitute the love of beauty for mere desire, to place the mind above the senses;

Figure 2.1. The genteel tradition at its best: theatricals at Hull House, 1920. **Jane Addams, the founder of Hull House, contended that performing culture enabled youth to rework and understand life situations and expand their repertoire of responses. (Source: Jane Addams Memorial Collection, Wallace Kirkland Papers, The University Library, University of Illinois at Chicago)**

but is not this the sum of the immemorial obligation which rests upon the adults of each generation if they would nurture and restrain the youth, and has not the whole history of civilization been but one long effort to substitute psychic impulsion for the driving force of blind appetite?" (30). "He who makes himself its vessel and bearer thereby acquires a freedom from the blindness and soul poverty of daily existence" (82).

Yet Addams's position differed in significant respects from that of the cultural conservatives. For one, she refused to denigrate youth's interest in sensation as unwarranted or necessarily untoward. She never refers to them as stupid or savage. Holding adults accountable for their fear of pleasure in the young, she asserted that "this fundamental sex susceptibility" suffused "the world with its deepest meaning and beauty," and furnished "the momentum towards all art" (18). Her ideal more closely resembled sublimation than repression. Addams wanted not denial but socially valuable outlets for sexual energy. The arts could be such a venue, since they provided a chance for the young to work out the inevitable conflict between hopes and realities. Beauty provided a means for a group to measure experience against tradition. Her universalist aesthetic was less conformity to received judgment than the act of judging together. Drawing on Friederich Schiller's play instinct, Addams envisioned art as a matter of doing rather than passive watching. What she most valued in art was its opportunity to allow for exchange, a criterion that led her to rank baseball as the highest of the arts. "Even the unquestioned ability which the theater possesses to bring men together into a common mood and to afford them a mutual topic of conversation, is better accomplished with the one national game which we already possess, and might be infinitely extended through the organization of other public games. . . . Does not this contain a suggestion of the undoubted power of public recreation to bring together all classes of a community in the modern city unhappily so full of devices for keeping men apart?" (95–96).

In contrast to Addams and Du Bois, growing numbers of intellectuals and artists saw the problem of culture as less the failure to realize nineteenth-century principles of beauty through democratic participation than the principles themselves. Rather than providing meaningful standards, critics charged, American conceptions of beauty failed to provide an aesthetic life of consequence. By the middle of the period, scathing criticisms of American culture appeared with increasing regularity. Commentators indicted the cultural environment for its misunderstanding of the human condition, its misplaced values, and its complacency. Bewitched by an excessive and scolding moralism, American beauty was unable to bring its promises to fruition. For all the genteel talk of the virtues of beauty, such critics as Van Wyck Brooks and George Santayana saw instead forces that segregated beauty from life as lived. Culture had become a thing reserved for Sundays, a direct consequence of its status as spiritual and transcendent.

Van Wyck Brooks's call for a renewal of American culture was the most influential among his contemporaries, becoming a staple of the group of critics and writers known as the Young Americans. Born in Plainfield, New Jersey, in 1886, the son of a stockbroker, Brooks graduated Harvard in 1907, where he had traveled in aesthete circles. The following year, he published his first book, *Wine of the Puritans*. As Casey N. Blake has definitively shown, Brooks's indictment originated in his anger at the failure of an older generation to make beauty count in the world. Like the genteel cultural arbiters with whom he broke, Brooks believed that beauty has a moral component. Rejecting the sunny uplift of sanctioned art as fatuous and useless, Brooks was nonetheless concerned that literature serve as a training ground for democratic citizenship, by binding people in imagination with others in whose fate they were implicated. Brooks wanted a literature that made sense of the world, integrating the fragments of modern life. To that end, he had little truck with modernist experiments, which he regarded as a self-indulgent refusal to attend to the social responsibility of clear and meaningful communication.[11]

Brooks's yearning for unity paralleled his effort to knit together his own polar interests. An aesthete who championed Tolstoyan ethics of social involvement, Brooks located the fatal flaw in American culture in the tendency to segregate beauty from the life of action so as to ensure its purity. A transcendent, ethereal art was incapable of integrating society, a need Brooks felt was especially acute in the United States because the nation had no history of medieval solidarity. Americans had only bits and pieces from Europe, which did not coalesce into "a point of view." With no guiding set of principles, art and literature were "excrescences," he wrote in *Wine*. Without the focal center of a lived culture, Brooks argued, American energy had become a destructive commercialism by default. In the most famous and misunderstood formulation of his 1915 *America's Coming-of-Age*, Brooks noted the separation of highbrow and lowbrow. His concern here was not a purely aesthetic one of taste cultures, but more precisely the disjunction between lofty ideals and workaday practice. Brooks's "genial middle ground" was his version of the English socialist William Morris's effort to repair the division between theory and practice that the capitalist division of labor created.

If the aesthete Brooks was opposed to utilitarianism, he nonetheless rejected efforts to lift "'Lowbrow' elements . . . to the level of the 'Highbrow" elements." The Lowbrow, after all, was the source of humanity, flexibility, and tangibility. Because the Highbrow lacked those qualities, refinement in the United States was little more than "a glassy inflexible priggishness on the upper levels which paralyzes life." Cultured Americans needed to recognize that "Tammany has quite as much to teach Good Government as Good Government has to teach Tammany." Like many in his circle, which included Randolph Bourne and Waldo Frank, Brooks took particular exception to Matthew Arnold's famed definition of culture as "the best that has been thought and said in the world," because it located culture in the past and not in vital American materials. Adherence to the cult of the best, Brooks charged, prevented genteel critics from seeing that Walt Whitman had created just such an art "in a fresh democratic ideal, based upon the whole personality."[12]

Harvard philosopher George Santayana doubted the wisdom of Brooks's strategy of integration. Although his "The Genteel Tradition in American Philosophy" (1911) ostensibly covered the same ground as did Brooks, his conclusions were considerably less hopeful about the ability for reform. Understood in the light of his general philosophical position, his criticism on the whole was designed less to foster a "genial middle ground" than to make beauty safe from the lures of the world. Committed to a naturalism in which the spiritual could only celebrate existence, not alter it, Santayana envisioned spiritual life as affirming one's subjection to higher and deeper forces. In such a scheme, beauty functioned by seizing hold of the "reality of sensation and fancy beneath the surface of conventional ideas, and then out of that living but indefinite material to build new structures, richer, finer, fitter to the primary tendencies of our nature, truer to the ultimate possibilities of the soul."[13] Such talk might sound like genteel uplift, but it was more concerned with protecting sensibility from the spirit of social improvement, which Santayana regarded as a falsely optimistic unity.

Santayana's rejection of integration marked his famed talk. His version of American cultural division split intellect from will. A strange concoction of a Puritanism that no longer acknowledged the universe was unknowable and a Transcendentalism in which the individualistic and egoistic elements prevailed, American culture was a moldy moralistic set of ideas that favored propriety over piety. Genteel uplift robbed American art of sensual pleasure. Instead of having clearness of form and "infinity of suggestion," American art was plodding, because it taught that "every sensation" was "merely a sign and symbol, a signal that something is to be done." So strong was the link between morality and beauty that American rebels only fitfully rejected the claims of gentility. The subjectivism of Poe, Hawthorne, and Emerson left them "morbid, or tinkling, or self-indulgent."[14] Whitman, on the other hand, lacked the guidance of reason and thus was a primitive who could do no more than describe experience as it came to him.

The genteel tradition also came under attack from a movement often said to be its heir, New Humanism. Led by Irving Babbitt of Harvard and *Nation* writer and editor Paul Elmer More, the movement might better be understood as a criticism of those who undermined the unified aesthetic by making fatal concessions to the forces that opposed it. In Babbitt's *Literature and the American College* (1908), *The New Laokoon* (1910), *Rousseau and Romanticism* (1919) and More's *Shelburne Essays* (1904–1921), the humanists proposed an aesthetic based on classical and Christian sources. The flaw in the American aesthetics, Babbitt and More argued, was the failure to recognize that humans were equal part spirit and animality. That dualism, not Darwinian flux, was constant throughout history. Genteel hopes in universal improvement were bound to be dashed. The best one could hope for was finding the measure of equilibrium from within. Rather than pursuing desire and locating itself in nature, humanity was better served by following the higher direction of the soul. The truly human balanced reason and imagination, and it was these qualities that humanists believed art should embody. By demonstrating perfection and equipoise, humanist art would restore what modern life and philosophy had ripped asunder.[15]

Babbitt charged that romanticism had destroyed the balance by embracing nature, celebrating passion, and elevating the self. Immanuel Kant did special damage, Babbitt contended, by separating authority and reason from imagination. Freed from governance, imagination ruled aesthetics; and the strange and exotic became, in fact, the norm. Rejecting the psychic restlessness of such modern romantics as Henri Bergson and Benedetto Croce as a reflection of the cult of speed and power of the material world, the New Humanists maintained that standards of art were unchanging because human nature was as well. In the end, however, the New Humanists may not have been concerned with aesthetics at all. Their most careful student, J. David Hoeveler, concludes that they too often confused literature with life, judging the former by the latter. Like the genteel critics scolded for their acceptance of romanticism, Babbitt could not help but regard aesthetics as a branch of ethics, holding that beauty lost most of its meaning when divorced from morals.

What mattered for many young Americans in the age of multiplicity was less the precise arguments of these criticisms than that they were advanced at all. Hailed somewhat incorrectly as liberators in advanced quarters, Brooks and Santayana spoke to a feeling that beauty had become a dreary duty. Their call for an art that engaged the vital forces of life and reanimated spirituality seemed to countenance departures. So too did the sexual politics of their analyses. Neither Brooks nor Santayana (a gay man) were fans of the strutting masculinity of the American will. Brooks and his fellow Young Americans rejected the heedless wastefulness of the pioneer and the grandiose scheming of the captains of industry. Yet neither Brooks nor Santayana was comfortable with the feminine. Brooks ended *America's Coming-of-Age* with the following: "When the women of America have gathered together all the culture in the world there is—who knows?—perhaps the dry old Yankee stalk will send forth shoots and burst into a storm of blossoms." Santayana followed suit, contrasting the female intellect as residing in a simulacrum, "a neat reproduction of the colonial mansion—with some modern comforts introduced surreptitiously," with the aggressive enterprise embodied by the skyscraper inhabited by the masculine will.[16]

Often forgotten in such indictments was that the nineteenth-century version of beauty was something of a compromise, a synthesis of opposite tendencies. It aimed at combining the senses with the mind, pleasure with morality, personal expression with social responsibility. In so doing, the genteel tradition put arts at the center of the good life. The call of genteel critics for pleasure to have purpose inadvertently opened the way for purposes to be pleasurable. For all the well-deserved vitriol the Young Americans directed at their genteel predecessors, they shared with them the hope that pleasures could be good and meaningful. The practices of beauty in the first twenty years of the twentieth century, however, never coalesced. Fragments of the old ideas remained, but instead of linking beauty with universal truth and ethics, the practitioners created an aesthetic multiverse in which art was at times embedded in life rather than idealized, frankly perspectival rather than universal, and amoral rather than uplifting.

Plebeian Beauty

Maintaining that no beauty could come from the incessant dwelling on the distasteful and the unpleasant, cultural arbiters in the late nineteenth century policed artwork for unattractive subject matter and salacious treatments. The boundaries of acceptability were fluid ones; no firm and fast rule separated art from mere sensuousness. Provided materiality was restrained, depiction of greed and sexual desire did not necessarily disqualify a work as beautiful. Nor could critics enforce their judgments with any great success. Mark Twain was originally greeted with great suspicion, condemned in many New England aesthetic circles as too plebeian and sensuous at midcentury, only to be hailed as an authentic American artist by the end of the nineteenth century. Cultural custodians were unsuccessful on other fronts as well. Despite instruction, Americans favored mindless pleasures, ones that were more sensual than ethereal and more rooted than transcendent. During the early twentieth century, some of the most enduring forms of popular pleasure originated or came to maturity. Ragtime, jazz, blues, comic strips, movies, amusement parks, and organized sports, which all failed the test of elevation, occupied a distinctive and growing portion of the aesthetic multiverse.

American literature had always shown interest in plebeian subjects. Nineteenth-century realism, after all, had staked its claim to art on its portrayal of the world as experienced, whether by ragamuffin Missouri orphans such as Huckleberry Finn or nouveau-riche mineral-paint kings such as William Dean Howells's Silas Lapham. By 1900, however, Howells's literary strictures had become synonymous with timidity. The novelist Gertrude Atherton accused Howellsian realism of being "bourgeois." Far from the democratic celebration it claimed to be, realism was "littleism," excessively rational, naively empiricist, and fearful of the body. When writing of plebeians, realists intended to tame rather than embrace life. Expurgating the sensual, realists missed the excitement, vigor, and contingency of life on its own terms. Realism had broadened the categories in its day, Atherton admitted, but it still relied on preconceived notions that divided the world into acceptable and unacceptable peoples, objects, and acts. Vital art had to eliminate such distinctions entirely.[17]

Atherton used *bourgeois* as a cultural rather than a social designation. The writer who contemporaries believed best managed to combine a plebeian concern with social oppression with a disdain for propriety was Theodore Dreiser. Born to a poor German Catholic Indiana family, Dreiser came to literature through a career in journalism. His first novel, *Sister Carrie* (1900), was the story of a small-town young woman who yearns for riches and fame. Based loosely on the experience of one of his sisters, who eloped with a cashier of a Chicago bar who had stolen money from the establishment's safe, the novel depicted Carrie Meeber's meteoric rise to stardom as an actress, a success that was often aided by her love affairs with men whom she eventually surpassed. The failure of Dreiser to detail the punishment that attended such acts prompted publisher Frank Doubleday, who had been in Europe on business when the book was accepted, to demand Dreiser withdraw it. When Dreiser refused, the company honored its contract but made no effort to publicize the book. The contretemps sent Dreiser into a tailspin for two years. He returned to fiction writing again in 1911 with the publication of *Jennie Gerhardt*. Gerhardt shares with Meeber an open sexuality, but her character is considerably different. Where Meeber is virtually a blank slate who assumes the shape of male desire, Gerhardt is less calculating and more devoted, staying true to her two lovers. Dreiser followed these up with two novels based on the life of traction magnate Charles Yerkes, *The Financier* (1912) and *The Titan* (1914), as well as a loosely worked autobiography of an artist driven by sex and success, *The "Genius"* (1915). The last became a cause célèbre when the New York Society for the Suppression of Vice attempted to have it banned.

Dreiser's prose is by turns the most aggravating and most enticing aspect of his fiction. It is often clunky and poorly constructed. His diction is frequently haphazard and inexact. Many passages read as if he ran to the thesaurus to find the most obscure word possible. His sentences often lack rhythm and pace. Yet the sheer torrent of words and the mass of details have a momentum of their own. No previous American writer conveyed with such excitement the force of the vulgar. At his best, which was quite often, Dreiser provides a map of the power of the American city. He has a sense for the newly emerging institutions of urban America. One finds in his pages descriptions of all manner of objects—restaurants, jewelry, gaslight, department stores, streetcars, the list is virtually endless. In Dreiser's prose, the city itself becomes something of a character—a churning collection of forces that ceaselessly makes and remakes the conditions of existence. Nor is Dreiser at all bashful about acknowledging human drives. His characters act naturally on their urges, sometimes barely bothering to justify or describe them. Frank Cowperwood, the protagonist of *The Financier* and *The Titan*, is without remorse as he destroys wives, lovers, and rivals in his seemingly unending quest for satisfactions. That Dreiser treated all these things as matters of fact, interesting in and of themselves, was one reason that the editor and journalist Floyd Dell could laud him for seeing beauty even in the ugliness of Chicago.[18]

Dreiser's critics saw his novels as the most repugnant naturalism, in which humans, driven by "animal passions," were incapable of reflecting upon them. H. L. Mencken countered that Dreiser's stories were in fact tragedies that detail what we desire but cannot possess. For Mencken, the tragedy of both Carrie Meeber and Jennie Gerhardt is that their seductions did not ruin them but set them upward in the world, where their aspirations exceeded their capacity.[19] Put another way, Dreiser understood the world of industrial capitalism as one in which a new psychology, which gentility dismissed as vulgar, was the order of the day. By displaying goods so prominently and making them the measure of the self, the economic and cultural system created a desire for possession of what one lacked. It was a system without end, a ceaseless machine of craving made all the more poignant because of the opportunities for possession. If gentility preached restraint and satisfaction with and acceptance of one's lot, Dreiser did not. He portrayed life as an endless process of the press of desire, efforts to satisfy it, and new dissatisfaction, whether because desire was frustrated or, just as likely, realization of desire enabled even more desire. He treated even the perception of beauty as a somatic reaction no more deliberated upon than the drives for success or sex. The "genius" Eugene Witla regarded beauty, success, and sex as inseparably intertwined and never fully capable of satisfaction.

Perhaps no form so failed to meet the criterion of elevation as American popular music. The predictable rhythmic and lyrical structure that had hardened into virtual requirements, treacly romanticism, and first-person lyrics of Tin Pan Alley earned much condemnation from serious critics. Nonetheless, the institution proved enormously popular. The profits to publishing firms and singers took a quantum leap in the first twenty years of the twentieth century. More significantly, the tunes have had a remarkable shelf life. "Bill Bailey, Won't You Please Come Home" (1902), "In the Good Old Summer Time" (1902), "Give My Regards to Broadway" (1904), "Take Me out to the Ball Game" (1908), "Alexander's Ragtime Band" (1911), "I Want a Girl (Just Like the Girl That Married Dear Old Dad)" (1911), "Oh, You Beautiful Doll" (1911), "Waiting for the Robert E. Lee" (1912), and "When Irish Eyes are Smiling" (1912) all date from this period. The conjunction of recording technology, new distribution patterns, and an influx of immigrant and ethnic talent resulted in an accessible yet flexible musical formula that provided the basis of popular music for years to come.[20]

The most striking use of low elements came from musicians working in the African American tradition. Black music made its most dramatic impact on white ears during the first twenty years of the twentieth century with ragtime. In 1899, Scott Joplin's "Maple Leaf Rag" became a nationwide hit, selling sheet music at a prodigious rate. For ten years, rags provided a boost to Tin Pan Alley, despite a chorus of critics who bemoaned their primitivism and association with houses of ill repute. Such criticism was far off base. Falsely reduced to syncopation, the accent of beats not normally stressed, ragtime was more than the broken rhythms and shifted accents that so caught the fancy of white listeners accustomed to rather conventional harmonic devices. In the hands of its leading practitioners, Joplin (1868–1917), James Scott (1886–1938), and Joseph Lamb (1887–1960), ragtime deployed an entire panoply of varied rhythmic resources, including the break, stop-time, and a variety of complex bass patterns instead of the usual march line. Drawing upon the whole range of African musical forms, particularly country dances, which they heard in their youth, the classic ragtime composers produced a vital music that aspired to depict elegant motion. In one sense,

Figure 2.2. The beauty of the vernacular: sheet music for Scott Joplin's "Sugar Cane." Ragtime, of which Joplin was the leading practitioner, combined plebeian and folk sources with innovative rhythms that placed accents on unexpected beats. Although never achieving the contemporary acceptance as art music that its composers desired, it gained popularity among a wide variety of listeners for its novel pleasures. (Source: The Lilly Library, Indiana University; reprinted with permission)

ragtime was an analogue to efforts among classical composers to preserve folk materials by building upon them. Like Ralph Vaughan Williams in England, Edvard Grieg in Norway, Anton Dvorak, and Bela Bartok, ragtime composers gave permanent form to indigenous styles.

That indebtedness no doubt accounted for the popularity of ragtime, but so too did the ways in which ragtime composers poured their sources into distinctive molds. White listeners often referred to early jazz as ragtime, but the differences between the two forms are significant. Improvisation, the hallmark of jazz, is absent in ragtime. So too is the muddying of notes. Composers demanded clean articulation and steady, elegant, controlled playing. Joplin, for instance, was insistent that ragtime delay release: "Play slowly until you catch the swing, and never play ragtime fast," he wrote. "It is never right to play Ragtime fast." Tempos could vary, but they did so within a highly disciplined structure. Played on the piano, in large measure because of the instrument's association with acceptable culture, classic ragtime often created musical tension by overturning expectations of the kind of sound effects produced by chords and octaves. Joplin, in particular, pressed new kinds of harmonies into service. The irony of ragtime is that its practitioners were never understood on their own terms. Joplin wrote a failed opera, *Treemonisha*, which aspired to demonstrate the fight between savagery and civilization within the Negro community. For his part, James Scott, in the words of his chroniclers, seemed dedicated to demonstrating that black men could create art music, an urge he revealed in such rag titles as "Grace and Beauty" and "Ophelia." For his pains, he became remembered as the master of the jig piano by white critics, and as too tied to foreign traditions and too enthralled by a rigid time scheme by later generations of jazz musicians.[21]

Ragtime prospered as long as it was linked to its folk sources. When it became simply a problem in musical composition, it gave way to new developments. At its height, however, it demonstrated the aesthetic pleasures in the variation of rhythm and harmony. It never achieved the spiritual ends its originators hoped it would, but it contributed to the emerging sense that so-called mindless pleasures were worth savoring. Beauty, Hiram K. Moderwell realized in a laudatory review of the form in the *New Republic* in 1915, no longer conformed to the old boundaries. Ragtime "carried the complexities of the rhythmic subdivision of the measure to a point never before reached in the history of music . . . has established subtle conflicting rhythms to a degree never before attempted in any popular music or folk-music and rarely enough in art-music . . . has gone far beyond most other popular music in the freedom of inner voices (yes, I mean polyphony) and of harmonic modulation." "And it has proved its adaptability to the expression of many distinct

moods." Those who denigrated people who liked it were, Moderwell concluded, simply elitists who lived in fear that others were having fun that they
could not control.[22]

The composer Charles Ives shared with the ragtime composers a sense
that plebeian sound had aesthetic potential. Linking plebeian with nature,
Ives staked out a ground that he hoped would overturn a feminized culture
that was sheer artifice. The influence of his bête noire, "Richy Wagner,"
whom Ives considered "a woman passing as a man," had created a deadened
ear. Ives's nature, however, was more Emersonian than Darwinian. Equating
the natural as the emblem of spiritual perfection, Ives associated his music
with the direct democracy of the New England town. The purpose of music
was to paint "pictures in music of the common events in the lives of common
people."[23] Ives reversed the genteel formula. Rather than rejecting the everyday for the sublime, Ives hoped to show the sublime in the everyday, by effecting what Leon Botstein has termed "the moral transformation of the vernacular material through art.[24]

To overcome deadened ears, Ives mixed the familiar and the strange. Like
his bandmaster father, Ives rejected slavish devotion to so-called musical
laws. His experimentation, apparently done with only minimal knowledge of
European musical developments, thus encompassed atonality, elusive quotations, quartertones, polytones, and a whole panoply of unconventional and
"incorrect" features. Ives had no compunction about borrowing "low" music
virtually verbatim. One can find ragtime, popular standards, and Protestant
hymns in Ives. *Contemplation of Nothing Serious* required the orchestra to divide itself into two separate ensembles, one of which played recognizable
melodies like "Hello, My Baby," while the other played dissonant pieces with
entirely different rhythms. Sequential juxtaposition, dissonant tonalities and
rhythms, would on its face seem elite high art, especially if *popular* is understood as "common taste as it is currently constituted." Ives, however, had another understanding of the concept. *Common* meant a common set of sources
melded together to penetrate beneath the surface of things. Realizing that
the nineteenth-century aesthetic synthesis was not viable, Ives hoped to
build a new unity from many sonic truths. In his song "Majority," for instance, dissonance dissolves into unison, a sentiment expressed in an original verse, which Ives later excised, that declared, "So men seeking common
life together for a season become as one."[25]

Less devoted to achieving commonality on spiritual grounds or concerned
with proving the aesthetic value of the plebeian were two new forms that
gained prominence during the first twenty years of the twentieth century. Because both comic strips and movies were first and foremost intended to

amuse large numbers of people, critics who thought entertainment incompatible with beauty charged that they pandered to the lowest tastes. Wary of instant gratification, genteel critics condemned the simple jokes, tricks of perspective, and melodrama on which the new mass amusements relied. Their accessibility made them especially dangerous for the young, who were said to lack moral and aesthetic discrimination. Behind much of the educated handwringing was a worry about delirious patrons.[26] Even the self-declared cultural democrat Randolph Bourne worried about the possible effects of movie-going, after seeing a particularly baleful fiction designed to inform patrons about the scourge of tuberculosis. The staleness of *The White Terror* prompted him to lament that mass entertainment provided little that acquainted men and women with their world or prompted them to think creatively about it. Still, Bourne recognized the aesthetic potential of the new form to reveal the mystery and excitement of the everyday.[27]

Originally peep shows, movies gained prominence as a novelty by concentrating on exotic sights and loosely connected sight gags. With the development of continuous stories, movies came into their own as a mass-culture form. In January of 1904, Rochesterians found themselves turned away from showings of *The Great Train Robbery* if they did not arrive early. Edward Porter's classic film was not the only popular success. Spurred by a new venue, the nickelodeon, the demand for films rose exponentially. Fashioned in Pittsburgh in 1905, storefronts showing films proliferated throughout the country, displacing vaudeville, variety shows, and plays as a prime entertainment. By early 1907, Chicago had 158 theaters exhibiting films, giving about forty shows a day. The "nickel madness" of 1905–1907 was primarily a working-class phenomenon. Exhibitors deliberately courted workers by charging a single affordable price, which meant seating was not segregated. Shown in modest venues that were deliberately designed to be unintimidating, in marked contrast to tony theaters for the middle class, movies succeeded among the urban working class because they were both accessible and pitched to their viewers' sensibilities.[28]

Almost as soon as they had become a national fixture, movies came under suspicion for the danger they posed to social health and for their lack of aesthetic quality. Most middle-class complaints centered on the prevalence of crime stories and adulteries (often of the rich and famous). Editorials blamed the romance and adventure (sex and violence) in movies for promoting crime, causing strikes, and generally inducing dissatisfaction with life. Critics singled out the graphic nature of images, the absence of words, and the juxtapositions of storylines to indict movies for failing to provide the contemplation and reflection that true beauty required. One critic, writing in the exhibitors' trade paper, declared that the "seething mass of human cattle" set the tastes that "have dominated, or at least set, the standard of American moving pictures."[29] Although some production companies angled for middle-class audiences with such attractions as new viewing spaces, rules of deportment, and films shorn of what a contributor to Moving Picture World called "repellent influences," the plebeian note still prevailed. As film historian Charles Musser concludes, the drive to tame the movies through review boards and commercial pressures could not fully shake the fantasies of sex, violence, and success that had tapped working-class sentiments and desires in the formative years of the art.[30]

This working-class spirit was most prevalent in the comedies. Criticized for their unmotivated, gratuitous violence, their anti-intellectual and repetitive gags, and their grotesque exaggerations, they nonetheless escaped censorship, because regulators regarded them as less serious. Slapstick offered audiences a whole host of pleasures, the most obvious of which was viewing unrestrained motion that often violated expectations of the physical world and rained down chaos on established order. The champion of the genre was Mack Sennett, whose famous Keystone Comedies were remarkable successes. Sennett's sensibility was pure anarchy, anticipating Groucho Marx's line from Horse Feathers "Whatever it is, I'm against it" by twenty years. Those in authority or who have claim to prestige and status look foolish in a Sennett film. He burlesqued melodrama, uplift, progress, patriotism, love for mothers, and Fords. His actors played directly to the camera, breaking the illusion of reality. If Sennett films did not cause imitation outside the theater, what historian Robert Sklar calls their "inventive, resourceful vulgarity" set a cultural tone that was decidedly not universal, uplifting, or ethereal.[31]

Sennett would have treated with disdain any suggestion that his work was beautiful, but his star comic would have been intrigued and flattered by the thought. It is such a commonplace these days to accord Charlie Chaplin high-culture status that it is worthwhile to remember that his early films were often dismissed by many critics as grotesque celebrations of low life. Daily Variety claimed in a review of Work (1915) that it, like all Chaplin films, was a mess. Wrote Motion Picture World of the Property Man: "Some of the funniest things in the picture are vulgar. They are too vulgar to describe; but are too funny to pass for vulgarity when only seen." A columnist in Harper's Weekly expressed dismay that Chaplin received $10,000 a week "for making grimaces, sitting in custard pies, hurling pancakes into human countenances, walking with strange anticks, and doing all manner of grotesque steps, which are enough, say those who have seen him, to make a cat laugh."[32] As late as 1919, Theatre Magazine could charge that Chaplin's work was based on simple repetition and that "the appeal of every Chaplin picture is to the lowest human instincts," particularly a psychology in which pain was treated as "diverting." Chaplin, the writer concluded, was hailed as a great artist only by incompetent people.[33]

Such criticisms were a response to the physicality, spontaneity, and rawness of Chaplin's work. In response to an appeal of the National Board of Censors that he devote his art to uplift, Chaplin promised reform. His films of the period nonetheless possessed plenty of cruelty, lechery, and slapstick. His characters often remain incorrigible and rarely acquire refinement or advance in the world. Much of Chaplin's work relied on techniques learned in English music halls, techniques that Chaplin and his defenders often gave high culture cover by calling them Elizabethan or Rabelaisian.[34] There was, however, always something more. Even as his post-1915 work made the vulgar elements less stark and graphic, Chaplin's milieu and viewpoint remained that of the working class. Sennett had his fun with the corruption and pretension of the rich but located no alternative. The British-born Chaplin, on the other hand, brought with him a finely tuned sense of distinctions, sensing in his major character's very dress how items signified difference. Where previous humor dressed the poor in clothes of the rich to signify their false pretensions to higher status, his famous Tramp's clearly salvaged oversized shoes, baggy pants, tight jacket, and bowler hat pointed to the structure of life that consigned him to the margins. His efforts to retain dignity as he teeters on the brink of survival seem less an inversion of the way things should be than a reminder of a human struggle. The character who infected the world with what one journalist dubbed Chaplinitis is engaged in a constant scramble for food, shelter, and companionship. In *Work*, Chaplin begins with a striking image. As a painter's assistant, he is pulling the cart carrying the equipment, while his boss rides. In *A Dog's Life*, he drew explicit parallels between the life of a dog and that of his tramp. As the film opens, Chaplin is lying asleep outdoors against a fence; a crosscut reveals the dog Scraps in the exact same position.

The psychological depth of the Tramp was part of Chaplin's effort to break free from the Sennett conventions. One key departure was the prominence of women in Chaplin's films. Where Sennett portrayed gender relations as unremitting warfare in which women were often demonized, Chaplin increasingly showed tenderness, even respect. Chaplin rarely won at love, at least not through traditional means of displaying wealth, proving his physical prowess, or asserting his position. Another crucial departure was his alteration of pace. Abandoning the unrelieved hectic pace of traditional comedies, Chaplin situated the Tramp in a world of recalcitrant and unobtainable

Figure 2.3. Proletarian art: Chaplin as a painter's assistant in Work (1915). **In his ability to tap the particulars of working-class conditions, Chaplin created an art that saw beauty in the vulgar rather than in the ethereal. (Source: George Eastman House)**

objects and alien people. The Tramp never ceased to be an outcast or at odds with privilege. Not quite at their mercy, he retains throughout a sense of self and imagination that animates the world around him into a slightly less hostile place. Chaplin himself put great emphasis on the ability of laughter to rest on identification of the audience with characters in a predicament. Accomplishing that was a matter of emphasizing not what happened, but the Tramp's feelings about it. David Robinson persuasively argues, "In the Keystone style, it was enough to bump into a tree to be funny. When Chaplin bumped into a tree, however, it was not the collision that was funny, but the fact that he raised his hat to the tree in a reflex gesture of apology."[35] With Chaplin, then, the key was negotiating the tensions between the merely sensuous and its possible meanings. Chaplin's success was to take the vulgar and not so much transcend it as demonstrate its human dimension.

Those who aspired to etherealize the common found they could use the new medium as well. With the dramas of D. W. (David Wark) Griffith, movies not only gained greater middle-class acceptance but, more importantly, took on a supple vocabulary that would refurbish the aesthetic of elevation. By combining a Jacksonian trust in the goodness of people with an insistence that the moving-picture camera was an instrument that enabled communication of the spiritual level, Griffith forged a way that mixed an exhibition of real life and the persistence of ideals. Where Chaplin demonstrated the dignity inherent in the struggle for existence, Griffith specialized in revealing the essential, inherent goodness of common folk. No genteel uplifter (his work scorned moral reformers as hypocritical intruders), Griffith deployed a panoply of finely honed aesthetic techniques to use the vitality of the sensuous to convey the significance of the ideal. At times Griffith became carried away with his mission, telling his company of actors and technicians that they had "gone beyond Babel, beyond words. We've found a universal language—a power that can make men brothers and end war forever." The purpose of art was to document his great concern, the drama of plebeian virtue under siege.

Born in Kentucky in 1875, Griffith was the son of a Confederate war veteran who seemed perpetually stuck in the past. In the course of a hardscrabble existence, the younger Griffith became an actor and a playwright. By the twentieth century, he was writing scenarios for the Biograph Film company, before making his debut as a director in 1908. Over the course of the next five years, Griffith turned out nearly 500 one- and two-reelers that included comedies, dramas of ghetto life, Westerns, and gangster films (*The Musketeers of Pig Alley* is often celebrated as the film that established the key elements of the genre). This work allowed him to hone his narrative skills and develop his mastery of a cinematic language. Commentators have sometimes erroneously credited Griffith with originating closeups, parallel cutting, artificial lighting, and use of a mobile camera. His true innovation was to think about storytelling systematically.[36] Breaking up traditional sequences into their component parts, Griffith reassembled those parts to make something new. Under Griffith, the shot, not the scene, became the building block. Cutting enabled Griffith to juxtapose events separated in time and space, making film an art of simultaneities rather than continuity. Jumps in time and space resembled cubist painting or automatic writing, but Griffith used them to underscore significance rather than to undermine it.

Few contemporaries thought as deeply about the aesthetic potential of film as Griffith did. Noting that audiences relaxed their rational minds and let the images wash over them, Griffith believed film communication was immediate and preconscious. An exclusively visual medium, movies communicated spiritually, a position that rested on Griffith's belief that eyes were organs of the mind rather than the body. As such, film could move beyond material reality and commonplace existence. Griffith signaled this status with the imaginative use of a number of filmic techniques, including the iris—a small circle within the larger frame that called attention to unexpected relationships—and a beam of light to highlight characters or objects to approximate the viewer's use of a spiritual eye to penetrate the truth of life.

In many ways, Griffith's work was steeped in melodrama. His films are chock-full of ill mothers, starving children, and women in peril, stock characters whose presence automatically signified virtue oppressed. Yet few could heighten the effect or evoke the pain of life as skillfully as Griffith. He honed such melodrama, imparting to it a special status by implying rather than showing, counting on the cascading images to build intensity. His most famous use of suggestion takes place at the end of Part I of *Birth of a Nation* when all the audience sees of the Little Colonel's homecoming is a view of his back with his mother's arms around his neck as he stands in the doorway. In scenes like that one, technique bolstered ideological commitments. More than most of his contemporaries in the film business, Griffith was animated by his belief that suffering was caused by greed and selfishness in high places. A considerable number of his early films for Biograph concentrate on the ways in which abuse of power in the industrial era has disordered American life. His *Corner in Wheat* (1909), based on the novelist Frank Norris's *The Octopus*, juxtaposes scenes of capitalist financial machinations with the actual production and links farmers' unrelenting and unrewarding toil to the structures of industrial America. Few movies of the era managed to show the connections between disparate activities so effectively or economically as Griffith did through his cuts from the speculators celebrating the corner, to the image of a ruined speculation, then to the farmers returning home empty-handed, and finally to the urban poor going hungry and beginning to riot when bread becomes unaffordable.

His exposure of greed was not a sign of political radicalism, at least of the socialist variety. Many Griffith films stress the necessity of individual propriety over collective and mutual action. Longing for the restoration of the virtue of preindustrial America, Griffith more often than not opts for what Scott Simmon calls sentimental hopes for lucky accidents. It is a measure of the limitations of Griffith's political vision that he could not locate any motor or agent for change. His epic *Intolerance* (1916) demonstrates the point. A combination of four stories—modern, Judaean, French, and Babylonian—interlaced and differently tinted, the film emphasizes the perfidy brought about by the prejudices that rulers promote. Against the villains, Griffith sets Eternal Motherhood, the symbol of endurance of humanity in the face of evil, embodied by Lillian Gish, who is shown comforting a baby while the intertitle shows the famous line from Whitman's *Leaves of Grass:* "Out of the Cradle Endlessly Rocking. Uniter of Here and Hereafter—Chanter of Sorrows and Joys." Griffith made the film as a response to critics of his *Birth of a Nation*, released the year before. The film, however, earned Griffith condemnation as a threat to the social order, because of his scathing portrayal of the alliance of oppression enacted in the marriage of a heartless industrial baron and his narrow-minded, social reformer wife. Even in the face of this threat, however, the film resists endorsing any social action, leaving primordial innocence strangely disembodied. Griffith succeeds admirably in dramatizing violence and portraying the ways in which illegitimate passions and unwarranted self-interest lead to tragedy. His strike sequence in the modern portion of the film builds dynamically with shots of shorter and shorter duration that move from the view of the strikers to their anxious families to the factory owner, shown in a long shot as a tiny figure dwarfed by a giant desk in a field of floor space. The sequence culminates in the shooting of strikers by the guards and drives home the forgotten brotherhood, the loneliness of greed, and the futility of resistance. Humanity may well need to change, but the upshot of the film is that time left humanity where it began.[37]

In large measure, Griffith's key subject was less class than gender. It is the tenuous nature of woman's role as moral beacon and purveyor of beauty that most interests Griffith. His working-class dramas revolve around the vulnerability of women outside the home. Outside the confines of domestic space and no longer protected by the family, women became sexual beings. Griffith's films associate this development with the breakdown of social harmony. Clearly uneasy with the unruliness of female desire, Griffith moved to contain, even punish it. Griffith often signified this shift from spirituality to sexuality by having his female characters glance into a mirror to inspect themselves. Punishment invariably followed. If females were not allowed to admire themselves, Griffith, on the other hand, paid special attention to the appearances of his female actors. Convinced that irregularities were signs of spiritual defects, he aimed at choosing lead actors whose beauty was innocent rather than sexual. As objects of beauty, Griffith's women were rooted in nineteenth-century notions of harmony, elevation, and morality. In contrast, Griffith embodied independence in less-than-perfect figures, at least as his work began to mature.

The nexus of morality, gender, and race was at the heart of Griffith's masterpiece, *Birth of a Nation* (1915). Predicated on the idea that the nation was born in the triumph of white supremacy, the film details the outrages of black transgression against home and hearth. After paying due homage to the sacrifices on both sides, the evils of slavery, and the generosity of the "Great Heart," Abraham Lincoln, *Birth* explores how the process of putting the bottom rail on top only threatened vulnerable female innocence, and with it, national unity itself. In casting the blond, classically guileless beauty Lillian Gish in the pivotal role of Elsie Stoneman, the daughter of a radical republican congressman, rescued from the clutches of a lustful mulatto by her Confederate veteran lover, Griffith emphasized both the ethereal beauty of white women and the dangerous sexuality of black men. Griffith's movie understood the "birth" of the title as the act of white men of both sections protecting the vulnerable and presexual from despoilment through the violent means of a heroic Ku Klux Klan.

Griffith's linkage of sexual innocence and racial purity tapped a deep strain in American culture and accounted for the tumultuous reception that white audiences gave the film. Karl Brown, Griffith's cameraman, described the February 8, 1915 premiere of *Birth of a Nation* as one in which "every soul in that audience was in the saddle with the clansmen and pounding hell-for-leather on an errand of stern justice, lighted on their way by the holy flames of a burning cross. . . . The audience didn't just sit there and applaud but they stood up and cheered and yelled and stamped feet until Griffith finally made an appearance."[38] Such acclaim was not universal. The National Association for the Advancement of Colored People charged Griffith's moral art was deeply immoral and untruthful. The National Board of Review concurred and attempted to suppress the film's more horrendous scenes depicting uncontrolled lust for sex and violence by African Americans. Griffith reacted bitterly, accusing his enemies of being uplifters who were determined to turn whites into property-less dependents and eager to legalize miscegenation. Such charges conveniently obscured the uncomfortable fact that most miscegenation had been the result of white male aggression. Like Ives, Griffith hoped to replace the false unity of gentility with the true unity of the common. In the end, however, the plebeians were more divided and less idealized than Griffith could admit.

Particular Beauty

According to nineteenth-century writers on aesthetics, beauty was not only spiritual, evoking ideals rather than materials; it was also universal, pointing beyond the partiality of view to the human condition writ large. Beauty was beauty irrespective of time and place. Critics explained the failure for artifacts to be proclaimed beautiful by universal assent as the consequence of perceptual deficiencies and partial vision. They located that partiality in preferences for music that was only rhythm, sculpture that lacked proportion and spirituality, and literature that was special pleading wrapped in tortured idioms. The judgment of inferior taste fell disproportionately on such marginalized groups as blacks, immigrants, and women. So ingrained were such critical habits that the art critic Frank Mather could find no greater condemnation of post-impressionism than that it borrowed from "recondite and barbaric models—negro sculpture, the neolithic and Bushman paintings, and the Javanese puppets. Against the academicism of culture they set the academicism of savagery."³⁹

Increasingly, artists and critics rebelled against Mather's concept of universality, finding it narrow and constraining. In its place, they celebrated what artists, musicians, and writers knew better—the particular. Early-twentieth-century aesthetic particularism had a number of sources: the establishment of ethnic cultural institutions, the insistence of marginalized groups that Mather's notion of the universal excluded them, and a new stress on the virtues of individualized expression. Particularism in beauty had no single agenda, and at times the various demands and interests clashed with one another. Yet their combined force in the early twentieth century had the effect of legitimating the notion that standards are the province of those who make and consume the art.

The ethnic cultural institutions that proliferated during the first two decades of the twentieth century negotiated a fine line between asserting group distinctiveness and aspiring to universality or at least commonality. Some aimed at sustaining the culture of the homeland in a hostile environment and in the process promoting group solidarity. Other "ethnic" arts were launched to demonstrate that the group was capable of producing beauty in the American grain. Many native-born champions of these cultures, however, missed these disparate motives and, with only a superficial understanding, marshaled them into an attack on both universality and propriety. Some responses were the cultural tourism of stifled Victorians who yearned for a liberating exoticism. Others turned to immigrant culture as a source of values to oppose American commercial culture. The journalist Hutchins Hapgood, for example, favorably contrasted a Jewish theater determined to face facts with the "empty farce and inane cheerfulness of the uptown theatres."⁴⁰

Much of Hapgood's *Spirit of the Ghetto* (1902) was a testimony to the virtues of Jewish provincialism. The provincialism that Hapgood discerned was of a special sort. Taking care to point out that it was a "mistake to think that the young Hebrew turns naturally to trade," Hapgood detailed the Jews' commitment to scholarship, their play with ideas, their commitment to truth. "The Spirit of the Ghetto is the spirit of seriousness, of melancholy, of

high idealism," he maintained. His ghetto is the ghetto of religion and intellectuals, detailing with the help of East Side resident Jacob Epstein's sketches
the various character types who populate the ghetto. For all his admiration
of Jewish life, Hapgood did observe a lack of sensuousness. "The Russian
Jew's lack of appreciation of completed beauty or of merely sensuous nature
is strikingly illustrated by the fact that there has never been a great expression of plastic art in his history. Painting, sculpture, and architecture are
nothing to the Jew in comparison with the literature and music of ideas. . . .
In nearly all the Jews of talent I have met there is the same intellectual consumption, the excitement of beauty, but no enjoyment of pure beauty of
form. The race is still too unhappy, too unsatisfied, has too much to gain, to
express a complacent sense of the beauty of what is."[41]

Lack of sensuousness was rarely a charge brought against black Americans.
In the face of legal segregation and a horrifying increase in racial violence,
African Americans developed a number of cultural forms that starkly demonstrated their determination not to abandon their particular sense of pleasure.
In addition to the ragtime composers, such black artists as the poet Paul Dun-
bar and James Weldon Johnson, the lyricist of "Lift Every Voice and Sing"
and the author of Memoirs of an Ex-Colored Person, skillfully melded the aesthetic forms championed by genteel critics with insightful evocations of
black experience. Black musicians of the Mississippi Delta, for their part,
fashioned a new aesthetic form, bringing together disparate strands of the
American sound tradition and African inflections and rhythmic emphases.
The blues drew on field hollers (nonlinear coded messages designed to evade
the understanding of white overseers) and jump-ups (rhythmic dance tunes)
to create a new musical vocabulary. Relying upon "bent" notes—emotionally
inflected pitches that do not fit precisely into Western scales, the music was
honed in work camps and juke joints. Lyrically, the blues concentrated on
failed love affairs, economic deprivation, and encounters with law enforcement. Often unexpectedly juxtaposing images, blues lyrics come in three-line
verses, with the second line repeating the first, and the third often being
quite different. The effect was to use rhythm as expressive rather than as discipline or coordination as in other music. Its moods, often expressed in
moans and sliding among pitches, gave a texture to the music that emphasized not so much its universality—although many of the themes very much
transcended their origin—as the specificity of point of view and the uniqueness of the cultural tradition in which it originated.[42]

The frank sexuality of much of the blues, its unusual rhythms and pitches,
and its use of the guitar earned the music a reputation as the devil's music
among respectable folk, both black and white. More secular efforts to parse

meaning have not reached consensus. Some analysts have seen blues as a folk music that expressed the sorrows and protests of a people denied citizenship rights and meaningful economic existence. As such, it has been celebrated for its unsoiled ability to capture the character of a people. Alan Lomax, who spent much of the 1930s and 1940s discovering blues singers and collecting blues songs, contends that they are "notable among all human works for their profound despair." Others, however, have seen the blues as less political than existential. Albert Murray, for one, sets himself against views that see the blues as the outcry of the victim. Rather he sees it as a statement about "confronting the complexities inherent in the human situation and about improvising . . . with such possibilities as are also inherent in the obstacles, disjunctures, and the jeopardy." It is, he contends, "a statement about perseverance and about resilience and thus also about the maintenance of equilibrium despite precarious circumstances."[43]

Despite efforts to contain it, the blues reached a larger audience in the first two decades of the twentieth century and a much larger one in subsequent years. The blues spread in part because of the effort of Memphis political leader Boss Crump to placate voters demanding an end to vice. Closing down the bars and bordellos where musicians had previously played spurred the creation of new venues for the music. Also aiding the diffusion of the blues was the advent of W. C. Handy. Handy, who had grown up in a religious family that rejected wilder, rougher music, was intrigued one day, as he sat in a rail station, by a man singing that he was "goin' where the Southern cross the dog," a reference to the spot in Moorhead, Mississippi, where the Southern rail lines intersected with those of the Yazoo Delta (known vernacularly as "the Yellow Dog") at ninety-degree angles. The odd reference, which would later take on cosmic and symbolic significance as the crossroads, and a sound Handy regarded as crude did not prevent him from admiring the vitality of the music. Adding elements of orchestration and a touch of Latin *habanera*, Handy scored hits with the "Memphis Blues" and "St. Louis Blues" in 1913 and 1914 respectively. If Handy aimed at diluting the rough-hewn sound with classical touches, he nonetheless kept such crucial elements of black music as call-and-response and bent notes. The success of recordings of his work among both white and black record buyers testifies to the potential of aesthetic particularism both to express the sentiments of the people from which it originated and to cross boundaries. Much to the dismay of purists of all sorts, the history of American popular music has been a story of mixing and melding, although not necessarily the democratic one that Du Bois envisioned.[44]

Women too advanced new claims to an aesthetic of their own. Long considered objects of beauty, they rarely earned credit from male arbiters of taste for possessing the ability to create it. Critics had noted their presence as writers and readers of certain kinds of fiction but had dismissed their tastes as inartistic and overly wrought. As historians have shown, the sentimental novel was something more complicated, a way in which women could speak to and for each other.[45] Often blamed for dampening the appeal of serious literature, the "woman's novel" reached the heights of popularity and influence during the middle decades of the nineteenth century. Yet it remained a staple of the American literary arts in our period as well, dominating the bestseller lists with such entries as Alice Rice's Mrs. *Wiggs of the Cabbage Patch* (1901), Kate Douglas Wiggin's *Rebecca of Sunnybrook Farm* (1903), Margaret Deland's *The Awakening of Helena Richie* (1906), and Eleanor Potter's *Pollyanna* (1913). Such works often acknowledged, if only to dismiss, new possibilities for women. Answering them with a decidedly feminist claim to the existence of a specific, independent female notion of pleasure were Mary Johnston's *Hagar* (1913) and Charlotte Perkins Gilman's utopian fantasy of a world without men *Herland* (1915).

Less overtly political but more aesthetically significant than Johnston's and Gilman's efforts were the novels of Willa Cather, Ellen Glasgow, and Edith Wharton, all of whom broke in significant ways from the traditions of the sentimental novel. Historians of sentimental literature have noted the potential of the form for subversion of gender expectations by shifting, if at times surreptitiously, power relations. Yet such subversive moments were always accompanied by more conformist inclinations that limited the success of the opposition. Cather, Glasgow, and Wharton, on the other hand, were reluctant either in their work or in their lives to see home and hearth as the sole pivot of women's lives. None regarded beauty as a strictly ethereal matter. Nor did they rely on traditional female qualities of sacrifice and nurturing as the basis of their best work. Much of their output in the early twentieth century may well be read as an indictment of society, in which being an object of beauty has serious consequences for women. *House of Mirth* (Wharton, 1905), *Virginia* (Glasgow, 1913), and *Song of the Lark* (Cather, 1915) are products of decidedly different sensibilities, but they share a sense of the cost to women of not being allowed to develop their own points of view unencumbered by expectations of what women should be and want. Cather, Glasgow, and Wharton all indicted universality as being at the bottom male-oriented—honoring male desires and enacting male conceptions in which women were objects rather than agents. Such positions overlapped with those of the emergent feminist movement, but the three were not uniformly supportive of organized female political action. Glasgow had marched in suffrage parades and had published her poem "The Call" in *Collier's*, which had as its refrain "Woman calls to woman to awaken! / Woman calls to woman to arise!" Wharton, on the other hand, dismissed feminist calls as foolish.[46]

Challenging the false universality of accepted norms of beauty was the impetus behind the modern dance of Ruth St. Denis and Isadora Duncan. The former began her career in what were known as Broadway leg shows, which had a reputation for being daringly revealing, if not particularly aesthetic. After visiting Coney Island in 1905, she presented *Radha*, which was an instant sensation, as a consequence of her ability to fashion "the curious combination of Delsarte dance movements, show business eroticism, and Coney Island exoticism into a novel and moving dance."[47] Duncan made the ballet her particular target. Rejecting its "delusion that the law of gravity does not exist" and its deformation of the "beautiful woman's body" by insisting upon an unnaturally thin form, Duncan danced barefoot in flowing toga robes in movements she claimed dated from ancient Greece and Rome.[48] She envisioned her work as a woman uniting body and soul, of natural movements revealing spiritual heights. The artist John Sloan spoke for many who adored Duncan: "I feel she dances a symbol of human happiness as it should be, free from unnatural trammels. Not angelic, materialistic—not superhuman but the greatest human love of life. Her great big thighs, her small head, her full solid loins, belly—clean, all clean—she dances away civilization's tainted brain vapors, wholly human and holy—part of God."[49]

For all her bohemian posture and flamboyant manner, Duncan's notion of female naturalness was less a departure from nineteenth-century aesthetic norms than her enthusiastic supporters claimed. Her understanding of the "natural female body" shared many of the ideals of uplift and moral transcendence of previous generations. She rejected earthiness in its more explicit forms. Overt eroticism violated her sense of art. To be legitimate, dance should exhibit, "no rhythm from the waist down, but from the Solar Plexus, the temporal home of the soul. . . . It seems monstrous that anyone should believe that the Jazz rhythm expresses America. Jazz rhythm," she concluded, "expresses the primitive savage."[50]

Feminist commitment to an independent viewpoint was apparent in the plays of the little theater movement. Designed to counter what proponents regarded as the lifeless, dull offerings of commercial theater and to bypass the rigid control exercised by mainstream producers and booking agents, little theaters were intended to make theater meaningful rather than an evening's diversion, relevant to the forces of life, and open to new ways of using the stage to express modern life. This joy in experimentation and dedication to authentic expression attracted amateurs and budding professionals alike. The growth was astounding. In 1912, there were nine little theaters in the country. Five years later, there were fifty. By 1922, the number reached some three hundred experimental theaters.[51] Two of the most famous in New York, the Washington Square Players and the Provincetown Players, were particularly amenable to feminist contributions. The more professional Washington Square Players, which usually specialized in European drama, scored the first sensation with Alice Gerstenberg's *Overtone*. The conceit of the play is to put both the conscious and unconscious selves of two women on stage at the same time. Ostensibly a meeting between the wife of a painter and his former lover, who had chosen to marry a richer man instead, the play details the struggle between the divergent selves as well as the two women. Against a polite banter between Harriet and Margaret, Gerstenberg sets the more straightforward, unguarded talk between the two women and their "primitive" selves, Hettie and Maggie respectively. The conscious selves are ostensibly polite to one another, even as they attempt to outmaneuver the other. The primitive selves are, on the other hand, crude, jealous, petty, and disdainful of social convention. In physically separating the primitive and cultivated selves on stage, Gerstenberg graphically conveyed how patriarchy prevented women from integrating desire with their presentation of self to others.

Susan Glaspell expanded on Gerstenberg's feminist insight about the consequence of patriarchy. Glaspell, with her husband George Cram Cook, founded and maintained the Provincetown Players, perhaps best known for the discovery of Eugene O'Neill. Begun in Provincetown among vacationing Villagers in 1915, it moved to New York in 1916. Unlike the Washington Square Players, the Provincetown crew, which enrolled such Greenwich Village luminaries as Floyd Dell, Mary Heaton Vorse, Louise Bryant, and John Reed, organized itself as an amateur collective in which art and life were to be merged. In theory antihierarchical, the Players democratically decided what to present and collaborated on production itself. By itself, Cook's ideal theater was not particularly feminist in orientation. Yet in light of the declared feminism of the Village and Glaspell's own talent, the original plays that the Provincetown Players presented were quite often explorations of female subjectivity. Glaspell's forte was the simple one-act play in which mood was evoked by inarticulateness. Beauty resided in the unseen and unannounced meaning in things. Objects that seemed quite ordinary reverberate with the meanings characters ascribe to them.

That tack is evident in her most famous Provincetown work, *Trifles* (1916), a tale of how women can discern a different truth from details that seem inconsequential or meaningless to men. The play is set in a farmhouse, where the Sheriff, his wife, the County Attorney, and Mrs. Hale, a neighbor, are looking for clues to the murder of John Wright, who was hanged in his sleep. His wife, Minnie, is the obvious suspect and has been taken to jail. When the four arrive, they note in passing that the housework is incomplete. For the men, this is a trifling thing, a failure of Minnie Wright to do her duties. For the women, however, the spoiled preserves, the poor stitching on a quilt, and unwashed dishes indicate a disturbed consciousness, a subjective rather than an objective terrain. Other clues indicate that John Wright demanded total possession of his wife, prohibiting her from communicating with others. In her sewing box, the women find a strangled canary wrapped in cloth. They surmise that Wright, who despised sound, had strangled the only thing that gave Minnie's life meaning, and in desperation, revenge, and anger she lashed out at her authoritarian husband. By attending to the meaning of small things, the women glean what puzzled the men, the motive for the crime. For Glaspell, the prohibition of communication and the failure to understand constituted the undetected crime.

Feminist playwrights were not the only artists of the early twentieth century to put a premium on consciousness as the source of aesthetic value. Many writers, artists, and musicians took their cues from discourses that conceived truth as a matter of perspective rather than as something objective. The goal of art was less to speak to all of humanity than to accurately reveal who one was and what one valued. Dismissing as unrealistic and illusionary the Arnoldian goal of seeing it clearly and seeing it whole, a new crop of artists and writers stressed instead the interior truths of the psyche, which by their very nature were partial. The new conception of beauty entailed more than acknowledging that different people saw reality differently. It also concentrated attention on the ways in which the interaction between events and the resources of the self could produce beauty. Portrayal of the workings of consciousness itself replaced faithful reproduction of the external world as the measure of aesthetic achievement. Under such a regime, self-expression was not an indulgence, but the purpose of representation. For partisans of aesthetic particularism, art that promoted authenticity—the squaring of act with the real or essential self—was one in which stimulation and pleasure trumped uplift, social obligation, and efforts to transcend limitations of self.[52]

Henry James's novels in the early twentieth century demonstrate this new aesthetic of subjectivity. Putting aside his realism of the 1880s and 1890s, James took a new interest in the ways in which the complicated, intricate, and often contradictory perceptions and feelings shaped reality.[53] In his twentieth-century novels, particularly *Wings of the Dove* (1902), *The Ambas-*

sadors (1903), and *The Golden Bowl* (1904), conventional action gives way to exploration of characters' minds. Our understanding of Paris in *The Ambassadors*, for instance, turns on the changing consciousness of Lambert Strether, a Massachusetts editor who travels there on behalf of his fiancée, Mrs. Newsome. His assignment is to bring back her son, Chad, to manage the family business and to remove him from a love affair he is conducting with a married woman. Strether's firm New England notions of right and wrong are no match for the aestheticism of France. He is unable to stay detached, to maintain his values amid the aesthetic attractions of Paris. The focus of the novel turns away from the events themselves, any objective determination of the characters, or the physicality of the setting to the ways in which Strether cannot get his bearings. Strether discovers that his knowledge was not an unproblematic perception of things, but one that was from its very inception rooted in his desires. What he finds disturbing at first is how transient and free-floating those desires can be. James writes of Paris in one of the best-known passages of the novel, "It hung before him this morning, this vast bright Babylon, like some huge iridescent object, a jewel brilliant and hard, in which parts are not to be discriminated nor differences comfortably marked. It twinkled and trembled and melted together, and what seemed all surface one moment seemed all depth the next." By the end of the novel, Strether has come to accept fluidity as the way of the world. Recommending to Chad that he remain in Paris, he returns to Massachusetts, less rigid and judgmental than before.

James was not a vitalist, but he shared with vitalists a sense of the subjectivity of aesthetic pleasure. Aesthetic vitalism, which appeared in the work of modernist painters, the new poets, and the photographer Alfred Stieglitz, asserted the validity of the fluctuating and ineffable quality of experience. Disdaining the idea of aesthetic perfection, vitalists looked to art to accomplish what a deterministic and hierarchical science could not: to preserve meaning in a spiritual space impervious to description. Vitalists opted for art because it depended upon intuition and better rendered immediate subjective experience. Because art prompted somatic reaction, it fulfilled the vitalist goals of escaping entrapping concepts. Vitalist-based art was the epitome of the particularistic interior aesthetic, aiming to stimulate what Matthew Baigell has termed the "endlessly continuous sense of creation within the mind of the beholder."[54] Once the self became the source and site of pleasure, maintaining a universal standard became well-nigh impossible.

The use of abstraction in the arts—particularly the concentration on form for its own sake—might seem the opposite of aesthetic particularism. Certainly, critics of abstraction complained about the coldness and impersonality of the dissection of the human form into its component shapes, comparing it to the efforts of scientists to reduce all phenomena to their most basic elements. Yet such criticisms captured only a portion of what the new arts intended to accomplish. In breaking with the accepted modes of representation, artists emphasized the personal understanding of form. As the painter Arthur Dove put it to a friend in 1913, abstraction allowed the painter to break "actual dependence on the object" and facilitate the "means of expression becoming purely subjective." Dove claimed he no longer observed in the same way, concentrating on the subjective sensations of form and color rather than passively registering objects as objects in the conventional manner.[55] Once the representation of the objective world ceased to be the sole goal of aesthetic expression, aesthetic multiplicity followed. As artists, musicians, and composers sought out a new vocabulary that often took the form of imploding the old forms, the early twentieth-century aesthetic world witnessed unexpected uses of color, strange juxtapositions of sound in both music and poetry, and rejection of the accepted tonal qualities and of perspective in painting. At times, the very notion of art as unique expression came into question, as when Marcel Duchamp submitted a toilet signed "R. Mutt" to an art show. In making the familiar strange, the new art strove less for universal assent than for an appeal to small coteries of like-minded people in the know.

Particularist pleasures of this sort were central to the photographer Alfred Stieglitz's contributions to American art. Born to a German Jewish family in Hoboken, New Jersey, in 1864, Stieglitz began his career advocating the aesthetic value of photography. Through his influential *Camera Work*, Stieglitz rejected both the prettifying photographic aesthetic that sanctioned layered effects and manipulation of the negative and the contention that a photograph was at bottom an objective record of the world. Influenced by the philosopher Henri Bergson, whom he published regularly, Stieglitz attempted to create a slice of meaning from the flux of life. That motivation spurred his famous photograph *Steerage*. Often taken as a record of the poignancy and vulnerability of immigrants, Stieglitz saw something else. In 1907 on a trip to Europe, he left the stuffy first-class deck to glimpse humanity in steerage. There, as he looked, he began to see life as a whole, or so he claimed. "A round straw hat, the funnel leaning left, the stairway leaning right, the white draw-bridge with its railings made of circular chains—white suspenders crossing the back of a man in steerage below, round shapes of iron machinery, a mast cutting into the sky, making a triangular shape. I stood spellbound for a while, looking and looking. Could I photograph what I felt, looking and looking and still looking? I saw shapes related to each other. I saw a picture of shapes and underlying that, the feeling I had about life."[56] In Stieglitz's view, the ability of an engaged self to capture the élan vital of the material and express the purity of the vision with expert craftsmanship had a political component, in the largest sense of the word. As he noted in 1914, such an art contrasted with the shoddiness and stupidity that he believed was in control everywhere. Critics of Stieglitz and his allies in the Photo-Secession movement—Edward Steichen, Gertrude Käsebier, F. Holland Day, and Clarence White—charged them with deliberate effacement of communication. Wrote one photographer of Stieglitz's aesthetic, "Nothing is artistic which is not outré, nothing beautiful which is not 'bizarre,' nothing worthy of attention which is not preposterous, nothing serious unless untranslatable."[57]

In 1908, Stieglitz shifted his aesthetic focus. His concern with shapes drew him toward post-impressionism. Having once disliked the distortions of Cezanne, he now embraced Matisse for his bold palette. Even before the Armory Show of 1913, Stieglitz was exhibiting abstract and modernist work in his "291" studio. And he began cultivating artists. Although his stringent personality often alienated them, he did create a community of Bergsonians. One painter who had intermittent relations with the Stieglitz set was Max Weber, a Russian Orthodox Jew who had studied with Matisse. Weber matched both Stieglitz's confidence and his insistent subjectivism. In an argument verging on animism, Weber held that "even inanimate objects crave a hearing, and desire to participate in the great motion of time." The flower, he continued, "is not satisfied to be merely a flower in light and space and temperature, [because] it wants to be a flower in us, in our soul." The upshot for Weber was that "things live in us and through us."[58] If few extended subjectivity that far, the impulse toward canvases, scores, and manuscripts in which beauty was personal, limited, contingent, and perspectival, and in which form was a medium of experimentation that Weber and his comrades pioneered, was an identifying feature of multiplicity in pleasure. Whether such multiplicity could foster meaningful communication remained an open question.

Amoral Beauty

Central to the aesthetic universe of nineteenth-century critics was the contention that beauty was the sign of morality. For the leading arbiters of taste, morality in art encompassed spirituality and universality, giving sensuous experience purpose and direction. Educated Americans understood moral art in a number of ways. The most literal construction was that art must represent the good in a straightforward way. The best art ratified accepted morals. Part of this impetus arose from worries that without guidance, pleasure would become anarchic. So worried were some regulators of morals that they extended supervision to children's playgrounds in the hope that rational recreation would build strong minds and bodies. Others understood a moral art as one that in some way enabled us to understand the world in which we live. From that starting point, evaluation concentrated on the type of world the artist or writer imagined. A work that enabled us to think imaginatively and productively about our lives qualified under this interpretation as moral art. During the early twentieth century, it was the first sense that was the more generally opposed. Artists and writers of many persuasions objected to demands for uplift on the grounds that such an art choked off the joy and denied the pleasure that they saw as essential to art. Audiences too gravitated to many mindless pleasures. It was the second sense that proved harder to jettison. Fewer artists, critics, and consumers accepted a purposeless art, one evaluated solely on its technique. Nonetheless, the defenders of *art pour l'art* were numerous enough to press home to cultural custodians the reality of an aesthetic multiverse.

One sign that men and women demanded a reevaluation of morality in art is the declining effectiveness of vice commissions in policing entertainment. *Succès de scandale* dotted the cultural landscape. Olga Nethersole, an English actress and the star and director of the French play *Sapho* faced prosecution for obscenity in 1900 for its less-than-circumspect depiction of sexual relations. Nethersole's willingness to play a woman who does not object when the hero carries her upstairs to the bedroom drew particular interest. The vice commission prevailed on the police to make an arrest, but demonstrations by the women of New York City led to an acquittal after fifteen minutes of deliberation.[59] Anthony Comstock may have successfully disrupted the 1905 performance of George Bernard Shaw's *Mrs. Warren's Profession*, but Shaw won the showdown when he coined the term "Comstockery" as a synonym for self-righteous censorship, a characterization that still haunts Comstock's reputation. The following year, the debate over morality was itself dramatized in William Vaughn Moody's *Great Divide*, which set Eastern refinement against Western "barbarism" and located energy in the latter. The Eastern woman wants a sublime abstraction; she desires the hero but believes, as is her training and her history, that pleasure requires suffering. The Western hero rejects the sentiment, proclaiming in a far cry from Victorian notions of morality as restraint and sacrifice, "our law is joy and selfishness, the curve of your shoulder and the light on your hair as you sit there say that as plain as preaching."[60]

If moral codes were less rigid, the complete uncoupling of ethics and beauty was harder for middle-class Americans to accept. Jane Addams, for instance, could praise the plays of Ibsen, Shaw, and Hauptman for dealing "so directly with moral issues that the moralists themselves wince under their teachings and declare them brutal." Addams held that many Americans took their morality this way because "the over-refined and complicated lives of city dwellers" led them to "recoil from intricate moral teaching and metaphysical creeds." Hungry for life, Addams concluded, they saw in such drama "definite instruction for daily living," a sign that among a significant portion of the American middle class even the most seemingly brutal and harsh work of art could be redeemed if one could locate a meaningful purpose in the pleasure.[61] Embracing an art that emphasized the pleasures of form alone, saw beauty in evil, or abandoned hope was hardly a majority pursuit in the early twentieth century.

Still, amorality in the arts was not uncommon in the broad-based attack on the straitjacket of uplift. Decadence had appeared in strength in the 1890s, and many of its practitioners were still active in the twentieth century. For many college students, the English aesthete Walter Pater was still an influential figure. Likewise, the critics James Huneker of New York and William Marion Reedy of St. Louis brought a new kind of aestheticism to the public. Reedy, who once opined that clocks all over the country were striking "sex o'clock," was especially important in nurturing new talent in his role as editor of the St. Louis *Mirror*. Amoral aestheticism received theoretical expression in *New Criticism* (1911), written by Joel Spingarn, a Columbia University professor of literature and, later, a prominent member of the executive board of the National Association for the Advancement of Colored People. Critical of aesthetics that restricted pleasure, Spingarn insisted that art was intrinsically valuable and could not be beholden to social or moral demands. Critics needed to attend to how well an artifact revealed subjectivity, Spingarn argued, by becoming one with the artist in feeling and reproducing it in themselves. Because Americans were too fearful of such art and accepted only artifacts that claimed to depict reality objectively, Spingarn concluded that the fundamental problem of American cultural life was that beauty was too sane. "The virtue of all art is that it is always more or less mad. All the greater is our American need of art's tonic loveliness, and all the more difficult is it for us to recapture the inherent madness without which she cannot speak or breathe. . . . How timid seemed our poetry and our drama and our prose fiction; how conventional and pusillanimous our literary and dramatic fiction."[62]

Better known was H. L. Mencken (1880–1956), Baltimore newspaper-man, editor, and critic and American champion of Friedrich Nietzsche. Mencken was particularly barbed in his rejection of uplift, which he saw as leaving life in these United States vapid and dreary. He valued Nietzsche most for the German philosopher's rejection of conventional morality, de-lighting in the characterization of Christianity as the epitome of a slave men-tality. Nietzsche meant that Christian injunctions to repress rather than ac-cept instincts separated humans from their own powers and crushed desires for greater control and mastery. A philosopher of multiplicity, Nietzsche cel-ebrated not the good and evil of traditional morality, but a flow of life that was, as he put it, the "will to power." Unleashing the will to power enabled domination and creativity and enriched existence. Where traditional moral-ity sought to limit human nature, Nietzscheans celebrated those who would reject denial and obligation and would instead act daringly, testing them-selves and soaking in experience. Nietzsche countered morality with an aes-thetics, seeing a frankly perspectival beauty as preferable to the misbegotten search for universals and absolutes. Only exceptional human beings could undertake such journeys, a point Mencken understood and championed.[63]

Mencken shared with Nietzsche a hatred for religion, women, and de-mocracy. Not surprisingly, he found progressive reform, which usually com-bined all three in various degrees, laughable. He indicted reformers for their condemnation of pleasure, seeing in uplift reformers' denial of their own im-pulses. Revolutionists, he declared, were only more boring reformers. Yet Mencken, like Nietzsche, was too aware of tragedy to accept claims of plea-sure for its own sake. He had scorn for bohemians, whom he saw as lacking a distinctive style, and he found the sexual revolution a bit tedious. He was ca-pable of writing about Spingarn's criticism that "beauty as we know it in this world is by no means the apparition in vacuo that Dr. Spingarn seems to see. It has its social, its political, even its moral implications. . . . To denounce moralizing out of hand is to pronounce a moral judgment." Even amorality, it seems, was something less than pure during the first twenty years of the century.[64]

Mencken was not the only critic of the morality of the "booboisie" to re-tain the link between some form of morality and beauty. So too did the nov-elist Theodore Dreiser. Although many contemporaries condemned him as amoral, Dreiser often was less free from purposeful aesthetic pleasure than it seemed. University of Illinois literature professor Stuart Sherman ignited a literary battle royal with Mencken when he accused Dreiser of indulging only pure sensuality and deficient moral insights. Only by deliberately suppressing evidence of moral impulses in American culture, Sherman believed, could

Dreiser conclude life was a jungle. Even the literary radical Floyd Dell, who had befriended Dreiser and praised his work in the mid-teens, concluded that Dreiser ultimately allowed too little space for the human will and encouraged a passive acceptance of life.[65] Dreiser himself seemed to confirm some of the worst fears of his critics. He often talked and wrote as if society were indeed subsumed under nature and humans were simply creatures with inexorable and unmodifiable biological needs. His novels are dotted with passages in which he comments directly on the blindness of human strivings and the weakness of human will. As Lester Kane tells his mistress Jennie Gerhardt in explaining his decision to abandon her in the face of public condemnation and potential disinheritance, "all of us are more or less pawns. We're moved about like chessman by circumstances over which we have no control."[66]

Dreiser's naturalism was far from total, however. He often railed against what he claimed was inevitable, hoping to effect justice—something that was possible only if humans could have some control of their fate. Competition may have been the way of the world, but Dreiser was not supremely indifferent to the lot of those who lost the race or those who were driven by desires they could not fully articulate or suppress. "Let no one underestimate the need of pity," he wrote in The Financier. Genteel pressure, as James West has demonstrated, did change the shape of Sister Carrie, softening its fatalism. One change to which Dreiser did agree was removing the ending in which the ruined Hurstwood mutters, "What's the use?" as he turns on the gas with which he will commit suicide. The ending published in 1900 has Carrie sitting in her rocking chair, dreaming of a happiness she may never feel. In its suggestion that Carrie's dreams and desires were destined never to be fulfilled, that her strivings would go unrealized, that beauty would be transitory, Dreiser demonstrated less indifference to her fate than something akin to sympathy. That sympathy appeared in an interview in which Dreiser contended that while he respected and even admired human desire, he was well aware how it could lead to folly. The point of his novels, he remarked, was to show that "all humanity must stand together and war against and overcome the forces of nature."[67]

Professor Spingarn may have thought American beauty too sane, but the majority of critics who viewed the International Exhibition of Modern Art by the Association of American Painters and Sculptors, better known as the Armory Show, disagreed. By their lights, the cubist, fauvist, and other post-impressionist work on display had links to political radicalism and amorality. Some, such as the critic Royal Cortissoz, proclaimed the show an invasion of degeneracy and insanity, calling it the art of Ellis Island. The New York Times placed modern art in a "general movement, discernible all over the world, to disrupt and degrade, if not to destroy, not only art, but literature and society, too." This general movement, the *Times* averred, included "anarchists in politics, the poets who defy syntax and decency, and all the would-be destroyers . . . with the pretense of trying to regenerate the world." Such folk imagine themselves democratic, the *Times* insisted, but they were "really trying to block the wheels of progress in every direction."[68] Henri Matisse may have drawn the most fire. Despite his efforts to assure American reporters he was an ordinary man with fairly ordinary desires, the critics Frank Mather and Kenyon Cox condemned his efforts to achieve childlike innocence as uncivilized and nasty, accusing him of deliberately courting ugliness in order to destabilize society and profit in the bargain.[69]

The critical success of the show has left Cox with a reputation as "hidebound," making him something of a victim of what historian of the show Milton Brown has termed "the sweep of artistic history."[70] Yet Cox was no simple reactionary. He had championed impressionism when it was offensive to established tastes and had liberal political views. Cleared of heated rhetoric, Cox's worry was less a matter of prudery than a concern about the antisocial, individualistic whimsy that he saw enshrined in the new art. Such an art would turn its back on presenting human possibilities and human communication. In line with a number of progressive political thinkers, Cox lamented the inclination to elevate self over society. "Art has a social function" Cox told the *New York Times*. "In all the great periods of art it has spoken to the people in a language that they understood and expressed what they would have it express. These men who would make art merely expressive of their personal whim, make it speak in a special language only understood by themselves, are as truly anarchists as are those who would overthrow all social laws. But the modern tendency is to exalt individualism at the expense of law. The Cubists and the Futurists simply exhibit a very extreme and savage form of this individualism, an individualism exaggerated and made absurd for the sake of advertising."[71]

Cox's equation of social function and morality stood opposed to painter Wassily Kandinsky's proposition that "a picture is but a given space where things of the moment which happen to the painter occur." In the years following the show, such views seemed more palatable to educated Americans. Art institutions changed as well, with the semi-official National Academy of Design, which embodied the aesthetic of reproduction and uplift, giving way to a new group of galleries, exhibition spaces, and schools.[72] The show prompted as well the intensified declaration of new art movements, replete with their own manifestos and standards. Pre-show aesthetic unity gave way to post-show aesthetic multiplicity. Yet whether aesthetic communities fully accepted art as an autotelic object, one that was self-contained, autonomous, and understood in reference only to itself, was less clear. Cox's morality and politics clearly lost ground in the wake of the show, but the usefulness still remained a criterion by which even those with advanced tastes evaluated art. Art patrons may well have replaced education of the moral sense with education of the senses as the goal of art, but the sense that art related to the good in the world was never fully jettisoned. As art historian Matthew Baigell notes, few Americans were ready to see the world as pure chance or gave up the idea that art should be a form of communication about the world.[73] The retention of morality in art might be seen in the split among many of the modern artists. Duchamp found Stieglitz much too concerned with the effects of art and much too interested in art effecting change, dismissing him as a moral Socrates. On the other hand, the painter John Marin, whose cityscapes hinted at moving buildings, denied he was an abstract painter at all, arguing that instead he valued "Health." He dismissed "the so-called abstractionist" for his lifelessness and lack of vital sexuality.[74]

Amoral aesthetics were the furthest thing from the mind of the artists whose movement eventuated in the Armory Show. Most historians trace the show to earlier dissents from the critical establishment. The first successful movement came from a group of painters from what was known as the Ashcan School, so-called because their rejection of the notion that beauty required elevated subject matter led them to paint scenes of urban life, dirt and all. The social realism of John Sloan, Robert Henri, George Bellows, Everett Shinn, George Luks, and Albert Glackens held that depiction of working-class life was more "real" and authentic. Eliminating much of the gloss and finish that was accepted as beauty, Ashcan artists aimed at capturing the vitality of industrial life. Although called "unhealthy" by some critics, their work more often than not captured the strength and resilience of the slum dwellers. Latter-day critics remain divided about whether Sloan and his compatriots remained connected to and sympathetic with their subjects. In the pre-show years, however, Sloan articulated both a sense of the independence of the artist to pursue individual vision and a socialist politics that led to his association with the radical magazine the *Masses*.[75] Not all Ashcan painters shared Sloan's politics, but nearly all objected to elitism and traditionalism that made art a thing of trifling amusement of the rich. To break the Academy monopoly, they sponsored their own shows in 1902 and 1904. The 1908 show, which proudly proclaimed "no juries, no prizes" was particularly successful, earning the exhibiting artists special plaudits. More dissident artists and critics joined planning for new shows, but fissures soon developed. Against the Ashcan interest in establishing American standards and their commitment to a representational art stood a diverse group who found such insistence to be provincial and limiting itself. Led by artists and critics such as Walter Kuhn, Walter Pach, who had studied with Matisse, and Arthur Davies, who specialized in symbolic dreamscapes, the non-Ashcan contingent struck out under the influence of Stieglitz and Gertrude and Leo Stein to champion a whole panoply of European post-impressionist work. It was the latter group, in part because they had better connections with donors and patrons, who set the tone.

Revolutionary though the cubist, fauvist, and other variants of post-impressionism were, they actually took up much less space in the hall than the outcry made it seem. Seven hundred of the nearly 1,300 artifacts on display were American in origin. Yet since the exhibit was arranged chronologically, all viewers would eventually gravitate toward European nonrepresentational art as the pinnacle of aesthetic achievement. Organizers set out to sell the new art as a logical progression in the history of art, normalizing many of its departures. Publicist Frederick J. Gregg in the preface to the catalogue lauded arts as a "sign of life," one that entailed both danger and development, of which Americans as a forward-thinking people should not be afraid. "To be afraid of life is to be afraid of truth, and to be a champion of superstition" was a sentiment that could very well appeal to bourgeois beliefs in progress and improvement.[76] Walter Pach seconded the endorsement, contending that representational art had exhausted its potential. Its conventions had become so hackneyed that the shapes it deemed acceptable could no longer convey the meaning of the modern world, making cubism an evolutionary development in the history of expression.

At other moments, the Armory Show champions emphasized the discontinuity of the new art. Painting, Pach argued, needed to achieve the purity of expression that architecture and music had already achieved by accepting rather than denying the artifice involved. Rather than efface their own subjective acts, as realism would have them do, artists could now be free to acknowledge their own craft. That acknowledgment could range from abstraction, in which the subject was form itself, to explorations of the vicissitudes of color in the recognition that hue was an essential tool of painting. Ultimately, the fashioning might yield to complete autonomy. Arthur Dove dreamt of creating a real thing in itself, that is, a thing that "does not remind anyone of any other thing and that does not have to be explained—like the letter A, for instance."[77] By ridding painting of reference to place and producing a work that was about itself, Dove's aesthetic was also jettisoning the old morality. Painting would no longer involve a sense of how to judge and act in the actually existing world. Rather, the

Figure 2.4. Poster for the 1913 Armory Show. **The show caused a sensation in the art world, acquainting Americans with such European developments as fauvism and cubism. Much of its significance lay in many artists' refusal to link beauty with morality. (Source: Smithsonian American Art Museum, Gift of Olga Hirshhorn)**

pleasure of such art would be in the act of observing creation, a pleasure that would be its own justification.

The technical issue over which the problem of morality was debated was one-point perspective, the convention that enabled two dimensions to appear to be three. Perspective gave proportion and established relative size. It depended upon a single stable point of view that in effect froze time. Critics of the technique claimed that this mainstay of painting was seeing by a one-eyed motionless person who was clearly detached from what she sees.

Perspective rarely accorded with the new visual science on how people actually saw. Movement of eyes and head happens almost involuntarily. The brain can isolate a view, but the solidity, fixity, and singularity of view is something of an abstraction. Perspective failed as well to account for the modern notion that viewer and view are part of the same field, that reality is interaction. Critics of post-impressionism at the Armory Show fastened on the absence of perspective as the basis of their claim that the technique, particularly of cubism, was poor. The absence of the convention was why Marcel Duchamp's *Nude Descending a Staircase* became the focus of such controversy. His overlapping planes obliterated one-point perspective, combining numerous ones that would have taken place over time. Nor did he provide cues to locate the body in space. Multiplicity is the governing element of reality. "Where's the woman?" asked ex-president Theodore Roosevelt, when escorted through the show by Davies on the day his rival Woodrow Wilson was inaugurated.

Duchamp explained his painting in terms of the aesthetics of purity, arguing that multiple views were truer to the reality of perception. "The reduction of a head in movement to a bare line seemed to me defensible. A form passing through space would traverse a line; and as the form moved the line it traversed would be replaced by another line—and another and another. Therefore I felt justified in reducing a figure in movement to a line rather than to a skeleton. Reduce, reduce, reduce was my thought."[78] But since Duchamp's was not the only nonrepresentational work at the show, the amused dismissal that the picture provoked owed much to the transgressive implications of the title. For nineteenth-century sensibilities, the nude was the female body etherealized. Nudes were, in theory at least, elevated and moral despite their nakedness. Usually gazed upon by rich men who could afford to buy the pictures, the spiritual coding of the nude allowed the sensual to be smuggled into the visual experience. In removing the sensual, Duchamp called attention to operation. His blurs seemed to mock. Nothing divine, uplifting, or moral could be located in them. The implied movement violated the decorum to which the convention aspired as well, as did the strange colors and ugly forms.

Reduction and flattening had the effect of eliminating hierarchy of elements. Without such a hierarchy, moral judgment was impossible. The technique was not solely a property of the visual arts. Gertrude Stein, who was one of the first Americans to encounter and embrace cubism, aimed for an artistic pleasure in which arranging shapes or, in her case, words was the prime undertaking. In treating words not as referents but things in and of themselves, Stein intended to jettison the cause and effect and emotion that was part and parcel of the moral view of art. Rejecting the novel of psycho-logical analysis, she vowed to kill the nineteenth century, "which was so sure of evolution and prayers, and esperanto and their ideas." This flattening pro-duced works of art that were plotless. They had, it seemed, no purchase on the world itself. They certainly did not aim to make ethics appealing. Hav-ing opted for analysis and reduction, this form of beauty rejected higher con-textual meaning. The amoral artist treated subjects coolly and dispassion-ately. Such a stance allowed Francis Picabia and Duchamp to praise America as the land of the future because it was the land of the machine. Picabia's fan-tasies of sex as literally a mechanical act (he painted pistons and other ma-chines engaged in thrusting, repetitive acts) were intended matter-of-factly, not as laments about the dehumanization of modern life.[79]

Such statements were disturbing not only to the defenders of unity but also to some who accepted multiplicity in the arts. Walter Lippmann, who had compared life's uncertainty to a cubist painting, had reservations about the new arts. Lippmann contended that modernists' inability to communi-cate rationally was a failure disguised as a virtue. The complete abandonment of moral considerations, Lippmann charged, opened the way for humans to be treated as aesthetic objects solely, judged and ranked by their beauty.[80] Lippmann's concerns were probably premature. Yet if amorality made only halting progress in American aesthetic life, it was nonetheless significant enough to contribute to the unraveling of aesthetic unity. The nineteenth-century art world was not quite the place of a unified standard of beauty that cultural custodians celebrated. However, the ability of middle-class aesthetic practice to approximate the precepts of spirituality, universality, and moral-ity that the cultural elite held sacred justified thinking that an aesthetic uni-verse did in fact exist. Early-twentieth-century developments shattered that fiction. The prevalence of the new mass culture, the prominence of particu-larist cultures, the spread of subjectivity and perspective in various arts, and the appearance of amoral pleasure for its own sake all challenged the domi-nant Arnoldian culture. The result was many competing beauties and an in-creasing sense that the confidences of the past would be difficult to restore. Those who tried to understand the self would face a similar situation.

Notes

1. Perhaps the most famous European discussion of American taste in the late nineteenth century was Matthew Arnold (*Civilization in the United States: First and Last Impressions of America* [Boston, MA: Cupples and Hurd, 1888]), who saw little of note, much to the chagrin of his American disciples. Neither did long-time editor

of the *Nation*, E. L. Godkin. See his *Reflections and Comments, 1865–1895* (New York: Charles Scribner's Sons, 1895). Arnold Bennett, "The Future of the American Novel," *North American Review* (January 1912), 231–52, offers a rebuttal. H. Wayne Morgan, *New Muses: Art in American Culture, 1865–1920* (Norman: University of Oklahoma Press, 1978), 121–23, discusses the American reception of impressionism.

2. Mary Warner Blanchard, *Oscar Wilde's America: Counterculture in the Gilded Age* (New Haven, CT: Yale University Press, 1998); and M. H. Dunlop, *Gilded City: Scandal and Sensation in Turn-of-the-Century New York* (New York: William Morrow, 2000). Dunlop documents how the claim of "art" enabled rich men to justify their intense gaze at the naked female form and to romp with scantily clad women in private, activities that were otherwise condemned.

3. Nineteenth-century aesthetic thought is the province of Edward Alexander, *Matthew Arnold, John Ruskin and the Modern Temper* (Columbus: Ohio State University Press, 1973); Dorothy Broaddus, *Genteel Rhetoric: Writing High Culture in Nineteenth-Century Boston* (Columbia: University of South Carolina Press, 1999); Robert Dawidoff, *The Genteel Tradition and the Sacred Rage: High Culture vs. Democracy in Adams, James, and Santayana* (Chapel Hill: University of North Carolina Press, 1992); Stephen Eisenman, *Nineteenth Century Art: A Critical History* (New York and London: Thames and Hudson, 1994); Lucian Krukowski, *Aesthetic Legacies* (Philadelphia: Temple University Press, 1992); George Lansing Raymond, *Art in Theory* (New York: G. P. Putnam's Sons, 1894); George Santayana, *The Sense of Beauty: Being the Outline of Aesthetic Theory* (New York: Charles Scribner's Sons, 1896); and George Santayana, "The Genteel Tradition in American Philosophy," in *The Genteel Tradition*, ed. Douglas Wilson (Cambridge, MA: Harvard University Press, 1967), 37–64.

4. Hamilton Wright Mabie, *Essays on Nature and Culture* (New York: Dodd Mead, 1896), 76–77.

5. Lawrence Levine, *Highbrow/Lowbrow: The Emergence of Cultural Hierarchy in America* (Cambridge, MA: Harvard University Press, 1988) details the sacralization process of expressive culture in the United States. M. H. Abrams, "Art-as-Such: The Sociology of Modern Aesthetics," 135–58, and "From Addison to Kant: Modern Aesthetics and the Exemplary Art," 159–87, in *Doing Things with Texts: Essays in Criticism and Critical Theory* (New York: W. W. Norton, 1989), explore the eighteenth-century English and German precedents.

6. *New York Times*, February 21 , 1875, quoted in H. Wayne Morgan, *New Muses: Art in American Culture, 1865–1920* (Norman: University of Oklahoma Press, 1978), 32.

7. The best known nineteenth-century articulations of the class and culture problem were E. L. Godkin, "Chromo-Civilization," *Nation* (September 24, 1874), 201–2; and Charles Dudley Warner, "What Is Your Culture to Me?" *Scribner's Monthly* (August 1872), 470–78. In addition to Levine, see Mary Ann Stankiewicz, "Chromo-Civilization and the Genteel Tradition (An Essay on the Social Value of Art Education)," *Studies in Art Education* (Winter 1999), 101–13; and Alex Zwerdling,

Improvised Europeans: American Literary Expatriates and the Siege of London (New York: Basic Books, 1998).

8. See Arnold Rampersand, *The Art and Imagination of W. E. B. Du Bois* (New York: Schocken, 1990), 27–47, for Du Bois's cultural training. Alvin Poussaint makes the elitist argument against Du Bois in "The Souls of Black Folk: A Critique," in W. E. B. Du Bois, *The Souls of Black Folk* (New York: Signet, [1903] 1969), xxviii–xlii.

9. Du Bois, *Souls of Black Folk*, 265. Subsequent references in the text.

10. Jane Addams, *The Spirit of Youth and the City Streets* (Urbana: University of Illinois Press, [1910] 1972). Subsequent references in the text.

11. Casey Blake, *Beloved Community: The Cultural Criticism of Randolph Bourne, Van Wyck Brooks, Waldo Frank & Lewis Mumford* (Chapel Hill: University of North Carolina Press, 1990), especially 99–121. See also James Hoopes, *Van Wyck Brooks: In Search of American Culture* (Amherst: University of Massachusetts Press, 1977); and Claire Sprague, *Van Wyck Brooks: The Early Years* (New York: Harper and Row, 1968)

12. Van Wyck Brooks, *America's Coming-of-Age* (New York: Doubleday, [1916] 1958), 16, 62.

13. George Santayana, *Interpretations of Poetry and Religion* (New York: Charles Scribner's Sons, 1900), 161.

14. George Santayana, "What Is a Philistine?" in James Ballowe, ed., *George Santayana's America: Essays on Literature and Culture* (Urbana: University of Illinois Press, 1967), 140.

15. I have drawn on J. David Hoeveler, *The New Humanism: A Critique of Modern America, 1900–1940* (Charlottesville: University of Virginia Press, 1977), for my portrait of the humanists.

16. Brooks, *America's Coming-of-Age*; Santayana, "Genteel Tradition," 44.

17. Gertrude Atherton, "Why Is American Literature Bourgeois?" *North American Review* 178 (1904): 771.

18. Douglas Clayton, *Floyd Dell: The Life and Times of an American Rebel* (Chicago, IL: Ivan R. Dee, 1994), 72. Dell's full evaluation may be found in "Mr. Dreiser and the Dodo," *Masses* 5 (February 1914), 162–64.

19. H. L. Mencken, "The Creed of a Novelist" (October 1916), in William H. Nolte, ed., *H. L. Mencken's Smart Set Criticism* (Washington, DC: Regnery Gateway, 1987), 248–56.

20. Larry Starr and Christopher Alan Waterman, *American Popular Music from Minstrelsy to MTV* (Oxford and New York: Oxford University Press, 2003), 1–38, 62–85.

21. I have relied on William J. Schafer and Johannes Riedel, *The Art of Ragtime: Form and Meaning of an Original Black American Art* (Baton Rouge: Louisiana State University Press, 1973); Hiram K. Moderwell, "Ragtime," *New Republic* 4 (October 16, 1915): 285–86, and Susan Curtis, *Dancing to a Black Man's Tune: A Life of Scott Joplin* (Columbia: University of Missouri Press, 1994).

22. Moderwell, "Ragtime," 285–86.

23. Charles Ives, *Memos*, John Kirkpatrick, ed. (New York: W. W. Norton, 1972), 95.

24. Leon Botstein, "Innovation and Nostalgia: Ives, Mahler, and the Origins of Twentieth-Century Modernism," in J. Peter Burkholder, ed., *Charles Ives and His World* (Princeton, NJ: Princeton University Press, 1996), 60.

25. Michael Broyles, "Charles Ives and the American Democratic Tradition," in Burkholder, 118–60, quotation from 127. Broyles suggestively argues that Ives's career in insurance, which he conceived of as democratic mutuality, set the tone for and limits on his politics which stressed both individuality and commonality. Broyles further notes that Ives was particularly affected by the infamous insurance scandals of the first decade of the twentieth century in which the lords of insurance joined other robber barons in the pantheon of progressive villains.

26. Gerald Mast, ed., *Movies in Our Midst: Documents in the Cultural History of Film in America* (Chicago, IL: University of Chicago Press, 1982); Lary May, *Screening out the Past: The Birth of Mass Culture and the Motion Picture Industry* (New York: Oxford University Press, 1980), 6–52; and Robert Sklar, *Movie-Made America: A Cultural History of American Movies* (New York: Vintage, 1975) provide a sample of complaints about the new medium. Edward Wagenknecht's *American Profile, 1900–1909* (Amherst: University of Massachusetts Press, 1982), a delightful memoir, indicates that even in the first decade of the twentieth century, solid middle-class youngsters enjoyed movies.

27. Randolph Bourne, "The Heart of the People," *New Republic* 3 (July 3, 1915), 233.

28. Charles Musser, *The Emergence of Cinema: The American Screen to 1907*, vol. 1 of *History of the American Cinema* (New York: Charles Scribner's Sons, 1990), 418–32.

29. *Moving Picture World* (September 23, 1910), 658, cited in Eileen Bowser, *The Transformation of Cinema, 1907–1915*, vol. 2 of *History of the American Cinema* (New York: Charles Scribner's Sons, 1990), 4.

30. Musser, *Emergence of Cinema*, 1:494–95.

31. Sklar, *Movie-Made America*, 104–9.

32. *Movie World*, quoted in Charles J. Maland, *Chaplin and American Culture: The Evolution of a Star Image* (Princeton, NJ: Princeton University Press, 1989), 15–16; *Harper's Weekly* (March 25, 1916), 300.

33. *Theatre Magazine* 30 (October 1919), 249.

34. Maland, *Chaplin and American Culture*.

35. David Robinson, *Chaplin, His Life and Art* (New York: McGraw-Hill, 1985), 116–21; Charles Spencer Chaplin, "What People Laugh At," *American Magazine* 86 (November 1918), 34, 134–37.

36. See, for example, May, *Screening out the Past*, 60–95. Tom Gunning marks the work of 1909 as especially crucial. Gunning holds that Griffith developed a way for the camera to serve as a narrator who is neither a character in the story nor a real person outside it but who provides comments nonetheless (Tom Gunning, *D. W.*

Griffith and the Origins of American Narrative Film [Urbana: University of Illinois Press, 1991]).

37. Scott Simmon, *The Films of D. W. Griffith* (Cambridge: Cambridge University Press, 1993), 155.

38. Karl Brown, *Adventures with D. W. Griffith* (New York: Farrar, Straus and Giroux, 1973), 94–95.

39. Frank Mather, *Nation* 3 (February 1902), 132.

40. Hutchins Hapgood, *The Spirit of the Ghetto* (New York: Funk and Wagnalls, 1902), 149.

41. Ibid., 37, 98, 110.

42. Among the significant discussions of the blues are Lawrence Cohn and Mary Katherine Aldin, *Nothing but the Blues: The Music and the Musicians* (New York: Abbeville Press, 1993); Francis Davis, *The History of the Blues: The Roots, the Music, the People* (New York: Da Capo Press, 2003); Alan Lomax, *The Land Where the Blues Began* (New York: Pantheon Books, 1993); Albert Murray, *Stomping the Blues* (New York: Da Capo Press, [1976] 2000); Giles Oakley, *The Devil's Music: A History of the Blues* (New York: Da Capo Press, 1997); and Robert Palmer, *Deep Blues: A Musical and Cultural History of the Mississippi Delta* (New York: Penguin, 1982).

43. Lomax, *Land Where the Blues Began*, 233; Murray, *Stomping the Blues*, 64.

44. Starr and Waterman, *American Popular Music*, 89–100. Bessie Smith and Louis Armstrong's *St. Louis Blues* (Columbia, 14064-D, 1925) is a particularly vivid rendition of Handy's art and a remarkable aesthetic and commercial success.

45. Catherine Gallagher, *Nobody's Story: The Vanishing Acts of Women Writers in the Marketplace, 1670–1820* (Berkeley: University of California Press, 1994); and Ian Watt, *The Rise of the Novel: Studies in Defoe, Richardson, and Fielding* (Berkeley: University of California Press, 1965), detail how women were crucial to the development of the English novel, even as their contributions were obscured and denigrated. Gillian Brown, *Domestic Individualism: Imagining the Self in Nineteenth-Century America* (Berkeley: University of California Press, 1990); Jane Tompkins, *Sensational Designs: The Cultural Work of American Fiction, 1790–1860* (New York: Oxford University Press, 1985); Mary Kelley, *Private Woman, Public Stage: Literary Domesticity in Nineteenth-Century America* (New York: Oxford University Press, 1984); and Ann Douglas, *The Feminization of American Culture* (New York: Alfred A. Knopf, 1977), explore the import of the sentimental novel in the middle of the nineteenth century in the United States.

46. Glasgow's poem "The Call" was published in *Collier's* (July 27, 1912), 21.

47. William B. Scott and Peter M. Rutcoff, *New York Modern: The Arts and the City* (Baltimore: Johns Hopkins University Press, 1999), 27.

48. Duncan, quoted in ibid., 31.

49. Sloan, quoted in ibid., 32. For a similar reaction from Floyd Dell, see Clayton, *Floyd Dell*, 76.

50. Duncan, quoted in Scott and Rutcoff, *New York Modern*, 42–43.

51. Michael Newlin, ed., *American Plays of the New Woman* (Chicago, IL: Ivan R. Dee, 2000), 12.

52. This paragraph draws on, from among other sources, Marshall Berman, *All That Is Solid Melts into Air* (New York: Simon and Schuster, 1982); Astradur Eysteinsson, *The Concept of Modernism* (Ithaca, NY: Cornell University Press, 1990); Andreas Huyssen, *After the Great Divide: Modernism, Mass Culture, Postmodernism* (Bloomington: Indiana University Press, 1986); Fred Matthews, "The New Psychology and American Drama," in Adele Heller and Lois Rudnick, eds., *1915: The Cultural Moment* (New Brunswick, NJ: Rutgers University Press, 1991), 146–56; Judith Ryan, *The Vanishing Subject: Early Psychology and Literary Modernism* (Chicago, IL: University of Chicago Press, 1991); Daniel Joseph Singal, "Toward a Definition of American Modernism," *American Quarterly* 39 (Spring 1987), 7–26; and Raymond Williams, *The Politics of Modernism* (London: Verso, 1989).

53. James's career is handled in Leon Edel's majestic five-volume biography (Lippincott, 195–72). Of interest are *The Treacherous Years, 1895–1901* and *The Master, 1901–1916*.

54. Matthew Baigell, *A Concise History of American Painting and Sculpture* (Boulder, CO: Westview Press, 1996), 210–11.

55. Dove, quoted in Robert Hughes, *American Visions: The Epic History of Art in America* (New York: Alfred A. Knopf, 1997), 344.

56. Stieglitz, quoted in William Innes Homer, *Alfred Stieglitz and the American Avant-Garde* (Boston, MA: New York Graphic Society, 1977), 70.

57. William Innes Homer, *Alfred Stieglitz and the Photo-Secession* (Boston, MA: Little, Brown, 1982), 36–37.

58. Weber, quoted in Baigell, *Concise History*, 219–22.

59. Judy Crichton, *America 1900: The Turning Point* (New York: Henry Holt, 1998), 78–85.

60. William Vaughn Moody, *The Great Divide*, in Newlin, ed., *American Plays of the New Woman*, 6.

61. Addams, *The Spirit of Youth*, 83.

62. See, among other discussions of decadence, Larzer Ziff, *The American 1890s: Life and Times of a Lost Generation* (New York: Viking Press, 1966); Melinda Knight, "Cultural Radicalism in the American Fin de Siècle: The Emergence of an Oppositional Literary Culture," PhD diss. (New York: New York University, 1992); and Cassandra Laity, *H.D. and the Victorian Fin de Siècle: Gender, Modernism, Decadence* (Cambridge and New York: Cambridge University Press, 1996). Hoeveler, *The New Humanism*, 60–63, contains a useful summary of Spingarn's debates with New Humanist Irving Babbitt. Milton Brown, *The Story of the Armory Show* (New York: Abbeville Press, 1988), 182–83.

63. Robert C. Solomon and Kathleen Higgins, *What Nietzsche Really Said* (New York: Schocken, 2000); Andrew Bowie, *Aesthetics and Subjectivity: From Kant to Nietzsche* (Manchester: Manchester University Press, 1990); Bernard Yack, *The*

Longing for Total Revolution: Philosophic Sources of Social Discontent from Rousseau to Marx and Nietzsche (Berkeley and Los Angeles: University of California Press, 1992). My understanding of Nietzsche's reception in the United States and by Mencken in particular is drawn from Melvin Drimmer, "Nietzsche in American Thought" (PhD diss., University of Rochester, 1965); Jennifer Ratner-Rosenhagen, "Neither Rock nor Refuge: American Encounters with Nietzsche and the Search for Foundations" (PhD diss., Brandeis University, 2003); and Manfred Putz, ed., *Nietzsche in American Literature and Thought* (Columbia, SC: Camden House, 1995).

64. H. L. Mencken, "Criticism of Criticism of Criticism," in *Prejudices: A Selection Made by James T. Farrell* (New York: Vintage, 1961), 10.

65. Hoeveler, *The New Humanism*, 10–20, covers the Mencken-Sherman dispute from the point of view of the New Humanists. Floyd Dell, "Mr. Dreiser and the Dodo," *Masses* 5 (February 1914), 162–64.

66. Theodore Dreiser, *Jennie Gerhardt* (New York: Penguin, [1911] 1994), 392.

67. Dreiser, quoted in David Shi, *Facing Facts: Realism in American Thought and Culture, 1850–1920* (New York: Oxford University Press, 1995), 246–50.

68. *New York Times* (March 17, 1913), cited in Brown, *Story of the Armory Show*, 167.

69. Kenyon Cox, "The Illusion of Progress," *Century Magazine* (March 1913), 39–43; Kenyon Cox, "The 'Modern' Spirit in Art: Some Reflections Inspired by the Recent International Exhibition," *Harper's Weekly* (March 15, 1913), 10; "Cubists and Futurists Are Making Insanity Pay," *New York Times* (March 16, 1913), 1.

70. My account of the Armory Show is derived from Brown, *The Story of the Armory Show*, Martin Green, *New York 1913: The Armory Show and the Paterson Strike Pageant* (New York: Charles Scribner's Sons, 1988), and Henry May, *The End of American Innocence* (New York: Oxford University Press, [1959] 1970). Brown's judgment of the inevitability of modern art can be found on page 44.

71. "Cubists and Futurists," 1.

72. In addition to Morgan, see also JoAnne Mancini, "'One Term Is as Fatuous as Another': Responses to the Armory Show Reconsidered," *American Quarterly* 51 (December 1999): 833–70.

73. Baigell, *Concise History*, 240.

74. Marin, quoted in Green, *New York, 4 1913*, 262.

75. Compare the judgment of Rebecca Zurier, *Art for the Masses: A Radical Magazine and Its Graphics, 1911–1917* (Philadelphia: Temple University Press, 1988), 38–41, with Scott and Rutcoff, *New York Modern*, 247.

76. Gregg, quoted in William R. Everdell, *The First Moderns: Profiles in the Origins of Twentieth-Century Thought* (Chicago, IL: University of Chicago Press, 1997), 327.

77. Dove, quoted in Hughes, *American Visions*, 343.

78. Duchamp, quoted in Paul Vitz and Arnold Glimcher, *Modern Art and Modern Science: The Parallel Analysis of Vision* (New York: Praeger, 1984), 130.

79. See, among others, Katia Samaltanos-Stenström, *Apollinaire, Catalyst for Primitivism, Picabia, Duchamp* (Ann Arbor: University of Michigan Press, 1984).

80. Edward Abrahams, *The Lyrical Left: Randolph Bourne, Alfred Stieglitz, and the Origins of Cultural Radicalism in America* (Charlottesville: University Press of Virginia, 1986), 167.

CHAPTER THREE

~

Selves

The early years of the twentieth century were difficult ones for that perennial of American culture, individualism. Although many still professed faith in the centrality of individual rights and responsibilities, more than a few commentators noted the increasing inability of a single person to work his way in the world. The growing importance of cities, national markets, and corporations in American life made it harder for individuals to proclaim their independence on traditional grounds. The constant interaction with strangers, the multiplicity of situations in which one found oneself, and the presence of faraway entities that had direct influence on one's fate made it all the more difficult for an individual to develop and maintain freedom from the control or influence of others. Such developments spurred challenges to the conception of the sovereign individual, which had been the primary formulation of the self during the nineteenth century. As questions about the origins of the self, its path to self-knowledge, its purposes and capacities, and its connections to others were reopened and reexamined, new versions treated the self as a project rather than an innate entity. Guiding that project were a cacophony of competing visions. By 1920, such novel discourses as social psychology, Freudianism and depth psychology, and feminism pointed to a brave new world in which the self was collectively forged, divided, and embodied.

Collectively made, divided, embodied selves contrasted with the prevailing view in nineteenth-century educated circles, which combined Descartes's notion that the self was primarily a thinking entity rather than a bodily one with the Scottish Common-Sense understanding of the self as a soul to whom right reason was addressed. This self was perforce interiorized, unique, and self-sufficient. The singular possession of each individual, this interior, disembodied self had a consistency and solidity that made it ultimately immune from the clutches of contingency. Its qualities did not vary with the situation in which it found itself or the social role that its owner played. A set of distinctive faculties and qualities over which the self itself tended, the self became responsible for its actions when an individual reached maturity. It was this self, the essential interior one that combined thinking and morality abstracted from multiplicity, which most thinkers took to be the "real person."[1]

The autonomous self was a cornerstone of much of nineteenth-century intellectual life. It was at the heart of understanding of society. Posited as existing prior to society, those independent selves were the prime movers in the creation of social institutions, bringing them together by voluntary agreement. By the same token, the autonomous individual was central to much moral theory. Moral action had meaning only if humans were free to act otherwise. Scottish Common-Sense located the source of morality in the ability of the unified soul to receive and embody moral sense. Consequently, defending and nurturing the autonomous self was a constant preoccupation of nineteenth-century middle-class cultural life. Social institutions such as family, school, and the law centered on creating and reinforcing the self-sufficiency and individual responsibility that befit independent selves. Middle-class Protestants trained their children for independence, steeling them with inner compasses that were to guide them through a sometimes hostile society. Though human-made, society often figured as an imposing alien edifice that intruded upon its originators. Protecting the ability of those originators to exercise their autonomy was, many argued throughout the nineteenth century, precisely the function of government. Law liberated the creative, autonomous agents in contradistinction to the traditional rights and claims of communities. Similarly, literary works stressed the significance of authenticity, of freeing oneself from restraining convention, tradition, or community norms.[2] At times, Americans so highly regarded the powers of a truly autonomous self that they attributed to it the power to overcome nature. Disease, as countless mind-cure advocates contended, was a matter of individual responsibility—a misplaced use of the mind.[3]

There was an underlying material basis to this autonomous self. Republican thought put great emphasis on property ownership as the guarantee of mastery, control, independence, and eventually the ability to be and govern oneself. Given the gender bias in the determination of productivity, it is not surprising that this autonomous property-owning independent self was marked male. Property distribution was probably never as widespread as the republican theorists of the self believed, yet the live possibility of property ownership gave American individualism much of its solidity and depth. The laments about proletarianization during the nineteenth century were, among other things, expressions of concern that without the ability to accumulate even a modest amount of productive property, the self would become nullified and vanish.[4]

Proletarianization was not the only force to buffet the sovereign individual during the course of the nineteenth century. Some of the precariousness of the interior self in an urbanizing, capitalist society was epistemological in nature. Nineteenth-century Americans were impressed with the difficulties that such selves had in engaging in commerce with other such constituted selves. Interior selves by definition could make themselves known to others only by acts, which could be fraudulent or inauthentic. Squaring interior selves with presented ones was a matter of some concern throughout the nineteenth century, as the number of sermons, advice manuals, and novels that dealt with the topic indicate. Nor was self-knowledge as easily come by as the assertions suggested. Contributing to the fragility of the prevailing conception were the intensifying subdivision of labor and the social interconnectedness, which made assertions of independence increasingly problematic, the rise of bureaucracies (the railroads, for instance, employed as many people in such white-collar jobs as debt service, scheduling, and ticket sales as in the blue-collar ones of engineer and fireman), the quickening of consumer society, the seeming ubiquity of the fashion system, and the number of different and potentially novel situations in which individuals found themselves in metropolitan life. Taken as a whole, the combined weight of these conditions reduced the viability of classic independence. Theorists began to talk tentatively about mass society in which the self was simply batted around by forces greater than a single person could withstand. A mass politics in which the "crowd" took on a life of its own undercut the republican politics in which autonomous, rational, and self-aware individuals made informed deliberations.[5]

Neither urbanization nor the concentration of property holding in and of themselves swept away the concept of the sovereign individual. Analysts searched for materials to refurbish the notion in new circumstances. Various notions of stakeholding or intangible property (such as John Commons's notions of ownership of a job, which is covered in chapter 4) might well have provided the basis, as Commons clearly hoped, for a reconstitution of the republican self. For a growing number of Americans, however, revision rather than reconstruction was the preferred path. Mere assertion of eternal verities seemed unable to account for how people experienced their world. A number of turn-of-the-century projects held that a unified, self-determining, transparent and disembodied self was inconsistent with the practices of modern life. Social psychology, depth psychology, and the new discourses of the gendered self undercut the very foundations of the autonomous self. These projects overlapped at various points but did not come to a synthesis. For some, the decline of the ethereal, self-creating, self-knowing self was yet another chapter in the overall tragedy of multiplicity. For others, it augured new kinds of responsibility, a more meaningful ethics, and real creativity.

The Social Self

Critical to the notion of the autonomous self was that elusive yet seemingly universal attribute of consciousness. Many philosophers, psychologists, and theologians attributed great significance to the ability of humans to recognize themselves as subjects, entities distinct from others. That humans could monitor their own state of mind and develop capacities for control and representation of the self constituted a key instance of self-government. In drawing ego boundaries and in choosing to act as one does, the argument went, an individual realized the indwelling potential of his or her self. Fully equipped with mental powers, the self was therefore independent, deriving principles of action from within itself. So important was consciousness that, as John O'Donnell notes, much mid-nineteenth-century academic psychology was devoted to isolating and defining the mental processes that constituted it, in an effort to banish notions of mechanical determination.[6]

The effort was only moderately successful. Scientific trappings notwithstanding, the result was often little more than minute inspection of the connection between stimulus and sensation that failed to acknowledge the full range of human mental processes. Meanwhile, neurological investigation continued apace. Although advocates of the so-called somatic style were unable to prove conclusively that physical changes in the brain accounted for changes in mental processes, they nonetheless produced results that made it increasingly difficult to sustain the notion that the mind was clearly dominant. Such findings led George Herbert Ladd, a Congregational minister-turned-psychology professor, and chair of the Yale Department, to worry that the mind had become "a mere stream of mechanically associated 'epiphenomena' thrown off from the molecular machinery of the cerebral hemispheres."[7]

The notion of the sovereign consciousness received a jolt from Darwinian evolution as well. By placing humans in a continuum with the rest of nature,

Darwin undercut the centrality that mind played in creating an absolute difference among species. Just as importantly, Darwin's orientation toward natural history and genetic explanations required an evolutionary account of consciousness itself. Investigators consequently switched their emphasis from what consciousness was to the "how" and "why" of it. As William James noted, consciousness would not have survived had it served no function for the species' adaptation to its environment. Indeed, mind was the most crucial characteristic in human engagement with circumstance. James's and similar views altered a crucial understanding of consciousness. Under the new scheme, it was more akin to a tool than an interior condition. Because it was first and foremost engaged in interaction, consciousness was as much part of the world as it was of the body that possessed it. In stressing the role of consciousness as mediating between the environment and the organism, this evolutionary psychology put a premium on understanding the interaction. Where Cartesian mind–body separation had established the self as an internal phenomenon, the new psychology gravitated toward what had previously been ruled out of court, social life. In contrast to a significant portion of nineteenth-century discourse on mind and self that concentrated explicitly on adult men (who, after all, were independent selves), the genetic approach focused on childhood and the origins of the self.[8]

Although autonomous and self-legislating, the classic self was no isolated Robinson Crusoe luxuriating in the sublime beauty of its faculties in supreme indifference to others. As Adam Smith had pointed out during the eighteenth century, men had all kinds of propensities to social interaction, the most famous of which was the imperative to truck, barter, and exchange. In the absence of others, such propensities would never be realized. In Smith's view, much of what the self did turned on human association. Smith argued in *Theory of Moral Sentiments* (1750) that the self possessed innate sociality. Smith held that this inbred sympathy allowed humans to feel compassion for others. We are capable of imaginatively identifying with others because we reconstruct others' experience as if it were our own. We need not have been tortured to feel for the captive.[9] This fellow feeling was both the source and guarantee of morality. Pleased by the fellow feeling we received from others, we act to induce it. In this moral version of the invisible hand, we achieve social good by acting in our self-interest, and we do so more reliably than when commanded by legislation or directed by moral exhortations. For all his concern with sociality, Smith still posited a self-determining, independent individual who was in society but not of it.

In time, Smith's sociability would develop into the contention that the self was formed in social interaction. As the breadth of social interactions

accelerated and people were continually influenced by events that they neither effected nor observed, and by people whom they did not know, the notion of the self-determining self, the author of its own fate, seemed less viable. In his classic *Principles of Psychology* (1890), William James suggestively
contended that any account of the self must move beyond its ability to recognize others. Noting the number of ways in which humans congregated,
James posited that the species was gregarious by nature. Taking the self to be
the sum total of what an individual could call his own, James included the
recognition one got from one's "mates." Such recognition constituted the social self and made possible self-respect. The self under such conditions was
not completely autonomous. In his brief discussion, James added hints of
multiplicity. The social self clearly varied with context. Observing that humans show different sides of themselves depending upon audiences, James
concluded that "properly speaking, a man has as many social selves as there
are individuals who recognize him and carry an image of him in their mind."
Such a condition presented both danger and promise, James averred. Concerned with authenticity, James glimpsed the unhappy possibility of a "discordant splitting, as where one is afraid to let one set of his acquaintances
know him as he is elsewhere."[10] Yet the social self could also empower an individual in social situations, acquainting him with new ideals and behaviors.

Josiah Royce, James's colleague in Harvard philosophy, was more thoroughly committed to the notion of a social self. Although no advocate of
multiplicity (his absolutism, as we saw in chapter 1, was predicated on the
notion of the ultimate unity of things), Royce nonetheless gave an extended
justification for a self that was changeable and determined. He did so in large
measure because he was dissatisfied on ethical and logical grounds with the
notion of an autonomous self. By Royce's lights, a self that was self-
determining made altruism, concern for and recognition of others, and in-
terpersonal communication seem odd and foreign inclinations, rather than
innate or inherent ones. In contrast, Royce insisted that we are inescapably
social creatures and that even the most private, personal, and self-regarding
act reveals traces of our social nature. Even the selfish man, after all, needed
to will the existence of others as the means to his desire. In light of the social nature of the self, the moral problem was not "Shall I aim to preserve social relations?" but rather "Which social relations should I preserve?"[11]

Royce staked his contentions about the social nature of the self on the argument that a self is impossible to know until and unless one knows a non-
self. We are aware of ourselves as selves, Royce maintained, only in social set-
tings. In the absence of others, we cannot make the implicit and explicit
comparisons we need in order to know who we are. When involved in ac-

tivities that do not involve contrasts with others, we tend to forget ourselves completely, Royce insisted. Directly challenging the traditional view of the autonomous self, Royce argued that consciousness of others is both logically and psychologically prior to our consciousness of our selves.[12]

Royce proposed suggestion and imitation as the mechanism through which the social self achieves consciousness. Imitation and suggestion begin, of course, when toddlers imitate significant others. The repetition of imitated acts not only gives children a repertoire of social skills, but also endows them with consciousness. It does so, according to Royce, because performance enables them to learn the inner meaning of the act, something mere observation does not. Royce insisted that imitation prompted consciousness when it was imperfect. The inability of the child to duplicate exactly the model's acts stimulates comparison between one's own acts and those of the model. The process enabled children to become aware of themselves as selves, realizing that they have a significant existence. In time, they come to realize that the acts and thoughts of the other will remain beyond their conscious control but that their own imitations are matters that the self can control.

The social self that imitation-suggestion and subsequent mechanisms of interaction underwrote raised a number of intriguing possibilities. Proponents championed it because it offered the allure of a self rooted in association, open to new experiences, interdependent with others. Such a self, if recognized and fostered, would be capable of adapting to a changing environment rather than hewing to outmoded a priori commitments. Such a self too would have multiple identities, opening the way for an enhanced set of experiences and an acceptance of a pluralistic society. Opponents, on the other hand, worried that a self so theoretically open to the world writ large ran the danger of becoming so plastic, so unfixed as to be in constant danger of dissolution. If there were no fixed self, they wondered, what then would claim rights or organize projects? Royce, for one, accepted the inevitable dissolution of ego boundaries. Noting that "what is denoted as non-ego this moment, and the contrasting ego we have in mind, is not at all the contrast we may be making an hour from now," Royce understood that a world filled with suggestion would render the self incomplete and that self would never be constant nor oblivious to influence from others. Free will, he conceded, may well be an illusion, a notion that fit nicely with his conviction that the world was held together by the Absolute.[13]

As Ruth Leys has demonstrated, imitation-suggestion had a powerful hold on American thought in the late nineteenth and early twentieth centuries. Although related ideas had long been floating around, imitation-suggestion crystallized with Gabriel Tarde's *Laws of Imitation*, published in 1890 and translated into English in 1903 by the anthropologist Elsie Clews Parsons. Imitation-suggestion challenged the division of body and mind by positing that people accounted for others through both perception and act. Emphasizing social interaction rather than self-government, the explanation openly opposed notions of the sovereign individual fully responsible for its own being.[14] As such, imitation-suggestion had political and cultural implications. Since it did not grant the chronological and epistemological priority of an autonomous, self-legislating self, imitation-suggestion implied that contracts were not a natural or given basis of social life. Rather, they were a kind of social construction, capable of being judged on how well they promoted social good rather than as an abstract right to be defended because they derived from natural individuals.[15] For another, as the work of social psychologists

Figure 3.1. Crowds. **Scenes such as this one of curb brokers outside the Wall Street Stock Exchange were common enough in the early twentieth century to prompt new notions of the self as social in nature. French theorists Gustave Le Bon and Gabriel Tarde, and American popularizers such as Gerald Stanley Lee, envisioned crowd psychology as proof that humans characteristically engaged in mindless copying. Pragmatist-influenced writers such as Charles Horton Cooley and George Herbert Mead saw greater possibilities in the social self. (Source: George Grantham Bain Collection, Library of Congress, LC-USZ62-93743)**

W. I. Thomas, Franklin Giddings, William McDougall, and Robert Park demonstrated, imitation-suggestion could account for social solidarities and broad similarities in behavior among homogeneous populations, suggesting that market relations and market values were not supreme. In an era of worry over differences, it could also be used to present a notion of how consensus might be achieved in times of ethnic and class conflicts and differentiation. Many feminists discerned in imitation-suggestion a liberating effect, in that it implied sexual differences were not inherited.[16]

Reformist impulses notwithstanding, much of the popularity of imitation-suggestion had much to do with fin-de-siècle worries about "mass society" and immigration. Imitation-suggestion played into fears of mindless masses who had no capacity for reason. If people were really "veritable copying machines," as social psychologist James Baldwin put it, the possibilities of manipulation were all too obvious. The point was made clearer in another French import that enjoyed a vogue in educated circles, Gustave Le Bon's *The Crowd: A Study of the Popular Mind* (1895). Much commentary drew an analogy between imitation-suggestion and hypnosis. Both Tarde and Le Bon had actually made reference to the process in their work. Tarde had compared the social state as a form of dream of command and action. "To have only ideas that have been suggested and to believe them spontaneous: such is the illusion of the somnambulist and such also of the social man."[17] Once dismissed as parlor trick and carnival spectacle, hypnosis began to attract serious interests among alienists and psychologists for its revelation of multiple selves. Imitation-suggestion advocates took special note of the way in which the subject of hypnosis seemed to vacate self in favor of that of the hypnotist, who seemed not to be recognized as the not-self.

The ambiguous status of imitation-suggestion can be seen in the work of publicist and essayist Gerald Stanley Lee. He had built a remarkable career as the popular expert on crowds and mass behavior, arguing that imitation and suggestion were at the root of all behavior. As Gregory Bush, his biographer, points out, Lee mixed reformist and manipulative impulses. Alternatively praised as Whitmanesque for his celebration of masses of people and criticized as the Svengali of western Massachusetts (his home base), Lee both praised collective action, especially in associations such as unions (at least at some phases of his career), and condemned it when it favored William Jennings Bryan, whom he regarded as a demagogue whose currency and social policies threatened the nature of things. His *Crowds* (1913), a mixture of both sentiments, was a tremendous best-seller. Lee envisioned imitation-suggestion as a containment strategy. The people united under the inspired and ethical leadership of men such as himself would, through the dynamism of the crowd, achieve the potential of democracy. As he wrote to the social-ist Eugene Debs, he valued the expert who could represent the people. Proper information, which would be provided by the president or advertising, com-bined with the proper emotional appeals would create "a vast pageant—a colossal silent spectacle of Us, of our people, of our ideas, of our Things—the things we pour our living into, the vast landscape or valley of Desire in the United States."[18]

The fluidity of the social self when encountering the "valley of Desire in the United States" was notably portrayed in Theodore Dreiser's *Sister Carrie*. Over the years, Dreiser's book has become a focal point in analyses of con-sumer culture and the social self that emerged, because its title character seems so filled with desire for things. Dreiser specialized in portraying the al-lure of the culture of display in urban America. He dwelt on the ways things sparkle and beckon. In classic naturalist fashion, the things take on a life of their own, animated by the reflection of Carrie's own absorption of the world of signs. Carrie, whose "craving her pleasure was so strong that it was the one stay of her nature," is always in the pursuit of the "not me." Full of desire, she is never at one with herself or her surroundings. Although the novel was cen-sured for its failure to punish Carrie's transgressions (she succeeds, while her former lovers Drouet and Hurstwood falter and decay), it also disturbed the sense of the rootedness of selfhood. The elements Dreiser put together—Car-rie's lack of domesticity, her success on the stage where she mastered the abil-ity to put on other selves, and her refusal to allow her working life to define her—were typical of a world in flux, where the boundaries of the self have indeed dissolved. Such a world was precisely what those dedicated to ad-vancing personal integrity found troubling, which is why the eminent realist William Dean Howells criticized the book as unrealistic.[19]

Academic discourse on the social self was less controversial than Dreiser's work, but no less keen to demonstrate that the self was formed in the web of interactions with others rather than a consequence of autonomy. The work of James Mark Baldwin, Charles Horton Cooley, and George Herbert Mead shared a commitment to a recognition of the centrality of contingency and context in self formation while taking care not to reduce the self to flotsam and jetsam on waves of change, buffeted by uncontrollable social forces. In the process of carving out a new discipline, the social psychologists endowed the social self with agency (the capability of initiating action), yet without the power of self-legislation (the self-sufficiency that underwrote the inde-pendent self). The social psychologists, in other words, interposed mediating factors in their notion of the self so as to demonstrate that modern life had created neither massified people nor anarchy, however difficult it was sometimes to pinpoint social motors. Their version of the self reflects their desire for an ordered multiplicity, one that repaired the social bonds that they believed industrial capitalism had undermined, but also one that encouraged individuation.

Royce applauded the merger of individual selves into what he termed the Absolute, an overarching transcendent ideal entity, as a sign of morality. Those who did not subscribe to his idealism, however, had to find their own mechanism to neutralize the potential dangers of the social self. For his friend James Baldwin (1861–1934), the task of squaring multiplicity with order proved a difficult challenge. Baldwin, who established psychology labs at Princeton, the University of Toronto, and Johns Hopkins, originally was attracted to the social self as the way to challenge Spencerian notions of utility. In his 1898 path-breaking *Social and Ethical Interpretations in Mental Development*, Baldwin argued that utility could not of its own accord explain the discrepancy between right and wrong acts. A self socialized in right and wrong, on the other hand, could do precisely that. Socialization, Baldwin contended, melded the self-regarding appetite with the natural propensity to imitate. The result was a child "turning out acts, opinions, decisions, which are based with more or less correctness upon models found in his social environment." By trying on varied ways of doing things, individuals developed a normal self. Imitation allowed selves to get a feel of what others did and to learn to "value the safe and sane."[20]

At the heart of Baldwin's theory of the social self were the unintended effects of imitation-suggestion. Regarding the development of the self as a compromise between individualism and collectivism, Baldwin saw imitation not only as a matter of experimentation in ways of doing things, but also as coming to grip with one's capacities to take what is present in others and make it over in forms "peculiar to one's own temper and valuable to one's own genius" (22–23). Baldwin contended that the self arises when the actions of others are capricious. As the child imitates, he or she learns that the bodies of others are not minds and that his or her own personality is also "two-sided; that he, too, is a mind on the inside, and that which others see of him on the outside is not the mind, but merely the physical person" (23–24). This discovery of mind impresses itself on the child as the recognition that he or she too has a mind and that it is this mind that others cannot see, just as he or she could not see or comprehend theirs. Thus, the child takes the presence of others over into himself or herself. Moments of emotional vividness drive home the point that acts have "personal, and not merely physical or bodily significance." Subjectivity results when children realize that the inner life of others is understood in terms of their own (24–25).

Children invariably read subjective experiences onto others. This dual process of self-awareness, in which others are thought of in just the same terms as the private self, and the private self in the same terms as other persons, makes it "impossible to distinguish them, so far as subjective terms is concerned. The thought of self is of a larger self which includes personalities in general; and the different persons, in all that which is not singular or characteristic of each, are fundamentally the same" (26).

Baldwin's notion of fundamental similarity was a version of Charles Horton Cooley's more extensive formulation. That Charles Horton Cooley, the son of famed jurist Thomas McIntyre Cooley and professor of sociology at the University of Michigan, should become one of the leading advocates of the social self is ironic. As historians delight in recounting, Cooley was a man of extreme diffidence and few friends, who was capable of going into a tailspin at the thought of entertaining anyone. Cooley's theory was not about gregariousness (he actually denied such an instinct existed), but about the development of the self in contact with others. He insisted in his two most famous works, *Human Nature and Social Organization* (1902) and *Social Organization* (1909), that the notion of a separate individual was an abstraction that never existed in nature. Likewise with society. Instead, there was human life, of which society and the individual were more akin to particular vantage points or ways of organizing experience than to dichotomous objects. Individuals and society were "simply collective and distributive aspects of the same thing, the relation between them being like that between other expressions one of which denotes a group as a whole and the other the members of the group, such as the army and the soldiers . . ."[21]

Cooley could maintain this position because he regarded both self and society as essentially mental images rather than objects. A child's "I" was less his or her body or muscular sensation than his or her imaginative reconstruction of social interaction. Society was likewise images of others that each of us carries around with us. "Society, then, in its immediate aspect, *is a relation among personal ideas.* In order to have society, it is evidently necessary that persons should get together somewhere; and they get together only as personal ideas in the mind. . . . Society exists in my mind as the contact and reciprocal influence of certain ideas named 'I,' Thomas, Henry, Susan, Bridget, and so on. It exists in your mind as a similar group, and so in every mind."[22] Cooley's argument made being real in a social sense a matter of being imagined, and made sociology, as Marshall Cohen has written, the imagination of imaginations. By treating self and society as ideas, Cooley found a way to link them, establish relations between them, and smooth the path toward explaining their mutuality. Cooley's social psychology was the counter to contractualism, which depended upon the creation of a new thing (society) from the agreement of autonomous beings. It also provided a way to stress the possibilities of social harmony. The social psychologists were not unaware of social conflict, but their working definitions inclined them to treat social bonds as normative.

Baldwin, for instance, saw human interactions as inclined toward a meshing of interests and interdependency. Each individual's apprehension of his own personal self and its interests involves the recognition of others and their interests, he argued. Because the individual "grows in personality and individuality by growing also in sociality," he does not have two lives—one personal and one social—but one, which is both personal and social at once. The social aspect linked an individual with others harmoniously, making intergroup conflict in society a temporary, nearly insignificant phenomenon that arose from misapprehension of fundamental similarity. "There is, on the whole, no general antagonism of interests. On the contrary, there is a concurrence and practical identity, at least in those great aspects of life which constitute the utilities of society, and motive the essential actions of men." Not surprisingly, he disparaged radical solutions and saw in business the generator of both social solidarity and progress.[23]

Baldwin, however, was not entirely convinced about the absence of antagonism of interests or about the obsolescence of the autonomous self. In the end, he was not happy labeling humans veritable copying machines. Imitation ensured social order but threatened social stagnation. To account for change, Baldwin distinguished among types of imitation. Plastic suggestion was a rather low level of learning in which everyone learned the same thing, and it was typical of primitive societies. Civilization, however, depended upon modification of the rule of plastic suggestion. That modification took the form of the creative individual, who reflexively imitated by making the acts of others over in "forms peculiar to one's own temper and valuable to one's own genius." Talented individuals were in fact failures as copying machines. Their failure, however, had social benefits, because they were Baldwin's propelling force of change. Such people needed arrangements that allowed the free exercise of personality, and free competition fit the bill for Baldwin. In good romantic fashion, he stood for the individual against the dormant contentedness and lifeless mediocrity of collectivism. Socialistic institutions, he wrote in 1912, were poised to squash individuality. "Even in his most valuable traits, his invention, his industry, his resourcefulness—in all his originalities, priceless gifts to society—he is being deprived of his individual birthright and made to conform to the collectivistic regulations."[24]

Baldwin's advocacy of individual initiative and dignity underscored his sense that social developments in the United States had swamped the balance between self and other that his theory of the embedded self meant to highlight. Society, by his lights, was not simply providing cues and opportunities, but preventing the formation of selves with repertoires. Not all social psychologists concurred with Baldwin's sense of society as an impersonal, omnivorous other. Both Charles Horton Cooley and George Herbert Mead saw the political problem as a growing absence of fellow feeling, or individualism run riot, and moved to foster collective and cooperative endeavors as more befitting the social self. Although Cooley occasionally extolled competition as the royal road to progress, he nonetheless favored a strong trade-union movement and democratic collective action that merged the "I into We," as he once put it.[25] For his part, Mead was even less enamored of competition, maintaining a long-standing connection to Jane Addams's Hull House and an active participation in community forums, civic commissions, and labor arbitration efforts.

The political positions of Cooley and Mead followed from their sense that imitation-suggestion was inadequate to describe the development of the self. Cooley criticized imitation-suggestion for its treatment of the self as passive receptor that faithfully aims to reproduce what it perceives. Cooley insisted that imitation-suggestion could not account for the purposive, teleological aims of humans. It failed to credit that humans are faced with multiple inputs and choose the ones they mimic. This active, motivated selection was to Cooley's mind the key element in the formation of a flexible social self, one that was more that a will-o'-the-wisp. "An intelligent child imitates because he has faculties crying for employment, and imitation is the key that lets them loose: he needs to do things and imitation gives him things to do."[26] From Cooley's vantage point, Baldwin had a passive mechanism of self-formation and mistook interaction for imposition. Remove the passivity, and you remove the dichotomy between self and society.

Which is what Cooley set out to do in his famous theory of the "looking-glass self." A reflexive self, the looking-glass self was the self that arose to consciousness by recognizing itself in the reflection it gleans from others. Cooley imagined children experimenting with controlling themselves and others by observing the connection between their own behavior and the responses of those in their environment. The looking-glass self was, in effect, a product of how an individual believes he or she fares in the imaginations of others. Arguing that what we call "me" is not "something separate from general life, but the most interesting part of it," Cooley saw the interchanges in imagination among people as absolutely crucial for the constitution of both self and society. "As we see our face, figure, and dress in the glass, and are interested in them because they are ours, and pleased or otherwise with them according as they do or do not answer to what we should like them to be; so in imagination we perceive in another's mind some thought of our appearance, manners, aims, deeds, character, friends, and so on, and are variously affected by it." This development of self in Cooley's schema was a tripartite process consisting of an individual's imagination of his or her appearance to others, supposition of what kinds of judgments others render, and "some sort of self-feeling such as pride or mortification."[27] Cooley thus proposed a mechanism whereby individuals engaged in a perpetual conversation in the mind between the self and its imaginary companions, an idea, perhaps, that appealed to someone who regarded himself as essentially shy. The individual gains confidence, feels humility, or experiences shame in light of how she imagines her audience's reaction to her. Adults, Cooley contended, do likewise, drawing upon a larger history and the lessons learned from previous imaginings.[28]

The constant interchange meant that the self was never fully identical with itself, constantly receiving and evaluating its reflection. But what did the evaluation, and what did the selection? Somewhere behind the social self some form of individual mind was making selection, contended George Herbert Mead in a 1930 article about Cooley's contributions to the concept of the social self. Mead concluded that Cooley lacked a genetic explanation of how the self arose in the social process. Cooley's social consciousness was an awareness of others, not an account of how social processes smoothed the way for the consciousness to be lodged as inner experience. In Mead's view, Cooley's notion that society was a set of personal ideas was based on the tacit assumption of a prior existence of a mind to do the imagining of others. As such, Mead concluded, Cooley's social self shared more with the autonomous self than Mead thought warranted. Mead, in contrast, aimed at more fully socializing the process of self-formation. When he declared, "Other selves come into existence first of all and later one becomes aware of himself," Mead was reversing the traditionally held order, introducing a level of multiplicity in the process.[29]

Mead (1863–1931) came from an academic family. His father held the chair of Sacred Rhetoric and Pastoral Theology at Oberlin College, and his mother later served as president of Mount Holyoke. That heritage did not immediately suggest a career path, however. Originally trained in Europe in physiological psychology, he eventually turned to philosophy. In 1891, Mead took a position at the University of Michigan in 1891, where he met John Dewey. Sharing with Dewey both an interest in Hegelianism and a commitment to a functionalist orientation, Mead moved with Dewey to the University of Chicago in 1894. A prolific thinker, Mead never synthesized his formulations on a wide variety of topics. Two of his major works are, in fact, publications of students' notes from his University of Chicago lectures. Mead scholars are not quite sure how exact the transcriptions are or how firmly Mead held some of his arguments. Those aiming to explicate Mead draw their arguments from disparate materials, spread across years. Such reconstruction gives Mead studies a touch of multiplicity, since there are, it seems, many "Meads."

There is agreement that Mead forged a concept of the social self that was neither originally internal nor purely reflective of its environment, thus avoiding what he saw as the weaknesses of Cooley's and Baldwin's models. Crucial to his formulation was his effort to account for the origins of self as an importation of a social object. In Mead's account, the self originated outside the organism in social interaction before it was internally adopted. This process was a consequence of the human status as problem-solving beings. Much of human action was habitual, but when habits failed to achieve desired ends, human adaptation to changing environment required interaction with others. To achieve their purposes within a social situation, humans gesture and vocalize. These gestures and vocalizations act as stimuli to others, signaling how we intend to act in a given situation. That in turn prompts responses from them, making us aware of the expectations of others. As we become aware of others, we develop the ability to take their positions, to know how they will react to our gestures and vocalizations and to surmise how they feel. Only then do we discover that we are also selves, possessing attitudes. We know our attitudes, Mead wrote in 1910, "because they are responsible for the changes in the conduct of other individuals."[30]

There was more to Mead's argument than that we develop consciousness because we see others react to us. One of the others to whom we react is ourselves. We exist first in the object world and then as a possession of ourselves. Mead's self was constructed and reconstructed in the give-and-take of social interaction "not by becoming a subject to himself, but only in so far as he first becomes an object to himself," which happens when the individual takes on the "attitudes of other individuals toward himself within a social environment or context of experience and behavior in which both he and they are involved."[31] This introjection of a social image occurs because of the power of language. In Mead's view, language entails not only words and meanings but vocalization. We react to our voice in effect as if it came from the outside. It stimulates us as it stimulates others.[32] Thus, we have conversations with ourselves, stimulating responses in ourselves that allow us to reflect on

our own activity. To be conscious in Mead's sense is to be able to call up others' response to ourselves and to reflect on its meaning.

This central inner conversation of consciousness takes place between
parts of the self that Mead entitled the "Me" and the "I." The former is the
self objectified to the self—the self available to consciousness. The latter is
not so much the subject as the site of an individual's novel responses. It does
active organizing, yet is never available to consciousness. The "I" might be
best thought of as the subjective attitude of reflection itself. It gazes on both
the objective image of the self and its own responses. "I" makes possible the
inner dialogue between the responses to others. "I" is the individual having
consciousness. As soon as it enters consciousness, the "I" becomes an object
and thus part of a new "Me."[33] Mead rejected the notion that the "I" was the
true self, the more fundamental, noting that without the images, memories,
and objects of the "Me," it could not function. One could not, he insisted,
have a subjective sense of self without constitution as social object.

Mead built multiplicity into his model of the self. Constantly adapting,
never quite capturable, it was a far cry from the essential self that Descartes
had made primary. Because the "Me" and the "I" never coincide, the individual is always in search of completion, never realizing it. At best, we live
with approximations and would profit from jettisoning the search for a true
self in favor of negotiation that was successful, enriching, adaptive. Self-
development was a combination of solidarity—a commitment to the social
organism in which one was entwined and through which one came to consciousness—and pluralism, an openness to others who were not incommen-
surate and outside the bounds of social life, since they shared the quality of
"otherness" with us. Both social solidarity and pluralism were implied in the
processes of becoming a self. The human ability to put oneself in the place of
others in the course of social living suggested that a self might prosper if it
multiplied the number of groups and number of selves it could mirror and develop.

Mead attempted to distinguish his self from the oversocialized self, a goal
apparent in his criticism of imitation-suggestion. He dismissed as illogical the
implication of imitation-suggestion that people were fully shaped by their environment. "When another self is present in consciousness doing something,
then such a self may be imitated by the self that is conscious of him in his
conduct, but by what possible mechanism, short of a miracle, the conduct of
one form should act as a stimulus to another to do, not what the situation
calls for, but something *like* that which the first form is doing, is beyond ordinary comprehension," he wrote.[34] Behavior, even that which appeared to

be direct copy, was by Mead's lights better understood as testing to find *appropriate* responses that called out desired behavior from the other. Royce and Baldwin erred, he argued, in thinking that mimetic identification with the actions of others immediately brings forth a self. Mead countered that children imitate only that which has meaning for them. Even smiling back at parents is not mechanical imitation but a search for meaning. As Ruth Leys has put it, "Mead makes imitation a phenomenon of discrete pregiven elements (or mechanisms), not the dissolution of boundaries; of temporal delay, not instant communication; of distance, not merger; and of cognitive self-representation, not blind, emotional identification."[35]

The concept of the social self opened analysis of individuality to multiple sources of influence, stressing the way selves and society were not necessarily polar terms. It expanded the boundary of the self and reoriented thinking about rights and legitimations. Yet it may well have been premature in its default position of integration between self and society. In part, their emphasis on process rather than structure led social psychologists to regard society writ small, the primary group rather than structural arrangements. Like Baldwin, Cooley often treated conflict as a mistake, a misunderstanding best solved through the face-to-face discussions of the primary group. Much of his writing on poverty concentrated not on struggle for access to sources of economic power but on the inadequate acquaintance of the poor to the operating norms of the social group as a whole.[36] Reasoning from social involvement to social harmony, social psychology was unprepared to regard social arrangement as inherently conflictual.[37]

The Unconscious Self

The social self, for all its changeability, was transparent to itself. Even as it searched for proper response, the Meadean or Cooleyan social self was eventually a unified one; the moment of uncertainty gave way to the moment of equilibrium. Neither theorist accepted the notion of unsocialized biological drives and impulses or the existence of motives unavailable to consciousness. That drives and emotions would be repressed and form alien and unknown forces within human personalities, compelling actors to behave in ways they neither understand nor control figured little in the theories of the social self. One key element of twentieth-century multiplicity was the proliferation of discourses that challenged the notion of the unified and knowable nature of the self on precisely those grounds. Notions of an unconscious self had floated around American thought in the nineteenth century, but during the first twenty years of the twentieth, such notions took on new respectability, in large measure because Freudian and other psychodynamic theories gave it a scientific imprimatur. In the process, Americans tamed Freudian insights, making the unconscious much less an example of multiplicity than a source of harmony.

The challenge presented by the unconscious to the autonomous individual revolved around the issue of the will. Nineteenth-century analysts designated the will as that capacity for effort against the line of greatest resistance. Those who possessed it were so in control of their faculties and capacities that they could steel themselves to duty regardless of pleasure or pain. Will was that faculty by which the autonomous self exercised its autonomy and assumed its responsibility. An unconscious, understood as a reservoir of desires and motives unknown to the self, threatened the stability, integrity, and self-knowledge of the self. A self driven by forces of which it was unaware could hardly be held culpable for its actions. Nor could it be fully disciplined by appeal to intellect or reason. Early-nineteenth-century discussion of the unconscious had conceptualized it as an untapped reservoir of potential, filled with hidden divine (or nearly so) forces. Such discourses as mesmerism and mind cure spoke glowingly of what Philip Cushman has labeled the enchanted interior. For Phineas Quimby (1802–1866), who claimed inspiration from the writings of Ralph Waldo Emerson, illness stemmed from incorrect ideas. Rejecting the notion that material conditions controlled individual lives, Quimby and his followers, which included Mary Baker Eddy of Christian Science fame, urged Americans to avoid identification with outer conditions and get in touch with the magnetic forces of the divine order that resided within. Such a position interiorized the Protestant ethos, making one responsible less to an external God than to one's own internal spirit that dictated individual wisdom.[38]

By the early twentieth century, most middle-class Americans generally accepted some version of an unconscious self. The first decade of the century was filled with therapeutic movements, self-help nostrums, and much publicity about the power of the hidden self. The press was filled with worries about the menace of nervousness, the mysteries of the mind, and the miracles of therapy. In 1905, readers had over a dozen choices of mental power books by prominent authors from which to choose. Those who felt paralyzed, apathetic, or lacking self-control could seek help from a slew of movements. There was New Thought, which traced its lineage back to Quimby and emphasized that the mind was not bound by natural laws but was instead a creative initiator. In the late nineteenth century, New Thought had a large number of female adherents who used it to stake out claims of women to possessing the ability to practice a distinctive spiritual science. It flourished in part because it emphasized the ways in which harnessed mental power could master the material world as well as unify a fractured and divided self. Among adherents at one time or another in their careers were the novelist Theodore Dreiser and the radical journalist Max Eastman. There was the Emmanuel movement, founded in Boston in 1906 by an Episcopalian minister, Elwood Worcester, and offering a form of suggestion therapy conducted by trained clergy. Worcester's version of the unconscious blended Transcendentalism, Schopenhauer, and Bergson. The subliminal self housed instincts that could be chaotic and compelling (Worcester seemed to have love and sexual attraction in mind) and therapeutic, supplying emotion and will. Once the psychologically afflicted jettisoned repressions and rote behavior, the subconscious could ply its healing powers, curing itself. These nonrational emotional sources were given a scientific boost in William James's 1907 article "The Energies of Men." Having had a hand in popularizing "The Hidden Self" (1890), James shifted the paradigm with his insistence that mental energy was abundant and once released it would propel human beings to higher achievements. Ever concerned with the nonquantifiable portion of human behavior, by the first decade of the twentieth century James had begun to emphasize the evanescence of the self, at times implying that selves were not always fixed to bodies.[39]

These developments ran counter to the conventional understandings of the men who in fact treated diseases of the mind. Their preferred paradigm was a somaticism in which disease was understood as maldeveloped brain function. According to the paradigm, lesions caused the nervous mechanism, which was powered by nervous energy, to break down. Eventually pathologists hoped to relate each symptom to a specified pathological condition. That hope, however, went unrealized. By 1900, somaticism was in retreat. Critics charged that the expected brain lesions were not present in a majority of cases and that the supposed links between the brain and cognitive functions were unproven. It was not at all clear that the same neurons or synapses were involved in two similar reactions to the same stimulus. Such findings led to charges that somatic cures, which were based on conserving and replenishing nervous energy, did little to address the mental problems they were supposed to solve. Others noted that somatic cures did not reduce the incidence of mental problems or show any tendency to relieve suffering based on investigations of reports from both patients and physicians.

Compounding the problem for somaticists was the proliferation of definitions of instinct. Researchers were aware that some behavior was automatic or nearly so in nature, but whether it originated as a patterned response to internal or to external stimuli was far from determined. How much purposiveness existed in instinct was a matter of some debate. Adding to the difficulties for somaticism, ironically enough, were the discoveries of August Weismann, who noted that germ plasma passed on unchanged from generation to generation. In challenging Lamarckianism—the notion that adaptations were inherited—Weismann undercut the melioristic strain of earlier generations of neurologists. According to historian Nathan Hale, the hereditarian approaches too became "more grotesque and vulnerable," a patchwork of contradictory classifications. The cumulative effect was to put the entire understanding of what constituted disease into question. As an increasing number of symptoms were placed under the rubric of neurasthenia, clinicians began to regard the diagnosis as untenable and searched for a way to understand mental and emotional difficulties that did not rely on a concept of finite nervous energy.[40]

With the decline of somaticism, clinicians embraced new ideas flowing from Europe. Sparked by such practitioners as Adolf Meyer, Morton Prince and Boris Sidis, who hailed from or who had been trained in Europe, American thinking turned to the contents of the mind itself as the source for malfunction. Drawing eclectically on Pierre Janet, various mind cures, Jamesian notions of the objectivity of thought, and imitation-suggestion, Americans fashioned a new paradigm that acknowledged a division between conscious and unconscious mental processes. The division was constructed so as to allow clinicians both to acknowledge and to tame multiplicity by subjecting the self to melioristic efforts. One of the most influential exponents of the new understanding was James Jackson Putnam (1846–1918), an eminent Bostonian physician who was both a friend and a compatriot of Royce and James and who was to become the standard bearer, albeit a less-than-orthodox one, of Freudianism in the United States. Putnam held that neuroses were rooted in forgotten childhood traumas. He insisted that theories that ignored the social dimension were bound to fail. Drawing upon much of the discourse of the social self, Putnam used imitation-suggestion to posit that patients afflicted with an inflexible internal censor actually suffered from incorrect and overly harsh introjection of the thoughts of others. As early as 1898, Putnam had contended that many mental and emotional disorders were sexual in origin, even when they were not recognized as such. Although he contended that doctrines that attributed neurosis to sinful acts and desires were "crude and dangerous" and held a Bergsonian-inflected notion of liberating life forces, Putnam's original therapeutic practice was relatively restrained. Rather than urging patients to gratify desires in the name of relief from an unremitting conscience, Putnam prodded them to give up their attachment to acting out morbid fears and indulging in morbid thoughts.[41]

Putnam was not the only person who saw sexual energies behind the unconscious mind prior to Sigmund Freud's 1909 visit to the United States. Throughout the late nineteenth century, there were a number of challenges to the accepted notions that individuals had only a finite amount of sexual energy and that wanton and wasteful expenditure would wreak havoc with civilization and exaggerate secondary sex characteristics. By century's end, there was much talk about the inexhaustible drive of sexual passion, the unnaturalness of Victorian attempts to refine and rechannel it, and the necessity for sexuality to be part of the expression and revelation of a true self. The work of two Englishmen, Edward Carpenter's *Love's Coming-of-Age* (1896) and the writings of Havelock Ellis, particularly *Man and Woman* (1894), *Sexual Inversion*, his study of homosexuality, and his mammoth *Studies in the Psychology of Sex* (the first six volumes of which were published between 1897 and 1910 in Philadelphia because of legal difficulties in England), were prime examples of a growing trend. Both boldly separated sexuality from reproduction, and both attacked prevailing social mores for creating a self divided between social pressure and instinctual expression. Although what Nathan Hale refers to as the "civilized morality" was far from vanquished in 1909, El-

Figure 3.2. Freud's Clark University lectures, 1909. **Among the notables pictured here are the philosopher William James (third from left, first row), the anthropologist Franz Boas (left, first row), and psychologist and president of Clark, G. Stanley Hall. Not pictured: the feminist and anarchist Emma Goldman. For all its postulation of universal drives, Freud's depth psychology introduced multiplicity into the study of the self by its insistence that the self was divided against itself, expressing universal conflicts in particular and unpredictable ways. (Source: Library of Congress; LC-USZ62-92136)**

lis's success among young intellectuals indicated that it was less hegemonic among the middle class than it had been twenty years earlier.[42]

Sigmund Freud's visit was not so much a turning point as an intensification and a sharpening of the debate over the nature of the unconscious. The trip, which thoroughly confirmed Freud's negative opinion of the form of life known as the United States, thrust his ideas into prominence and made him a celebrity of sorts. Among the notables attending his Clark University lectures were William James and Emma Goldman. Although his general introduction made the unconscious less untamable and inexorable than he would later depict it, his portrait of a self divided between drives and social expectation presented a self that did not comprehend its totality. In broad strokes, Freud laid out the power of an unconscious that made itself known indirectly. In his fifth lecture, he maintained that neurosis came from the arrest of sexual development, exacerbated by squeamish and puritanical social attitudes that refused to acknowledge its natural character. He contended, quite opposite to the view that social psychologists advanced, that civilization made demands that made life too hard for most people. They adjusted by replacing reality with fantasy to an abnormal extent, achieving through dreams and wishes what they really wanted. Even in dreams, Freud contended, the desires were not straightforwardly expressed, but rather articulated in a symbolic language whose grammar was not so easy to decipher. Sexual desire for the opposite-sexed parent—the desire Freud came to regard as universal—was almost always re-inscribed, available only through chains of association.

The Freudian self mixed the universal and the contingent. Personality arose at the intersection of culture and nature but did so almost serendipitously. There was no generalized way the tension between drive and social prohibition was negotiated in the Freudian scheme. It depended on how individuals experienced and remembered and how they constructed individual interior languages and assigned valences to objects. Symbolic meaning was entirely personal and often idiosyncratic. Although some associations seemed widespread (the link between feces and money, for instance), no unified principle seemed to structure this language, a point Freud recognized in his comment that sometimes a cigar is just a cigar. Such narratives had, as Eli Zaretsky notes, no social shared meaning. More likely than not, the Freudian self could not ever be fully integrated, divided as it was among social expectations, inexorable drives, and personal responses.[43]

In the years following his Clark talks, Freud would remap the self and its mechanisms. At Clark, Freud put forward, at least in part, a view that Americans could interpret as optimistic. Successful treatment of neurosis was possible with cathartic discovery of the thwarted wish. Making manifest the wishes that were unacknowledged and freely choosing whether to gratify them constituted the goal of treatment. Countering fears that freeing repressed desires and drives would create anarchy, Freud argued in the course of his lectures that rather than illicit desires swamping morality, the effect would be nearly the opposite. When made conscious, wishes would lose much of their energy, which would then be available to be used in other, more socially productive ways. Offering sexual sublimation rather than sexual repression, Freud presented a body of thought that Americans could interpret as simple, practical, even potentially optimistic.[44]

The Clark Lectures contained other themes, ones that suggested less harmonious outcomes. In the years following his 1909 visit, Freud extended those elements in which all humans could reasonably hope to achieve was a dampening of the clash between inexorable drives and social prohibition of uncontrolled sexuality. Therapeutic practice had acquainted him with the limitations of cathartic experience as the fount of insight, and with the cunning of resistance. The upshot was that the unconscious would still function as a somewhat unwelcome guest. Much turned on Freud's notion of sexuality. Freud construed sexuality to mean not just specific acts, but independent impulses whose aim was to produce pleasure from a sensitive body area. He termed this desire to achieve bodily pleasure from nongenital orifices and areas polymorphous perversity. This formulation of pleasure was at the heart of his controversial theory of infant sexuality. Until educated in social mores, children sought gratification by stimulating various body parts. How those impulses would find expression depended upon life histories, which were by definition varied and not easily classifiable. That even socially normal people had such drives—a claim that was also quite controversial—suggested that humans could never be transparent to themselves. In denying such inclinations, humans living in society became possessed of a self not governed by time, logic, or inhibition. Freud's use of material other analysts dismissed —dreams, slips, jokes—revealed a glimpse of the nonrational, illogical self. Even at his most optimistic, Freud regarded reason as a thin reed on which to prop human prospects.

In locating the origins of multiplicity in infant sexuality, Freud presented a challenge to lay and medical observers alike. There were, of course, complaints from moralists who saw Freud's work as overly materialistic. The physician Francis X. Dercum fumed in 1914: "What must we think of the wounding of the feelings of a sensitive and innocent nature when to a loving son or daughter is suggested an incestuous love for the mother? What injury can be greater than to give to one of the most beautiful relations in human life the most shocking and the vilest of interpretations?" Opponents connected Freudianism to occultism, cubism, and Jews. There were less agitated, more reasoned objections. At issue was less the existence of infantile sexuality—most evolutionists assumed something like it must exist—than the Freudian argument for its centrality in the formation of self and its incessant, unquenchable quality. A number of researchers argued, for instance, that Freud's notion of the persistence of drives was logically dubious, if not unsustainable. Other impulses dissipate when attention is directed elsewhere. Freud, they contended, gave no indication why the pleasure principle should be so particularly enduring and unmodifiable. Nor did he give full credence to drives being products of learning as well as instincts. To opponents, Freudianism opened the floodgates of multiplicity, undermining the autonomous self. Princeton philosopher Warren Fite argued in 1916 that Freud emphasized "not the personality expressed in sober and reflective judgment; not the conscious self, but the demon that rules when I am off my guard."[45]

Such objections did not dispose of the Freudian unconscious. Indeed, Freud's popularity seemed to accelerate with the criticism. Spurred by analysts' own astute self-promotion, psychoanalysis flourished as a singular revelatory process that revealed the true self. It achieved a prominence in the United States that far surpassed its acceptance elsewhere, in large measure by remaking Freud as the analyst of multiplicity within unity. Freudianism in the first two decades of the twentieth century rode the currents of the repeal of reticence by giving to those who embraced it a certain frisson of liberation while at the same time safely guiding individuals toward uplift and progress. Or so public discourse would have it. By the middle of the second decade of the twentieth century, psychoanalysis had become a tool for self-realization rather than a therapy for classical neurosis. In the December 1915 *Vanity Fair*, Floyd Dell called psychoanalysis "the greatest discovery made by intellectual conversationalists since Bergson and the International [sic] Workers of the World." That same year his fellow *Masses* editor Max Eastman published an article in *Everyman's* that extolled Freudian psychology for its ability to give those who suffered from paralyzed will a meaning to life. Sounding like a hawker of patent medicine, Eastman proclaimed "Are you worried? Are you worried where there is nothing to worry about? Have you lost confidence in yourself? Are you afraid? Are you depressed, nervous, irritable, unable to be decent-tempered around the house? . . . Do you suffer from headaches, nausea, 'neuralgia,' paralysis or any other mysterious disorder . . . ?" He lauded Freud for finding a way to sink "a shaft into the subconscious region and tap it of its mischievous elements." Little was said about resistance or transference—the ways in which the patient was said to map his neurosis on the analyst during the course of treatment. It is hard to find a popular

treatment of Freud in these years that captures his sense that the goal of therapy is to replace neurosis with common unhappiness. During the war years,
the unconscious did take on a less enchanted, more haunted quality. The prevailing notion, however, was of an uncanny and powerful region, which in
the mold of Quimby was a source of power for success and happiness. Repressions were, in this new atmosphere, more wasteful than compensatory.
Ridding oneself of these obstacles would, most gushing journalists noted, allow new energies to flow freely.[46]

If more circumspect than journalists, American analysts also interpreted
the Freudian unconscious so as to shape and contain a number of the implications of Freudian contingency. Attuned as a consequence of their clinical
experience to the unpredictability of the unconscious, yet not unaffected by
discourses of the enchanted interior, American practitioners were far from
strict Freudians in the early years of psychoanalysis in the United States. Although many defended the hypotheses of infantile sexuality and polymorphous perversity against all comers and were willing to engage in rough
polemics against doubters, most American analysts rarely embraced what
seemed the pessimistic conclusion of a permanently divided self. American
eclecticism resulted in a series of deviations designed to lessen the hold of the
unresolvable conflict between nature and culture. Some analysts, such as
Samuel Tannenbaum, advocated what Freud labeled wild analysis—the advocacy of gratification of repressed urges—so as to allow expression of the
true self. Gratifying repressed urges was embraced in a number of quarters as
daring liberation from social restrictions, a recasting of the romantic belief of
a whole self that flourished when fully expressed. Others, like Putnam and
Smith Jelliffe, who resisted the call for indulgence in sexuality as cure, could
portray sexuality freed from repression and properly expressed as splendid,
even spiritual. Defining sex as any human contact, "actual or symbolic with
another person" that involved any sensory area for the purpose of "productive creation," Putnam called it "one of the universal properties and glories
of all living things." Perhaps more significant was the depiction of the unconscious as a carrier of potentially beneficent and compensatory forces and
the interpretation of sublimation as an operation guided by the will and subject to therapeutic manipulation.[47]

Putnam was always a bit miscast as Freud's designated American
spokesman for the psychoanalytic movement. His Bergsonian vitalism, his
sense of the possibilities of mind creating life, and his neo-Transcendentalist
fusion of moral and natural laws all made him less than satisfied with the deterministic aspects of Freudian thought. He objected forcefully to the orthodox drift toward rigidity, indicating to William James that the "alternative is

surely between a gross materialism and a truly personalistic universe with love and hope in it from the start." In contrast to Freud's notion of the often antagonistic relation between individual and society, Putnam envisioned a more benign relationship with the universe infusing the mind of the individual. Civilization, Putnam continually maintained, was something more than the sublimation of sexual instincts; it was the product of the life force.[48] Putnam viewed the human condition as divided between the drive for self-expression and the sense of its impossibility. He saw the goal of life as the realization of the self's permeability and continuity, an optimistic outlook that sat uneasily with Freudian pessimism.[49]

Given this prevalence of a vitalist current that commended a self that ultimately submerges itself with life itself, in which divisions in the end make conscious what had previously been unconscious, in which sexuality—however broadly understood—did not hold the privileged position, it is not surprising that many American analysts were attracted to the work of Carl Jung in the years following the Clark talks and Freud's subsequent reworking of the mental geography. The Americans and the Swiss theorist shared objections to the sexualization of the libido. Jung spoke to American objections to a theory that concentrated on the animal nature of humanity. Jung's reinterpretation on the grounds that the spiritual, like the biological, had "inviolable rights" dovetailed nicely with the psychiatrist William Allenson White's notion that sexuality was but one expression of primordial energy and yielded to evolution and progress as the source of sublimation. Jung and the Americans both owed a debt to Bergson's life force and to his notion of "true" memory as the unconscious survival of personal memories. Jung's substitution of problems in achieving life tasks for Oedipal conflicts as the central cause of mental disturbances resonated with American psychiatrists' theories.[50]

Both medical and lay audience alike took to his notions of a collective unconscious and the psyche as self-correcting. Jung's depth psychology, with its leaven of exotic elements from Asian myths, appealed to many as a counter to the perpetual war of instinct and society at the heart of Freudianism. Having set themselves against a narrow, official Western tradition, the Young Americans were fascinated with the seeming eclecticism and exoticism of Jung's references. By the late teens, many denizens of Greenwich Village regarded Freud as old hat and Jung as the cutting edge. Only Putnam's sense that Jung was personally dictatorial kept him from becoming a full-fledged Jungian. Others, such as Smith Jelliffe, shared none of the reservations.[51]

The vitalist current eschewed determinisms and pointed to the power of the mind. It presented as welcoming the flux of existence and thus constitutes a form of multiplicity of the self in which change, creation, and energy are constants in life. Like the social self of Mead and Cooley, the analytical self countered notions of hereditarian and somatic determinism in which identity was fixed at birth. It thrust the self into the world and located its constituent parts in practice. Yet in its embrace of growth and the delights of multiplicity, American discourse moved steadily to guard against a negative multiplicity in which biology and social practice were never at one with one another. Freudian discourse placed desires in another realm and made them only partly recoverable and only partly extinguishable. Even as many Americans were eager to jettison a conception of the self as self-contained and defined once and for all, they were less ready to embrace a self that could not fully change or fully know itself. Understanding the issue as a choice between gross materialism and human-created love and hope, American analysts by and large opted, as did many of their fellow citizens, for the latter. They did so in the hope that they could segregate a productive from a destructive multiplicity. Whether creativity and freedom could so easily be achieved was, as the final years of the 1910s were to demonstrate, a dubious proposition.

The Gendered Self

Biology was destiny, went the Freudian aphorism. It was a proposition that had culture-wide assent. Nineteenth-century Americans may have regarded the self in Cartesian terms as Mind, not body, but they were quite aware that the type of body one had was no insignificant matter. Nowhere was this more apparent than in the matter of sex. Few middle-class Americans doubted that men were different from women, each sex having a distinct set of qualities, inclinations, temperaments, and capacities. If sexual difference did not create a unique self, Americans did believe it defined the parameters in which that self would develop. For somaticists, deficiencies in the female body had dramatic repercussions. Each internal organ was connected by nerves to the spinal cord and to other organs. The irritation or infection of one organ could excite and distort others. Particularly prone to distortion was the uterus, which was the seat of hysteria and other maladies.[52] This susceptibility to exhaustion virtually dictated the female role of nurturing and prohibited strenuous exertion of limited energies, especially sparse mental ones. The female self thus had to develop and function within a bodily form that limited the amount of energy available for mental and analytical tasks. Indeed, it is no exaggeration to say that the prevailing view of the autonomous self was deeply gendered, since only men had bodies that were capable of sustaining autonomy.

Gender ideology was not particularly consistent. Although popular writings held women were less prone to extremes of emotion and were often thought more emotionally stable than men, those same writings were not reluctant to claim that women were also more influenced by their emotions than men and ultimately to be incapable of transcending their feelings. Thought to be patience personified, women were nonetheless regarded as incapable of prolonged efforts of attention. The logical flaws of gender ideology did little, however, to weaken the general consensus that different types of bodies generated different kinds of selves. More effective in challenging the assumption that Man and Woman were easily classified was the burgeoning feminist movement.

Part political and cultural protest and part intellectual development, the feminist movement of the first two decades of the twentieth century constituted a direct opposition to nineteenth-century notions that the female body

Figure 3.3. Suffrage march past the grave of Susan B. Anthony, Rochester, New York, 1910. **The demand for the vote was only part of the feminist movement of the early twentieth century. Arguing that the female body should not inhibit the development of the female self, such feminists as social psychologist Jessie Taft and the anthropologist Elsie Clews Parsons envisioned female liberation as a rejection of the categories of gender and an adoption of multiplicity. (Source: Rochester Historical Society)**

constituted an object that restrained the development of the self. By insisting that folk and scientific wisdom about female capacities constituted constricting stereotypes, early-twentieth-century feminists presented a nuanced
portrait of human potential. Feminist thought insisted in the main that the
assignment of psychological qualities to bodies was arbitrary, oppressive, and
destructive, both to those with female bodies and to society writ large. Gender, feminists maintained, was the mode by which selves were contained. In
its stead, a significant number of feminists offered a multiplicity that deliberately rejected the boundaries of a gendered self. The multiplicity of early-
twentieth-century feminism was a multiplicity that selves and bodies were
unfinished, not assigned by nature or bound by social expectations. This departure was most apparent in the embrace of pleasure, rather than of duty or
obligation, by many feminists. Although some influential feminists such as
the Swedish writer Ellen Key argued for female emancipation on the basis of
a special propensity for nurturing while at the same time celebrating female
sexual expression in and outside of marriage, other feminists denied that the
female self was naturally self-sacrificing. Hoping to advance conditions by
which those with female bodies could express and act upon their desires,
early-twentieth-century feminists put forward positions that aimed at extending the meaning of autonomy.[53]

As Nancy Cott has persuasively argued, feminism as both a way of seeing
and a movement was a creation of the early twentieth century.[54] Prior to the
twentieth century, the prevailing ideology came from something called the
woman movement, which even as it campaigned for full citizenship and social rights nonetheless saw gender distinctions as fixed and meaningful. Although nineteenth-century advocates of rights for women sometimes constructed their arguments on the grounds of common human rights that
should be available to all regardless of gender, the woman movement, as the
singular suggests, saw women as a group united by common qualities, inclinations, capacities, and, by extension, interests. Allowing those characteristics fuller public scope was a central impetus of nineteenth-century agitation.
A significant number of suffragists argued for the vote on the grounds that
women's maternal and nurturing qualities made them better citizens, in concert with pleas for elemental human justice on the basis of human rights. In
light of the ways in which industrial capitalism affected family life, the argument held that the vote was a logical extension rather than a blatant violation of women's suitability for the domestic sphere.

Feminists, often referred to with an exaggerated French spelling, *feministe*,
to accentuate their departure, denied the assumptions of the argument. So-
called feminine qualities, they asserted, were matters of history and conven-

tion—conventions that presumably were alterable. Human liberation depended upon jettisoning notions that the formation of selves arose from fixed sources and followed a set, unchangeable pattern. At issue for feminists was as much the achievement of self-development as the acquisition of power. For many feminists, the purpose of the latter was to advance the former. Feminist power, therefore, would enable women to enjoy the fruits of multiplicity, transcending the restrictions that gender rules had placed on women. As Marie Jenny Howe, the woman who organized the first clearly feminist group, Heterodoxy, in New York City in 1912, put it, "We intend simply to be ourselves, not just our little female selves, but our whole big human selves."[55]

Achieving human selves meant ignoring and destroying those cultural imperatives that consigned people with female bodies to a passive existence of nurturing, consumption, and, most of all, protection by and deference to men. In her remarkable PhD dissertation in social psychology, written under the direction of George Herbert Mead at the University of Chicago, *The Woman Movement from the Point of View of Social Consciousness*, Jessie Taft laid out the argument in greater depth. Drawing on Mead's theory of the social self, Taft laid out the distinctive way in which female self-consciousness was formed. Understanding and anticipating the gestures and reactions of others, women, like other social actors, took on the characteristics ascribed to them. Girls, Taft insisted, came to the realization that awareness of themselves as females entailed valuing modesty and eschewing inquisitiveness. Modesty and incuriosity led to self-denial and fear of change, leaving women with narrow personalities. Change required in effect remaking cultural expectations. Economic independence and legal equality, no matter how welcome and just, would make few inroads on the fundamental problem. In good social-psychological fashion, Taft held that the point was to create conditions in which all people could "feel within themselves as their own the impulses and points of view of all classes and both sexes." That goal seemed utopian to Taft, and she foresaw the continual conflict and social division. "All of this hopeless conflict among impulses which the woman feels she has legitimate right, even a moral obligation, to express, all of the rebellion against stupid, meaningless sacrifice of powers that ought to be used by society, constitutes the force, conscious or unconscious, which motivates the woman movement and will continue to vitalize it until some adjustment is made."[56]

The feminist movement had indeed expanded beyond the drive for the vote. In mid-February 1914, Heterodoxy organized two public meetings to explore understandings of the new orientation. The first, held February 17, dealt with "what feminism means to me" and included such speakers as the socialist Crystal Eastman, schoolteacher Henrietta Rodman—who had achieved prominence by opposing the ban in New York City against married schoolteachers—and the journalist George Creel. The second, held three days later, dealt with "breaking into the Human Race" and mentioned the rights to work, to convictions, to one's own name, and to ignore fashion, among others. What a world would look like wherein those rights were achievable was the subject of Charlotte Perkins Gilman's *Herland* (1915). Gilman had provided the intellectual underpinnings for a good deal of feminism with her 1898 volume, *Women and Economics*. In the book, she applied Darwinian notions of evolution to argue that the overemphasis on sexual selection in the United States had resulted in the exaggeration of the feminine traits. Contending that women as a class had no natural aptitude for homemaking, she excoriated the waste entailed in the enforced female segregation from the productive world. *Innocence*, she maintained, was simply another word for ignorance. Ignorant was something that the women of Herland were decidedly not. The novel is the story of an all-female country in which women propagate by means of parthenogenesis. Without men, there are no gender roles. This absence confuses the three male aviators who happen upon the nation, and they take their time to get their bearings. They are amazed to see women organizing and running a country and are at pains to understand why such women are not emotionally vulnerable and physically inferior. Gilman takes special note of the health and strength of women not constrained by misunderstandings of the abilities of their body. The swaggering braggart of the group consistently finds himself easily subdued and outpointed by the women of Herland. Uninhibited by preconceptions and social demands for conformity to a limited set of roles, the women of Herland are free to develop their human selves. Since home and motherhood are, in concert with Gilman's socialist inclinations, part of a society in which nurturing was built into all social institutions and shared by the community at large, the women of Gilman's novel make selves unencumbered by the social expectations that would normally accompany the kinds of bodies they possess. Although as is typical of a utopian novel, the individuation of the denizens of Herland is minimal, Gilman did advance the possibility that a social self could pick up cues in which gender did not prescribe only a few types.[57]

Herland is a world with little sexuality or sensuality. Gilman herself was not fond of the sexual expression of the New Women of the early twentieth century. It was the feminist assertion of sexual rights that represented the frontal assault on modesty and was the most-remarked-upon aspect of the movement in the early twentieth century. Feminists embraced the pursuit of sexual pleasure, hitherto considered inappropriate and improper, on the grounds that women were entitled to the same opportunities for enjoyment as men. Rejecting notions that women were incapable of such pleasures, feminists understood sexuality as a form of expression and thus a component of self-building. In feminist thinking, sexual compatibility went hand-in-hand with the right to trial marriages and accessible and equitable divorce. Partnership should, they asserted, be a matter of choice, not duty. Feminist liberation would press humanity forward to the achievement of what at the time was regarded as the human sex—the free, equal, and nonhierarchical relationship between men and women. Sexual pleasure would free the self from the constraints of the mind and make the self a matter of the active body rather than the biologically given one.[58]

It was this possibility that made birth control so crucial an issue for feminists in the 1910s. In its prewar incarnation, birth control embodied a feminist rejection of ascribed self. Begun by Margaret Sanger as a way to free working-class women from the burdens and dangers of continual childbearing (so that they might struggle for socialism, Sanger's original pet project), the birth control movement raised the possibilities of a sexuality freed from procreation and of female pleasure escaping the bounds of male control. Working-class women eventually proved lukewarm to Sanger's project and were especially alienated by her disdain and condescension, which intensified after the Great War. Sanger's rival in the birth control movement, Mary Ware Dennett, hinted at the great potential of birth control when she spoke of the "joy" that the banishment of pregnancy worries would bring to both participants. The term evoked spiritual ecstasy and intensity, something not previously associated with sexual release. Fearful of the destabilizing possibilities of uninhibited sexual expression, opponents turned to law enforcement to suppress birth control pamphlets. Cultural conservatives may well have exaggerated the threat to social order that the end of sexual repression constituted, but the full range of their anxiety revealed the cultural stakes in the new morality. Opponents viewed the expression of female desire as an unnatural rejection of the social cohesion that depended on female renunciation. By contending that female selves had an equal right to pleasure as male ones, feminists posited selves that effected social transformation while opening possibilities for personal expression. Critics noted, not without reason, that public sex talk drained away the mystery, refinement, and spirituality that the Victorians attributed to sexual matters. As dance crazes and movies spread throughout the period, many middle-class Americans saw an inexorable tide of personal excesses, disdain for decorum, and the erosion of the distinction between the higher self of the spirit and the lower one of the body.[59]

Feminist claims that human nature was gender-neutral advanced an argument that Mary Wollstonecraft and John Stuart Mill had originated. Part of the liberation of women, then, meant jettisoning as degrading and artificial traits and orientations regarded as feminine. What made the feminist position during the 1910s unique was that it did not rest on universality alone. Rather than simply claiming to be genuinely human and leaving it at that, feminists also argued that history and social pressure had created a group that had specific needs and interests that universal claims, cleared of their gendered nature, could not meet. Success depended on the ability of women, divided and stratified as they were, coming together and saying "we." Achieving such balance and escaping the restricted selves that came with female bodies proved more difficult than some of the blithe feminist rhetoric both men and women deployed throughout the 1910s.[60] This was especially true in some of the arrangements that male and female feminists concocted among themselves in the early twentieth century. Companionship on the basis of equality was honored more in the breech than in fulfillment. Trial marriages and free love hurt women more than men. Careers and self-fulfillment did not mean an end to the politics of housework. As the Greenwich Village writer Floyd Dell admitted in his more candid moments, feminism appealed to many men because it promised new playmates.[61]

Such results were not altogether surprising to the most articulate feminist theorist of the period, the anthropologist Elsie Clews Parsons. A woman of substantial means, with secure connections to the New York social and financial elite, Parsons chafed from a very early age at the restrictions placed on her gender. Her rebelliousness made itself felt not only in her determination to earn an advanced degree, which she did under the direction of Franklin Giddings in sociology at Columbia in 1899, but also in her insistence to combine both settlement house and intellectual work with motherhood. In the early part of her career, Parsons's touchstone was Tarde, whose *Laws of Imitation* she translated into English in 1903. Parsons found Tarde congenial for a number of reasons. She relished his celebration of exceptional people, among whom she included herself. More importantly, she regarded Tarde as opening the possibilities for the multiplicity of the self. She read Tarde as a celebrant of modern life, who saw potential in the many objects that the self could draw upon to imitate. Parsons's respect for difference was only to grow with her later acquaintance with Franz Boas and the circle of anthropologists then just beginning to articulate cultural relativism, and with her own ethnographic investigations of the Indians of the Southwest. In a moment of optimism, she saw prolonged imitation that characterized metropolitan life as eventually resulting in the "purest and most potent individualism and a consummate sociability."[62]

Potent individualism and a consummate sociability were not likely to emerge from the social arrangements that the American middle class had made for itself, Parsons argued in her 1906 ethnographic discussion of her own tribe, *The Family*. By this time married to a New York congressman and political ally of Theodore Roosevelt, and a mother of two, Parsons caused a scandal by portraying the American family not as the cornerstone of civilization, but as tribal in its beliefs, superstitions, and customs. Like Gilman, Parsons saw the family as burdening women in their efforts to be initiators of social progress. In her criticism of family life, Parsons clearly drew upon Veblen, whose *Theory of the Leisure Class* she praised for its depiction of women as a caste. As a caste, middle-class women were dependent upon men for their status and sense of self. Much to the anguish of her reviewers, Parsons criticized the enforced lack of female usefulness, women's conspicuous leisure, their enslavement to possessions as the only source of identity, and their consequent failure to realize sex solidarity. Urging an end to prescribed status, Parsons outlined a plan in which women were self-creators, fully productive citizens who entered the marriage relationship only after a trial period.[63]

Parsons's controversial recommendations in the last eight pages of her book hinged on her growing awareness of the virtues of cultural relativism. Free selves need environments of toleration, Parsons averred. She had come to that position after having observed firsthand how, best intentions aside, settlement-house workers imposed their unbending sense of right and wrong on the communities with which they worked. Their judgments did not foster the local initiative they ostensibly wanted, but rather, local inhabitants' resignation and withdrawal. That experience had kindled in Parsons a sense that American society was more restrictive and tradition-laden than its official rhetoric made it out to be. In a series of prewar writings, she detailed how American cultural attitudes about sex limited the free and full development of the self. Parsons contended that women's embrace of sexual pleasure would have the effect of overcoming the dependency embedded in marriage. By seeking out pleasure in both trial and legal marriages, women could effect a meaningful separation of private desires from public parental responsibilities. Like other advocates of sexual freedom for women, Parsons believed that the end of patriarchal morals would open the way for male–female relations rooted in genuine affection, sincerity, and authenticity. In an optimistic mood, Parsons believed that such a strategy would enable women to avoid the traps that snagged nineteenth-century feminists, who found themselves on the defensive about sexuality. Far from a dedicated libertine, Parsons in 1906 saw trial marriage as a way to strengthen monogamy, developing, in the words of her biographer, complex, independent personalities fit to educate children. As monogamous relations were most conducive to emotional and intellectual development and health, it would be sensible to encourage early trial marriage, which would aim for permanency but would allow no-fault divorce.[64]

Parsons had no illusions about the difficulty in realizing her liberationist aspirations. Male self-interest, female acceptance of claims that their position bestowed upon them comfort and protection, and general fear of change of social habits thought to be natural all militated against immediate overturn of the sex regime. Even her erstwhile allies, the suffragists, were affected by cultural norms, Parsons noted. She was especially critical of arguments for suffrage that held female voting would inject various needed female qualities into the public sphere. Parsons had no objection to the pacific life (she was an ardent opponent of American entrance into World War I) or to nurturing (although her daughter often bemoaned her mother's failure to be interested sufficiently in her social launching). Rather, she was convinced that the association of women with essential qualities was the basis of the woman problem. Liberation, she countered, depended upon eliminating the category of woman itself. In this argument, which anticipated late-twentieth-century positions, Parsons drew upon her reading of Henri Bergson and Ernst Mach. From Bergson, she took the idea that restrictiveness had its origin in intellectual categories imposed on life to create unities. From Mach, whom she encountered through Robert Lowie and the anthropological circle around Boas, she gleaned an understanding of the ego as highly provisional, a heuristic device that temporarily allowed individuals to orient themselves. Her three books of the 1910s, *The Old-Fashioned Woman: Primitive Fancies about Sex* (1914), *Social Freedom* (1915), and *Social Rule* (1916), may well be taken as extended reflection on feminist multiplicity in which she aspired to sever the link between self and the female body but also to argue for a selfhood that was so fluid and changeable as to be almost evanescent. In all three books, Parsons set out to understand how human societies assigned selves to particular types of bodies.

Parsons held that human societies generally were deeply wary of anomalies and had a passion for classification. The unclassifiable, that which escaped boundaries, was a source of great anxiety. Yet because humans were indeed sociable creatures, they ran the risk of association with those different from themselves. Whereas her instructor Giddings had lauded consciousness of kind as a natural phenomenon, Parsons in fact saw it as socially constructed to the degree that men devised categories that enable them to classify and regulate those who are different. Social categories gratified the will to power, subjecting the classified individual to control by others. It was, therefore, "not hard to see why the classification of women according to sex has ever been so thorough and so rigid. As long as they are thought of in terms of sex and that sex the weaker or the submissive, they are subject by hypothesis to control. Just as soon as women are considered not as creatures of sex, but as persons, sexual regulations cease to apply. . . . Their womanliness must never be out of mind, if masculine rule is to be kept intact. . . . The more thoroughly a woman is classified the more easily is she controlled."[65] The goal of Parsons's feminism was to dismantle the classification system, creating a moment in which fluidity resisted the defining and controlling hand of patriarchy. If women lived in opposition to imposed categories and viewed these defining elements of the self as "only temporary expedients for practical purposes," the effect would be to open the self to anomalies. A society in which the "willingness to change [will be] a recognized virtue, a criterion in fact of morality" and differences in others "will no longer be recognized as troublesome or fearful" constituted Parsons's ideal.[66]

Parsons's goal of escaping classification was perhaps the fullest expression of multiplicity in the understanding of the self during the early twentieth century. Her rejection of foundations as constricting and her positing as ideal a self that was only contingent offered little room for a unitary principle. Her radical multiplicity took her further than either the social psychologists or the depth psychologists. The former challenged the singularity and self-creation aspect of the autonomous self, and the latter took on the notion of its unity, yet both retained elements of unity in their conceptions of the self. The social self, while in dialogue with others, was implicated in the common life. The Freudian self, divided between biology and culture, nonetheless played out universal dilemmas. Parsons, in contrast, aspired to a self that was permanently provisional, acting out incessant individuation.

Parsons's writings on the self were also part of her intervention in debates within the discipline of anthropology. At issue was whether psychology or structure should be the focal point of the investigation of peoples. Was the key to explanation of human interaction a matter of mental acts or material relations? Parsons opted for psychology in large measure because it better spoke to her sense of liberating multiplicity. Structure often meant historical determinism that left less room for adaptation. In this predilection, Parsons shared much with the architects of the social self. They construed "social" to designate a field of action in which an individual engaged with and was observed by others. Of special interest were the meanings that social actors assigned to the interaction. Cooley and Mead, for all their political commitments, were less disposed to treat the society as a set of structural and institutional arrangements that produced and deployed power. Those who undertook that task in the early twentieth century found the old syntheses almost as problematic as the notion of the autonomous, disembodied self. Such recognition gave a particular character to early-twentieth-century reform.

Notes

1. Valuable discussions of the notion of the self in the nineteenth century include John Burnham, "The Fragmenting of the Soul: Intellectual Prerequisites for Ideas of Dissociation in the United States," in *Paths into American Culture: Psychology, Medicine, and Morals* (Philadelphia: Temple University Press, 1988), 11–24; James E. Block, *A Nation of Agents: The American Path to a Modern Self and Society* (Cambridge, MA: Belknap Press of Harvard University Press, 2002); Philip Cushman, *Constructing the Self, Constructing America* (New York: Addison-Wesley, 1995); Karen Halttunen, *Confidence Men and Painted Women: A Study of Middle-Class Culture in America, 1830–1870* (New Haven, CT: Yale University Press, 1982); Daniel Walker Howe, *Making the American Self: Jonathan Edwards to Abraham Lincoln* (Cambridge, CT: Harvard University Press, 1997); John O'Donnell, *The Origins of Behaviorism: American Psychology, 1870–1920* (New York: New York University Press, 1985); Jeffrey Sklansky, *The Soul's Economy: Market Society and Selfhood in American Thought, 1829–1920* (Chapel Hill: University of North Carolina Press, 2002); and Cushing Stout, *Making American Tradition: Visions and Revisions from Ben Franklin to Alice Walker* (New Brunswick, NJ: Rutgers University Press, 1990).

2. The assumption of individualism in legal thought is documented in Lawrence Meir Friedman, *American Law* (New York: Norton, 1984); James Willard Hurst, *Law and Social Order in the United States* (Ithaca, NY: Cornell University Press, 1977); and, from a position that explicitly stresses the intellectual and philosophical, rather than the economic as such, roots, see the insightful Susanna L. Blumenthal, "Law and the Modern Mind: The Problem of Consciousness in American Legal Culture, 1800–1930" (PhD diss., Yale University, 2001). The standard discussions of literature are Lionel Trilling, *Sincerity and Authenticity* (Cambridge, MA: Harvard University Press, 1972); and M. H. Abrams, *The Mirror and the Lamp: Romantic Theory and the Critical Tradition* (New York: Oxford University Press, 1953), and *Natural Supernaturalism Tradition and Revolution in Romantic Literature* (New York: Norton, 1971).

3. See Ann Braude, *Radical Spirits: Spiritualism and Women's Rights in Nineteenth-Century America* (Boston, MA: Beacon Press, 1989); Philip Cushman, *Constructing the Self, Constructing America* (New York: Addison-Wesley, 1995); Donald B. Meyer, *The Positive Thinkers: Religion as Pop Psychology, from Mary Baker Eddy to Oral Roberts* (New York: Pantheon Books, 1980); Gail Thain Parker, *Mind Cure in New England from the Civil War to World War I* (Hanover, NH: University Press of New England, 1973); and Beryl Satter, *Each Mind a Kingdom: American Women, Sexual Purity and the New Thought Movement, 1875–1920* (Berkeley and Los Angeles: University of California Press, 1999).

4. For quite different valuations of such a view of the sovereign self, which nonetheless point to the centrality of property ownership, compare James Livingston, *Pragmatism and the Political Economy of Cultural Revolution, 1850–1940* (Chapel Hill: University of North Carolina Press, 1994), especially 45–81, and Sklansky, *Soul's Economy.* For the continued relevance of small property ownership in the Progressive Era, see Robert D. Johnston, *The Radical Middle Class: Populist Democracy and the Question of Capitalism in Progressive Era Portland, Oregon* (Princeton, NJ: Princeton University Press, 2003).

5. In addition to the Burnham, Cushman, Livingston, and O'Donnell volumes cited above, see Roy F. Baumeister, "How the Self Became a Problem: A Psychological Review of Historical Research," *Journal of Personality and Social Psychology* 52 (January 1987): 163–76; and John P. Hewitt, *Dilemmas of the American Self* (Philadelphia: Temple University Press, 1989), for discussions of the transformation of the American self at the turn of the century.

6. O'Donnell, *Origins,* 60–72

7. Ladd, quoted in ibid., 135.

8. James's contributions to evolutionary psychology are explored in John Burnham, "The New Psychology: From Narcissism to Social Control," in *Paths into American Culture: Psychology, Medicine, and Morals* (Philadelphia: Temple University, 1988), 69–93; John Burnham, *Paths into American Culture: Psychology, Medicine, and Morals* (Philadelphia: Temple University Press, 1988); John Burnham, "The Mind-Body Problem in the Early Twentieth Century," in *Paths into American Culture: Psychology, Medicine, and Morals* (Philadelphia: Temple University, 1988), 25–40; O'Donnell, *Origins;* Cynthia Russett, *Darwin in America: The Intellectual Response, 1865–1912* (San Francisco: W. H. Freeman, 1976).

9. Given recent defenses of torture, a Smithian view needs explain why this innate sympathy is often such a weak obstacle to objectively immoral behavior.

10. William James, *The Principles of Psychology* (Cambridge, MA: Harvard University Press, 1983), 281–84.

11. Josiah Royce, *Studies of Good and Evil: A Series of Essays upon Problems of Philosophy and of Life* (New York: D. Appleton, 1899), 215.

12. Ibid., 203. Royce continued the discussion in *The World and the Individual* (New York: Macmillan, 1900). The best discussion of Royce's views and the one on which my account has drawn is James Harry Cotton, *Royce on the Human Self* (Cambridge, MA: Harvard University Press, 1954). The definite biography is John Clendenning, *The Life and Thought of Josiah Royce* (Madison: University of Wisconsin Press, 1985).

13. Royce, *Studies of Good and Evil,* 210–34.

14. Ruth Leys, "Mead's Voices: Imitation as Foundation; or, the Struggle against Mimesis," in *Modernist Impulses in the Social Sciences,* ed. Dorothy Ross (Baltimore: Johns Hopkins University Press, 1994), 210–35.

15. For Jeffrey Sklansky, the erosion of contractual explanations was a regressive development that ultimately replaced discussions of material interests with analysis of collective mental life.

16. See Leys, "Mead's Voices." The feminist use of imitation-suggestion is discussed in Rosalind Rosenberg, *Beyond Separate Spheres: Intellectual Roots of Modern Feminism* (New Haven, CT: Yale University Press, 1982); and Desley Deacon, *Elsie Clews Parsons: Inventing Modern Life* (Chicago: University of Chicago Press, 1997).

17. Tarde, quoted in Leys, "Mead's Voices," 211. Royce concurred: "Take away a man's conscious longing for freedom, or for what he thinks to be his self-will, and you find, as his 'Hidden Self,' a being far more completely at the mercy of social suggestion than he had consciously supposed himself to be, a being whose whole nature, for the moment appears to be fulfilled in a deep dependence upon his social guides. And, in his dream, as it were, his hypnotist has now become the one representative of these guides. But the abiding lesson for us is that, as the hypnotizer is to his drowsy and plastic subject, so is society itself. Here . . . is for me the lesson of hypnotic research." Quoted in Leys, "Mead's Voices," 220.

18. Gerald Stanley Lee, "Lords of Attention," unpublished essay quoted in Gregory W. Bush, *Lord of Attention: Gerald Stanley Lee and the Crowd Metaphor in Industrializing America* (Amherst: University of Massachusetts Press, 1991), 123.

19. Dreiser did get a positive review from William Marion Reedy of the St. Louis *Mirror*, who was intrigued by "the strong hint of the pathetic in banale situations which is more frequent than often imagined." Reedy was especially taken with how the novel was both impossible and breathtakingly true. See, among others, Lester H. Cohen, "Locating One's Self: The Problematics of Dreiser's Social World," *Modern Fiction Studies* 23 (1977): 355–68; Livingston, *Pragmatism*, 137–57; and Walter Benn Michaels, "*Sister Carrie's* Popular Economy," *Critical Inquiry* 7 (1980): 373–90.

20. James Mark Baldwin, *The Individual and Society; or, Psychology and Sociology* (Boston, MA: Richard G. Badger, 1911), 21. Subsequent references in the text.

21. Charles Horton Cooley, *Human Nature and the Social Order* (New York: Charles Scribner's Sons, 1902), 36–37.

22. Ibid., 119. Emphasis original.

23. Baldwin, *Individual and Society*, 28–32, 118.

24. Ibid., 89. See also page 152 for his discussion of individual initiative as the basis of social progress.

25. On Cooley's politics, see Charles Hunt Page, *Class and American Sociology from Ward to Ross* (New York: Dial Press, 1940); and Marshall J. Cohen, *Charles Horton Cooley and the Social Self in American Thought* (New York: Garland, 1982).

26. Cooley, *Human Nature and the Social Order*, 63.

27. Ibid., 179–92, quotations from 184.

28. Cohen, *Cooley and the Social Self*, 139–50.

29. Mead, quoted in Rosenberg, *Beyond Separate Spheres: Intellectual Roots of Modern Feminism*, 134. For Mead's evaluation of Cooley, see George Herbert Mead, "Cooley's Contribution to American Social Thought," *American Journal of Sociology* 35, no. 5 (March 1930): 693–706. Mead commentary is large, and growing larger. See Mitchell Aboulafia, *The Cosmopolitan Self: George Herbert Mead and Continental Philosophy* (Urbana: University of Illinois Press, 2001), and *The Mediating Self: Mead,*

Sartre, and Self-Determination (New Haven, CT: Yale University Press, 1986); Ian Burkitt, *Social Selves: Theories of the Social Formation of Personality* (London: Sage, 1991); Gary A. Cook, *George Herbert Mead: The Making of a Social Pragmatist* (Urbana and Chicago: University of Illinois Press, 1993); and Hans Joas, *G. H. Mead, a Contemporary Re-Examination of His Thought* (Cambridge: Polity Press, 1985). For a discussion of the political dimensions, see also Dmitri Shalin, "G. H. Mead, Socialism, and the Progressive Agenda," *American Journal of Sociology* 93 (1988): 913–51; and Mary Jo Deegan, *Jane Addams and the Men of the Chicago School, 1892–1918* (New Brunswick, NJ: Transaction Books, 1986).

30. George Herbert Mead, "Social Consciousness and the Consciousness of Meaning," *Psychological Bulletin* 7 (1910): 403.

31. Mead, quoted in Burkitt, *Social Selves*, 36.

32. George Herbert Mead and Charles W. Morris, *Mind, Self, and Society from the Standpoint of a Social Behaviorist*, ed. Charles W. Morris (Chicago: University of Chicago Press, 1990), 69.

33. Mead lays out the argument in "The Social Self," especially pages 140-44, "The Mechanism of Social Consciousness," in *Selected Writings: George Herbert Mead*, ed. Andrew J. Reck, 134–41; and *Mind, Self, and Society*, 151–79.

34. Mead, quoted in Leys, "Mead's Voices," 219.

35. Leys, "Mead's Voices," 225.

36. Cohen, *Cooley and the Social Self*, 150–85.

37. For a different view of Mead's politics and the political potential of his work, see Shalin, "Mead and the Progressive Agenda."

38. Cushman, *Constructing the Self*, 119–25.

39. New Thought and the Emmanuel Movement are treated in Eric Caplan, *Mind Games: American Culture and the Birth of Psychotherapy* (Berkeley: University of California Press, 1998); Cushman, *Constructing the Self*, 118–49; Nathan G. Hale Jr., *The Beginnings of Psychoanalysis in the United States, 1876–1917* (New York: Oxford University Press, 1971), 225–49; Tom Lutz, *American Nervousness 1903* (Ithaca, NY: Cornell University Press, 1991); and Satter, *Mind*. James's article was his presidential address to the American Philosophical Association and was published in *Science*, N.S. 25 (No. 635), 321–32.

40. Hale, *Beginnings of Psychoanalysis*, 47–99. For a discussion of the rise and fall of the popularity of neurasthenia, see Lutz, *American Nervousness 1903*. Lutz suggests that neurasthenia disappeared for cultural reasons. As marginal populations began to show signs of neurasthenia, the diagnosis no longer had the cachet it had formerly possessed. Likewise, Lutz argues, it was very much at odds with the new consumerist ethos in which husbanding energy was replaced by self-expression.

41. Hale, *Beginnings of Psychoanalysis*, 133–41; and Jeffrey S. Brown, "Vitalism and the Modernist Search for Meaning: Subjectivity, Social Order, and the Philosophy of Life in the Progressive Era" (PhD diss., University of Rochester, 2001), 121–282.

42. John Burnham, "The Medical Origins and Cultural Use of Freud's Instinctual Drive Theory," in *Paths into American Culture: Psychology, Medicine, and Morals*

(Philadelphia: Temple University, 1988), 52–64; John Burnham, "The Progressive Era Revolution in American Attitudes toward Sex," in *Paths into American Culture: Psychology, Medicine, Morals* (Philadelphia: Temple University Press, 1988), 150–66; Hale, *Beginnings of Psychoanalysis*, 217–20; and Kevin White, *Sexual Liberation or Sexual License: The American Revolt against Victorianism* (Chicago: Ivan R. Dee, 2000).

43. Eli Zaretsky, *Secrets of the Soul: A Social and Cultural History of Psychoanalysis* (New York: Alfred A. Knopf, 2004).

44. Sigmund Freud, *Introductory Lectures on Psycho-Analysis*, ed. James Strachey, trans. James Strachey (New York: Norton, 1989); Freud's trip and its meaning are discussed in Hale, *Beginnings of Psychoanalysis*, especially 3–20, and Saul Rosenzweig, *Freud, Jung, and Hall The King-Maker: The Historic Expedition to America (1909), with G. Stanley Hall as Host and William James as Guest* (Seattle, Toronto, Bern, Gottingen: Hogrefe and Huber, 1992).

45. Hale, *Beginnings of Psychoanalysis*, 274–312; Warner Fite, "Psycho-analysis and Sex-Psychology," *Nation* 103 (August 10, 1916): 127–29.

46. Hale, *Beginnings of Psychoanalysis*, 401–8. See also John Demos, "Oedipus in America: Historical Perspectives on the Reception of Psychoanalysis in the United States," in *Ourselves/Our Past: Psychological Approaches to American History*, ed. Robert J. Brugger (Baltimore: Johns Hopkins University Press, 1971).

47. Hale, *Beginnings of Psychoanalysis*, 338–41.

48. Brown, Vitalism and the Modernist Search for Meaning, 181–85; Hale, *Beginnings of Psychoanalysis*, 368–81.

49. Brown, "Vitalism," 253–64.

50. Caplan, *Mind Games: American Culture and the Birth of Psychotherapy*; Hale, *Beginnings of Psychoanalysis*, 354; Eugene Taylor, "Jung before Freud, Not Freud before Jung: The Reception of Jung's Work in American Psychoanalytic Circles between 1904 and 1909," *Journal of Analytical Psychology* 43, no. 1 (January 1998): 97–114. White was especially influenced by Bergson's famous image in chapter 3 of *Mind and Memory* of the inverted memory cone.

51. See Ross Wetzsteon, *Republic of Dreams: Greenwich Village, The American Bohemia, 1910–1960* (New York: Simon and Schuster, 2002), chap. 1; and Mabel Dodge Luhan, *Movers and Shakers* (Albuquerque: University of New Mexico Press, [1936] 1985), 439–57.

52. This account of the sexual component of the nineteenth-century view of the self draws, among others, on Cushman, *Constructing the Self*, especially 105–6; Rosenberg, *Beyond Separate Spheres: Intellectual Roots of Modern Feminism*; and Cynthia Russett, *Sexual Science: The Victorian Construction of Womanhood* (Cambridge, MA: Harvard University Press, 1989).

53. Key's most influential work in the United States was *Love and Marriage; with a Critical and Biographical Introduction by Havelock Ellis* (New York: G. P. Putnam's Sons, 1911), and *The Woman Movement* (New York: G. P. Putnam's Sons, 1912).

54. Nancy Cott, *The Grounding of Modern Feminism* (New Haven, MA: Yale University Press, 1987).

55. Howe, quoted in ibid., 39. See also Judith Schwarz, *The Radical Feminists of Heterodoxy: Greenwich Village, 1912–1940* (Norwich, VT: New Victoria Publishers, 1986).

56. Jessie Taft, *The Woman Movement from the Point of View of Social Consciousness* (Chicago: University of Chicago Press, 1916), quoted in Rosenberg, *Beyond Separate Spheres: Intellectual Roots of Modern Feminism*, 141–42. The argument appeared in briefer form as "The Woman Movement and the Larger Social Situation," *International Journal of Ethics* 25 (April 1915): 328–45. Commentary on Taft's work can be found in Rosenberg and James Livingston, *Pragmatism, Feminism, and Democracy: Rethinking the Politics of American History* (New York: Routledge, 2001), 71–78.

57. Charlotte Perkins Gilman, *Herland* (New York: Pantheon, [1915] 1979). Gilman's life is detailed in Ann Lane, *To Herland and Beyond* (New York: Pantheon, 1990).

58. In addition to the Rosenberg, *Beyond Separate Spheres: Intellectual Roots of Modern Feminism*, White, *Sexual Liberation or Sexual License?*; and Donald B. Meyer, *Sex and Power the Rise of Women in America, Russia, Sweden, and Italy* (Middletown, CT: Wesleyan University Press, 1987), see Christine Stansell, *American Moderns: Bohemian New York and the Creation of a New Century* (New York: Metropolitan, 2000) for an insightful discussion of the centrality of feminism to Greenwich Village and the vicissitudes of sexual liberation. For the class dimension of sexuality in the Progressive Era, see Ruth Rosen, *The Lost Sisterhood: Prostitution in America, 1900–1918* (Baltimore: Johns Hopkins University Press, 1982).

59. Sanger's career is detailed in David Kennedy, *Birth Control in America: The Career of Margaret Sanger* (New Haven, CT: Yale University Press, 1970). See also Carole R. McCann, *Birth Control Politics in the United States, 1916–1945* (Ithaca, NY: Cornell University Press, 1994).

60. Cott, *Grounding of Modern Feminism*, 3–50.

61. Leslie Fishbein, *Rebels in Bohemia: The Radicals of* the Masses (Chapel Hill: University of North Carolina Press, 1982), 71–92; Douglas Clayton, *Floyd Dell: The Life and Times of an American Rebel* (Chicago: Ivan R. Dee, 1994), 72–77; and Elizabeth Wilson, *Bohemians: The Glamorous Outcasts* (New Brunswick, NJ: Rutgers University Press, 2000), 69.

62. Parsons, quoted in Deacon, *Elsie Clews Parsons*, 36–37.

63. Ibid., 47–54; Elsie Clews Parsons, *The Family: An Ethnographical and Historical Outline with Descriptive Notes, Planned as a Text-Book for the Use of College Lecturers and of Directors of Home-Reading Clubs* (New York: Putnam, 1906).

64. Deacon, *Elsie Clews Parsons*, 64–66.

65. Elsie Clews Parsons, *Social Rule: A Study of the Will to Power* (New York and London: G. P. Putnam's Sons, 1916), 54–56.

66. Elsie Clews Parsons, *Fear and Conventionality* (New York and London: G. P. Putnam's Sons, 1914), 209–17.

CHAPTER FOUR

~

Collectivities

The predominant nineteenth-century understanding of social life, like those of truth, morality, beauty, and the self, assumed at bottom society was a unified entity. Most social scientists and commentators held that human aggregates were rule-bound entities that demonstrated consistency, wholeness, and harmony, at least in the long run. Disorderly and centrifugal elements in the large scheme of things gave way to integrative and cohesive forces. In matters of politics, social life, and group dynamics, Americans generally favored theories that took equilibrium and unity as the norm. That inclination was present in racial thought and political economy, two of the major discourses upon which Americans drew to explain social structure. Racial thought looked to inherited, essential features to explain intragroup cohesion and group difference. Race endowed members with distinct traits and set limits on what group members could achieve. For its part, the discourse of political economy discerned natural law at work in the myriad acts of production, distribution, and consumption. As John Wenzler has demonstrated, the American variant maintained that there was an equivalence of moral and natural law. Distrustful of the "dismal science" of Malthus and Ricardo, Americans maintained that a bountiful nature would yield abundance rather than scarcity, leading to propositions that group interests complemented rather than clashed with one another.[1]

The momentous changes of the nineteenth century at first did little to shake the confidence in unity among its proponents. They often subsumed sundry alterations in social life under general principles of development. It was not uncommon for defenders of the notion of social wholeness to maintain that given the proper racial composition of a population or the reliance on the proper social arrangements, such as a respect for the working of an equilibrium-seeking market and an enlightened government that respected natural relations and liberated the energies of a free people, progress would follow. Many subscribed to notions of history in which material and moral improvement seemed written into the scheme of things. With its implication of evolutionary change, Lewis Henry Morgan's tripartite scheme of human divisions—savage, barbarian, and civilized—and Herbert Spencer's influential notion that heterogeneity in function spurred overall development were two such theories that discerned singular meaning in ostensibly disparate phenomena.[2]

Yet confidence in unity was less secure by the end of the century. Militating against confident assertions in harmony and progress was the persistence of such disturbances as economic depression, class conflict, and ethnic and racial clashes–disturbances that theory held should have dissipated. As University of Chicago sociologist Albion Small noted in his 1905 *General Sociology*, any efforts to recoup unity had much to take into account:

> The production of wealth in prodigious quantities, the machine-like integration of the industries, the syndicated control of capital and the syndicated organization of labor, the conjunction of interests in production and the collision of interests in distribution, the widening chasm between luxury and poverty, the security of the economically strong and the insecurity of the economically weak, the domination of politics by pecuniary interests, the growth of capitalistic world-politics, the absence of commanding moral authority, the well-nigh universal instinct that there is something wrong in our social machinery and that society is gravitating toward a crisis, the thousand and one demands for reform, the futility or fractionality of most ameliorative programs—all these are making men wonder how long we can go on in a fashion that no one quite understands and that everyone feels at liberty to condemn.[3]

Multiplicity in the social sciences took the form less of arguments for many societies (or no society at all) than contentions that the integrative rules were either not given or universal. As empirical evidence rendered the old truths about human aggregates less viable, an increasing number of analysts challenged the premise that disparate phenomena could be reduced to a single governing principle. Heterodox theories emerged in the relatively new discipline of sociology, anthropology, and economics that bracketed the assumption of unity, concentrated on the empirical, and advanced provisional and flexible conclusions. Those who advanced the new multiplicity interro-

gated such building blocks of the old social science as the primacy of economic class and the disinterestedness of government. The new emphasis on
context and contingency led pluralists to mount significant challenges
against both race theory and classical and neoclassical political economy.
Recognition of the limitations of totalizing explanations helped foster an unprecedented number of political and social reforms, as many activist Americans moved away from the dream of complete reconstruction of society that
they associated with the nineteenth-century utopian reform tradition.

Theories of the piecemeal did not, however, signal the demise of harmony
as a goal. The concentration on the sources of social unity was still central to
the investigation of social structure in the early twentieth century. Not only
did theories of multiplicity have to contend with refurbished versions of
racial thought and classical economics, but many investigators who accepted
the new importance of contingency and context still held out hope that harmony was achievable, or at least asymptotically approachable. For such leading lights of American sociology as Franklin Giddings, Edward Ross, and Albion Small, owing perhaps to the clerical backgrounds of many of their
families, the existence of moral bonds in keeping together social life amidst
conflict were crucial. Relying on institutions of association and commitment
to fellow feeling as countervailing forces in need of strengthening, they managed to square their understanding that the natural mechanisms of harmony
no longer operated with their hope that new sources could be found.

Transnational America

The one characteristic of human populations that nineteenth-century
thinkers thought guaranteed cohesion and unity was "race." The term dated
from the sixteenth century and denoted, as one modern-day scholar has put
it, "the biological transmission of innate qualities or all pervading natural
phenomenon, an awesome and mysterious primordial force, operating mechanically or organically, materially or spiritually, through all historical and
prehistorical time." Race created a common sense that individuals were
"linked in some eventless way by common blood, climate, soil, Kultur, language, mental disposition, or some commonplace feature."[4] Or as University
of Chicago anthropologist Frederick Starr articulated the matter in 1900,
"race characteristics are physical, mental, and moral."[5] The term, therefore,
defined a group by melding physical attributes and long-standing cultural
practices and attitudes. Race had outward markers—hair type, skin color—
that acted a synecdoche for something inward and essential that shaped
those who had belonged to the group. Given the sweep of the word *race*, it

was quite common during the nineteenth century to hear talk of the "Irish" or "Jewish" race. The reduction of races to the core five was a process that took well into the twentieth century to become generally accepted.

So defined, "race" made groups and individuals within them subject to natural laws. "Race" helped explain intragroup unity and intergroup difference. Many nineteenth-century versions of the concept possessed a certain flexibility in their ability to capture population change as well as population stability. The Lamarckian current insisted, for instance, that acquired characteristics were inheritable. Races developed, many writers contended, as a consequence of adaptation. Once developed to meet environmental demands, traits could be passed along. Lamarckian views knit the social and physical and nicely complemented views of progress, at least under some readings. While keeping notions of superiority and inferiority, Lamarckian racialism allowed for a dominant race to absorb others. Such views dampened much of the opposition to the initial upsurge in second-wave immigration in the 1870s, even as suspicions percolated about many of the customs and practices the immigrants brought with them. If newcomers were not capable of being assimilated, Lamarckian race theory held out the hope that their offspring could be domesticated. The muckraker Jacob Riis made such an assertion in his famous *How the Other Half Lives* (1890), when he urged environmental change so as to help Americanize newcomers.[6] Yet Lamarckian views had an underside. Absorption might not be positive. Habits might not drift upward. Pollution was a possibility—one that seemed more likely to Anglo-Americans as the nineteenth century came to a close.

Such worries demonstrate that "race" was nearly always a hierarchical designation, enabling invidious comparisons among groups. As the Lamarckian elements fell by the wayside, the race concept suggested permanency in traits, which went a long way to explain why some failed to advance or to conform to social norms. By the early twentieth century, racial traits were said to include, among other things, the propensity for violence and lust on the one hand and the inclination toward courage and culture on the other. So the University of Chicago's Starr could contend that environment alone could not explain behavior, particularly crime statistics. "Conditions of life and bad social opportunities cannot be urged in excuse. In Chicago the conditions of life for Italians, Poles, and Russians are fully as bad as for the blacks, but their criminality is much less. The difference is *racial*."[7] Where once so-called primitive peoples were thought to reason falsely, by the early twentieth century critics taxed them with lacking reasoning power altogether and capable of acting by instinct alone.

Under the impress of Darwinism, race was seen as a matter of survival. Groups that did not improve would invariably become extinct. Frederick L. Hoffman, whose *Race Traits and Tendencies of the American Negro* (1896) was awarded a prize by the American Economic Association, declared that the message of "moral statistics" was that reform was impossible. The proper course was to let degeneracy take its natural course. Hoffman's degeneracy thesis was not the only view of dark-skinned people. Republican-leaning anthropologists exhibiting Filipinos at the 1904 St. Louis World's Fair, on the other hand, decreed that the specimens should not wear their native loincloths, because such clothing signified incapacity for any civilization, a conclusion that ran counter to the stated justifications for American occupation. Less contested than the dress of the Filipinos was the extensive racial testing of peoples at the fair. Over 1,100 people had their bodies observed, measured, and ranked.[8] Racial measurements had propelled modern development in statistical technique undertaken by Karl Pearson (correlation coefficient) and Francis Galton (correlation regression), who fashioned such tools to bolster their insistence that racial inheritance was the central determinant of human aggregate behavior. Both Englishmen were firmly convinced that Great Britain was in danger of being drowned by unfit racial stock; for them, the United States was in an even more perilous condition. It was Galton's 1901 Huxley Lecture, "The Possible Improvement of the Human Breed under the Existing Conditions of Law and Sentiment," that founded the science of eugenics.[9]

"Race" increasingly became unalterable destiny with the eclipse of Lamarckian biology. The first blow was struck by August Weismann, who in *Uber die Vererberung* (1883) and *Vorträge über Descendenztheorie* (1902) located the heritable stuff in impermeable germ plasma. Weismann argued that the body was divided into germ cells that transmitted information, and somatic cells that did not. Aiding this challenge was the rediscovery of the work of Gregor Mendel. In showing that traits were either dominant or recessive, Mendel established a mechanism that ruled out acquired characteristics. For racialists, "race" was increasingly a matter of body, not language, history, and custom. Or rather, heredity was the determinant of group dynamics from which social entities flowed. Columbia anthropologist William Ripley wrote in his definitive *Races of Europe* (1899), "Race denotes what man is"; politics, caste, class, and religion merely denoted what men did.[10]

For all their insistence that race was biologically based destiny, analysts nonetheless had difficulty indicating its purview. All the measurement of noses, cranial volume, and nerve endings yielded no pure racial elements.

Figure 4.1. Racialism: Mrs. Wilkins teaches an Igorotte boy the cakewalk at Filipino exhibit at the 1904 St. Louis World's Fair. **Although under challenge from anthropologists who dismissed the concept of race as scientifically meaningless, racial ranking remained a staple of American social thought and practice.** (Source: Missouri Historical Society, St. Louis Louisiana Purchase Exposition, World's Fair Presentation Album 9, Plate 657)

James Ridpath conceded in 1893 that "few of those characteristics have been found to be sufficiently constant to furnish an invariable and scientific principle of division. In the present work the color of the human body has been taken as the most invariable criterion of race character, and on that fundamental fact, assisted by other physical traits and by intellectual peculiarities of development, particularly by the great fact of language, the classification has been made."[11] Ripley also conceded the absence of pure raciality. "Race, in the present state of things, is an abstract conception, a notion of continuity in discontinuity, of unity in diversity. It is the rehabilitation of a real but directly unattainable thing." Intermarriage, migration, mutation meant, he concluded, that "at the present time rarely, if indeed ever, do we discover a single individual corresponding to our racial type in every detail. It exists for us nevertheless."[12]

Ripley's insistence that race mattered, even if its components cannot be isolated and identified with any degree of certainty, suggested that the concept was honored as much for its ability to amalgamate disparate observations as for its precision. Dispelling its scientific basis was the consequence of the work of another Columbia anthropologist, Franz Boas. He had trained as a naturalist in his native Germany but also imbibed a great deal of the Herder-Humboldt tradition of cultural analysis that stressed the specific genius of peoples. Emigrating to the United States in 1886, Boas did fieldwork among the Indians of the Pacific Northwest and was employed at the Museum of Natural History before joining the Columbia faculty in 1896. Sometimes known as the founder of modern American anthropology and lauded for his commitment to the concept of culture, Boas came to that position tentatively, abandoning his racialist presumptions slowly. Nonetheless, his ability to put racial science to empirical test rather than take it on faith opened ways to talk about human differences without the teleology and biology upon which race talk rested. The anthropological circle that grew around him at Columbia challenged directly the outright essentialism of the concept of race and aspired to substitute in its place a discourse about peoples that jettisoned a singular way to evaluate groups for a pluralism that recognized multiple standards of evaluation.

Like many of his generation, Boas took note of physical characteristics of groups and often compared them on that basis. Well into the twentieth century, he was observing cranium size and implied that it was in some way related to mental acuity. He did not, however, specify the connection and was insistent that the racialist conclusions were unwarranted. His 1894 article "Human Faculty as Determined by Race" struck a new note in the discussion and was to provide the groundwork for a reevaluation of fixity in human

types. Boas contended first and foremost that no race has exclusive possession of any characteristic. Variation within groups was as great as variation
among them. The distribution of traits was diffuse. If African noses and fore-
heads resembled those of animals slightly more than whites, there were other
characteristics where the proximity was the other way around. He noted that
"overlapping of variations is significant in so far as it shows that the existing
differences are not fundamental."[13] Boas located two basic errors in racialist
thinking. The first was the equation of a level of civilization with the propensity or aptitude for civilization. It made more sense to account for differing
achievements on the basis of historical circumstances, which "appear to have
been much more potent in leading races to civilization than their faculty."
Because contingency weighed so heavily, we have no grounds "to assume that
one race is more highly gifted than the other" (229). But that assumption was
precisely what racialist unifiers did take for granted. In linking aptitude for
civilization to a greater perfectibility, they inferred, according to Boas, that
"every deviation from the white type is considered a characteristic feature of
a lower type" (222).

Boas made more thorough criticisms of racial typology in the twentieth
century, taking them apart from the inside, as it were. Working for the
United States Commission on Immigration, Boas set out to test whether immigrants retained type or assimilated after living in America. His criteria
were not customs but the very physical markers that were central to racial
analysis. Measuring the heads and bodies of high school students, Boas found
that children of immigrant parents born in the United States could, in fact,
change physical type. His most compelling piece of evidence, at least by prevailing terms of evaluation, had to do with what many anthropologists had
regarded as a key and stable indicator, the cephalic index. The cephalic index measured the ratio of skull length to width. The approach of children to
the norm, argued Boas, demonstrated that climate, diet, and living conditions were as significant, if not more so, in the determination of the person
as biological inheritance. Boas's findings did not eliminate race talk among
educated men and women (much less in the culture as a whole), but they did
make it harder to contend that race alone was the building block of human
type and the template from which human practices arose. In place of the centrality of race, Boas proposed a set of standards that fostered multiplicity and
which stressed the flexibility and open nature of human capabilities.

There were those then and subsequently who charged that Boas was motivated by the ulterior motive of defending the inflow of his fellow Jews.
Whatever the truth of the charge, Boas did strike out on a path that undid
the prevailing synthesis by separating biological traits from human practices.

His indictment of race originated in his long-held suspicion of the teleology embedded in racial science, particularly the universalist history on which it depended. Part of the stock argumentation of racial theorists was that similar traits found in populations widely dispersed and separated from one another could be explained only by the single cause of race. Boas countered that similarities among populations need not indicate similar makeup or inheritance. Like effects could have unlike causes. One certainly could not assume a racial connection because different peoples had the same technology, customs, or word for marriage. The similarities most likely flowed, Boas maintained, from contacts. In placing diffusion at the center of his accounts, Boas shifted the foundation of group characteristics from biology to history, and from a single cause to many. In light of the unstable relationship people had to their racial designation (Boas retained racial terminology throughout the first twenty years of the twentieth century, even as he shrank its purview), biology was not destiny. Europeans had no permanent monopoly on civilization or the ability to innovate and develop, a point Boas had made in 1894 when he claimed that European expansion "cut short the growth of the existing independent germs without regard to the mental aptitude of people among whom it was developing."[14]

In uncoupling race and practices, Boas did not adopt a full-blown cultural multiplicity. Racial thought had held human types were incompatible with one another. Its refutation opened the way to maintain that peoples could converge, a tack that Boas promoted throughout the early twentieth century. An ardent assimilationist, Boas in the early twentieth century was not a relativist as the term is currently understood. Although he avoided the judgmental distinctions that made one people inferior to another, he was not hesitant about labeling certain *practices* primitive or civilized. No group had a monopoly on the best ways of living, but Boas had no doubt in the prewar years that some ways were more productive for humans than others. Since physical differences were relatively unimportant in determining capacities of individuals, Boas fervently argued that neither German Jews nor Americans of African descent should be or could be denied access to the dominant cultural resources of their respective countries. In light of the possibilities of convergence, which were greater as contacts and interchange increased, Boas held that ethical solidarity was the only logical and humane response to the problem of difference. He articulated the point in his 1906 talk at Atlanta University, which informed a predominantly black audience (including W. E. B. Du Bois) of historic African achievement hitherto unknown to white and black alike. Those whose ancestors built kingdoms and worked iron when Europeans lagged behind surely were capable of being productive citizens in the United States.[15]

The inability of the concept of race to acknowledge multiplicity prompted many analysts to search for an alternative explanation for both differences among groups and cohesion within them that did not have its biological or evolutionary connotations. By 1920, the term that was the most viable alternative was "culture," a word well known for having myriad meanings. On the one hand, Americans were well acquainted with the Arnoldian notion of the "best that has been thought and said in the world." Culture on this meaning constituted an attainment and differentiated the cultivated from the uncultivated. Culture freed humans from control by such outside forces as nature or instinct. On the other, the German *Kultur* connoted the particular spirit of a people and the patterns of thought and behavior that characterized them. All peoples qualified as having culture, although some were clearly superior to others. Herder, for one, deliberately posited *Kultur* in opposition to the French term *civilisation*, which connoted polish rather than essence and universality rather than particularity. The social science term, which drew heavily on the German formulation, emerged haphazardly in the first decade of the twentieth century. Boas had used the concept as a counter to evolutionary understandings, but he did not fully spell out the concept until *Race, Language, and Culture* (1930). By that time, he was writing in response to his students' formulations, which in turn were taken from hints he littered throughout lectures and articles. The number of definitions proliferated to such an extent that by midcentury A. L. Kroeber and Clyde Kluckhohn found over fifty different ones.[16]

Although emphases differed, *culture* as used by early-twentieth-century social scientists highlighted a set of common understandings, values, beliefs, and orientations. Jettisoning the singular determining power of nature in race theory, Boas and his students deployed the culture concept to emphasize how different peoples responded to nature in diverse ways. Boas maintained that people were not born with their culture fully formed; they grew up and into it. In treating culture in pragmatic fashion as a tool to solve problems, anthropologists constructed the concept as the intersection of preconception and situation. Because the activities that counted as culture were the consequence of particular, situated peoples, each with their own experiences, needs, and values, cultures were generally speaking unique. Formed by chance contact and creative response to environmental challenges, cultures were, therefore, not specific instances of general rules. Where nineteenth-century anthropologists used race in the plural and culture in the singular, the Boasian school that included Robert Lowie, Edward Sapir, Alfred Kroeber, Elsie Clews Parsons, and Alexander Goldenweiser reversed the plural and singular and the valence on each term. For nineteenth-century racial thinkers, culture was a uniform ideal against which peoples were measured. For social scientists of the early twentieth century, cultural practices could be understood only in reference to the context in which they occurred. Where nineteenth-century race-based thinkers saw deviation from the norm as the basis of judgment, early-twentieth-century social scientists saw that same diversity as testimony that humanity shared the ability to make a culture.[17]

In linking culture to contingency, Boasians and like-minded analysts also rejected much of the hierarchy that accompanied racial assessments. The task was less to rank peoples than to understand the contingencies that went into making their beliefs and practices. Boas maintained in his *Mind of Primitive Man* (1911) that nonindustrialized, non-Westernized peoples do not lack reason or reason incompletely, but rather reason by a different set of rules that fit their circumstances and history. In Boas's telling, primitives demonstrated the whole gamut of thinking processes. They abstracted, condensed, and deduced just as Western peoples did, but they did so from different premises.[18] The political scientist Arthur Bentley had a similar point in mind when he accused Herbert Spencer of "civilization bias." He meant that Spencer took "the content of feelings as they are found today and set them up as the standards of feelings for all races and all times." That bias had enabled Spencer to proclaim that sympathy was necessary for the progress from primitivism to modern industrial societies. Bentley retorted that Spencer had simply created an abstract concept by fiat and had misunderstood the meanings that concern for others meant in specific circumstances. Indeed, Bentley charged, one might in fact argue with equal validity the opposite. The "primitive clan" will be "bloodthirsty in war but never lets its humblest member suffer from hunger while a luckier mouth is filled," a fact that rendered sympathy incapable of explaining anything, especially in light of the disregard often shown the suffering of the modern-day poor.[19] By the end of the Great War, Boas and his circle had begun articulating a view in which judgment of a culture depended upon the terms, standards, and circumstances of the culture itself.

If early-twentieth-century anthropologists delighted in debunking contentions of general laws governing humanity, many did regard individual cultures, on the other hand, as displaying unity. To talk of a culture was to subsume a tremendous number of diverse activities under the rubric. For culture to substitute for race as a source of group cohesion, its tools must be understood in a reasonably similar way by the people who deploy them. Clearly, language was a crucial shared resource. One could hardly be said to be culturally French if one did not understand the language. Yet language was hardly sufficient to define a culture. Making a culture from the values, ideals, rituals, and relationships that a group of people hold requires that the composite of elements mesh, at least in some way. An American culture, as opposed to American society or the American nation, implies a common orientation. Extracting that orientation was no easy task. Even the least complex human group presented to analysts a wealth of material. Indeed, one reason that many early-twentieth-century anthropologists rejected complexity–simplicity judgments was their understanding that so-called primitive societies had more detailed customary and ritualistic behavior than do advanced ones. Michael Elliott has noted that most of Boas's work consisted of detailed field notes, which Elliott contends constituted Boas's reluctance to grant primacy to any particular set of activities as the basis of what allowed a people to identify themselves as such.[20]

How unified and integrated a culture was remained at issue. Writing in 1920, Lowie lampooned the "superstitious reverence" afforded Western culture, since it was "a planless, hodgepodge," a thing of "shreds and patches."[21] In *Culture and Ethnology* (1917) and *Primitive Society* (1920), Lowie laid out a view of culture that stressed the unintegrated, fragmented quality of the cultural entity. Others turned to a people's spirit or genius as the crucial point of unity. Edward Sapir explicitly argued the position. Best known in this regard for his 1924 article "Culture, Genuine and Spurious," Sapir mixed many of the latent facets of the emerging social science definition with influences from such Young American critics as Randolph Bourne and Van Wyck Brooks, with whom he socialized in the 1910s. In 1919, he began a trial run on the formulation in the *Dial* with "Civilization and Culture." Separating culture as a collection of social facts from the Arnoldian culture of taste and refinement, he proposed a version of culture as the most characteristic aspects of the social group. As he put it in the 1924 version, culture is made up of "the general attitudes, views of life and specific manifestations of civilization" that bestow upon a "particular people its distinctive place in the world." By concentrating on the spiritual and integrative functions of culture, Sapir's definition envisioned culture as ideally producing harmony. Those that failed to do so, that failed to express something distinctive about a people, were less likely to become a genuine culture in Sapir's view.[22]

Sapir's notion that culture expressed the genius of a people turned on what that genius was. His emphasis on unity often led him to a view of some cultural practices as authentic and pure, and others as corrupt. Sapir did not hesitate to label some cultures better than others based on his criteria of the degree to which prevailing norms allowed for both harmony between individual and society and full individual expression. Culture resolved conflict, integrating men and women with their society, in Sapir's view. Reflecting a concern of the ways in which industrial life ripped asunder those patterns of life that warmly embrace individuals and left in its wake alienated and divided lives, Sapir ironically mirrored Arnold in his hope that genuine, authentic, and meaningful culture constituted an antidote to anarchy. Like Brooks and Bourne, Sapir had little use for the products of mass culture. Suspicious of their quality, Sapir doubted they could genuinely provide meaningful experiences that overcame the tendency toward alienation or mindless conformity in modern life.[23]

Judgments of authenticity constantly attended discussions of culture. In large measure, the inclination to regard each part as exemplifying the basic or essential principles made it easy to see culture as a kind of person writ large, possessing average or typical traits. Since culture was above and beyond individuals, it might also assume the role of an imprinting device. Alfred Kroeber articulated the rudiments of this argument in 1917 when he introduced his idea of the "superorganic," a term he chose to avoid the Germanic connotations of "culture." Sapir and Lowie, among others, rejected the argument on the grounds that the notion of impersonal patterning smacked of an unwarranted determinism and that Kroeber failed to provide a mechanism by which this entity acted upon humans.[24] His effort, however, pointed to the way in which culture could become alienated from the people who lived it and take on an impersonal, singular quality.

The culture concept was particularly meaningful to those who were committed to reconstructing American nationality in light of mass immigration. In contrast to such fin-de-siècle flaneurs as Henry Harland, editor of the *Yellow Book*, who went in search of the exotic, twentieth-century pluralists saw new resources for a new community. Jane Addams predicated her Hull House work on the supposition that the community that she and the residents of the Nineteenth Ward were building together required a respect for the cultural resources that immigrants brought. Aware that urban, industrial life negated the viability and meaning of much that immigrants brought with them, she aimed in Boas's terms for assimilation—not the imposition of new practices but providing information for the creative response to environmental challenges. Many of the activities of Hull, such as the Labor Museum and the national celebrations, were designed to link past and present by reconstructing experience. Assuming that "the things that make men alike are finer and better than the things that keep them apart" and could overcome "the less essential differences of race, language, creed, and tradition," Addams even hoped that the newcomers to American culture, whom she often referred to as "cosmopolitan," might show Americans a way out of their racial problems. "Doubtless these difficulties would be much minimized in America, if we faced our own race problem with courage and intelligence, and these very Mediterranean immigrants might give us valuable help. Certainly they are less conscious than the Anglo-Saxon of color distinctions, perhaps because of their traditional familiarity with Carthage and Egypt."[25]

Pluralism took other forms in the first two decades of the twentieth century. Some retained a familial relationship to the romantic notion of the premodern as more natural and authentic. In "Democracy versus the Melting-Pot" (1915), Horace Kallen made multiplicity itself the best hope for American life. Kallen worried that the various Americanization campaigns had boiled out group distinctiveness, leaving in their wake a rather bland morass of standardized, deracinated individuals attuned only to accumulation and conspicuous display. Celebrating ethnic groups for their premodern traits, Kallen viewed those traditions as an obstacle to massification and to a politics of class hatred. He offered ethnic enclaves as an alternative to the disharmony and commercialization of modern life. These enclaves, Kallen contended, would function like an orchestra in which each ethnic group "is the natural instrument, its spirit and culture are its theme and melody, and the harmony and dissonances and discords of them all make the symphony of civilization."[26] Kallen was unclear, however, on who wrote the score and who was the conductor. His equation of ethnicity with the premodern is a reminder that early-twentieth-century pluralism did not always jettison stereotypes or dispense with notions of purity.

A more sustained argument for multiplicity could be found in Randolph Bourne's "Trans-National America" (1916). Written at the height of the campaign to suppress hyphenated Americanism, the essay and its companion, "The Jew and Trans-National America," took direct aim at those arguments for ethnic purity that rested upon a notion that immigrants had no inherent talent. Denying a people had either a monopoly on a given quality or were so accomplished as to not need an infusion of new ideas and values, Bourne saw pluralism as a mode of democratic practice that could be achieved when Americans dropped the notion that the Anglo-Saxon was the norm and others were deviant. If "freedom means a democratic cooperation in determining the ideals and purposes and industrial and social institutions of a country, then the immigrant has not been free, and the Anglo-Saxon element is guilty of just what every dominant race is guilty of in every European country: the imposition of its own culture upon the minority peoples."[27] Pointing to the problems of the white South and the "tasteless, colorless fluid of uniformity" of the upper Midwest, Bourne, a New Jersey native who had the chauvinism of his adopted home, New York, asserted that Anglo-Saxons simply had no standing to claim superiority.

Like Kallen, Bourne saw commercialized culture as a threat to the functioning of the republic. Believing that culture was necessary to root people and give them resources, Bourne criticized those who were immersed in mass culture as "cultural half-breeds," a phrase that indicates how deeply embedded the rhetoric of purity was for even Bourne. Like Sapir (and Arnold), Bourne worried that "disintegrating nuclei" and "flotsam and jetsam" would result in anarchy. Bourne's transnationalism was a cosmopolitanism in which cultures federated through a transnational weave, combining threads of "living and potent cultures." Bourne envisioned less a melting in which the old is boiled away than an overlapping of autonomous cultures in which people reflected "the peculiar gifts and temperament of the people." Yet his was not a backward-looking celebration of the earthiness and authenticity of the peasantry, since transnational weaving required acclimation and adjustment. The weave, he conjectured, would be the equivalent of a rich and varied college catalogue. Bourne hoped his formulation would allow for dual and triple loyalties, shifting under circumstances, and construct the United States as the cosmopolitan nation par excellence. Yearning for unity in multiplicity, Bourne asserted that the "attempt to weave a wholly novel international nation out of our chaotic America will liberate and harmonize the creative power of all these people and give them the new spiritual citizenship."[28]

Black Americans were less interested in a new spiritual citizenship than in claiming the rights of the old political one. Becoming full-fledged participants in American life meant negotiating the ways in which race and culture talk impinged on their lives. In contrast to the sometimes insouciant playfulness with which Greenwich Village bohemians talked of culture, black Americans were faced with the more serious task of challenging a racism that became increasingly malevolent in the late nineteenth and early twentieth centuries. The predominant discourse of race had branded black Americans as incapable of assimilation, inherently inferior, prone to immorality and even extinction. Although there was little chance that black Americans would be able to escape adverse judgments of their racial identity by whites, race talk did hold one advantage for Americans of African descent. It provided a basis for group solidarity and an assertion of difference from whites. The paradigm of culture had its virtues for the oppressed as well. It contested judgments of their inferiority and stressed their adaptability. Throughout the hard-pressed years of the early twentieth century, black discourse drew on both race and culture in efforts to work out viable responses to difficult times.

Although debated among black and sympathetic white intellectuals, the matter was not purely an intellectual one. Nor was it one in which Americans of color had free choice. In *Plessy v. Ferguson* (1896), the Supreme

Court upheld a racial understanding of full citizenship rights. "Legislation," held the majority opinion, "is powerless to eradicate racial instincts, or to abolish distinctions based upon physical differences, and the attempt to do so can only result in accentuating the difficulties of the present situation. . . . If one race be inferior to the other socially, the constitution of the United States cannot put them upon the same plane." For the Court, the theoretical right to vote (political rights) was all the Constitution could grant; equal access to public accommodations, schools, hospitals and any other place where the races might mix was not required.[29] The lone dissenter, Justice John Harlan, predicted that the decision would "stimulate aggressions more or less brutal on the rights of colored citizens." As the intensification of segregation, the lynching, and the Wilmington, Memphis, Atlanta, Springfield (Illinois), East St. Louis, and Chicago riots demonstrated, the years following *Plessy* were violence-filled. In light of the escalating violence, the cultural task for black Americans was to find weaknesses in race discourses. At times, they relied on the Boasian strategy of separating race from culture, petitioning for inclusion. At others, they exerted claims on the basis of difference.

The race–culture tension was brilliantly captured in James Weldon Johnson's *Autobiography of an Ex-Colored Person* (1912). Johnson was the first African American admitted to the Florida bar, a school principal, lyricist of "Lift Every Voice and Sing," and executive secretary of the NAACP from 1920 to 1931. His novel, which was published anonymously and so "passed" as an autobiography, is itself a tale of passing. A talented, light-skinned African American composer and pianist is in the South to hunt up musical material that he intends to turn into a classical composition. His mastery of Arnoldian culture enables him to contemplate becoming the nation's first black classical composer and demonstrating in the process that race and culture were not identical endowments. That goal is derailed when he witnesses a black man burned alive in the town square. The event prompts him to pass (or more precisely, not to dissuade anyone from assuming he is white), to avoid the "label of inferiority pasted across my forehead." His decision, the narrator tells us, was motivated by shame "at being identified with a people that could with impunity be treated worse than animals. For certainly the law would restrain and punish the malicious burning alive of animals." In Johnson's novel, neither race nor culture reliably marked identity or separated people from one another with absolute certainty. Efforts such as lynching to enforce purity had the ironic effect of prompting those who faced the possibility of death to manipulate the divisions.[30]

Passing was not an option for an entire people, of course, and dealing with the multiplicity of race and culture was a task facing black leaders of the period. Booker T. Washington's strategy of self-development combined racial pride with racial assumptions. On the one hand, Washington was hopeful that black improvement would eventuate in changes in white attitudes. In his famous Atlanta Exposition Speech in 1896, Washington had conceded that in social matters there was no need for mixing and no need for black people to undertake intellectual pursuits, which under the circumstances of segregation seemed unlikely to allow them to prosper. In the speech and his autobiography, *Up from Slavery,* Washington accepted black cultural inferiority, which he ascribed to such historical circumstances as slavery and African origins. His Lamarckianism, however, led him to believe that the differences between races were not permanent. Christianity and the work ethic civilized barbarous people, and he urged pride in accomplishment and self-sufficiency as ways to build strong black communities. He hoped that such success would undercut the degeneracy theories.[31] By the middle of the first decade of the twentieth century, however, Washington had altered his historical perspective, which in turn increased his celebration of the distinctive contributions of his people. Where once he had accepted notions of African inferiority, an acquaintance with the new anthropology led him to maintain that Africa was the cradle of civilization.

Washington's great rival for leadership among black Americans, W. E. B. Du Bois, struggled with the meaning of race as well. In 1897, Du Bois penned

Figure 4.2. The brilliant W. E. B. Du Bois in 1919. **Editor of *The Crisis,* the journal of the National Association for the Advancement of Colored People, Du Bois struggled with the meaning of race during the first two decades of the twentieth century. At times he accepted it as a meaningful biological designation that allotted similar characteristics to like peoples; at others, he viewed race as a convention intended to create artificial distinctions and invidious comparisons. (Source: Library of Congress, LC-USZ62-16767)**

"Conservation of Races" in which he treated races as agents of history. Each race had its own history and its own capabilities. Du Bois did indeed criticize the biological definition of race, on grounds that "great as is the physical unlikeness of the various races of men their likenesses are greater," contending that "color, hair and bone go but a short way toward explaining the different roles which groups of men have played in Human Progress." At the same time, however, Du Bois deployed many of the categories of racial thinking, using the language of essence and talking of racial solidarity as if it had a biological basis that separated peoples. He envisioned human history that brought about race differentiation as a "growth, and the great characteristic of this growth has been the differentiation of spiritual and mental differences between great races of mankind and the integration of physical differences." How race and culture meshed was crucial in charting the future of the nation and black identity. "Am I an American or am I a Negro? Can I be both? Or is it my duty to cease to be a Negro as soon as possible and be an American? If I strive as a Negro, am I not perpetuating the very cleft that threatens and separates Black and White America? Is not my only possible practical aim the subduction of all that is Negro in me to the American?"[32] That choice between a national allegiance in which race should not matter (but all too frequently did) and embracing the seemingly unbridgeable differences that race defined were behind his famous question in Souls, "How does it feel to be a problem?" Du Bois saw that problem affecting not only black political and social prospects, but black consciousness as well. Black Americans lived with a permanent sense of division, the consequence not of their racial inheritance but of how their racial lives had been shaped by history. Blacks lived both within and outside the Veil, his figure for the ways in which blacks remained unseen, unacknowledged, and unknown. Blacks knew and even at times shared American understandings, but their legal separation made them outsiders without a firm sense of belonging.[33]

In Meadean terms, black men and women knew themselves only from their reflection from whites. Yet Du Bois pointed out how distorted the reflection was, in that it obscured a recognition of African American contributions in expression, creativity, and work. The tension between Negro and American was not, Du Bois concluded in Souls, fully resolvable. Black Americans could not opt for one pole or the other. They might accept their dual nature and effect a Hegelian synthesis in which their new identity, steeled by struggle, would become more knowing and more vital. Du Bois's synthesis was simultaneously racial and cultural. "He (the Negro) would not Africanize America, for America has too much to teach the world and Africa. He would not bleach his Negro soul in a flood of white Americanism, for he knows that Negro blood has a message for the world. He simply wishes to make it possible for a man to be both a Negro and an American, without being cursed and spit upon by his fellows, without having the doors of Opportunity closed roughly in his face."[34]

As the years went on, Du Bois talked less about the meaning of Negro blood and felt less torn by the conflict between being a Negro and being an American. The escalating riots and lynching and his own engagement with Boas generated a new set of particularist claims and raised growing doubts about Americanism.[35] In "The Souls of White Folk," written for the *Independent* in 1910, Du Bois maintained that racial differences were at bottom cultural ones. Whites, he contended, had made the paleness of their bodies "fraught with tremendous and eternal significance." The privilege of white skin, Du Bois maintained, was so ingrained that even liberal philanthropists defended it, charging blacks with impudence when they showed no deference. Five years later in his sweeping history of dark-skinned people in *The Negro* (1915), Du Bois rejected race as a meaningful category. Asserting that "no scientific definition of race is possible," he accepted that there were "differences, and striking differences . . . between men and groups of men." In good Boasian fashion, however, he maintained that "they fade into each other so insensibly that we can only indicate the main divisions of men in broad outlines."[36] No absolute physical line marked out "the darker part of the human family." Emphasizing a shared history to a far greater extent than he had in "Conservation," Du Bois argued that those who could trace their ancestry to Africa were inheritors of special spiritual gifts that had resulted in specific cultural forms. Showing his "nationalist" side, Du Bois argued for the defense and extension of those forms as the basis of political organization. Justice was less a matter of universal rights and even less a matter of natural ones.

> There is slowly arising not only a curiously strong brotherhood of Negro blood throughout the world, but the common cause of the darker races against the intolerable assumptions and insults of Europeans has already found expression. Most men in this world are colored. A belief in humanity means a belief in colored men. The future world will, in all reasonable probability, be what colored men make it. In order for this colored world to come into its heritage, must the earth again be drenched in the blood of fighting, snarling human beasts, or will Reason and Good Will prevail? That such may be true, the character of the Negro race is the best and greatest hope; for in its normal condition it is at once the strongest and gentlest of the races of men: "Semper novi quid ex Africa!"[37]

Race talk was unifying in that it applied a single standard to explain group differences and provided a ready-made answer to the problem of solidarity. Yet it had also introduced a crippling hierarchy that consigned people to place and mapped their possibilities on the basis of certain key signifiers such as hair type or skin color. Culture talk presented a countervision by pointing to multiple causes for the lack of similarity among peoples and to the possession of spiritual resources by all groups. As such, it opened the possibility of less hierarchical ways to talk about differences. To defeat the racialism that fastened "intolerable assumptions and insults" upon people of color, Du Bois pinned his hope on peoples linked through a long history of shared practices and belief. Their success, Du Bois contended, might well augur a new kind of unity to replace the defective old one.

Order and Change

The depression and political crises of the 1890s, as tumultuous as they were, did not banish notions of harmony from American social thought. They did, however, spur a recognition that the sources of harmony were not as fully natural as previous discourses had made them. If strikes, overproduction, and corporations were "disturbing agents," they were exogenous factors that had become fairly embedded in the social landscape. An account of their effects and the ways that they transformed rules were clearly on the agenda. For some, like Thorstein Veblen, these conditions of industrial life were the centerpiece of a new economic science. Holding that harmony was no longer possible without the overthrow of what he called the price system—the system of private ownership and profit seeking, Veblen was constantly aiming to find ways to square humanity's biological endowments and its social arrangements with the constancy of change. At times, Veblen's multiplicity was such that he fretted that even such a deep transformation would not resolve an essential conflict between human acts and intentions and a changing and often resistant environment.

Few shared Veblen's evaluation of the state of existing social life or his commitment to a broad-ranging transformation. Most social analysts rejected those goals as too universal and abstract and too neglectful of the sources of health that were currently available for use. Given their attention to the moral bonds that held society together, many social scientists evaluated the social problem of the late nineteenth century as the weakness of institutions of social interaction and the limited intensity of fellow feeling. Reform, therefore, would be well served by strengthening them. Even William Graham Sumner, the author of the "Absurd Attempt to Make the World

Over," who did not minimize the centrality of struggle in social life, envisioned ways in which social norms acted as a brake on conflict. Sumner had little use for activist government, holding that intervention for one was an injustice to another social agent. For all his celebration of the market as an impartial dispenser of justice, his late-nineteenth- and early-twentieth-century writings also contained the recognition of the power of nonmarket folkways that enabled obedience to authority and social solidarity.[38]

Most of the social theorists whose work set the parameters of twentieth-century multiplicity did not share Sumner's belief that competition was a mechanism of equilibrium. Albion Small saw it as something of a destabilizing element, primarily on moral or ethical grounds. He regarded the clash between employers and employees as real, but a mistaken apprehension of the social situation. At stake were less material differences that radicals saw as permanently dividing the social life of industrial capitalism than competing ethical approaches. Rejecting laissez-faire as selfish anarchy, and socialism as amoral stifling of individuality, Small held out the hope that conscious, collective purpose would involve a rational commitment to the common good. "We find the center of conflict which is the life of society, not in perpetual trial of strength between permanently defined classes, but we see the merging of these earlier alignments into incessant reassortment of classes in perpetual conflict for moral control of the terms of co-operation." If only men and women would discern their interest in cooperation, in taking the best of enterprise and the best of collective endeavor, the synthesis would result in "more and better life by more and better people."[39] There was, however, no guarantee that people would realize their interest or that realizing it, they could effect it.

Whether integration of individuals and society was simply a matter of cooperation was a central question posed in W. I. Thomas's and Florian Znaniecki's *The Polish Peasant in Europe and America* (1918–1920). Thomas was born a minister's son and lived most of his youth in Tennessee. Educated at the University of Tennessee, he spent 1888 in Germany, studying ethnology. At the University of Chicago, where he taught in the first sociology department in the United States, Thomas concentrated on studies of racial and gender problems. His 1907 study, *Sex and Society*, was one of the first to dispute hierarchical conclusions typical of biological approaches to the capabilities of men and women. Thomas's success with empirical, comparative work rather than the grand theorizing common to the fledgling discipline earned him the directorship of the Helen Culver Fund for Race Psychology. Culver, who endowed Hull House, gave Thomas a grant of $50,000 to study immigrant groups in Europe and America, "to determine as far as possible what

relation their home mores and norms had to their adjustment and malad-
justment in America."[40] In the course of the project, he met Znaniecki, a
Polish nationalist working with the Polish Emigrants Protective Association.
In 1914, Znaniecki moved to Chicago, where they wrote the famous methodological statement that served as an introduction.

The methodological statement was designed to carve out a mode of investigation that avoided both excessive psychologizing (that is, methods that
held that deep-seated and unalterable states of mind explained acts of immigrants) and objectivist accounts that explained immigrant and working-class
behavior by material deprivation and the absence of key institutions or values. The latter was especially common in the early twentieth century. Settlement houses and the famous Survey of Pittsburgh, which included investigations of some seventy investigators, including the radical Crystal
Eastman and the reformist economist John Commons, detailed the physical
nature of poverty and the legal and institutional environment in which the
urban poor lived. What such surveys had failed to register, Thomas and
Znaniecki maintained, was the subjective experience of those conditions—
the meanings that actors ascribed to those conditions, and how those meanings influenced actions. Rejecting the notion that poverty automatically led
to deviant behavior by the sheer weight of its existence, the two set out to
demonstrate that a better explanation could be built by showing how subjective and objective factors affected each other. To that end, they differentiated values from attitudes. The first were the set of prevailing group rules
about how individuals were to act. These were any "social datum" that serves
as an object of meaningful activity. Values confront individuals "as it were,
from the outside." Such rules "constitute with regard to their objective significance a certain number of more or less connected and harmonious systems which can be generally called *social institutions*." The totality of institutions constituted the social organization of the group. Attitudes, on the other
hand, were "a process of individual consciousness which determines real or
possible activity of the individual in the social world." Attitudes were acquired orientation toward values. They were inclinations and meaning that
were always in the process of being defined by individuals, not preexisting
dispositions. Social action was the result of the interplay of attitudes and values, the outcome of which was never predetermined.[41]

In studying the mutual action between individual understandings and
group norms, Thomas and Znaniecki detailed how individual Poles who em-
igrated to the United States experienced what they termed social disorganization. By "social disorganization," they had in mind less diseased or deformed attitudes and the absence of values than the lack of fit between norms

and acts. Or, as they put it, a "decrease of the influence of existing social rules of behavior upon individual members of the group." The story they told was how a set of values designed to keep society together through the direct supervision of individuals gave way to ones that counted on society cohering through the exercise of voluntaristic, rational attitudes. The authors created a portrait of a traditional Poland in which "the marriage group" exercised control over individual behavior, with an eye toward guaranteeing family solidarity and mutual help. The group judged acts on how well they served the well-being of the group as a whole. The emphasis in Polish social life in the Old Country on obligation, rather than individual accumulation or achievement, created a psychology of dependence and gave behavior a rigidly conformist cast. This social formation could not withstand market relations, which undermined authority and fostered economic rationality and the pursuit of personal pleasure. The process begun in Poland and Germany intensified in the new world. Thomas and Znaniecki documented the contrast between the new attitudes, developed under the impress of Americanized values, and the old ones, by citing letters to Poland from laborers in America who wanted to keep their wages rather than repatriating them.[42]

The failure to make sense of the new group norms brought from Europe did not, Thomas and Znaniecki insisted, uniformly or automatically lead to confusion and demoralization. To be sure, there were alienated Poles who could no longer recognize any connection between their action and the world around them. Drawing upon the pragmatist-inflected contention that attention is increased when environmental change undercuts habit, Thomas and Znaniecki understood the process of planting in the United States as an opportunity to solve problems rather than a decline or tragedy. The social disorganization of Polish Chicago could also lead to new possibilities for individuals to develop new capacities and to establish or reorganize social life. The key to the development of new attitudes built on viable values was the ability of peasants to learn to separate economic from social considerations, "the substitution of the principle of exchange for the principle of help."[43] Part of the process that eased this transition was the development of ethnicity. Thomas and Znaniecki treated the new ethnic institutions and allegiances as human-made things in response to a new environment rather than as the consequence of preexisting reflex or instinct. Where others saw ethnicity as an obstacle to or a brake on adaptation to modern life, the authors gleaned in the ethnic character of boardinghouse, parish, and mutual benefit society a path to a new social situation in which peasants could indulge their desire for new experience, recognition, mastery, and security in the midst of the breakdown of the primary marriage group.

Figure 4.3. Immigrants. **In the work of W. I. Thomas and Florian Znaniecki, immigrants such as these faced in the United States a particular lack of fit between norms and acts. Studying social disorganization in Poles in Chicago, Thomas and Znaniecki treated ethnicity as a creative response to a new social life, rather than as a preexisting reflex or instinct, thus opening the way for a new fluidity in social thought. (Source: George Grantham Bain Collection, Library of Congress, LC-USZ62-26543)**

In treating social action as voluntary individual response, *The Polish Peasant* laid bare the dynamics of the relation between individual and society. As noted, that response was by no means singular. They laid out a number of possible attitudes that immigrants could adapt to the social situation, ranging from conformist acceptance of American values, to Bohemian rebellion, to one they called creative, which resembled Bourne's pluralism. Thomas and Znaniecki were not uncritical proponents of either the melting pot or acquisitiveness, and they seemed to favor a pluralist response. Thomas had a well-developed sympathy for deviants and marginal figures (and ironically because of a scandal became an outcast himself). Yet their concentration on the conflict between individual and society colored their interpretation of Polish social life. Because they defined rationality as the recognition of the separation of economic and social spheres, they rarely noted conflicts between groups. So they treated the fondness of one Pole for socialism as little more than a backward-looking effort to re-create a no-longer-viable set of group values. Strikes they tended to attribute to individual alienation. Class relations were of little moment; Thomas and Znaniecki did not differentiate between profit-seeking and wage-taking attitudes, seeing both as an extension of control over the environment. Yet Poles were conscious of these differences. They were also well aware of the intervention into family life by lords in Poland and the bloody struggles against their rule in the beginning of the twentieth century. Similarly marginal in their account are trade unions in America, a particular oversight, given that Polish labor was crucial to organizing efforts in Chicago meatpacking plants and therefore quite observable.[44]

One implication of Thomas and Znaniecki's work was that the struggle between group and individual would never fully cease. Group efforts to enforce conformity would, they suggested, always come up against efforts to evade what would come to be constraints. Outcomes could never be established by fiat or theory but could be determined only on a case-by-case basis. Rejecting the notion of the individual as a "definite, firm, positive, foundation for individualized feelings and ideas" as overly abstract and something of a fiction, Arthur Bentley argued that harmony between groups was an unlikely outcome.[45] In his provocative *Process of Government: A Study of Social Pressures* (1908), Bentley treated groups as the primary building block and individuals as the consequences of the intersections of many groups to which they belonged. Individuation was therefore highly adventitious and unstable, dependent upon the shifting nature of intersection and the possibility of proliferation of groups. Analysis must therefore concentrate on the spectrum of relations among humans, their actions with and upon each other. So, Bentley concluded, "President Roosevelt" can be understood as a "very large amount of official activity, involving very many people," a "certain number of millions of American citizens tending in certain directions" (176, 322).

Bentley's notion of society was similarly unorthodox. Society, he maintained, was not a superindividual, and hence it had no motivations as such. His multiplicity was especially noteworthy in his repeated contention that there was no single motor of life that could explain history. Material factors such as food and sex were not sufficient to indicate why groups took the social action that they did. By Bentley's lights, very little group behavior was directed toward augmenting production and reproduction.[46] Nor were ideals adequate to the task in Bentley's rendition; they were simply "talk," too separated from what was the truly social. Feelings, faculties, and ideals were not definite things in or behind society, working upon it as causes, he insisted.[47] This misapprehension of the constitution of social life explained why both socialist appeals to material interests and idealists' invocation of the common good failed to sustain political movements.

Bentley countered with an analysis that was considerably more antifoundational than those of the materialists and idealists. Rather than scout for motives, Bentley placed emphasis on action itself. Society, he insisted, was a collection of a proliferating number of groups. He defined this building block of social analysis as a "certain portion of the men of a society, taken, however, not as a physical mass cut off from other masses of men, but as a mass

activity, which does not preclude the men who participate in it from partic-
ipating likewise in many other group activities."[48] To qualify as a political
group, men and women must act in concert to advance or secure valued objects and conditions. In line with his disapproval of materialist and structural
analysis, Bentley maintained that groups were not preexisting entities, defined by predetermined or transcendent interests determined by specific positions in the social structure or by their relations to the means of production.
One could know interests only by the goals that groups sought. In the absence of such action, Bentley regarded claims about the interests and even
the existence of groups as metaphysical. Analysis could not assume a singular working or capitalist class. It had to verify particular actions empirically.

Bentley's multiplicity was a consequence of this empirical testing. Noting
the proliferation of valued ends and objects, he argued that groups were
evanescent in their way, forming and reforming in the quest for satisfaction
of new goals. Because humans belonged to many groups, some of which were
conflicting, Bentley took "criss-crossing" as a hallmark of a social life in
which integration and unity were elusive goals. Although he was a bit obscure on the matter, Bentley did hold that some groups were more basic, potentially brought together by economic or ethnic similarities. Yet these underlying groups, as Bentley labeled them, were not directly political. They
did not always act in concert or sustain political groups. Thus, for instance,
Bentley contended that the failure of the First International indicated the
lack of substantial political existence of the proletariat. It was, he continued,
not surprising therefore that Karl Marx failed to arrive at an adequate definition of a class.[49] What interested Bentley was the tendency of groups to be
"freely combining, dissolving, and recombining in accordance with their interest lines" (359). Bentley's analysis cut against grand schemes of reconstruction. Since society was but the collection of groups, and since different
groups valued different actions, no Archimedean point above interest was
possible. Claims to speak for universal or general interest, Bentley argued,
mystified this central point. Not only was Bentley suspicious of socialist
claims about the working class as the universal class, he was also certain that
crisscrossing would undercut any unified collective action.

Shorn of ideals as a normative force, Bentley's version of politics was of a
constant tussle of groups of shifting composition and interests. Harmony as
nineteenth-century social thinkers envisioned it gave way to the multiplicity of process. History was always becoming, never arriving at any predetermined goals or ends. By making politics a matter of interest group struggle
over resources to achieve values, Bentley could assert that government was
not something outside society but immersed in it. That argument put him at

odds with those who understood government as the impartial regulator of interest, a referee between contending parties. Not so, Bentley countered, the state was the agent of interest, albeit not of a class or even a region but the shifting coalition of groups. The shifting coalition of groups meant that Bentley was less worried than some about concentration of power. Crisscrossing and the evanescence of groups meant that rule was never absolute in the long run and always contested.

Although Bentley saw constant struggle over interest, his model, much like the invisible hand in the market, took what he called the adjustment of interests as the general condition of political life. As Bentley noted, "order is bound to result, because order is now and order has been, where order is needed, though all the prophets be confounded" (267). That order did not always arise from the conscious recognition of its need by actors. It was, Bentley averred, sometimes quite accidental as a consequence of the ways in which opposing groups interacted in efforts to achieve values. Sometimes groups would achieve ends that would obviate the need for the group. Other times groups modified their ends when faced with the contending groups. At yet other times, the valued object proved not so worthwhile. Even violence, which would seem on its face to be a failure to adjust interests, was in Bentley's view not particularly exceptional as a technique to achieve ends. In one passage, he saw little difference in kind between violence and rhetoric and logic that prompted clamor or dogma.[50] The use of violence was the result of rulers' failing to recognize a political group. Once rulers recognize outlying groups, the groups become part of the group process, and adjustment follows. Despite "some tremendously strong underlying group interests," he wrote, "we have nevertheless frequent evidences of the giving way of the fortifications of one set of groups at the assault of another, and the freeing of the executive from class domination. We have avenues of approach through the government such that the class tendency can only advance to a certain degree before being overwhelmed, and that degree one which probably falls far short, except in most exceptional temporary cases, of the degree in which a resort to violence as the only effective technique becomes necessary" (358).

For all his disparagement of romantic reform, Bentley could not completely abandon his ideals of economic justice. Having spent the 1890s worried about the poverty he observed in European slums, he built amelioration into his system. Socialism would not succeed in the United States, because the process of adjustment of interests and the dissolution of groups, including the working class, would make working-class rule of interest only to a rump of radicals. But cooperation and forms of public ownership would proceed surreptitiously because the underlying group would force some adjustment from other groups. Not revolution but compromise would be the end of the socialist movement, since compromise "is the very process itself of the criss-cross groups in action" (208). In the end, the multiplicity of the process of government kept within the tracks of the present.

Bentley's pluralism of competing interest groups would in later decades become conventional wisdom among sociologists and political scientists. In its own time, *The Process of Government* was often disorienting to its readers. The dismissal of the motive force of ideas and his reduction of ideals to a matter-of-fact achievement of interest struck at the link between moral and natural law that had underwritten harmony and progress. When a similar analysis was offered to account for the origins of the United States, the reaction among the public was far from tempered. In his *Economic Interpretation of the Constitution* (1913), Charles Austin Beard (1874–1948) argued that interests, not ideals, were at the root of the campaign to replace the Articles of Confederation. This contention drew the ire of those who thought it insufficiently appreciative of the high-mindedness of the founders. The challenge of Beard and a number of like-minded historians who came of age in the early twentieth century was not solely a disagreement about motives of historical actors. The new history took issue with a vision of that past as a singular, unified story that demonstrated the harmonious working-out of general principles.

Born in Indiana, Beard graduated DePauw University in 1898. In his undergraduate and postgraduate days, he subscribed to the prevailing notion that traced democracy to the German forests.[51] His racialism, which included an acceptance of segregation, soon gave way to an interest in the struggles to control the means of wealth. Crucial in that transformation was academic work in Oxford. There he encountered Walter Vrooman, who emphasized the separation of ethics from history (a position that Beard ostensibly accepted, but whose implications he often resisted) and who treated history as the study of groups, not exceptional individuals. Also influential in Beard's new outlook was the work of two Columbia University colleagues, Edwin R. A. Seligman and James Harvey Robinson. Seligman had penned a pamphlet in 1902 entitled the *Economic Interpretation of History*, which drew upon Karl Marx's historical understanding but disdained his economics and politics. Seligman contended that changes in economic institutions changed the categories by which people understood their world. Property, he contended, determined politics because men would act to protect their form of property and to extend both its returns and its social dominance. Seligman insisted that moral and ethical choices were real but must be seen as "essentially social in their origin and largely conditioned in their actual sphere of operation by the economic relations of society."[52]

Robinson was the leading proponent of the "New History," which set it-self against an understanding of the past as the work of particularly forceful individuals and the concentration first and foremost on state building. In contrast, the New History contended that history itself was all that humans had accomplished. "In its amplest meaning, Robinson wrote, "History in-cludes every trace and vestige of everything that man has done or thought since first he appeared on earth. . . . Man is more than a warrior, a subject, or a princely ruler; the State is by no means his sole interest."[53] In expanding the scope of history, Robinson and his New History compatriots also shifted the terms of explanation. Previous historiography had treated the past not only as a singular story, whether it be of progress or the advance of liberty, but also one understandable by values or concepts thought to be transhistorical. The New History, in contrast, emphasized recovering context, paying partic-ular attention to the particular and contingent forces at work in a given sit-uation. It was context, they argued, that bestowed meaning. New Historians emphasized the transience of such phenomena of belief rather than celebrat-ing eternal verities. Robinson was consequently wary of viewing history as a repository of values, at least universal ones. Denying that "conditions remain sufficiently uniform to give precedents a perpetual value," he maintained that change had so accelerated in modern times that mining the past for guidance ran the risk of viewing "present problems with obsolete emotions" and settling them "by obsolete reasoning."[54]

Given the complexity of the past, historians were not so much recorders as interpreters. Historical accounts were made from the selection of particu-lar facts. Historians, the argument of the New History went, selected facts for contingent reasons. They came to the past not to see it clearly and see it whole, but to understand something that their own context had helped them see as significant. In emphasizing both the agency and situatedness of the his-torian, the New History made history a discourse of multiplicity, since the past was no longer a self-evident tale of progress to which the chronicler sim-ply gave voice. No longer universally true, it was, under New Historian aus-pices, a report from a particular and limited vantage point. If the writing of history was an active process in which the flow of events lacked a firm foun-dation, Robinson nonetheless did not believe that anything was possible or that radical breaks were likely. Because society was "infinitely more conser-vative than the individual," he maintained that "a sudden general change is almost inconceivable."[55]

Beard's history of the making of the Constitution combined Bentley's in-terest group notion with Seligman's economic basis to demonstrate Robin-son's point about context. That the American state was a product of those who stood to benefit from their holdings in the public debt and enshrined their defense of a particular type of property in the document directly challenged the view that had dated to the early nineteenth century that the Constitution was the expression of orderly liberty, a spiritual endowment that restrained the chaotic disorder of the Confederation period. As one of the leading lights of political science, John W. Burgess, put it, the Constitution overcame the "usurpation" by the states of the sovereignty of the people of the nation and set forth the groundwork for the American state to engage in its "transcendent mission" to perfect "the Aryan genius for political civilization."[56] Beard regarded this position as so much metaphysical mystification that substituted a normative belief designed to justify existing institutions for an account of the actual forces at work. By his lights, the Constitution was an eighteenth-century document that did not necessarily meet twentieth-century needs. Its adoption was an episode in the continuous process of competition between interest groups, not an absolute moment of truth.

Beard was not entirely clear what the episode meant. On the one hand, he seemed to charge that the Constitution was the work of men out for their main chance, whose interests extended no further than using the power of the new government to protect their investment in securities and in the manipulation of money values. Yet he leveled no such charges of narrow self-interest against the two major figures in the writing and defense of the founding document, Alexander Hamilton and James Madison. When critics noted that opponents of the Constitution often had larger holdings of public securities than did proponents, Beard fell back on an argument that delegates spoke for a capitalist "class" interest since the Constitution had made possible both a national polity and economic development, two consequences that were immensely instrumental in creation of profit-bearing property and profit taking. Beard was also aware that the clash between Federalists and Anti-Federalists, and subsequently between Hamiltonians and Jeffersonians, did not always break down neatly. The agrarians, who at times seemed anti-capitalist in their insistence on self-sufficiency and independence, were also graspers after the main chance, not to mention slaveholders. Jeffersonians, he argued in his subsequent book, *Economic Origins of Jeffersonian Democracy* (1915), were no simple democrats. Their debt did not make them any more prone to egalitarianism, Beard concluded. Tracing the fight between types of property into the new republic, Beard concluded that neither party wanted to "cherish the people" by lifting the restrictions on voting and office holding. Describing how Jefferson slave-owning planters had rallied the "agrarian masses" for their own benefit, Beard saw a contest between two interest groups rather than the moral struggle that he had at times implied was at stake. Such a conclusion both punctured a view of the American past as ultimately harmonic and progressive, and cast doubt on how usable the past might in fact be.[57]

In Beard's telling, conflict over property had been a fairly constant facet of American history. The neoclassicism to which most professional American economists subscribed viewed that conflict as a misapprehension of a fundamentally just order in which harmony and unity were the most logical outcome. John Bates Clark enunciated the American position in *The Philosophy of Wealth* (1885) and *The Distribution of Wealth* (1888), apparently independent of Austrian marginalism to which it bore great resemblance. Rising to the challenge of the redistributive economics of Henry George, Clark set out to demonstrate that corporate capitalism, all things being equal, delivered distributive justice. In order to show that returns to economic actors corresponded to their contribution, Clark diverged from the labor theory of value of Adam Smith and David Ricardo, which had established the foundations of classical political economy. He maintained that goods were exchanged with one another not on the basis of the comparative labor they embodied, but the relative utility of objects exchanged. Utility clearly varies from individual to individual, depending on circumstance and predilection, but it becomes measurable as a value in Clark's rendition by the price that seller and buyer assign to the last incremental or marginal commodity. The wonder of impersonal exchange is that it normalizes different desires, a formulation that also had the virtue of undercutting the moral claims of labor to more product on the grounds of having been the source of value. Complementing the theory of value was Clark's further contention that capital as well as labor was responsible for something vital in the process of psychic satisfaction. Returns to capitalists were therefore not, Clark argued, the result of monopoly advantage or exploitation. In the real world, of course, there was imperfect competition and friction, as he called it in analogy to the physical world of Galileo. And it was the job of reformers to remove that friction through regulation of markets, mandatory arbitration, and minimum wage laws.[58]

Although quite successful in transforming the discipline of economics, the harmonies and equilibria of Clark's imaginary world did not please every investigator of economic life. Some known as institutionalists charged that Clark's idealization was an abstract formulation that did not apprehend the world as actually lived, because it bracketed contingencies and treated economic institutions as natural rather than as historically developed. For men and women such as the University of Wisconsin's John Commons and his students, which included the daughter of jurist Louis Brandeis and the son of

Social Gospeler Walter Rauschenbusch, Wesley Mitchell, and eventually Clark's son, John Maurice, the point of economic science was to understand how the interaction of institutions shaped economic behavior. What neoclassical economics regarded as exogenous, institutional economics regarded as endogenous. Economics would be incomplete until it recognized that production and exchange varied according to their institutional setting, which in turn must be recognized as changing in response to particular problems. In the hands of its most provocative practitioner, Thorstein Veblen, institutional economics challenged not only the formalism of prevailing economic thought, but also the sense that society was at bottom a unified and harmonious association. In its modern guise, Veblen argued, society was better understood as based on force and fraud to maintain the privilege of a few.

Best known for *Theory of the Leisure Class* (1899), Veblen was always an outlier among American academics. Born in Minnesota in 1857, Veblen studied with both Clark (at Carleton) and Sumner (at Yale). Years of unemployment followed, but Veblen did manage to land a position at the University of Chicago. Political and personal problems followed him from Stanford, the University of Missouri, and the New School for Social Research. Developing a reputation (most likely unwarranted) as a libertine, Veblen was far from a hail-fellow-well-met. His mordant wit, which, despite his denials, is on display in *Leisure Class*, was the characteristic for which a later generation of radicals honored him. His portrait reveals a man sporting an out-of-date suit and an unruly head of hair, a stance that many have attributed to his obvious disdain for convention. As his children have testified, Veblen's dislike of waste was thorough, extending to his insistence that they wear sturdy, rather than fashionable, shoes and clothes. The attention lavished on his personal style and nonconformity has drawn attention away from the sweeping nature of his project. Veblen aimed at countering an economics rooted in ideas of natural law with one more attuned to the contingency and disharmony of social life. In recasting the study of production and distribution as the cultural history of material life, Veblen posited a world in which progress was not the consequence of existing economic arrangements but possible only through their overthrow.[59]

In charging the predominant economics was more metaphysical than scientific, Veblen had in mind its failure to take note of Darwinian contributions to science. According to Veblen, both classical and neoclassical economics evoked natural law as explanation. Conventional economics attributed to nature both purposes (which is what the assertion that markets seek equilibrium amounted to) and moral worth ("disturbing factors" such as regulation of rail rates, taxes, tariffs, or unions wrongly tampered with the law). In assuming that the action of economic agents tended to result in harmony in the absence of exogenous factors, the old political economy remained uninterested in those aspects that a science predicated on the reality of change and adaptation regarded as the proper object of study. Conventional economics misapprehended as well the nature of economic actors. The dominant strain of thought depended upon a hedonism in which human beings were mere registers of pain and pleasure and acted to avoid the first and seek the second. Drawing upon the pragmatist-inflected social psychology, Veblen put emphasis on agents who formulated their own ends and consciously deployed means to achieve them. Rather than assume harmony, Veblen maintained, a scientific economics needed to chart the social environment in which economic activity occurred.[60]

To construct his alternative account, Veblen drew upon prevailing anthropological understanding of different stages in the broad sweep of human history. Veblen differentiated among them less on the basis of technological advances than upon their social organization. In the first, savagery, the full complement of human instincts came into play. Veblen singled out three that helped meet the evolutionary task of survival—workmanship, which focused attention on the most efficient means to adapt to the material and social environment—idle curiosity, and parental bent. In light of the general scarcity, everyone worked to his or her utmost, and the product was distributed relatively equitably, Veblen maintained. Although primitives often hewed to animistic understandings of the world in which they imputed purposes and intentions to inanimate objects, Veblen believed that by and large they were attuned to material fact. This social and cultural life of instinctual expression and relative equality was fragile, however. Once conditions allowed for surplus, the necessity for all to work lessened, and the peaceable habits of savagery proved ill suited for the new environment. In Veblen's view, property ownership then emerged, and with it the will to dominate typical of the barbarian. Among the first items of property, Veblen theorized, were women captured in warfare.[61]

In contrast to the celebrations of ownership as a natural propensity in most other economic discourses, Veblen stressed what he called its conventional or invented nature. Defining ownership as "the customary right of use and abuse over an object," including claims on all the products of labor, Veblen set out to show its implications for social life. As the origins of property became obscure, men came to regard property as having rights that could not be violated without doing damage to natural law.[62] Manipulating this entity to its own benefit was the key actor in Veblen's anthropological economics, the leisure class. Veblen conceived the leisure class as distinguished

Figure 4.4. Conspicuous consumption. It was such display that led Thorstein Veblen to posit that the owning class maintained its power by manipulating the human tendency to emulation. Viewing society as riven with rival orientations, Veblen challenged notions that society was an ethical entity, ultimately unified and integrated. (Source: Library of Congress, LC-USZC2-521)

not so much by its lack of exertion or its propensity to take long vacations than by its manipulation of cultural symbols to exploit the surplus. Part of the cultural arsenal of the leisure class was its marking work as irksome rather than as the efficient manipulation of means to ends. This cultural shift earned prestige for those who could demonstrate that they did not need to work. By flaunting its lack of productivity, by insisting on the superiority of spiritual to material pursuits, and by ostentatiously displaying its wealth, the leisure class secured its cultural dominance. Veblen filled *The Leisure Class* with an entire catalogue of items from his own day that demonstrated "conspicuously wasteful honorific expenditure": manor homes, great retinues of servants, ornately ornamented silverware, carvings on walking sticks, and unusual breeds of dogs. Capitalists, he meant to show, were not so much agents of progress as barbarian remnants who ruled through assertion of status rather than through contracts negotiated by equals. Industrial society ran on waste, which he defined as the expenditure of energy that "does not serve human life or human well-being on the whole" and as a result worked against the well-being of most of its members. For all his protestation that his work was a neutral scientific account, the very contrast with conventional conclusions made his findings a particularly stinging indictment.[63]

Particularly haunting was the mechanism by which the leisure class maintained its rule. Veblen pointed often to force and fraud, but he also noted the way in which leisure-class rule had tapped into the human tendency to emulate others. Veblen treated conspicuous consumption as noteworthy because it was an impulse that was not confined to the elite. Because people take their cues from others, what he called the underlying population acted in accord with the prevailing canons of repute. In the modern world, these standards were pecuniary, Veblen noted; items confer prestige to owners on the basis not of the material needs they meet but of their price tags. From Veblen's vantage point, the nascent advertising industry resembled the medieval church in its promulgation of a "propaganda of the faith" in the sales pitch and its studied ignorance of "material facts with the same magisterial detachment."[64]

Veblen's conception of conspicuous consumption has been the most contentious of his claims. Critics, then and now, have accused him of dismissing aesthetic enjoyment (an interesting complaint about someone who wrote his first academic paper on Kant's *Critique of Judgment*), ascribing a single motive to consumption behavior that clearly has many causes, and of missing that fashion often percolates from below. Some of the criticism has validity but often considers Veblen's argument in isolation. Veblen was not so much interested in the fashion system as he was in the ways that pecuniary values became so widespread and the position of the leisure class so respected that the force and fraud on which the nonworking class lived went by unnoticed or became a condition to which everyone seemed to aspire.

Where sociologists such as Albion Small perceived an ethical order bounding society, Veblen saw a society riven by different orientations or "spiritual attitudes." In his emphasis on attitudes, Veblen stood in contrast to Marxists, who emphasized objective interest stemming from a material relation to the means of production. On the one hand, Veblen identified the primary role of business in shaping industrial society. Business was the instrument of the leisure class, and it embodied a pecuniary orientation in which the accumulation of money for its own sake was the prime value. Bolstered by a belief in natural law, business relied on capital to enhance its standing. Capital pecuniarily considered was a tool to "engross, or 'corner,' the usufruct of the commonplace knowledge of ways and means by taking over such of the requisite material as may be relatively scarce and relatively indispensable for procuring a livelihood under the current state of the industrial arts."[65] In contrast to business stood industry, which was driven by the human need to guarantee well-being. Pecuniary values never fully extirpated the commitment to productive efficiency, in large part because survival and adaptation depended upon it. Veblen located the most thorough commitment to industry in those workers and engineers who actually manned the industrial process. Because their daily activity made use of "capital industrially considered," the common inheritance of humanity reducible to "mechanical, chemical, and physiological effects," and subjected them to the discipline of the machine, they were less prone to imputing human purposes to nature. In his most optimistic moments after the Great War, Veblen envisioned a new set of habits inculcated by the machine process that would create a commitment among producers of various ranks to an "industrial republic" in which cooperation more attuned to the capabilities of an interdependent system of production flourished.

Veblen pinpointed the tension between business and industry as the cause of the periodic economic crises to which the Industrial Age seemed prone. He painted a scenario in which the inability of businessmen to receive the expected rate of return on capital goods led them to restrict production (Veblen termed it withdrawing efficiency or sabotage). In manipulating supply to maintain values, businessmen pitted their own desires for a profit rate that bequeathed the customary dignity against the material needs of the community. Veblen located one cause of economic crises in the incomplete understanding of capitalists. Influenced by pecuniary values, they took rates of return in which circumstances inflated the value of capital goods beyond their actual earning power as normal and expected. In time, the increased efficiency of machines coming on line and rising wages would lower the value of those capital goods and the returns that businessmen received from them. At that point, they decided that "industrial production was no longer worthwhile from the immaterial perspective of business." To continue production would be to risk the pecuniary magnitude of one's holdings upon which one's standing rested. The prevalence of sabotage in defense of pecuniary repute created an economy that tended toward stagnation. Veblen did see countervailing possibilities in permanent war, monopolization—which would allow businessmen to maintain the profitability of older investments by slowing the pace of innovation and restricting competition—or a producer seizure of power when workers and engineers decided that it was ridiculous to sacrifice the material well-being to the spell of ownership, in effect recalling and revitalizing the savage mode of cooperation at a higher plane.[66]

Unlike most of his contemporaries, Veblen doubted social peace was possible. The incompatibility between pecuniary and industrial values ruled out anything approaching a resolution. This tension-filled organization was perhaps fitting for the human species that had its instinctual heritage deformed by life in civilization. Even had the instinct of workmanship, idle curiosity, and parental bent not been damaged and deformed by centuries of barbarism, Veblen doubted humans could ever match their response to the environment to which they struggled to adapt. "Whatever is, is wrong," he commented in *Leisure Class*.[67]

Few bodies of American social thought on offer in the early twentieth century as thoroughly rejected the postulates of harmony and progress as did Veblen's. His confrontation with the contingencies involved in the understanding of human association resulted in a rejection of modes of study that assumed unity and which proceeded from abstract postulates. Only Bentley was as dedicated to rooting out vestiges of metaphysics in analysis. Few others discerned how illusions could promote a false moral order to give society an appearance of coherence. Yet hard-boiled as Veblen was in exposing the illusions of unity, he often missed the significance of contingencies. In setting business in opposition to industry, he underestimated the difficulty of engineers in overthrowing their interest in the former for a more complete commitment to the latter. His trust in science as providing a totally different framework than the metaphysics of capitalism did not register the ways in which science was not impartial or neutral. This was especially apparent in his contention that machine discipline inculcate habits that would lead workers and engineers to overthrow the price system. Technology, contra Veblen, often embodied leisure-class interests in its very construction, degrading the work process through subdivision. That degradation has had effects that Veblen did not reckon. Factory regimes on the shop floor and in the office have prompted worker acceptance of the irksomeness of labor, which in turn has made employment simply a means to the purchase of items of prestige, a result that might not have entirely surprised Veblen.

Social Justice

Where Veblen talked about overturn, most Americans in the first fifteen years of the twentieth century settled on reform. The actions that counted as efforts to channel betterment were myriad. They included moral crusades to restrict prostitution and ban liquor, and campaigns to ameliorate working conditions by various voluntary associations motivated by a new conception of citizenship. For the first time in American history, men and women enlisted the federal government to enforce reform, commending it to inspect food and drugs for purity, outlaw specific practices that were regarded as restraint of trade, and take an active role in managing the national economy through centralized banking, corporate regulation, and collection of income taxes.

This collection of reform efforts at the beginning of the twentieth century has long gone by the name progressivism. Few topics have caused historians of the United States as much consternation as has the reform impulse of the early twentieth century. There has been little agreement on its essential impulses, its goals and methods, or the social character of its personnel. Taken as a whole, the literature on early-twentieth-century reforms has emphasized both the extension of popular participation through the devices of referendum, recall, and popular election of senators and the reliance on the rule by commissions of experts and by such unelected officials as city managers. The dispute has extended to debates over the nature of corporate property. For some historians, the lawyer Louis Brandeis, who wanted to disperse productive property widely, remains the prototypical progressive. For others, Walter Lippmann, who believed that large-scale, consolidated enterprises could be regulated to produce a public-service capitalism, qualifies. Complicating matters is the effort of both parties to claim the moniker of progressive at some point during the first decade and a half of the twentieth century. When Theodore Roosevelt launched a third-party challenge in 1912 under the banner of the Progressive Party, the standard bearers of the two established parties vigorously disputed that his was the true version of progressivism. The Democrat Woodrow Wilson, for his part, always referred somewhat dismissively to Roosevelt's party as "the New Party."[68] Not surprisingly, progressivism has spawned a slew of creative interpretations, from Richard Hofstadter's status anxiety thesis in which progressivism originated with small-town, middle-class professionals who were motivated by the threat to their repute that industrial capitalism posed, to Robert Wiebe's organizational synthesis in which the impetus for rationalization of the economy came from the new professional class of experts, to Martin Sklar's corporate liberalism in which the legitimation and dominance of corporate property formed the central thrust of the period and politicians responded by melding liberalism with the new capitalism.[69]

Efforts to square the circle have been unavailing. Peter Filene has argued that, given all the contradictions, historians should dispense with the notion of a progressive movement and concentrate on the various components that made themselves felt politically and socially in the early twentieth century. Daniel Rodgers has argued in a somewhat similar vein that progressive developments might best be understood as consisting of different streams or tendencies that functioned as an unstable coalition.[70] Rather than search for the essential progressive—a near impossible task, given that the practice of era reforms involved coalitions in flux, congregating some people together for certain purposes and other people for others—we might instead inquire how multiplicity came into play in the profusion of reforms of the first two decades of the twentieth century. Many, perhaps most, of the folks whom one or another historian has termed a progressive rarely considered multiplicity at all. As the name *progressive* suggests, they remained by and large committed to a view that there was a predictable direction to history. Not all thought that direction was guaranteed or written into the nature of things, but their own intervention to hasten the arrival of the golden day was by and large undertaken confidently, with a sense that their standing at Armageddon, as Roosevelt put it in 1912, drew upon resources that made success highly probable. Many engaged in political action because they saw their principles temporarily stymied and wanted to remove the obstacles. A significant minority, however, agreed with Walter Lippmann's proposition that Americans "were immigrants in the industrial world" who had "no authority to lean upon" and therefore had to place all their principles into question.[71]

Even those progressives most certain that their principles correctly apprehended social life wondered whether the universality of the self-correcting economy was still operative. Since the economy was the social arena par excellence and a dispenser of social justice, the problem of economic and social justice was a central concern of early twentieth-century reform. For some progressives, the problem of economic justice was a matter of usurpation of power, of corporate greed, and concerted efforts to prevent the market from working. For others, the market ceased to have any unifying heft, and they turned their attention to regulation that depended upon conscious intervention and deliberate integration of the economy.[72]

For progressives, socialism was definitively *not* the royal road to social justice. Although a number of Progressive Era economic thinkers such as Herbert C. Adams, Richard T. Ely, and Edwin R. A. Seligman had flirted with

Figure 4.5. Progressivism in action: arbiters in the coal strike of 1902. **A confusing phenomenon that brought together many currents of thought, progressivism was a definite rejection of a belief in the natural unity of economy and society. (Source: George Grantham Bain Collection, Library of Congress, LC-USZ62-32674)**

socialism in the 1870s and 1880s, especially during and immediately after their postgraduate work in Germany, none emerged in the twentieth century as an advocate for a Veblenian overthrow of the price system, a Debsian workers' state, or a Bellamyite collective economy. In part, as Mary Furner has documented, the shift was a result of political and occupational threats from wealthy trustees and officious university administrators, who found such advocacy an abomination. Faced with expulsion from the academy, many recanted previous enthusiasms or trimmed their sails.[73] Most progressives were not academics, nor did they seriously flirt with socialism, despite the criticisms of some opponents. Their fundamental complaints were moral ones. Socialism, by their lights, was materialistic and had no use for the building of a moral order. Many objected to what they took as its denial of individuality and individual responsibility.[74]

Socialism, or at least most versions of it, was not particularly appealing to those who were more attuned to the prospects of multiplicity. Indeed, they indicted socialism for having the same false commitment to unity as classical and neoclassical economics. For William Weyl (1874–1919), economist and one of the founders of the *New Republic*, Marxist, or as he tellingly labeled it, absolute, socialism treated class conflict as an eternal, implacable condition of capitalist societies. Weyl contended that absolute socialism was committed to an either/or world. It was therefore another a priori system of thought that deduced from first principles that private property "automatically, inevitably, and always leads to exploitation." Weyl found the proposition as foolish as the notion that markets always yielded just results. Distribution, he concluded, was less a matter of "absolute right" than "relative utility."[75] Absolute socialism was wrong to insist on absolute immiseration of the working class when empirical observation indicated an increase in the standard of living. Absolute socialism was equally incorrect in calling for proletarian revolution. That call ignored the crosscutting of identification, the continued relevance of the petty bourgeoisie, particularly farmers, and a new democratic vision that transcended class. The way forward, Weyl argued, was by judging on a case-by-case basis whether social utility was best served through increased taxation of unearned increment, regulation, or takeover. "Progress will become adjustment by the gradual adaptation of production to social uses, rather than a complete overturn, either violent or peaceful, either rapid or slow, of our industrial habits and implements."[76]

For Weyl and like-minded reformers, then, social justice required a shift to production for need rather than for private gain. That in turn meant a redefinition of property as something other than the right to absolute use by an individual. That right, critics claimed, had brought baleful consequences. Absolute property rights had fostered a culture of selfishness. They had encouraged competition rather than cooperation, which had led to the social and political inequalities that had prompted the crisis of the 1890s. Since private rights reigned supreme, efforts to prevent overproduction had failed, as no one allowed his property to be subject to command by others. Not surprisingly, Weyl condemned absolute private property rights as the generator of excess and waste and an antisocial individualism.[77] His colleague Walter Lippmann excoriated unchecked private property used for personal accumulation for failing to serve civilization. If few agreed with Veblen that property rights were metaphysical illusions, many progressive thinkers agreed they were conventional. The circle around the *New Republic*, which included Lippmann, Weyl, and Herbert Croly, forcefully argued that since humans, not nature, created property rights, people could modify or even abolish them in certain circumstances as overwhelming social need dictated. Many came to this conclusion by applying the reasoning of the Supreme Court, which had awarded rights to the most prominent social "individual" of the period, the corporation. Mutability of property rights was one position that united anticorporate progressives with trust regulators.[78]

The effort to rework property rights took two separate but intertwined forms: limitations of individual (and corporate) property and the creation of social property. The former involved limiting claims by individuals against the well-being of others. Pure food and drug laws, safety inspections of factories, and tenement laws all were instances in which absolute private rights were subjected to the test of general welfare and modified accordingly. Progressives suffered a setback early on in the period with the Lochner decision. In *Lochner v. New York* (1905), the majority held that in the matter of setting working hours for bakery workers, the state had no right to use police powers to override the right of the individual to liberty of person and freedom of contract. Denying that general concern for healthful work was at stake, the majority warned that if the statute were held valid and liberty of contract overturned, "there would seem to be no length to which legislation of this nature might not go." Oliver Wendell Holmes, while professing himself agnostic on the question of laissez-faire, articulated a sense common among progressives attuned to multiplicity that rights were not natural or unalterable. In tune with his suspicion of abstract and absolute legal principles, Holmes argued that the Constitution "is not intended to embody a particular economic theory, whether of paternalism and the organic relation of the citizen to the State or of laissez faire," reasoning that accounted for his famous line that "the Fourteenth Amendment does not enact Mr. Herbert Spencer's *Social Statics*."[79]

The concept of social property was one of the progressive contributions to American political economy. Building on populist notions of "natural monopolies," essential commodities in which competition was either unfeasible or risky, progressives expanded the purview of government ownership. New ventures in municipal transportation, waste disposal, and water supply created a small, yet significant, sphere of social property based on the sense that the polity constituted the legitimate property holder of those services that people needed collectively to live. Picking up populist arguments, progressives offered similar proposals for railroads and banks, but the opposition of entrenched interests made realization unlikely. Some progressives even saw possibilities for social property in the corporation itself. Reworking Veblen's contrast of business with industry as the separation of management and ownership, Walter Lippmann saw the development as a step along the way to production for public use, thus fulfilling his colleague Weyl's sense of social justice. Lippmann came to this conclusion because he believed that the drive for production and efficiency of managers and engineers would eventually overcome the drive for profit of the absentee owners, missing how productivity gains augmented a profit in which modern management often had a stake.[80]

Public and municipal ownership was not the only expansion of property rights proposed during the first two decades of the twentieth century. Accepting that property gave men a stake in the polity and inculcated worthy social virtues, John Commons (1862–1945), professor of economics at the University of Wisconsin, constructed an argument to re-create republican political economy by substituting property rights in intangibles for lost rights in the tangible property that republican theorists originally had in mind. As Karen E. McCally has demonstrated, Commons's innovation was to use the expansion of property rights that had justified corporate property to argue that workers had legitimate property claims to jobs and to the formation of unions.[81] Those rights stemmed not from universal or absolute rights, but from ones that arose in particular contexts. This generation of new but perfectly legitimate rights allowed Commons and his students to provide justification for such social justice measures as minimum wage laws, unemployment insurance (which accrued to those who had earned job rights when laid off), and pensions.

Commons's emphasis on context and contingency was central to his position. Arguing that the only natural right was that the material of nature belonged to God, the deeply religious Commons held that every man was entitled to the resources necessary to preserve his physical capacities and to nurture his spiritual ones. Markets, on the other hand, were the creation of governments, which used their legal and political powers to bring them into being. As such, the laws of distribution were themselves conventions.[82] Because Commons accepted many of the propositions about scarcity, he needed to demonstrate that honoring workers' claims could be met from available resources without completely negating other claims on those resources. In making his case, Commons took advantage of the refutation of the long-standing wage-fund theory. For much of the nineteenth century, economics had earned its reputation as the dismal science, because prevailing thought held that there was only a finite amount of the national product available for wages. Overspending that fund would yield debt and economic stagnation, because less would be available for reinvestment. Marginalists such as John Bates Clark had argued convincingly that wage rates and hiring were determined, not by past production, but by expectations of the future. That was good as far as it went, Commons argued, but Clark's notion of natural market equilibrium as the dispenser of justice erred, because it defined justice tautologically. What was needed to establish justice was an independent, nonmarket standard. Challenging the notion that wages were an objective or natural measure of the worth of labor, Commons argued that wages, like all other economic transactions, flowed from the man-made laws of distribution embedded in the institutional framework of a given society. Rather than a harmony of interests, Commons saw continual conflict of interests in which a workable mutuality was the best possible outcome. To achieve that workable mutuality, Commons turned to the common law rather than to social engineering, relying upon that which allowed laborers to establish the value for their labor, their property right in a livable income.[83]

Wages were traditionally regarded as something quite different from property rights. Indeed, in some traditions, people drew wages because they had no property. Commons defined property differently. Property, Commons contended, was not an exclusive relationship between a person and a thing, but a social relation among people over the use of things. The legal foundation of property changed during the nineteenth century, Commons argued, when the courts recognized property as entailing not just the use of things, but intangibles as well. The courts consistently held that the law protected not only the use of objects, but also their potential use. So corporate property included not only the right to use its capital goods but also "good will" —the right to expected income earned in the free conduct of commerce. That expected income could become part of the process of capitalization of the company, which is why the value of the stock always exceeded the value of the tangible assets. Commons pointed out that workers had what amounted to property rights in their ability to labor. Freedom of contract meant that workers could sell or withhold their labor, if they so chose. As such, workers were protected not only in wages earned, but in wages expected. The property right in work also authorized the right of association, so workers could combine as freely and legally as capital could, leveraging the value of their property in income by acting collectively. Similarly, Commons had no objection to immigration restriction on the same grounds. From Commons's point of view, a compulsory minimum wage, pensions, and unemployment insurance were the equivalent of dividends that accrued to capital.

Commons defined a right as a claim that imposed obligations on others to respect particular behaviors. The right to free speech, for instance, requires others to allow an individual to speak. As such, it is a social matter, and open to negotiation. The recognition that rights were mutable led other progressive reformers to campaign for a cultural and intellectual change to strengthen efforts to heal divisions. During the early twentieth century, there was much talk about a new citizenship. The term was a vague one, but it meant something on the order of a rejection of individualism. In the first two decades of the twentieth century, criticism of the long-standing staple of American culture as a cover for self-regard intensified. Where once Americans unambiguously celebrated the pioneer spirit of exceptional individuals who tamed the wilderness, the advocates of what was known as social democracy pointed to the selfish exploitation of resources that such pioneering wrought and offered as a substitute to the community building and interdependence that was the true mark of pioneer life. For the new democracy to succeed, many progressive social thinkers maintained, the "we" feeling must prevail, which they interpreted as the transcendence of interest. Jane Addams had argued to that effect during the Pullman strike and had used her feeling to explain to her friends why she was not a socialist.[84] Achieving the transcendent social ethos led advocates to avoid rights talk in favor of an emphasis on community. Mary Follett went so far as to assert in *The New State* (1918) that the achievement of social consciousness would abolish the antiquated notion of individual rights, because obeying the group "which we have helped to make and of which we are an integral part is to be free because we are then obeying ourself." She yearned for a time when the state "must be no external authority which restrains and regulates me, but it must be myself acting as the state in every smallest detail of life."[85] Few writers erased the boundaries between public and private as thoroughly as Follett did, yet she was not alone in drawing upon the notion of society as a moral order. In one sense, of course, the new morality countered the multiplicity of interests that industrial society had generated and the myriad of people now thrown together. At times, the new social citizenship seemed to augur public provisioning on the grounds that a great society cared for all its members. At other times, it treated different or unwelcome behaviors as a sign of inadequate socialization on the part of immigrants or prostitutes. It led others to condemn notions of self or sectional interest as unnecessary, unwarranted, and regressive.[86]

Although Walter Weyl's notion of the new democracy shared a good deal with more conventional progressives, his concept indicated that he also was more accepting of multiplicity. Like most progressives, Weyl understood the development of social feeling as crucial to an active and meaningful democracy. To that end, he bemoaned the effects of "the unique standard of pecuniary preeminence." The goal of the new democracy, Weyl maintained, was, on the other hand, the liberation of possibility from the calculus of the commodity exchange. "We must throw over our conceptions of cost and value (which measure wealth by effort) and must accept new ideas of utility (which measure wealth by pleasure and satisfaction). We must recognize that we have the social wealth to cure our social evils—and that until we have turned that social wealth against poverty, crime, vice, disease, incapacity, and ignorance, we have not begun to attain democracy." Where Weyl dissented from many other progressives was his resistance to the defining social feeling as unanimity or a belief in a unifying common good that transcended interest and class. The social goal, Weyl argued, was not so much the achievement of a single unifying end but the creation of commonly determined meaning, a "common action and a common lot," as he put it (160). Unlike such better-known progressive writers as David Graham Phillips and Ray Stannard Baker, Weyl did not recoil from working-class action or political movements that did not proclaim the general interest in transcendental or universal terms. To be sure, Weyl doubted the exclusive concentration on class interests among "absolute" socialists and worried about violence in strikes (although he was quick to point out that there was more violence in industrial accidents than in industrial actions). Coalitions, he argued, would achieve progress and could not be pure from a class viewpoint, yet he also argued that progress would come when those injured by the present setup spoke in their name and pushed for "life, health, leisure, a share in our natural resources, a dignified existence in society" against "the opposition of men who hold exorbitant claims upon the continent" (161).

Like Bentley, Weyl saw conflict of some sort as both resistant to eradication and central to the practice of democracy. Progressives, he contended, could expect multiplicity, not full-blown unity, in social feeling. "Solidarity," he warned those for whom social unity was a precondition of political action, "is not a thing constant and invariable. It is a resultant of attracting and repelling forces. It is a fluctuating quality depending upon fundamental causes and upon transient phenomena. Solidarity exists, and its existence is the vital fact of social life, but nowhere in the world is there an absolute solidarity, or an absolute lack of solidarity. Solidarity grows and declines, flows and ebbs, becomes greater and smaller. Solidarity is relative, not absolute" (241–42). Weyl did hope, however, that the new society might cohere when men and women took on new identities as the old, class-based ones became exhausted or stymied. Like his companion at the *New Republic*, Walter Lippmann, Weyl saw as crucial both the growing importance of new groups of professionals, who bridged the old gaps between classes, and the new centrality of consumerism. In positing pleasure and satisfaction as goals of associated activity, Weyl had in mind both aesthetic and political goals. Recognizing that Americans might act in concert to correct ills as taxpayers (property owners), laborers, or consumers, Weyl saw that last grouping as the most promising "since even those who do not earn wages or pay direct taxes consume commodities" (249–50).[87] How capable these new identities were in generating relative solidarity would be put to the test during the Great War. So too would the place of multiplicity in American thought and culture.

Notes

1. John Wenzler, "Transcendental Economics: The Quest to Harmonize Economic and Moral Law in Nineteenth-Century American Social Thought" (PhD diss., University of Rochester, 1998), is an insightful account of the American school of economic thought.

2. On Morgan, see Carl Resek, *Lewis Henry Morgan, American Scholar* (Chicago: University of Chicago Press); and Daniel Moses, "Lewis Henry Morgan's 'Barbaric Yawp': The Making of a Victorian Anthropologist" (PhD diss., University of Rochester, 2001). On Spencer, see Jonathan H. Turner, *Herbert Spencer: A Renewed Appreciation* (Beverly Hills, CA: Sage, 1985); David Wiltshire, *The Social and Political Thought of Herbert Spencer* (New York: Oxford University Press, 1978); and E. L. Youmans, *Herbert Spencer on the Americans and the Americans on Herbert Spencer* (New York: Arno Press, [1882] 1973).

3. Albion Small, *General Sociology: An Exposition of the Main Development in Sociological Theory from Spencer to Ratzenhofer* (Chicago: University of Chicago Press, 1905), 653.

4. Ivan Hannaford, *Race: The History of an Idea in the West* (Baltimore: Johns Hopkins University Press, 1996), 3. See also Lee D. Baker, *From Savage to Negro: Anthropology and the Construction of Race, 1896–1954* (Berkeley and Los Angeles: University of California Press, 1998); Franz Boas, *Race and Democratic Society* (New York: J. J. Augustin, 1945); Thomas F. Gossett, *Race: The History of an Idea in America* (New York: Oxford University Press, 1997); Matthew Pratt Guterl, *The Color of Race in America, 1900–1940* (Cambridge, MA: Harvard University Press, 2001); Matthew Frye Jacobson, *Whiteness of a Different Color: European Immigrants and the Alchemy of Race* (Cambridge, MA: Harvard University Press, 1998); Horace M. Kallen, *Culture and Democracy in the United States: Studies in the Group Psychology of the American People* (New York: Boni and Liveright, 1924); Daniel J. Kevles, *In the Name of Eugenics: Genetics and the Uses of Human Heredity* (New York: Knopf, 1985); Adam Kuper, *Culture: The Anthropologists' Account* (Cambridge, MA: Harvard University Press, 1999); and George W. Stocking, *Race, Culture, and Evolution: Essays in the History of Anthropology* (New York: Free Press, 1968).

5. Starr, quoted in Baker, *From Savage to Negro*, 59.

6. Jacob Riis, *How the Other Half Lives* (New York: Charles Scribner's Sons, 1890), especially chapters 5, 9, 10, 12, 24, and 25.

7. Starr, quoted in Baker, *From Savage to Negro*, 59.

8. George Stocking, "The Dark-Skinned Savage: The Image of Primitive Man in Evolutionary Anthropology," in *Race, Culture, and Evolution: Essays in the History of Anthropology* (New York: Free Press, 1968), 110–32. For Hoffman, see George M. Fredrickson, *The Black Image in the White Mind: The Debate on Afro-American*

Character and Destiny, 1817–1914 (New York: Harper and Row, 1971), 249–56. For the debate during the St. Louis World's Fair over Filipino dress, see Baker, *Savage to Negro*, 68–71.

9. Hannaford, *Race*, 325–31.

10. Ripley, quoted in Hannaford, *Race*, 326.

11. John Clark Ridpath, *The Great Races of Mankind: An Account of the Ethnic Origin, Primitive Estate, Early Migrations, Social Evolution, and Present Conditions and Promise of the Principal Families of Man*, vol. 1 (Cincinnati, OH: Jones Brothers, 1893), xli–xlii.

12. Ripley, quoted in Hannaford, *Race*, 325.

13. Franz Boas, "Human Faculty as Determined by Race," in George Stocking, *The Shaping of American Anthropology, 1883–1911: A Franz Boas Reader* (New York: Basic Books, 1974), 227–28.

14. Boas's attack on racial typology as a result of his immigrant studies can be found in Franz Boas, "Instability of Human Types," in Gustav Spiller, ed., *Papers on Inter-racial Problems, Communicated to the First Universal Races Congress Held at the University of London, July 26–29, 1911* (Boston, MA: Ginn, 1912), 99–103. His speculation on history and development was initially sketched out in Boas, "Human Faculty as Determined by Race," 226–27.

15. Susan Hegeman, *Patterns for America: Modernism and the Concept of Culture* (Princeton, NJ: Princeton University Press, 1999), 35–57; Vernon J. Williams Jr., *Rethinking Race: Franz Boas and His Contemporaries* (Lexington: University Press of Kentucky, 1996), 3–52.

16. A. L. Kroeber and Clyde Kluckhohn, *Culture: A Critical Review of Concepts and Definitions* (Cambridge, MA: Peabody Museum, 1952). Raymond Williams famously called "culture" one of the "most complicated" words in the language (Williams, *Keywords: A Vocabulary of Culture and Society* [New York: Oxford University Press, 1985], 76–82). Discussions of culture abound. In addition to the Baker, Hegeman, Kuper, Stocking, and Vernon Williams volumes already cited, I have also drawn upon Terry Eagleton, *The Idea of Culture* (Oxford: Blackwell, 2000); and Michael A. Elliott, *The Culture Concept: Writing and Difference in the Age of Realism*, Critical American Studies Series (Minneapolis: University of Minnesota Press, 2002). Kuper, having witnessed the culture concept become a justification for apartheid in his native South Africa, is particularly attuned to the flaws of culture as an analytical tool. Walter Benn Michaels dismisses the entire concept as a surreptitious discussion of race in *Our America: Nativism, Modernism, and Pluralism* (Durham, NC: Duke University Press, 1995). Hegeman forcefully challenges Michaels's reading, while retaining an awareness of the limitations of the culture concept, 193–213.

17. See Kuper, *Culture: The Anthropologists' Account*, 12–15; and Hegeman, *Patterns for America: Modernism and the Concept of Culture*, 47–49, 85–87.

18. Franz Boas, *The Mind of Primitive Man* (New York: Macmillan, 1911).

19. Arthur Bentley, *The Process of Government: A Study of Social Pressures* (Evanston: Principia Press of Illinois, [1908] 1949), especially 45–46.

20. Elliott, *Culture Concept*, 20–34.

21. Lowie, cited in Kuper, *Culture*, 61.

22. Edward Sapir, "Civilization and Culture," *Dial* 67 (1919), 233–36, and "Culture, Genuine and Spurious," *American Journal of Sociology* 29, no. 4 (1924): 401–29.

23. Hegeman, *Patterns*, 93–103.

24. A. L. Kroeber, "The Superorganic," *American Anthropologist* 19, no. 2 (April–June 1917): 163–213. A. A. Goldenweiser rejected the cultural determinism in "The Autonomy of the Social," in *American Anthropologist* 19, no. 3 (July–September 1917): 448. Sapir rejected its metaphysical aspect in "Do We Need a 'Superorganic'?" *American Anthropologist* 19, no. 3 (July–September 1917): 442–43.

25. Jane Addams, *Twenty Years at Hull House* (New York: Signet, [1910] 1961); Mary Jo Deegan, *Jane Addams and the Men of the Chicago School, 1892–1918* (New Brunswick, NJ: Transaction Books, 1986) is a defense of Addams's pluralism.

26. Horace Kallen, "Democracy versus the Melting-Pot, *Nation* (February 18, 1915), 190–94 and *Nation* (February 25, 1915), 217–20. The orchestra quotation is from page 220. Guterl, *Color of Race in America*, 84.

27. Randolph Bourne, "Trans-National America," in *War and the Intellectuals: Essays by Randolph S. Bourne, 1915–1919*, edited by Carl Resek (New York: Harper Torchbooks, 1964), 112.

28. Ibid., 122.

29. Brook Thomas, ed., *Plessy v. Ferguson: A Brief History with Documents* (Boston, MA: Bedford Books, 1996) contains the decision, dissenting opinion, supporting documents, and a wonderful discussion by Thomas of the difference between political and social rights.

30. My discussion owes much to Michael Berubé, *What's Liberal about the Liberal Arts? Classroom Politics and "Bias" in Higher Education* (New York: W. W. Norton, 2007), 159–79.

31. Williams, *Rethinking Race*, 59–61.

32. W. E. B. Du Bois, "The Conservation of Races," *American Negro Academy Occasional Papers*, no. 2, 1897, http://www.webdubois.org/dbConsrvOfRaces.html, par. 4, 5, 9, and 14. Cited 15 February 2007. Du Bois's position has been subjected to great debate. Wilson Jeremiah Moses, *The Golden Age of Black Nationalism, 1850–1925* (New York and London: Oxford University Press, 1988), and Kwame Anthony Appiah, *In My Father's House: Africa in the Philosophy of Culture* (New York and London: Oxford University Press, 1993), 28–46, find Du Bois's position confused and relying upon conflicting standards. Thomas Holt, "W. E. B. DuBois's Archaeology of Race: Rereading 'The Conservation of Races,'" in Michael B. Katz and Thomas J. Sugrue, eds. *W. E. B. DuBois, Race, and the City: "The Philadelphia Negro" and Its Legacy* (Philadelphia: University of Pennsylvania Press, 1998), 61–76 challenges views that emphasize Du Bois's inconsistency and his entrapment in Victorian modes of thought, opting instead for seeing the address as a "postmodern" reading of race as "a social, political, and historical construction of the modern era, linked to the expansion of European capital."

33. This and similar arguments led to the charge that Du Bois was a marginal man, a damaged mulatto. See Daryl Michael Scott, *Contempt and Pity: Social Policy and the Image of the Damaged Black Psyche, 1880–1996* (Chapel Hill: University of North Carolina Press, 1997), 1–17.

34. W. E. B. Du Bois, *The Souls of Black Folk* (New York: Signet, [1903] 1969), 3–4.

35. Although doubtful about possibilities of American life, especially in its present configuration, Du Bois was throughout his career torn between universalist and particularist impulses. At times, his Marxism took on universalist dimensions. These, however, constantly tussled with his nationalist ones. See David L. Lewis, *W. E. B. DuBois*, vol. 2, *The Fight for Equality and the American Century, 1919–1963* (New York: Henry Holt, 2000).

36. W. E. B. Du Bois, *The Negro* (New York: Henry Holt, 1915), 7.

37. Ibid., 146.

38. On Sumner, see Bruce Curtis, *William Graham Sumner* (Boston, MA: Twayne, 1981), and Charles Hunt Page, *Class and American Sociology from Ward to Ross* (New York: Dial, 1940). William Graham Sumner, *Folkways; a Study of the Sociological Importance of Usages, Manners, Customs, Mores, and Morals* (Boston, MA: Ginn, 1907), lays out Sumner's understanding of the noneconomic component of collective life.

39. Small, quoted in Page, *Class and American Sociology*, 135.

40. W. I. Thomas in Herbert Blumer, ed., *An Appraisal of Thomas and Znaniecki's The Polish Peasant in Europe and America* (New York: Social Science Research Council, 1939), 103. Biographical details from Eli Zaretsky, "Editor's Introduction," W. I. Thomas and Florian Znaniecki, *The Polish Peasant in Europe and America* (Urbana: University of Illinois Press, 1984).

41. Thomas and Znaniecki, *Polish Peasant*, 58–59.

42. As Eli Zaretsky notes, Thomas and Znaniecki concentrated on czarist-ruled Poland. Their account would have been different had they looked at the immigration from Austrian and Prussian Poland. Immigrants from the latter came in families; those from the former, as single laborers.

43. Thomas and Znaniecki, *Polish Peasant*, 1, 181.

44. Zaretsky, "Editor's Introduction," 20–23.

45. Bentley, *Process of Government*, 169–70.

46. Ibid., 92–93.

47. Ibid., 167–72.

48. Ibid., 211. See also p. 271, where Bentley asserts again that "interest is nothing other than the group activity itself."

49. Ibid., 460.

50. Ibid., 442.

51. Details of Beard's life have been taken from Ellen Nore, *Charles A. Beard: An Intellectual Biography* (Carbondale: Southern Illinois University Press, 1983).

52. Edwin R. A. Seligman, *The Economic Interpretation of History* (New York: Columbia University Press, [1907] 1961), 133.

53. James Harvey Robinson, *The New History: Essays Illustrating the Modern Historical Outlook* (New York: Macmillan, 1912), 6, 9. For a discussion of the New History, see John Higham, *History: Professional Scholarship in America* (Baltimore: Johns Hopkins University Press, 1989); Ellen F. Fitzpatrick, *History's Memory: Writing America's Past, 1880–1980* (Cambridge, MA: Harvard University Press, 2002); Peter Novick, *That Noble Dream: The "Objectivity Question" and the American Historical Profession* (Cambridge and New York: Cambridge University Press, 1988).

54. Robinson, *New History*, 17–18, 22.

55. Ibid., 64.

56. John W. Burgess, "The American Commonwealth: Changes in Its Relation to the Nation," in *Political Science Quarterly* 1 (1886): 12–34.

57. Beard, quoted in Nore, *Beard*, 60–61. Vernon Louis Parrington forged a Beardian interpretation of American literature and thought, contrasting the interests against the people in his momentous *Main Currents in American Thought*, published in the 1920s but conceived earlier. See Richard Hofstadter, *The Progressive Historians: Turner, Beard, Parrington* (New York: Alfred A. Knopf, 1968); and Hall Lark, *V. L. Parrington: Through the Avenue of Art* (Kent, OH: Kent State University Press, 1994).

58. The most succinct and telling analysis of Clark can be found in Wenzler, "Transcendental Economics," chapter 7. See also James Livingston, "The Social Analysis of Economic History and Theory: Conjectures on Late Nineteenth-Century American Development," *American Historical Review* 92, no. 1 (1987): 69–95; and John F. Henry, *John Bates Clark: The Making of a Neoclassical Economist* (New York: St. Martin's Press, 1995).

59. The following account of Veblen comes from Joseph Dorfman, *Thorstein Veblen and His America* (New York: Viking, 1934); John P. Diggins, *The Bard of Savagery: Thorstein Veblen and Modern Social Theory* (New York: Seabury, 1978); Dorothy Ross, *The Origins of American Social Science* (New York and Cambridge: Cambridge University Press, 1991); Cynthia Russett, *Darwin in America: The Intellectual Response, 1865–1912* (San Francisco: W. H. Freeman, 1976); Rick Tilman, *The Intellectual Legacy of Thorstein: Veblen Unresolved Issues* (Westport, CT: Greenwood, 1996).

60. Thorstein Veblen, "Why Is Economics Not an Evolutionary Science?" *Quarterly Journal of Economics* 12, no. 4 (July 1898), 373–97.

61. Thorstein Veblen, *The Theory of the Leisure Class* (New York: Penguin, [1899] 1967), 212–45. See also Thorstein Veblen, *The Instinct of Workmanship and the State of Industrial Arts* (New York: B. W. Huebsch, 1912), and "The Beginnings of Ownership," *American Journal of Sociology* (November 1898), 352–65.

62. Veblen, "Beginnings of Ownership," 364.

63. Veblen, *Leisure Class*, 96–97.

64. Thorstein Veblen, *Absentee Ownership and Business Enterprise in Recent Times: The Case of America* (New York: B. W. Huebsch, 1923), 319.

65. Thorstein Veblen, "On the Nature of Capital," in Thorstein Veblen, *The Place of Science in Modern Civilisation and Other Essays* (New York: Viking, 1919), 332. See

also "Industrial and Pecuniary Employments," in the same volume; and Veblen, *The Theory of Business Enterprise* (New York: Charles Scribner's Sons, 1915).

66. Veblen, *Theory of Business Enterprise*, 374–400.

67. Veblen, *Leisure Class*, 217.

68. Brett Frelhinger, *The 1912 Election and the Power of Progressivism: A Brief History with Documents* (Boston, MA: Bedford/St. Martin's, 2003), 19.

69. In addition to Richard Hofstadter, *The Age of Reform: From Bryan to F.D.R.* (New York: Vintage Books, 1962); Robert H. Wiebe, *The Search for Order, 1877–1920* (New York: Hill and Wang, 1967); and Martin J. Sklar, *The Corporate Reconstruction of American Capitalism, 1890–1916: The Market, the Law, and Politics* (Cambridge and New York: Cambridge University Press, 1988), see also Michael E. McGerr, *A Fierce Discontent: The Rise and Fall of the Progressive Movement in America, 1870–1920* (New York: Free Press, 2003); Glenda Elizabeth Gilmore, *Who Were the Progressives?* (Boston, MA: Bedford/St. Martin's, 2002); Daniel T. Rodgers, *Atlantic Crossings: Social Politics in a Progressive Age* (Cambridge, MA: Belknap Press of Harvard University Press, 1998); and Eldon Eisenach, *The Lost Promise of Progressivism* (Lawrence: University Press of Kansas, 1994).

70. Peter G. Filene, "An Obituary for 'The Progressive Movement,'" *American Quarterly* 22 (Spring 1970): 20–34; and Daniel Rodgers, "In Search of Progressivism," *Reviews in American History* 10 (1982): 113–32.

71. Walter Lippmann, *Drift and Mastery* (Madison: University of Wisconsin Press, [1913] 1985), 118.

72. Sklar, *The Corporate Reconstruction of American Capitalism, 1890–1916: The Market, the Law, and Politics*, 1–85; Eisenach, *The Lost Promise of Progressivism*, 138–86; and Rodgers, *Atlantic Crossings: Social Politics in a Progressive Age*, 78–111, have detailed discussions of the ways in which this latter group of progressives responded to an industrial corporate economy through hopes that maintaining constant supply through regulation and industrial consolidation would end the problem of overproduction, guarantee profits, and thus remove wages as the crucial and most vulnerable component of economic life. The latter two deal as well with the creation of new forms of provisioning that were placed on the political agenda during the first fifteen years of the twentieth century.

73. Mary O. Furner, *Advocacy and Objectivity: A Crisis in the Professionalization of American Social Science, 1865–1905* (Lexington: Published for the Organization of American Historians [by] the University Press of Kentucky, 1975).

74. See Page, *Class and American Sociology*; and Dorothy Ross, "Socialism and American Liberalism: Academic Social Thought in the 1880s," *Perspectives in American History* 11 (1977–1978): 5–79.

75. Walter Weyl, *The New Democracy: An Essay on Certain Political and Economic Tendencies in the United States* (New York: Macmillan, 1912), 168–85, quotations from 184–85.

76. Ibid., 185.

77. Ibid., 41–46.

78. Throughout the late nineteenth century, courts had protected corporations from regulation by states and localities by holding that for purposes of law, corporations were individuals and thus protected by the Fourteenth Amendment against infringement of rights to due process and property holding. See discussions in Rebecca Edwards, *New Spirits: Americans in the Gilded Age, 1865–1905* (New York: Oxford University Press, 2006); Robert G. McCloskey, *American Conservatism in the Age of Enterprise: A Study of William Graham Sumner, Stephen J. Field, and Andrew Carnegie* (Cambridge, MA: Harvard University Press, 1951); Sklar, *The Corporate Reconstruction of American Capitalism, 1890–1916: The Market, the Law, and Politics*; and Mark W Summers, *The Gilded Age, Or, The Hazard of New Functions* (Upper Saddle River, NJ: Prentice Hall, 1997).

79. *Lochner v. New York*, 198 U.S. 45 (1905).

80. Lippmann, *Drift and Mastery*, 36–42. Public-service capitalism, rooted in the separation of ownership and management, is a trope of long standing in American social criticism, from Veblen to Lippmann in our period to Adolph Berle and Gardiner Means in the 1930s to John Kenneth Galbraith in the 1950s and 1960s. For a discussion of the lineage, see Howard Brick, *Transcending Capitalism: Visions of a New Society in Modern American Thought* (Ithaca, NY: Cornell University Press, 2006).

81. Karen McCally, "'A Bundle of Rights': The Commons School and American Social Policy, 1905–1945" (PhD diss., University of Rochester, 2001).

82. Commons's Christianity imbues all his work. His earliest and most explicit statement is *Social Reform and the Church* (New York: A. M. Kelley, 1967 [1894]).

83. As McCally demonstrated, Commons had begun his career at Indiana and Syracuse University advocating a right to work, which angered trustees. His later work was more circumspect in this regard.

84. See Jane Addams, "A Modern Lear," *Survey* 29 (November 2, 1912): 131–37, and *Twenty Years at Hull House*, 154–97.

85. Mary Parker Follett, *The New State: Group Organization, the Solution of Popular Government* (New York: Longmans, Green, 1918), 199, 210. See also Marc Stears, *Progressives, Pluralists, and the Problems of the State: Ideologies of Reform in the United States and Britain, 1909–1926* (Oxford and New York: Oxford University Press, 2002).

86. This criteria leads Eldon Eisenach to read Woodrow Wilson out of the progressive camp. Wilson was interested in maintaining sectional political economies rather than national ones and promoted self rather than social interest as the key to social peace, claims Eisenach. John Milton Cooper concurs, arguing that Roosevelt wanted to transcend interests and Wilson wanted to harmonize them. Wilson, he avers, had no sense of the public good as something apart or separate from interests that he believed to be eradicable (Eisenach, *Lost Promise of Progressivism*, and John Milton Cooper, *The Warrior and the Priest: Woodrow Wilson and Theodore Roosevelt* [Cambridge, MA: Belknap Press of Harvard University Press, 1983], especially 210–40).

87. Michael McGerr notes the role of consumerism in the politics of the Progressive Era, not only in the well-noted passage of pure food and drug and meat inspection

laws, but also in the failure of conservation to take hold and progressive appeals to social unity to be successful after the emergency of the war (McGerr, *Fierce Discontent*, 158–82, 300–301). Weyl himself noted that the consumer movement was more successful as a political than an industrial movement, noting the general inability of boycotts to produce long-lasting change in working conditions.

CHAPTER FIVE

War

By 1915, multiplicity had become a prominent feature in American cultural and intellectual life. Never before had contingency, local truths, and particular beauties been as prominent as they were in the early twentieth century. This change was far from complete and did not go unchallenged. Efforts to recoup unity ranged from opposition to the Armory Show to a refurbished and increasingly insistent racialist thought. Opponents of multiplicity exaggerated, however, when they branded it a species of nihilism. Few of those who rejected absolutism jettisoned laws or regulation entirely. If the social self opened the human personality to new identities, those identities on inspection proved to be not so much different from the ones that most Americans had already possessed. If the economy was not really self-correcting, neither was it so directionless and irregular that it could not be mastered. Most who rejected economic orthodoxy in the early twentieth century were not prepared to abolish private property (as opposed to restricting it) or to suspend market relations. The contribution of multiplicity to American intellectual life was less that its presence resulted in immediate sweeping changes in practice (although in such matters as art, social thought, and morality, those who operated from the assumption of multiplicity departed quite significantly from the norm) than that it provided justification for experimentation.

The First World War presented a stern test for the vitality of multiplicity in American cultural life. Not only did the issue of entering the war involve crucial problems of politics and morality, but the scope of the war effort made it difficult for most Americans to avoid its impact. In fighting a modern war, the state endeavored to organize and reorganize American life, sometimes to dramatic effect. The war crisis unsettled routines, expectations, and peace-time relations, raising the question whether the acceptance of many truths and goods was useful or an encumbrance. Hewing to multiplicity under such circumstances made many uneasy, and they embraced creeds that offered a more unified view of the world. Others kept their commitment to multiplic-ity, seeing the war as proof of the inability of a general, overarching truth to provide valid explanations or to establish uniform judgment about what course of action to take in regard to the war. Because pragmatism, mod-ernism, and the new social sciences had emphasized contingency, their prac-titioners read the war crisis differently. John Dewey, George Herbert Mead, Charles Horton Cooley, and Henri Bergson were among the leading plural-ists to support the war. Thorstein Veblen, in his own peculiar way, did as well. Franz Boas, Randolph Bourne, and Elsie Parsons, on the other hand, opposed it. All justified their positions on the war in terms of their multiplicity, even though some admitted in the aftermath that they missed the full extent of the abstractions and absolutism embedded in the war effort.

The status of multiplicity in American culture resembled a war within the war. Not only did those whose work advanced multiplicity differ among themselves, but those who were uneasy about the direction of a culture that lacked a singular foundation in truth and value saw in a war effort a chance to roll back the advances of multiplicity. Victory, they argued, required na-tional unity around a singular standard. In their effort to remove discordant elements, cultural traditionalists found an ally in the government, which un-dertook not only to organize production and classify and examine the popu-lation in order to match personnel to war needs but also to guide public opin-ion and regulate moral behavior to shield Americans from elements that would drain their fervor for the war. In efforts ranging from the Committee on Public Information (the Creel Committee, so called after its head, the muckraking journalist George Creel), which was designed to regulate the flow of knowledge, to Loyalty League campaigns to reform "hyphenated Americans," to purges of shop-floor radicals as saboteurs of production, to the strict Espionage and Sedition Acts, many Americans warred on difference. The drive for uniformity was extensive. Anthropologists, cinematographers, restaurateurs, and young women in search of a pleasant morale-boosting evening with a military man were among those whose activities prompted in-tense scrutiny for signs of unacceptable pluralism.

Cultural conservatives could not, however, restore unity by fiat. With the Armistice, much of the urgency disappeared, as did the commitment of many

Americans. Much to the chagrin of those who believed in the need for general principles and unwavering standards, multiplicity remained a significant part of American thought and culture, even if it could not claim to be the predominant strain. In such phenomena as Carl Becker's pessimism, which he modeled on Henry Adams's, the seeming solipsistic language experiments in poetry of Ezra Pound, and the strange forms of the painter Max Weber, multiplicity assumed an orientation that rejected most every sort of generalization or synthesis.[1] That form of multiplicity was not the only one on offer. John Dewey and Jane Addams, for their part, took note of the failures of postwar reconstruction, but neither embraced unity or the multiplicity of incommensurability. In surviving as a feature of cultural and intellectual life, the impetus to accept plurality made many Americans suspicious of claims that all fit together. The endurance of multiplicity ensured that American culture would continue to negotiate between the general and the specific, the one and the many.

Debating the War

In autumn 1914, most Americans either thought the war would be a short affair or considered it yet another example of European degeneration hardly worth bothering about. By 1915, those attitudes gave way to a full-scale American debate about the Great War. That debate was a multifaceted affair in which those who had long argued for unity in thought and morals and those whose work undercut such assumptions often found themselves in unanticipated alliances. For the former, deciding how to respond to the war was relatively straightforward. It was, depending upon one's absolute principles, a righteous struggle or a hideous crime. The first position was that of the elites of the Republican Party and old-line members of the middle classes of the Northeast. As former president Theodore Roosevelt presented the argument, the war was a matter of moral clarity. German militarism was aggressive and shamefully unprincipled. German atrocities were outrages against civilized codes of conduct, all the more so because the perpetrators expressed no remorse for their subjugation of neutrals. Unopposed, German imperial advance posed a danger not only to the legitimate commercial interests of the United States, but also to the preservation of an ethical order to which the United States was committed by its very nature. Americans were honorbound, Roosevelt maintained, to resist the Central Powers. Brooking no effeminate doubts, which he regarded as corrosive as German aggression was immoral, Roosevelt was only the most prominent of voices that early on sided with the Allies.[2]

Wilsonian neutrality also derived its strength from its moral vision. Driven less by pacifism than by the premise of American moral innocence for the bloodshed, Wilson and his supporters based their original noninvolvement on their sense that the war stemmed from European corruption and nationalist rivalries in which the United States had no stake. As revisionist historians Gordon Levin and William Appleman Williams have pointed out, Wilsonian internationalism rested on the supposed contrast between the competitive struggle that dominated European diplomatic maneuvering and the open and cooperative nature of American efforts.[3] The editors of the liberal *New Republic* lacked Wilson's moral certainty, but they too saw no American interest in the war, save ending it. Early on, editor Herbert Croly indicated that his interest in the war was "becoming more and more a matter of seeking its probable results in making over the European international system," a position that implied the unhealthy and unproductive nature of the war aims of the European belligerents.[4] Even sensational reports of German crimes in Belgium did not immediately convince Americans that the war was an existential struggle in which the United States could not remain on the sidelines.

Wilson's conviction that the United States embodied a unique integration of progress and morality remained part of his intellectual arsenal, even as he reluctantly concluded that war was inevitable and potentially uplifting. Convinced that American actions were morally commendable because untainted by any thought of gain, Wilson articulated aims in his war message to Congress that committed the United States to holding other nations to standards of morality similar to those that governed relations among moral persons. Despite later charges of rigid Wilsonian moralism, the president was far from alone among his contemporaries in applying moral codes to foreign policy. Very few Americans entered the debate with the realist outlook that George Kennan and Hans Morgenthau would later use to condemn Wilsonianism. Particularly revealing was the morality that Wilson and his supporters championed. In calling for "peace without victory" and "making the world safe for democracy," Wilson defined morality as a matter of renunciation, assuming the principles were universal and relatively straightforward to apply. Wilson's certainty derived from a set of unifying assumptions. Not only did he take for granted that humanity agreed on what constituted higher interests in the abstract, but he also supposed that the peoples of the world could view the conflict from a disinterested perspective and would act accordingly to secure the agreed-upon higher interests. "Only free peoples," he maintained, "can hold their purpose and their honor steady to a common end and prefer the interests of mankind to any narrow interest of their own."[5]

Among academic supporters of the war, the indictment of German behavior soon became entwined with the politics of intellectual orientation. In the emerging indictment, Central Power criminality was not the simple venality of leaders, but a consequence of deep-seated cultural inclinations. By their lights, Germany was the absolutist state par excellence, beholden to no laws outside its province and claimant to a monopoly on Truth and Morality. The claim of the German state to embody ultimate principle, spurred on by a corps of philosophers that legitimated it, allowed it to demand the total allegiance of its people. Ironically, as autocratic and centralized as Americans thought it to be, Germany also exemplified the faults that academicians had attributed to multiplicity. Without guiding standards, they charged, the self became the standard and judge of truth, and so convinced of its righteousness, it would confuse desires with rights. Christian Gauss of Princeton pointed not only to the aggressive German character (a clear holdover of racialist thought) but also to the blind loyalty that filled the void left by the rejection of the common-sense version of truth and morality. "We are fighting *das Deutschtum*. And what is *das Deutschtum*? It is the mystic conception of the mission, the power, and the privileges of the German people which is to be realized by the German state. It has no principles. It is above them."[6] The philosopher Arthur Lovejoy, who had opposed pragmatism on grounds of its incoherent fluidity, echoed Gauss's analysis. As early as 1914, he had seen the war as an epic struggle to fend off German threats to civilization. Reacting to letters defending German acts in Belgium, Lovejoy accused such German intellectual signatories as Max Planck and Georg Simmel of being mere servants to power. The Germans had clearly abandoned any commitment to detached consideration and were driven by the wrongheaded notions about the virtues of an absolutist state. Eventually, Lovejoy concluded that "in spite of England's many past sins against the light, any serious weakening of the British Empire would be an incalculable and irreparable loss to the material and the higher moral interests of the United States, and to the cause of free government throughout the world."[7]

Lovejoy's assertion that the war was an extraordinary moral struggle figured into his position on academic freedom. In charge of drafting a statement on the issue for the fledgling American Association of University Professors, Lovejoy made clear that the unique nature of the war required suspension of normal rules of conduct. The report endorsed the logic of total war, arguing that universities were not immune from the necessity of supporting war aims. To do otherwise was to "desire the triumph of moral evil in the world." Responding to those who argued that protecting only one side of an argument was not protecting free inquiry, Lovejoy responded that universities could not allow themselves to be in a position that would "bring about the defeat and dishonor of the republic and do immeasurable injury to the cause of freedom throughout the world." In Lovejoy's view, universities faced an absolute choice between becoming an agent of the state or becoming its enemy. In vastly overestimating both the scope of antiwar sentiment in the academy and the effect that sentiment could have on the war effort, Lovejoy and his compatriots ironically demonstrated the power of contingency in human affairs. As Carol Gruber has noted, Lovejoy's defense of the necessity of violating principles that one would have observed in "normal" conditions replicated that of the German intellectuals whom he had stridently criticized in 1914 for failing to detach themselves from their context so as to evaluate events critically.[8]

In terms of its moral certainty, the pacifism of the American Union Against Militarism (AUAM) mirrored that of war advocates. A coalition of such gentry figures as Amos Pinchot and Oswald Garrison Villard and labor radicals such as Crystal Eastman and Florence Kelley, the AUAM was predicated on the notion that war had no moral standing. To engage in it was to answer wrongdoing with wrongdoing, members contended. Taking lives, they averred, did not redress grievances. Aware that a military created pressure to use it, members of the AUAM opposed the preparedness programs of 1915 and 1916 as training in aggression and breeding grounds of irrationality. They were particularly keen to prevent military action against Mexico, which had been bruited about as a response to Pancho Villa's raids and the political uncertainty in that country. AUAM members regarded war agitation as the consequence of the immature masculine strut of Roosevelt and his allies, and not as the basis of a moral policy.[9]

It was this position that John Dewey criticized for its misleading absolutism. It was predicated, he held, on "the tendency to dispose of war by bringing it under the commandment against murder, the belief that by *not* doing something, by keeping out of a declaration of war, our responsibilities could be met." This, Dewey declared, was "a somewhat mushy belief in the existence of disembodied moral forces which require only an atmosphere of feelings to operate so as to bring about what is right, the denial of the efficacy of force, no matter how controlled, to modify disposition; in short, the inveterate habit of separating ends from means and then identifying morals with ends thus emasculated."[10] Those who abjured war under all circumstances, Dewey continued, failed to make the distinction between force, the energy required to realize purposeful action, and violence, the use of means inappropriate or counterproductive for the desired end. Squeamishness about force was little more than "moonstruck morals."[11]

George Herbert Mead launched a similar pragmatic attack on conscientious objection. Pacifism, he contended, ran against human nature, since as an empirical matter humans have always engaged in conflict. Mead doubted that so dominant a human trait could be sufficiently suppressed or sublimated to make the use of force under any conditions abhorrent. As a progressive who believed that individuals had social obligations to protect the community, Mead saw the conscientious objector as holding a doctrine that "renders martyrdom almost inevitable, when his country is involved in a war that seriously threatens its existence or whatever values the country insists on fighting for."[12] In light of the inability of the government to devise an acid test of sincerity of such rather irregular and minority beliefs, Mead held it perfectly justified in enforcing conscription laws. Otherwise, pacifists would be removing themselves from the community in the same way tax evaders did. Although Mead went further in allowing debate than Lovejoy (he granted people the right to agitate against conscription laws, but not to prevent their enforcement), he was concerned to preserve the right of the community to regulate and protect itself:

> War brings about exceptional conditions. For a war may involve the very existence of the country itself. Questions of policy which are debatable and must be debated under a democracy, if they involve the war itself and its successful conduct, cannot be debated while it is going on. Such discussion may very well involve a serious weakening of the country in its fight and even lead to its defeat, and the loss of the very institutions of democracy itself. No government in war time can suffer a movement at home against the armies of the country and their conduct, any more than it will give way willingly before the enemy in the field.[13]

Mead, like Dewey, indicted war opponents as purists who would have the United States simply withdraw from the world so as not to sully itself. Men such as Sen. Robert La Follette (R-Wisc.) And former secretary of state William Jennings Bryan unrealistically proposed to shut down commerce so as to avoid German U-boats and British blockades. By the same token, Mead charged, their eagerness to label Britain and Germany both autocracies on the basis of the existence of the British monarchy and landed aristocracy and limited suffrage rights was an absolutism that failed to make meaningful distinctions. Beyond its lack of realism, the neutrality of the La Follette–Bryan variety was also tacit support for the Prussian autocracy, since it robbed the allies of needed goods. In the logic of total war, Mead contended that not adopting the cause of the allies "meant becoming the unwilling and ignominious allies of Germany and Austria. There would probably have been no instance in the recorded history of the world in which the very failure to act would have been such decided action, and an action so contrary to the intent of the agents."[14] Denying the possibility for action independent of the two sides, Mead reduced pragmatic problem solving to an either/or proposition. Faced with such a choice, Mead himself opted reluctantly for war, seeing it as a principled choice to duplicate abroad the form of rule that was deeply rooted at home.[15]

As Terrance MacMullan has demonstrated (and Dewey and Mead reluctantly admitted), Jane Addams arrived at a pacifist position without recourse to absolute principles. Rather than insisting that killing under any and all circumstances was a sin, Addams and her compatriots in the Women's Peace Party (later, Women's International League for Peace and Freedom) argued pragmatically that war was incapable of resolving problems. Addams rejected the contention that war led to good, much less optimal, solutions for individuals or for nations. A "limiting experience" that provided no uplifting test for soldiers, it had no purchase on adjudicating the international political and economic problems that lay behind the war. Why, she asked, did the problem of building a railroad to Baghdad or securing a corridor to the sea necessarily result in war? Much of her argument was patiently empirical, attempting to document how war thoroughly stymied human needs. She was convinced, MacMullan has forcefully argued, that war would introduce the unpragmatic "deceptive cry of mock patriotism: 'our country, right or wrong' that forestalled the intelligent search for solutions." It would enforce not the constant testing and adaptation that pragmatists prized, but operation from first principles. Addams was certain that war fever would roll back democratic reform and tighten the control of undemocratic elements in the quest for unity.[16] Addams in effect rejected a bad unity for a good one. Her sense that war had no efficacy as a problem-solving device and could be replaced by meaningful and real arbitration of grievances was based on the proposition that it was possible to find a common ground between the contending parties.

Universalist sentiments were capable of generating positions on the war that did not rely on a blanket condemnation of force. Such was the case of Felix Adler, the founder of the Ethical Culture movement. Adler's ethical culture was based in Kantian notions of obligation. Abjuring utilitarianism in morals, Adler and the ethical culture movement judged acts by the degree to which they measured up to a transcendent standard of perfection, which few did. Adler was especially concerned that people respect others as legitimate ends and grant them freedom for development. Acknowledging the crimes of the Central Powers, Adler nonetheless maintained that those bad acts did not settle the matter of motives. By Adler's lights, neither side met the criteria of moral behavior. Rejecting the pacifist contention that militarism was the cause of the deep flaw in civilization that produced a war of such ferocity, Adler located the cause in the imperialist struggle for domination, of which the Great War was only the most current, albeit most violent, manifestation. As long as commercialism inculcated the spirit of aggression, and as long as "strong peoples permit themselves to prey on the weaker peoples of the earth, on the false plea that they are spreading civilization," militarism would not be expunged from the repertoire of human behavior. The great powers on both sides had failed to respect the uniqueness of others and did little to aid subject peoples to engage in more direct expression of their essential qualities. Belgian acts of cruelty in the Congo did not justify or cancel out German ones in Belgium, Adler insisted, but they demonstrated that no combatant had properly held civilization in trust. Protecting that kind of civilization was the goal toward which power should be directed, not opting for some "lesser evil."[17]

Adler needed only to apply his ethical culture to oppose the war. Those who started with the assumption that the way to live in the world could not be determined a priori were faced with the task of justifying their position without recourse to universal abstract principles. For them, the war was less a specific instance of a general consideration than a new problem in the continuation of life. What is striking about the heated debates is that both pro- and antiwar pluralists justified their position as a struggle against both political and philosophical absolutism. At stake was overcoming threats to the ability of humans to respond creatively and experimentally to the world. Where they differed, of course, is the source of that threat. Advocates of American intervention regarded Germany as the avatar of absolutism, prone to aggression by ideology and training. In addition to disputing that Germany alone among the combatants was responsible for absolutist politics, war opponents charged that the very techniques and institutions needed to fight the war were bound to enforce a coercive regimentation. The dispute over how profitably to understand the implications of multiplicity in the face of war was at issue in the famed Randolph Bourne–John Dewey disagreement over the war. Although not quite a debate, in that Dewey did not directly respond to Bourne's position, their differences have long been a mainstay of American cultural and intellectual history, and for good reason. Not only did this episode raise questions about the relations of intellect and power, it dealt with the best way to evaluate social justice and to act to achieve it. In assertions about the duty to the community and the nature of society, Bourne and Dewey batted back and forth different understandings about the way in which multiplicity affected the premier question of the day.

For Dewey and like-minded antifoundationalists, support for American entrance into the war on the side of the Entente could not, of course, follow from the assertion that entering the war was an absolute good, self-evident, or "common sense." It had to be tested on the basis of ends and means. As such German acts as the escalated U-boat campaign of 1916–1917 and the Zimmerman Note, which promised Mexico land in exchange for an alliance with Germany, began to encroach on American rights and prerogatives, a number of progressives reconsidered their earlier understanding of the war as the conflict of rival imperialisms. The refusal of the German government to honor agreements, its decision to forgo all negotiation by late 1916, and its frank rejection of even the appearance of democracy led many progressives and pragmatists to conclude reluctantly that the proposition that both sides were equally guilty of violating American rights and had equally unpalatable war goals was untenable. Although not denying Great Britain and France's transgressions, those associated with the *New Republic* and such independent intellectuals as Thorstein Veblen and Carl Becker were more prone to dismiss them as "technical" and to consider Central Power acts as considerably more brutal and more dangerous to America and the world. That danger stemmed less from the immediate likelihood of German occupation of American soil than from German aggression preventing Americans from engaging in legitimate activities abroad. A German victory would, as well, establish the validity of force of arms and aggression as solving disputes. Well before the declaration of war aims, Dewey and his compatriots began building the case that the war involved not only political and social ends, but philosophical ones as well. At stake was not simply the expansionism of German autocracy, but the absolutist ideas that authorized it. We might see their understanding of the war as an effort to make the world safe for multiplicity by clearing away the traditional overgrowth that had made blind allegiance, hierarchical decision making, and inflexibility seem natural and self-evident. Prowar pragmatists and pluralists hoped that it would be possible to fight absolutism in democratic ways in which warranted action, tested and retested by consequences, would eventuate in a national solidarity that was less commanded than earned.

Crucial to the intellectuals' war effort was the reconfiguration of Germany and its works. Although the United States and Germany had a dust-up in the late nineteenth century over German desires to ply its influence in Latin America, Germany had occasioned little demonization prior to the war. Indeed, among intellectuals, Germany often held pride of place for its cultural and intellectual achievements. A large number of academics had received their doctoral training in Germany. Many university presidents had opted for the German research model over the English liberal arts one. The new physics was quite inconceivable without German participation. German social programs had attracted considerable admiration among American reformers. Much of the new psychology had links to German discoveries. Nor would "culture" have made headway as a concept without the contributions of German-born Franz Boas. These and sundry other German cultural traits were influential in establishing John W. Burgess's early wartime position. A historian and political scientist who had negotiated German–American exchange professorships, Burgess defended Germany as a vanguard of civilization that was reacting defensively against Allied efforts to quarantine the nation in the Balkans and the North Sea, in his 1915 volume *The European War of 1914*. His loyalty seemed less to Germany as such than to imperial Germany. When Franz Boas asked Burgess to join him in publishing a letter in support of a hands-off policy toward the revolution of Rosa Luxemburg and Karl Leibknecht, he scornfully refused.[18]

Few liberals shared the judgment of G. Stanley Hall that Germans were totally deficient in human feeling, but they did hold that German social and political arrangements were particularly poisonous. Thorstein Veblen's analysis was especially at pains to demonstrate the point. Veblen recognized the mixed motives and imperial desires of Britain, France, and czarist Russia, and he had no use for patriotism, holding that it was another example of invidious comparison and the struggle for prestige. He did, however, single out Germany as a special case of evolutionary deformation, a case where elements unsuited for the new environment had managed to maintain power. *Imperial Germany and the Industrial Revolution* laid out how a barbaric ruling class, driven by invidious motives, harnessed the power of a unique industrial scheme. German industrial power benefitted from its late arrival (a typically Veblenian reversal of conventional wisdom), which made it all the more capable of expropriating from the underlying population.[19] The Junkers therefore were especially free to engage in vicious imperial aggression, and they cemented their hold by a unique state in which fealty to a feudal monarch had become transformed into subordination to the collective strength vested in a divinely appointed emperor. By use of an imperial tariff policy, compulsory military service, and a government system of industrial tutelage, the Prussian ruling class developed a superior fighting machine. For Veblen, this was "cultural reversion" with a vengeance. So pressing did Veblen find the need to oppose this tendency that he put aside his usual ironic detachment to serve the war effort in the Food Administration. Perhaps Veblen's commitment to the defeat of Germany can be gauged by a letter his wife wrote his teenage daughter Ann in 1918. "The 'present day' 'Radicals' in America are mostly pro-German passifists [sic] & Bolsheviki and are no friends of ours. . . . You must keep in mind that we are most bitterly opposed to any kind of pro-German propaganda or sympathizers."[20]

However fervent Veblen's support of the war may have been (and there is reason to think it less strong than his wife's account), the mixed reception accorded *Imperial Germany* is indicative of its author's unwillingness to jettison his mode of dealing with contingency. In seeing Germany as an extreme example of malformed development, Veblen did little to whitewash Allied transgressions and bestow the mantle of indivisible goodness on them. Like other Veblenian writings, the book was fierce in its criticism of those who were so stuck in metaphysics and absolutes that they were incapable of adapting to the environment. George Creel recognized the value of Veblen's attack on both the German state and the German aristocracy and distributed the book through the auspices of the Committee on Public Information. Others found it a tacit justification of "Hun" aggression, primarily because of Veblen's barbs about the atavistic conditions of the Allies. No such divided response greeted Veblen's next venture, *Inquiry into the Nature of Peace* (1917). Begun even before American entrance, the book indicated that the war had multiple facets and that the fight against Germany was only one of them. Veblen argued that patriotism could not lead to the general benefit, because the gulf in material interests of the leisure class and the underlying population was so great that it could not be bridged by any common enterprise. Writers to the *New York Times* called the book too dangerous to let undergraduates read. Theodore Roosevelt wanted Veblen clapped into jail for his caustic dismissal of patriotism as mere habit, his insistence that common folk were manipulated against their own interests by their leaders, and that peace required an elimination of the very institutions that Roosevelt and his allies believed they were defending.[21] In the end, Veblen could not rest satisfied with an analysis that exculpated the price system by laying all the blame on German aggression.

In testimony to the different understandings of multiplicity in social analysis, George Herbert Mead found Veblen's view of patriotism too absolutist for his taste. Taking Veblen to task for construing patriotism purely negatively, Mead objected most strenuously to one element in Veblen's social thought that resisted unity: Veblen's contention that society as currently constituted was inevitably and always divided against itself. Mead pointed to signs that he thought demonstrated the possibility of unity and charged that Veblen failed to recognize any principle of social growth or positive social force that tended toward democratic control, a charge not entirely true of Veblen's immediate postwar work. By concentrating primarily on material advantages, Mead contended, Veblen wrongly concluded that humans gained no advantage out of the structure of society. He failed entirely to recognize the "consciousness that comes with the feel of the greater values that belong to more complete community life." Where Veblen saw force and fraud, Mead insisted in 1918 there was community solidarity. Veblen's yearning for the end of capitalism, Mead maintained, was too simple and abstract, uprooting the positive with the negative. In contrast, he lauded the reconstruction program of the English Labor Party that did not abolish private property but proceeded slowly and experimentally to combine a number of forces to expand social property in education, sanitary science, and improved housing.[22]

Dewey's treatise on German philosophy, *German Philosophy and Politics*, paralleled Veblen's *Imperial Germany*. Both applied elements of their prewar work to the current situation, and both located dangerous adherence to the absolute in German culture. Although Dewey began with German ideals rather than German productive relations, he shared with Veblen a sense that Germany was plagued by the malady of metaphysics. Dewey traced the fatal wound in German culture to the dualism that Immanuel Kant had introduced into German culture. Kant rigidly separated the inner and outer worlds and celebrated the self over the latter. In addition, Kantian ethics championed obligation to the transcendent, disinterested morality and dismissed any act with regard to personal interest as inherently impure and compromised. Dewey found the combination lethal. Wrote Dewey, "the gospel of a Duty devoid of content naturally lent itself to the consecration and idealization of such specific duties as the existing national order might prescribe. The sense of duty must get its subject matter somewhere, and unless subjectivism was to revert to anarchic or romantic individualism (which is hardly in the spirit of obedience to authoritative law) its appropriate subject matter lies in the commands of a superior."[23] Because German culture lacked an ethics in which humans derived their moral worth from outcomes in the world, German philosophy was driven by an unblinking desire to realize the ideal. Germans located the manifestation of the ideal in the state, which made for self-righteous militarism and ceaseless aggression. Although clearly sympathetic with the Allies, Dewey claimed the book was not designed as brief for the war as much as a warning of the dangers of absolutism as such.[24]

Prowar liberals may have, as David Kennedy argues, supported the war provisionally with an awareness of the possibilities for failure, but quite a few convinced themselves to support the war by imagining the possibilities of reform at home as well as abroad.[25] In both public rhetoric and private correspondence, many seemed to have confused the ideal America with the real, underplaying the strength of antireform forces and overestimating popular commitment to social transformation. For many pragmatists, *New Republic* intellectuals, and pluralists, making the world safe for democracy was more than a propaganda slogan; it defined the ends and means of the war itself. A war conducted democratically would invariably extend democracy at home. Walter Lippmann allowed himself a number of enthusiasms, conjuring up a sense that the war could create a commitment "as never before to the realization of democracy in America." He insisted that the war would lead to a confrontation with American "autocracies" in Colorado mines and steel industries and new interests in ending the sweatshops and slums. The National Women's Trade Union League of America saw the war as an opportunity to nationalize rails, strengthen collective bargaining, and "conscript wealth."[26] W. E. B. Du Bois, for his part, hoped that black support for the war would redound to the dissolution of legal inferiority.[27] Du Bois endorsed the war as much from the fear that blacks could not risk being outside the national consensus as from the hope that the war itself would eventuate in real racial reform.

Randolph Bourne entertained no such hopes. His face disfigured by a forceps delivery at birth and suffering as a child from spinal tuberculosis, which left him a hunchback, Bourne was well schooled in discourses of multiplicity, having attended the Columbia of Dewey, Boas, and Beard. He made a name for himself as an incisive essayist, whose series on "Youth" declared permanent opposition to the encrusted traditions of Victorian certainties. His reports on the Gary, Indiana, schools, which Bourne thought attempted to put Deweyan educational theories into practice, captured the excitement of learning by melding thought and action. As critics have noted, his famous wartime writings bear the mark of personal slights delivered by former allies and friends alienated by his opposition to the war. During the run-up to the war and during the war itself, Bourne was marginalized at the *New Republic*, and other venues soon closed as well, either by editor choice or by government action. Having been persuaded by Dewey of the virtues of pragmatism, Bourne was especially disturbed by Dewey's failure to recognize absolutism when presented with it. Yet more than personal relations were involved. Critics, then and now, have honored Bourne as insisting that the office of the intellectual was that of speaking truth to power. In the conjuncture in which they were made, Bourne's criticisms were a reminder that prewar multiplicity could take the world to be more plastic than it was. Bourne's essays called pragmatists to account for taking antifoundationalism to mean that history could be easily directed. In positing the war as a destructive, intractable force, Bourne sounded a warning about how easily people could abandon rea-

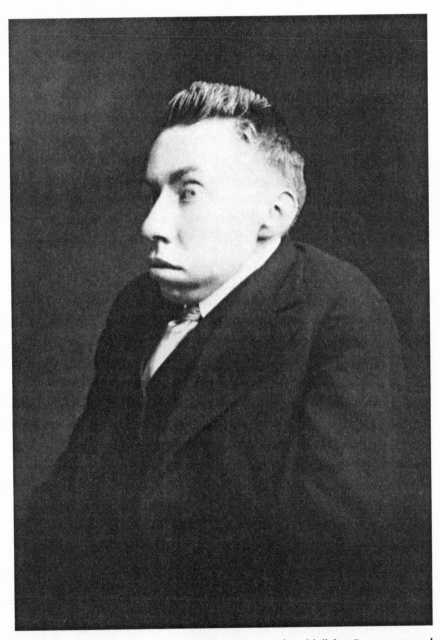

Figure 5.1. Randolph Bourne. A fierce proponent of multiplicity, Bourne opposed American entrance into the war on the grounds that it was bound to destroy democratic and pluralist movements. His stance was often a lonely one, as many of his fellow pragmatists supported the war effort, which Bourne savagely analyzed in a number of trenchant articles in 1917 and 1918. (Randolph Bourne Papers, Rare Book and Manuscript Library, Columbia University)

son and allow themselves to be swept along by the promise of achievement and harmony.[28]

Bourne's dissent from the accommodation to the war was thorough. He rejected as far too unsupple and dogmatic the growing consensus about the cultural deficiencies of Germany. Objecting less to the political criticism than to the sweeping explanation of cultural deformities as the cause of German imperialism, Bourne penned a reminder that German philosophical idealism was more elastic and viable than the single-minded devotion to duty that Veblen and Dewey presented. Bourne argued that German group dynamics might well be construed as cooperation and seen as a useful antidote to the excessive individualism that progressives had long bemoaned. Likewise, Bourne maintained, German research pointed to a higher learning that English liberal-arts dilettantism did not. More centrally, Bourne believed that German idealism and hermeneutics opened up more possibilities for creativity than a crabbed English empiricism could muster. German idealism, with its emphasis on the reality of mental events, gave rise to moral and intellectual adventure that Americans could well use. Deweyan pragmatism, he contended, could well hold in check its dangerous tendencies. It spoke ill of intellectuals, claimed Bourne, to allow their feelings about German conduct in the war to shape their understanding of all things German.[29]

Bourne's indictment of the war was not, as Harold Laski subsequently argued, a standing at Armageddon and philosophizing about the "abstract injustice of war." Bourne was certainly no pacifist, at least in the traditional sense, since he wrote of conscientious objection that it was archaic, a stiff formalism of a "godly grandmother" who absolutely forbade anything passionate.[30] Nor was his refusal to support the war a matter of a desire to maintain some pristine purity by avoiding being tainted by the imperfect Allies. To the contrary, Bourne's writings were filled with schemes designed to promote specific collective acts that would affect the war and help bring about a more democratic peace, rather than one of exhaustion in which enmities would continue to grow. Much of his condemnation of the war had to do with the ways in which American power was not used in securing a just peace when it could have been brought to bear on the belligerents. Wilson and the liberals eschewed the virtues of "armed neutrality," refrained from making American entrance to save the British commonwealth contingent upon any Entente concessions, and shied away from making a common cause with the war-weary left of the Central Powers to end the war.[31] Having chosen not to do so, the nation became agents of Entente designs and subject to the chaos of war itself. Bourne may very well have been incorrect about the political likelihood of achieving his ends with his means, but his arguments were practical in the sense that they aimed at influencing practice by taking measure of the constellation of forces and adjusting responses accordingly.

Bourne's criticism of prowar liberals and pragmatists rested on their misapprehension of the nature of the war. They were, he contended, far too confident that they could run the war for democratic purposes. Their confidence yielded little in wartime and much less in peace. Such results were not at all surprising to Bourne, because the war, after all, was in the hands of those who cared little for democracy in peacetime. The patriots who had never been concerned about the horrors of capitalist peace had during the war crisis found a "large fund of idle emotional capital to invest in the oppressed nationalities and ravaged villages of Europe. Hearts that had felt only ugly contempt for democratic strivings at home beat in tune with the struggle for freedom abroad."[32] Liberals had failed to advance any meaningful plans for the extension of democracy, Bourne charged. The vaunted League of Nations hardly fit the bill, because it sanctified existing nation-states and denied international economic justice. "In a world which requires recognition of economic internationalism far more than of political internationalism, an idea is reactionary which proposes to petrify and federate the nations as political and economic units."[33] As he famously remarked in "Twilight of the Idols," his impassioned critique of prowar pragmatists, "if the war is too strong for you to prevent, how is it going to be weak enough for you to control and mold to your liberal purposes?"[34] Whether the result of some trust in the impersonal workings of history (which would constitute a belief in absolute law that pragmatism was supposed to challenge) or in the beneficent omniscience of Wilson (a belief for which Bourne could discern no evidence), liberals' support for the war was a signal retreat from prewar commitments.

American intellectuals had come to such a pass in Bourne's rendition because, having come to multiplicity by stressing how contingent things were, they overestimated the plasticity in the world. On the one hand, pragmatists prided themselves that their commitment to problem solving meant verification rather than reference to preexisting principles. On the other, they valued constructive purposive action that molded materials to an end. Quietism was, by this rendering, "an acute moral failure to adjust." What Bourne termed the inexorable gave pragmatists the intellectual equivalent of an allergic reaction, because it removed choice and control. Pragmatists could hardly deny the reality of the war, and were inclined to accept it, but retained their firm (but false) sense that they could control it and turn it to their creative purposes. "To talk as if war were anything else than such a poison," Bourne wrote in one of his angriest passages at Dewey and Mead's wartime philosophic justifications, "is to show that your philosophy has never been confronted with the pathless and the inexorable, and that, only dimly feeling the change, it goes ahead acting as if it had not got out of its depth. Only a lack of practice with a world of human nature so raw-nerved, irrational, uncreative, as an America at war was bound to show itself to be, can account for the singular unsatisfactoriness of these later utterances of Dewey."[35]

The result of such callow belief in the plasticity of the world was to replace values with technique, Bourne charged. In viewing the world as process, many of the younger intellectuals (Bourne had in mind less Dewey and Mead themselves than their followers who had joined the war efforts) had made adaptation to reality a mark of high seriousness and purpose. Their creative intelligence was entirely technical, and they had lost the ability to think creatively about ends. Dewey thought about values, Bourne allowed, but had never indicated just how values were created. Tabling the question had made growth and activity ends. "The defect of any philosophy of 'adaptation' or 'adjustment,' even when it means adjustment to changing, living experience, is that there is no provision for thought or experience getting beyond itself. If your ideal is to be adjustment to your situation, in radiant co-operation with reality, then your success is likely to be just that and no more. You never transcend anything. You grow, but your spirit never jumps out of your skin to go on wild adventures."[36]

Bourne himself had little stirring counsel for the antiwar remnant. His essays in *Seven Arts* were landmarks of angry analysis that endeared him to subsequent generations of radicals, but his description of his own attitudes were resigned, less outwardly oppositional than internally resistant. His own sense was that all that was left to war opponents was to be aloof, to not obstruct the war but not spiritually accept it either. "We are tired of continued disillusionment, and of the betrayal of generous anticipations. It is saner not to waste energy in hope within the system of war-enterprise. One may accept dispassionately whatever changes for good may happen from the war, but one will not allow one's imagination to connect them organically with war."[37] In the face of the intrusive state apparatus, the elimination of outlets for his work, his alienation from his former comrades, and his own growing sense of persecution, Bourne was increasingly at odds with his world in the little time that remained to him. (He died in December of 1918, a victim of the flu epidemic.) He found no patterns of progress, either universal or particular. Bourne feared that until the war fever ran its course, an empowered reactionary idealism would put the creative potential of multiplicity in jeopardy, in part by concerted attacks on creativity and in part by creative minds acceding to the logic of victory above all else. Bourne found little reason to hope that when the inevitable excesses prompted Americans to call a halt that the resources to rebuild the creative aspects of cultural life would be available.

Multiplicity's Fortune

Bourne's pessimism about the postwar fate of multiplicity had much to do with the concerted effort for social and cultural uniformity that had begun even before the declaration of war in 1917. By late 1914, war advocates and preparedness leagues had connected the conflict in Europe to what they perceived as American disunity. For many, the war was not solely a matter of turning back German aggression and guaranteeing international comity. It also entailed reversing fissiparous tendencies in American life. Envisioning their struggle as a fight to save civilization, cultural conservatives regarded the proliferation of difference as corrosive, promoting anarchy and strife. In a process akin to Freudian condensation, those who yearned for a unitary culture linked discourses and practices that were unconnected with one another and combined them into a single force. It was not uncommon, for instance, for opponents of multiplicity to consolidate modern art and Bolshevism, although the goals and assumptions of each development were quite different. In light of the erosion of many cultural unities, conservatives vigorously opposed the undesirable indiscriminate blending of cultures as an act of aggression against the existing majority culture. One of the attractions of the war was that the effort promised to reunite the American people, calling them back to selfless service and moral conviction. The *North American Review* informed its readers that the war would counter an America in which too many had become "degraded in gluttonous realization," . . . "putting self above patriotism" and "feeding off our own fat instead of mulcting lean Chautauquans." The war would be a necessary "test of body, of mind and of spirit." War, the magazine concluded, was "curative, not destructive, a blessing not a curse." Such rhetoric of transcendent national interest and the unswerving commitment to a singular, unquestionably moral goal is one reason that historians have considered the war as the high point of progressivism as well as its downfall.[38]

The war for unity brooked few exceptions. Understanding unity as similarity in thought and deed, those who led the campaigns to reconstitute American life were constantly on the lookout for those who subscribed to different truths or held different values. Of special importance was the understanding of patriotism, which even before the declaration of war included allegiance to the state and support for martial virtues. Theodore Roosevelt's condemnation of the hit song of 1915, "I Didn't Raise My Boy to Be a Soldier" is instructive. A direct response to the preparedness campaigns, the song imagines the horror of mass death and asks in its chorus, "Who dares to put a musket on his shoulder / To shoot some other mother's darling boy?" And enjoins "nations [to] arbitrate their future troubles." The sentiment was anathema to Roosevelt, whose reaction combined his sense of disorder in sexual relations with his racial animus. Such women built weak, disordered men, Roosevelt declared. Women who opposed war belonged "in China—or by preference in a harem—and not in the United States."[39] That apparently included his old compatriot in the Progressive Party, Jane Addams. When Addams delivered her talk of July 9, 1915, "Revolt against War," which stressed the lack of heroism in the senseless slaughter of trench warfare and the restiveness of the men who were fighting it, Roosevelt branded her an "evil enemy" of the country, the modern-day equivalent of a Copperhead, an ironic charge given her father's worship of Lincoln. Roosevelt was not alone in his criticism of Addams. Having once been revered as "America's only saint," Addams found herself under attack as a threat to national purpose and a purveyor of unnatural ideas. By her own account, the attacks left her isolated, vacillating between self-pity and self-righteousness.[40]

When the United States did enter the war nearly two years later, the campaigns for national unity became in part the province of the national government. Under the auspices of the Committee on Public Information (CPI), the war to make the world safe for democracy became a war *for* commonality in deportment and belief. Nations at war had, of course, tried to unify their populations, but the scope of the committee's activities in regulating and shaping the flow of information was unprecedented in American history. The committee melded the progressive urge for national unity with the absolutist hope to steer the diverse elements of American public opinion into a coherent whole. Founded to provide honest information that its supporters believed was the lifeblood of a deliberative democracy, the committee urged its "Four-Minute" speakers to use atrocity stories and placed ads in large-circulation magazines urging readers to report to the Justice Department those "who spread pessimistic stories or cried for peace." If the CPI aimed at persuasion, other arms of the government meant to coerce unity. The suspension of mailing rights by Postmaster General Burleson, the utter disregard for civil liberties by Attorney General Gregory, and the passage of the Espionage and Sedition Acts, which severely limited political discussion, were particularly noteworthy. At times Wilson made gestures to rein in the more exuberant enforcement, but such pronouncements as his 1917 Flag Day speech, which promised "woe to the man or group of men that seeks to stand in our way," set the tone, neutralizing his condemnation of excesses.[41]

As Christopher Capozzola has argued, government regulation dovetailed with the American tradition of citizen vigilance and community policing. Owing much to the republican obligation to participate in the polity, the tradition had provided the impetus for such progressive reforms as Prohibition. The tradition presumed a fairly unified and uniform community, so that under the press of war, vigilance became vigilantism. With security fears heightened, the criteria for difference expanded, the amount of surveillance assumed unprecedented levels, and the efforts to remove offenders escalated. As Capozzola demonstrates, such acts always had a quasi-legal standing in many American communities, a condition that persisted throughout the war despite the official condemnations of vigilantism as un-American. Given the desire to turn back multiplicity, words were unlikely to have much effect. Indeed, the levels of violence continued after the war. Overt brutality abated by 1920, but efforts at coercion did not.[42]

Vigilance and defense societies caught no German agents during the war (at least no one was convicted of the offense). They did achieve greater success in regulating social differences. The drive for uniformity to fight the war invigorated racialist thought. Those of German origin, who had previously been a well-admired people, particularly bore the brunt. Methodist Bishop William Quayle, in the course of declaring that the United States was at war not against Junkers or the Kaiser but the German people, declared that "the German race are the strongest, most pertinacious, and dangerous on earth. . . . In the long run, unless we and our allies set our house in order and excise the cancer of party warfare, the German will dominate the world." Racialism also made itself felt in the worries about divided loyalties. Many arguments proceeded from the assumption of racial imperatives that compelled primitive attachments to land and blood. Such mainstream journals as the *Saturday Evening Post* and *Literary Digest* urged a unity that was ostensibly rooted in shared ideals but often devolved into purging "the scum of the melting pot" that had infiltrated American schools, universities, and the press. Campaigns to eliminate German-language instruction from school curricula and German music from concert halls followed. More comical was the 1910s version of "freedom fries," the renaming of sauerkraut as "liberty cabbage."[43]

The lynching of the German American Robert Prager in Collinsville, Illinois, was tragic. Prager, who had actually tried to enlist in the navy after the declaration of war, came to his end at the hands of a group of drunken miners, who accused him of disloyalty. The miners who perpetrated the crime admitted their involvement (and their alcohol use), but the jury of their peers scarcely deliberated before deciding on their acquittal. One juror was heard to declare that no one could doubt their loyalty now. As E. A. Schwartz has recently demonstrated, the remark had deeper resonances than usually allowed. Schwartz contends that the mob contained men who had recently found themselves under ethnic attack, charges that had intensified during a recent strike. Many in the mob believed, not entirely without reason, that Prager was a company spy trying to break the walkout. The miners, in effect, earned acquittal by proclaiming their unity and deflected charges of radical difference by murdering someone even more vulnerable.[44]

German Americans were not the only group that the editorialists at the *Saturday Evening Post* considered scum in need of purging. Those who formed the so-called second wave of immigration from southern and eastern Europe also found themselves under suspicion. Prevailing theory held that such folk were dangerous to national unity, because their genes could pollute racial stock and because they lacked the ability to grasp American ideals. Theodore Roosevelt went so far as to endorse plans to limit the breeding of "the worst stocks, physically and morally." Not all those who worried about racial multiplicity endorsed the eugenic solution. The immediate issue in the war years was the problem of dual loyalty. While Randolph Bourne lauded dual loyalties as adding cosmopolitanism to American provincialism, cultural traditionalists and war advocates saw only the unraveling of unity. Roosevelt was insistent that stamping out dual loyalties was not only a wartime matter. The future of American civilization depended on it. "There must be no sagging back in the fight for Americanism merely because the war is over," Roosevelt declared. "Any man who says he is an American, but something else also, isn't an American at all. We have room for but one flag, the American flag, and this excludes the red flag, which symbolizes all wars against liberty and civilization, just as much as it excludes any foreign flag of a nation to which we are hostile. We have room for but one language here, and that is the English language, for we intended to see that the crucible turns our people out as Americans, of American nationality, and not as dwellers in a polyglot boarding-house; and we have room for but one soul loyalty, and that is loyalty to the American people."[45] Although George Creel was personally suspicious of the motives of old-stock nationalists and xenophobes, his worry about unity led him to organize "Loyalty Leagues" through the Division of Work with the Foreign-Born. These leagues sponsored rallies and pageants to acquaint immigrants with American traditions but also attempted to discourage certain kinds of cultural difference. Other government agencies were less benign, asking employers to take stock of the nationality of their employees and to report suspicious behavior.[46]

Not surprisingly, racial vigilantism was especially acute during and after the war. Lynching and rioting, of course, were characteristic of racial relations after 1890. The war and postwar years saw intensified conflict, the result of tensions caused by the beginning of the Great Migration of blacks from the South in search of wartime employment. Major eruptions occurred in East Saint Louis and Houston in 1917, Chicago and Omaha in 1919, and Tulsa in 1921. Between the Armistice and January 1920, according to John Hope Franklin and Alfred A. Moss Jr., seventy-six blacks were lynched, ten of whom were still in their military uniform. In Phillips County, Arkansas, white organizations took control of the legal system itself to suppress the black sharecroppers of the Progressive Farmers and Householders' Union of America. In the course of the gun battles that followed, perhaps as many as two hundred people died. A trial in which black defendants were not allowed counsel and the right to call witnesses on their behalf resulted in conviction of all sixty-nine. The bloodshed in North and South, the failure of the Wilson administration to respond meaningfully, the de facto segregation in the North, and the job bar in industry all dashed the hopes of W. E. B. Du Bois and the National Association for the Advancement of Colored People that endorsement of the war and demonstration of African-American patriotism

Figure 5.2. The war to end multiplicity. **Striking copper miners in Bisbee, Arizona, many of whom were sympathetic to the Industrial Workers of the World, are rounded up to be herded onto trains and deposited in New Mexico. The Bisbee incident was only one of numerous efforts undertaken to create unity during the war by suppressing difference. (Courtesy of the Arizona Historical Society/Tucson AHS #43174)**

would ameliorate tensions, lead to obedience to the law, and allow for a greater measure of black progress.[47]

Labor radicals too became an object of surveillance and repression. Workers who expressed doubts about or opposition to the war were harassed, fired, and blacklisted. In a case that was to become a cause célèbre among radicals and civil libertarians, Industrial Worker of the World member and San Francisco railcar strike leader Tom Mooney was indicted and convicted of planting a bomb that killed several people during a San Francisco preparedness campaign in 1916, on what Felix Frankfurter concluded was probably perjured testimony. Union organizers found themselves accused of lacking commitment to the war cause if they made any efforts to help form unions or redress worker grievances. In the notorious Bisbee, Arizona, case county sheriff Harry Wheeler and the local citizens rounded up nearly 1,200 striking copper miners, herded them onto a train, and left them in railcars in Hermanas, New Mexico, with little food and water. Despite its members' general hatred of the war, the IWW took no official position, hoping to forestall repression. The strategy was unsuccessful. Organizers were beaten or killed in places such as Centralia, Washington, and Butte, Montana. Despite efforts to arbitrate and to control labor–management conflicts after the bloody wars in the mines in Colorado and the institution of a no-strike pledge in return for boosted wages and government recognition, American labor relations remained vicious.[48]

Efforts to stamp out multiplicity extended to the unprecedented campaign to create a uniformly moral fighting force. As the war began, President Wilson received many entreaties from mothers who worried that military life would expose their sons to moral influences that were, as one correspondent put it, "worse than death." This concern led to an abandonment of the long-standing policy of allowing soldiers and sailors sexual release. Policing the sexual lives of both the armed forces and women attracted to men in uniform aimed at returning the United States to the absolute standard of behavior and thought that many had believed characterized public life in the nineteenth century. To enforce the new single standard in which men and women both restrained their animal passions, the government established the Commission on Training Camp Activities (CTCA), headed by Raymond Fosdick, who had formerly headed the Rockefeller-funded Bureau of Social Hygiene. Fosdick and those who supported the CTCA believed that sexual purity complemented, reinforced, and guaranteed the high ideals for which the war was fought. Such beliefs provided the justification for posters that accused of treason those who got venereal disease. Surveillance did not stop at the camp gates; it also included the behavior of women. The federal government undertook extended campaigns to limit male–female interaction and to provide wholesome entertainment throughout the war years. When molding character failed, recourse to coercion to achieve moral uniformity followed. As a complement to the CTCA, the government established the Committee on Protective Work for Girls, which was charged with removing women from areas around camps so as to keep soldiers from temptation. These campaigns made use of the discipline of "the feeble-minded" to commit promiscuous women to mental institutions. Medical inspection and even sterilization could follow. Policing multiplicity in sexual behavior resulted in such extraordinary efforts as social workers hiding in the bushes of Boston Commons to stop unacceptable fraternization. Over 15,000 women were detained as threats to national security.[49]

Even the most seemingly rarefied precincts of cultural and intellectual life were not immune from efforts to achieve unity. Convinced of the power of high culture, partisans treated it as another front in the war. Works that violated prevailing standards faced charges of relativism and accusations that their work made it more difficult to stand firmly against Central Power perfidy. In literature, challenges to the identity of morality and beauty and to the sovereignty of the individual were, critics maintained, undercutting the domestic fight for civilization. The famed Stuart Sherman–H. L. Mencken contretemps touched upon not only the novels of Theodore Dreiser, which Sherman decried and Mencken defended, but the nature of morality, patriotism, and truth. In a 1915 article in the *Nation*, Sherman, a professor of literature at the University of Illinois and an ally of the New Humanists, linked Dreiser's novels to German culture and to a slew of sins of multiplicity. Lampooning Dreiser's attack on Puritanism, Sherman railed against Dreiser's amoral naturalism as an intellectual mainstay of Kaiserism. As Henry May and Joan Shelley Rubin have noted, there was irony here in that the defender of uplift and ideals was himself quite doubtful in private about a war to fight for them. Mencken replied acidly in *A Book of Prefaces* (1917). Sherman zeroed in on Mencken in November of that year, making note of his love of "Teutonic-Oriental pessimism and nihilism in philosophy, of anti-democratic politics, of the subjection and contempt of women, of the *Herrenmoral*, and of anything but Anglo-Saxon civilization." Sherman continued his polemic during his work for the Creel Committee, producing a pamphlet that historian Henry May concluded fixed "the image of the immoral, subversive, polyglot, materialist, decadent, pro-German intellectual."[50]

Universities were not ivory-tower refuges from the turbulence. Although many had proclaimed a commitment to free inquiry in the early twentieth century as a reaction against efforts of corporate donors to dictate policy, university presidents and boards of trustees expected scholars to aid the war effort, and often punished those who resisted. Among the most prominent targeted were the labor economist Scott Nearing, who was dismissed from the University of Toledo (where he had landed after being summarily dismissed from the University of Pennsylvania in 1915 for his support of labor unions and socialism) and the economist-sociologist Emily Balch, author of the 1910 volume *Our Slavic Fellow Citizens*. Balch had taken a leave of absence from Wellesley to work for international arbitration of disputes and the establishment of a system of international colonial administration, which resembled what was to become the mandate system of the League of Nations. In 1918, the board of trustees terminated her contract. Nearing ran afoul of conservatives and progressives alike. His *Great Madness: A Victory for the American Plutocracy*, which indicted the war for dragging "human beings from their tasks of building and improving, and push[ing] them en masse into the category of destroyers and killers," for the selfish interests of a few, enraged war supporters for its dangerous promulgation of doubt and its denial of the universal justice of the war. Wrote a minister who had been his ally in progressive fights in Toledo, "Scott Nearing should shut up and stay shut up. He should not mislead or deceive the people who have not had the educational advantages he has had. There was a time in the country when a pro and con discussion of peace or war was allowable. But when the country is thrust into war it is no time to preach disloyalty or to talk dissension. Men who do are guilty of treason. They are traitors."[51]

At Columbia, similar sentiments moved President Nicholas Murray Butler and the board of trustees. The august Butler had been a power in the Republican Party, running as Taft's vice president in 1912. Prior to the war, Butler had been an advocate of international arbitration conferences and had been influential in persuading Andrew Carnegie to establish an endowment for peace. When the war came, however, Butler regarded multiplicity as a poor platform from which to fight a war. Fighting against a vicious and absolute enemy required an intellectual and political unanimity. There was no room for "any among us who are not with whole heart and mind and strength committed to fight with us to make the world safe for democracy," he told the graduates of the class of 1917. The board of trustees resolved that "the unqualified loyalty to the Government of the United States be required of all students, officers of administration and officers of instruction in the University as a condition of retaining their connection with the University." It granted Butler the power to enforce the resolution, and he used it to dismiss or discipline a number of scholars, including the irascible social psychologist James McKeen Cattell, who had written a letter to three U.S. congressmen requesting that they vote against sending American troops to fight in France.[52]

Nor were dismissals of dissenters the only ways that the academy enacted a politics of unity. Academics produced work designed to bolster the war effort. Perhaps boosted by a heightened sense of excitement of being in the "real world" after the cloistered prewar years, many willingly lent their talents in service to the state. In the case of the historians, the newly created National Board for Historical Service (NBHS) aimed to put into practice the New History precept that history was a matter of creating a usable past. If the NBHS did not approve work that portrayed history as the unfolding of transcendental truth, it also produced little that caught the complexities of the past as it related to the present moment or indicated the provisionality of historical accounts. For the most part, "usable past" meant something that boosted morale. Histories of Germany more often than not relied upon generalization that fit nicely with propaganda. Other academics lent their talents to more immediate problems. John Commons wrote a pamphlet designed for working-class Wisconsites designed to defeat socialist congressman Victor Berger's bid for senator, entitled "Scheidermann and Berger—The Arch Traitors to Socialism and Democracy." Commons, economist Richard Ely, and University of Wisconsin president Charles Van Hise attacked war opponent Robert La Follette and tried to get the NBHS to do likewise. Gruber concludes that as professors, the prowar academics would have better served their country by maintaining the critical intellect so as to "protect and promote the very values and freedoms in whose name the fight was being waged."[53] Ely and Commons had never conceived of themselves as free-floating intellectuals above the fray or committed to the abstract ideal of inquiry. Long yearning to make their ideas effective, they never saw critical intellect as a matter of defending independence. Even after the war, when regrets abounded, the Wisconsinites saw their war work as one with their prewar work for the state.

As devastating as suppression could be for its targets, the banning and firing ran its course by 1920, prompting remorse in its aftermath. During the war, AUAM member Roger Baldwin established the National Civil Liberties Bureau, in the hope that the liberal commitment to free speech that had developed during the early teens in struggles for birth control and solidarity with the IWW would continue during the war. The organization became the American Civil Liberties Union in 1920. Likewise, some academics opposed the use of power to dictate intellectual life. Charles Beard, himself a hesitant supporter of the war, left Columbia in protest of President Butler's policies. Beard joined with other dissidents to form the New School for Social

Research. The American Association of University Professors eventually reevaluated its principles of academic freedom, rejecting Lovejoy's more insistent formulations of patriotism. Subsequent political crises in the twentieth century would result in similar demands for unity, many of them successful. Yet the presence of organizations constituted in the aftermath of the war arguably had a mitigating presence on efforts to enforce intellectual unity in the political sphere.[54]

Campaigns for unity often floundered after the war. In politics, the meaning of the unity during the war was a matter of debate. During the armed conflict, the two major parties ostensibly put partisan jostling for advantage aside, to fight the common foe. Yet Republicans bristled under Democratic control and railed against what they took to be the timidity of Wilsonian war efforts. By the time the Versailles Treaty came to the Senate for ratification, the Republican sniping had turned to open opposition, fanned by Wilson's shutting them out of the delegation. In part because they had never been moved by Wilsonian internationalism in the first place, Republicans found much fault with the treaty. The left flank of Wilson's coalition was not much happier with many of the concessions that Wilson made to the old European order, although Wilson probably had less leverage with Britain and France than his critics believed. Few besides devoted Wilsonians regarded the war as redeeming the promise of history. If the leader of the Republican opposition, irreconcilable Henry Cabot Lodge of Massachusetts, lacked the universalist impulses of Wilsonian progressives, he nonetheless had his American exceptionalist version of unity. The League, he charged, was a contraption, "the mechanical appliances of the rhetorician" that would only interfere with the realization of American promise. "We all respect and share these aspirations and desires [of peace]," proclaimed Lodge, "but some of us see no hope, but rather defeat, for them in this murky covenant. For we, too, have our ideals, even if we differ from those who have tried to establish a monopoly of idealism." Convinced that the United States was the world's best hope, a land of ordered liberty, Lodge opposed the League on the grounds that it interfered with natural processes. Lodge's justification for other political positions, including his conservative political economy and immigration restriction, had rested on straightforward unifying principles, which the war had not shaken.[55]

Part of Lodge's original opposition in fact came from the treaty's original provisions on immigration, which he and other nativists feared would limit the ability to regulate the influx of outsiders. Efforts to induce hyphenated Americans to forgo dual identities were only partially successful at best. While immigrants did indeed flock to classes on citizenship and English, which had been the demand of immigration restriction leagues, and enthusiastically attended the parades and rallies to support the war effort, most kept to ethnic enclaves during and immediately after the war. As their increased willingness to strike during the 1919 wave indicates, immigrants did not convert to the one-hundred-percent Americanism urged on them (at least not the portion that rejected unions and community solidarity for individualism). For many, hyphenation remained viable and meaningful, allowing them to oscillate between the ways of the United States and the ways of their community. The failure of the war to Americanize ethnics to the satisfaction of cultural conservatives was a prime reason for the 1921 and 1924 immigration laws, designed to limit Eastern and Southern European immigration. The laws were intended to stop the ethnic and racial multiplicity, but the success of the endeavor was not entirely clear.[56]

The ability of moralists to effect uniform standards of restraint in sexual mores were, to all appearances, unavailing. Peace did little to stem the decrease in the marriage rate or the increase in that of divorce. Nor did the various campaigns to ensure sexual propriety put a halt to sex talk in the immediate postwar years. Traditionalists continued to bemoan racy talk and the public deportment of single women, who seemed to abandon the modesty that middle-class custom expected them to uphold. Setbacks did not diminish efforts to recreate an impermeable wall between private behavior and public display. The banning of the first installment of James Joyce's *Ulysses* in 1918 was only the most prominent of such efforts.[57]

The problem of depiction of sexuality was but an aspect of the larger endeavor to establish the contours of beauty. Despite wartime and postwar efforts to shape expressive culture, genteel uplift did not flourish after the war. To be sure, the war itself was still celebrated in popular culture, often by soldiers or ambulance operators, as a heroic effort and a grand adventure. Much other popular culture had little of the fragmentation, uncertainty, and despair that many have seen as the cultural legacy of the war. Nineteen-nineteen was, after all, the year of *I'm Forever Blowing Bubbles* and *Lad: A Dog*, two examples of aesthetic objects that conjured a world of order and reassuring morality. Nonetheless, the forms that had created an aesthetic multiverse before the war continued apace. Jazz and blues continued to gain in popularity, despite warnings of their dangers. Nonrepresentational art gained a new prominence in the art market as a number of the number of supporting institutions—museums, dealers, critics, and the like—took up its cause. Movies retained and expanded their popularity. Advocates of uplift thought they had achieved some leverage with the legal approval of review boards. *Mutual Film Corp. v. Industrial Commission of Ohio* (1916), a case that revolved around the ability of the state of Ohio to prohibit the importation of films it deemed dangerous, had denied movies the protection of the First Amendment (in large measure because the plaintiffs argued for it only haphazardly, concentrating their case on the rights of property). The decision did not prove the panacea that regulators hoped it would be, however. In urban areas in particular, the boards lost their clout, falling into disuse or losing government support. The letdown resulted in the immediate postwar years in a proliferation of movies that aesthetic traditionalists considered salacious or subversive. Their agitation for new national enforcement powers intensified, boosted by a number of Hollywood scandals. The industry forestalled the threat by undertaking self-regulation in 1922.[58]

Perhaps no development shook cultural conservatives as much as the Bolshevik Revolution. Indicting Bolshevism as the epitome of a culture loosed from its moorings, opponents charged the socialist revolutionaries with favoring such evils as the abolition of morality, the eradication of the individual by society, and an attraction to violence, a consequence of their blatant destruction of private property. On the first glance, American Bolsheviks might seem to be cultural conservatives in their commitment to unifying principles. Bolsheviks certainly did think history operated according to a set of laws that those with proper insight could master. In the long-term, few believed that history was messy, however contingent any given moment might be. Yet it was the contingency that did matter for supporters of the revolution. The war, by their lights, had exposed the contradictions of capitalism and made its overthrow possible. In contrast to the socialists of the Second International, revolutionists rejected the belief that history had to arrive through stages in order to achieve socialism. Instead, they celebrated the ability of the Bolsheviks to seize the moment and take advantage of the outright failures of the bourgeoisie to serve the role that history had assigned them. Russia, by all objective measures, was not prepared for socialism. The Bolsheviks had not, however, passively accepted the unfolding of history; they had jumped it forward. Many treated history as an exercise in problem solving, working within a set of parameters and with a set of forces that were both identifiable and impersonal. As the optimism of 1918 that history could be shaped faded, American Communists confronted their own problems of multiplicity: the difficulty in organizing the working class, the schisms and purges within the movement, and the tensions with the Comintern over whether local or universal conditions should dictate strategy. Originally holding that practice and theory need inform each other, American communism often became a vestige of an absolutist culture in which members tried to impose theory on practice.[59]

Neither the revolutionary progress of the Bolsheviks nor the evolutionary progress of liberals much appealed to J. Gresham Machen, a theologian at Princeton and leading opponent of religious liberalism in the 1920s. Before the war, Machen had objected to the postmillennialism of liberal Protestantism. Postmillennialism, the belief that Christ would come after a thousand-year millennium, was part of the teleological view of history of liberals, who were convinced that amelioration was the way of the world, and provoked them to aid the path to perfection. They applied this narrative frame to the war itself, regarding it as the ultimate uplift project that would eradicate international evil. Although some Social Gospelers such as Walter Rauschenbusch found the militarism of preparedness inconsistent with their moral commitments, dissenters among liberal Protestants were in the minority by 1917. The war presented a challenge to Fundamentalists, those who subscribed to the basic tenets laid out in twelve volumes between 1910 and 1915, which included the inerrancy of scripture, the virgin birth, the substitutionary atonement of Christ, Christ's bodily resurrection, and the historicity of the miracles. Lukewarm at best about the war, they had little use for the reformist effort to create earthly perfection, seeing in the senseless brutality confirmation of their belief in the innate corruption of humankind, a position that opened premillennialist Christians to the charge of a lack of patriotism.[60] Charges of a lack of patriotism eventually prompted Fundamentalist congregations to accede to the war effort.

Despite his personal friendship with Woodrow Wilson, Machen opposed American entrance into the war. He wrote his mother that the high-flown rhetoric was merely a cover for British aggrandizement. Abhorring the bloodthirstiness of American militarism that made him feel a "man without a country," Machen urged a gospel-based "production of mutual respect and confidence among equal nations." These sentiments did not prevent him from serving as a YMCA chaplain in France. That experience only confirmed his opposition to postmillennialism. No sane person could experience warfare and conclude that progress was the way of this world or that Satan was gradually retreating before the advance of the kingdom of God. Rather, Machen concluded that the illusion of human reform had led to the disaster. Machen's distaste for multiplicity was evident in his postwar dispute with the liberal theologian Harry Fosdick. Fosdick noted the postwar falling away from religion and laid the blame on the outdated, unscientific doctrines such as biblical inerrancy and virgin birth. Machen countered in a May 1919 Princeton address, "The Church in the War," that the source of church failure was a moving away from certain basic principles of divinity and a dalliance with a multiplicity that rested on experience. Experience-based theology,

Machen contended, had made religion perfectly disposable, because it dropped any notion of the reality of sin or personal salvation. In its place, it substituted what he called "paganism"—the emphasis on "healthy and harmonious and joyous development of human faculties." Joy, he countered, was not a matter of increasing human faculties, which were inherently flawed and uncontrollable, but of placing oneself in the call of God, which was available only through repentance.[61]

Although reluctant in the immediate postwar years to throw in his lot with Fundamentalists, whom he saw as too anti-intellectual and solely devoted to an unwholesome reaction against all of modernity, Machen clearly sounded a rejection of progress unusual in American cultural and intellectual life. Machen indicted liberal Protestantism for celebrating human potential and ignoring human sinfulness. In trusting in a science limited by human perception, liberals secular and otherwise ignored divine governance, Machen maintained. Liberals failed to evince any concern with the central point of religion, the salvation of individual souls. Talk of society and social conditions only highlighted their indifference. Machen charged that their replacement for salvation was a collectivism that was an unnatural intrusion into personal life. Lacking foundations in the divine Word, liberal Christianity would repeat its errors, ratifying the normlessness of modern life and permitting, even encouraging, an oppressive and deadly uniformity in the name of improvement and perfectibility.

The war also did not shake the absolutism of the New Humanists, who concluded that the pointless carnage and failed ideals were the consequence of the fatal trust that progressives placed in nature, which the humanists found unharnessed and destructive. Rather than striving for equipoise to keep human dualism in check, modern-day culture had hankered after improvement without reckoning the obdurate forces that prevented it. The war only accentuated the humanist sense of flux in the world and intensified their commitment to integrating reason and imagination. Although the war was hardly a major point in Babbitt's 1919 *Rousseau and Romanticism*, it takes little extrapolation to discern how the war only confirmed him in his sense of the dangers of romantic idealism. Babbitt asserts that the danger of Rousseau was the danger of naturalism. Adopting Rousseau's celebration of the natural had undercut the ability of modern cultures to construct barriers against irrationality and criminality. In accepting romantic assumptions of natural goodness and emotional authenticity, Babbitt charged, moderns had, without realizing it, spurred the tendency to search for external scapegoats and to blame society for all ills. In light of the irrationality unloosed by the war, those complaints took on special piquancy. Setting themselves against those who had oscillated from exhilaration to despair, New Humanists insisted that classical balance was the only way to recoup meaning.

Most intellectuals and artists were more inclined to rework their understanding of multiplicity than to take up the faith of Machen or the classical dualism of the humanists. Those whose work had advanced an understanding of multiplicity before the war were confronted yet again by the seeming pointlessness of the slaughter and the unfulfilled promises of the aftermath with the question of how extensively combinable were particular truths and values. Was the world a patchwork of observations and disparate theories in which the fragmentation of the human community and the inability to sustain any collective project to meet human needs were the way of the world? Or was multiplicity itself provisional, a condition that reflected contingencies of human understanding and practice that did not necessarily rule out efforts to build more modest syntheses and engage in meaningful action? The multiplicity of lament announced itself with the publication and literary success of Henry Adams's *Education*. Largely finished by 1907, the manuscript circulated privately in part because Adams judged its tone to be too markedly bitter and pessimistic for a public still committed to cheerful uplift. Published in 1918 after Adams's death in March, the book was an immediate bestseller and won the Pulitzer Prize for Autobiography in 1919. Others retained a sense that multiplicity and diversity implied more commensurability than Adams allowed. Tabling whether the many truths and beauties were ultimately reducible to identity, they set out to discover how truths worked in contingent moments or situations. If the attitude of those who thought multiplicity went all the way down was despairing, that of those who bracketed the question of how combinable truths and beauties ultimately were had a sense of provisional hope as they approached the postwar world. What was missing in the immediate postwar years was the innocent optimism of what Greenwich Villager Floyd Dell had called the "lyric years," in which playfulness and change were regarded as following easily from the breakdown of the culture of unity.[62]

The war certainly dampened Carl Becker's exuberance. In the wake of the war, Becker found Adams's pessimism and resignation an attractive posture. Writing to his friend William E. Dodd in 1920, Becker declared that the war was "inexplicable on any ground of reason or . . . even of intelligent self-interest," leading him to conclude that all that remained was a futile scramble for power. Such a conclusion represented a retreat from his position in the war in which he was an active participant in the endeavors of the Creel Committee. Although too intellectually honest to accept the simplifications of the war as simply a fight between democracy and autocracy, Becker was nonetheless capable of penning some purple anti-Prussian prose. Adams's book seems to have crystallized certain doubts Becker had long entertained over the efficacy of reason. Adams confirmed his sense that events were not fully knowable, and thus not fully directed or apprehended. John Higham notes that Becker had always had something of a "deracinated air," torn between his scientific drive for significant generalization and his realization that the work of history was always intertwined with mutable values. Those values, Becker recognized, colored not only the ends for which one strove or the interpretation one gave to facts but also what we count as facts—a view that expressed an antifoundationalism unusual for the human sciences.

Becker's Adamsian pessimism was less apparent in his immediate postwar public writing. His *United States: An Experiment in Democracy* had liberal doses of the progressive paeans to the uses of intelligence. It also had hints that intelligence was particularly hard to come by and that events and developments all too often spun out of control. Ending his discussion with the conflicting demands of liberty and equality, Becker doubted that the two could ever be made to integrate, especially in industrial matters. Taking a page from John Commons, Becker saw property itself as a governmental creation, but one that could no longer be distributed along Commons's lines. The power of the dominant classes required, he posited, the intervention of the government on behalf of the masses but would most likely result in the destruction of representative government itself. If the government could achieve some equality, Becker would scarcely question it. "But it is well to remember that governmental intervention may be quite legitimate without being quite adequate; and recent events have made it abundantly clear that the problem which confronts us is not one involving industrial liberty only, but political liberty as well. If, therefore, industrial liberty is to be achieved through the action of a beneficent government, we need to be quite sure that the government is beneficent; if the state is to give us equality, we need to know whether it is likely, in the process, to deprive us of liberty" (323). Gone was any possibility of achieving the common good, the progressive's dream. What representatives "too often legally represent is a group of people without any definite common will to be expressed; what they have to deal with are groups of people who can get their will expressed only by using their extra-legal economic power as a means of dictation" (328). Even were the proletariat to grasp the levers of power, its rule would be problematic at best. "What the dominant class . . . really fears . . . is an all-powerful government which it does not control; what it desires is an all-powerful government which can be used primarily in the service of its own interests. A genuine friend of mankind, one who estimates civilization in terms of the spiritual as

well as the material life, has little to hope for from the conception of an absolute state for which obedience is the only virtue and force the only test of
right" (331).[63]

Becker speculated that historical accounts would require jumbled narratives, a conclusion that postwar literature enacted. One of the sensations of
1919 was James Branch Cabell's *Jürgen: A Comedy of Justice*, a fantasy-laden
account of a medieval pawnbroker, who searches the past for justice outfitted
with a middle-aged man's head and a young man's body. This quest takes him
through numerous mythic kingdoms and has him assume such stations in life
as duke, king, and even pope. The sexual innuendoes were sufficient to lead
John Sumner, the head of the New York Society for the Suppression of Vice,
to charge Cabell and his editor with violation of state obscenity laws. Sumner's actions made Cabell a celebrity in many quarters, a sure sign that the
integration of beauty and morality on which much nineteenth-century aesthetics had rested increasingly lacked viability. Just as significant as *Jürgen's*
sensuality was the aimlessness and purposelessness the novel portrayed. Jürgen finds no justice and little to sustain faith that it exists. Written in a
mixed prose-verse style, *Jürgen* spoke to the inability to root oneself in this or
any other world.[64]

Although written in much less florid prose, Sherwood Anderson's *Winesburg, Ohio*, another sensation of 1919, shared with *Jürgen* a portrait of a world
in fragmentation. A series of narratives, only intermittently related, *Winesburg* details the hidden, often tragic, travails of village life. Anderson's characters live lives of isolation from both others and themselves. Whether the
frustrated intellectual or the homosexual who struggles to submerge his fears
of desire, they find little in the way of meaning to help them negotiate a
world that has been drenched in the acids of modernity. One sees the isolation in the ways the stories are discontinuous and in which human connection is evanescent and insufficient. Even moments of connection, such the
sexual coupling between George Willard and Helen White in the penulti-
mate story, are moments of flux and dislocation. Prompted by their own desires and their loneliness, which was in part a result of their unfulfilled aspirations for "sophistication" (the title that Anderson gave their story), they
managed to take hold "of the thing that makes the mature life of men and
women in the modern world possible," but only for a moment. In the next,
George leaves Winesburg for an uncertain manhood.

Anderson signaled his lament at fragmentation in his introduction, entitled "The Book of the Grotesque," a work of a writer whose characters had
all become incongruous and misshapen, although we are told not all were
horrible. This lost book, Anderson maintains, was a classic statement of

multiplicity. The book revolved around a single thought: that "in the beginning when the world was young there were a great many thoughts but no
such thing as a truth. Man made the truths himself and each truth was a composite of a great many vague thoughts. All about in the world were the truths
and they were all beautiful." People prized the truths by possessing and mo-
nopolizing them. Single truths made them grotesque. As Anderson's writer
explained, "the moment one of the people took one of the truths to himself,
called it his truth, and tried to live his life by it, he became a grotesque and
the truth he embraced became a falsehood." Warning of the danger of making a single truth absolute, Anderson nonetheless offered little to suggest that
negotiating multiplicity would yield happier outcomes.[65]

American social science had never doubted that the truths of social life
were synthesizable in some fashion. Neither Thorstein Veblen's rejection of
classical economics as metaphysics nor Franz Boas's dissent from evolutionary anthropology resulted in a characterization of human affairs as ruled by
serendipity or flux. Jettisoning universal laws, valid in all times and places,
did not lead the leading social scientists to avoid explanation or the search
for meaningful syntheses. Veblen, for instance, had always thought that different societies possessed similar qualities and operated along similar lines. To
talk of barbarian pursuits or to scout out the survivals of savagery, after all,
was to see some unity amidst all the contingencies and particularities. Veblen
was not alone. Franklin Giddings, the doyen of the Columbia sociology department, spoke for most in the profession when he envisioned that sociology would enable analysts to comprehend intentions as thoroughly as physicists had discerned physical laws. As late as 1922 his counterpart at the
University of Chicago, and sometimes rival, Albion Small, saw in science a
way to have a "completely objective representation of the totality of phenomena in all their relations." For Small, social science was still predicated
on "the conscious and unblushing acceptance of experience as a coherent reality."[66]

Small's position, however, lost its position of dominance in the discourse
in the postwar years. In prewar years, Small's grand theory had faced opposition from those who thought it too ethereal and speculative. His student
Luther Bernard was an outspoken advocate of a study of human aggregates
that dealt exclusively with social facts and abjured conjectures about objects
that could not be isolated. Sociology that tended toward social theory was,
Bernard and his rebellious classmate Edwin Sutherland confided to one another, meaningless moralizing. Indeed, as early as 1906, Small had surveyed
practicing sociologists about their view of reality, only to find the question
dismissed as irrelevant and metaphysical. Bernard's scientistic approach gath-

ered favor in the war and immediate postwar years in large measure as a re-sult of the newfound employment in war-related commissions for govern-ment and industry. In place of discussions about social wholes and moral uni-ties, the objectivist wing, which included Small's successors at the University of Chicago, Ernest Burgess and Robert Park, opted for precise observation, a narrowing of the questions addressed, and a rigid separation of fact and value on the grounds that these were of two different orders of existence. In stud-ies confined to how things worked rather than why, the new discourse took on a new multiplicity, allowing a thousand studies to bloom. Even Small gave ground in the postwar years, conceding that his absolutist notion was rooted more in faith than in science as it was then conceived.[67]

Rejection of "soul stuff," however, did not mean that the new objectivism completely abandoned its aspirations toward unity. If objectivist social scien-tists discarded, at least initially, the effort to see it whole, they were nonethe-less unswervingly loyal to their method as holding not one of the ways to truth about aggregate behavior, but the only way to it. In their effort to re-strict their findings to objects that could be observed and tested and to re-sults that could be replicated, the objectivists drained their investigations of such imprecise concepts as intention, on the grounds that it was far too ab-stract. In place of discussion of assimilation, the postwar generation of social scientists looked to particular behaviors such as saving or the purchase of cer-tain consumer goods. Such a formulation indeed operationalized abstract concepts, but since people do have intentions and do ascribe meanings, it was not entirely clear how explanatory a social science that forsook subjec-tivity was. Despite its formal banishment, the impulse that Small had made explicit did not totally disappear. Advocates for science writ small nonethe-less held onto the distant hope that once science had sorted out all problems, reform would naturally follow. Piecemeal truths in some unspecified way and at some distant time would create a larger one by virtue of their unimpeach-able status as scientific. If the war intensified the multiplicity entailed in the investigation of social phenomena, it did not fully eradicate the appeal of unity. Although the new objectivists did not offer the principle to which the many truths were to be integrated, more than a few were reluctant to accept randomness or disintegration in social affairs.[68]

At times during and after the war, the culture concept lost some of its sup-pleness. Although successful in a number of circles in casting doubt on the explanatory power and unifying potential of race, Boas and his students did not fully succeed in driving out racialist thought as an explanation for differ-ences among human groups. Spurred by war tensions, the campaigns to end hyphenated Americanism, and reaction to the strike wave of 1919, nativists pushed for immigration restriction on racialist grounds. They made their case with reference to a refurbished, often pseudoscientific basis. Others used not race but culture to make the case. Indeed "culture" had figured heavily in the case for war, much to the chagrin of Boas. Where his students had used the concept by and large to connote the diversity of human associations and the diverse possibilities that resulted from human activity, opponents used the term to signify the entity that shaped individuals within a group in specific and definitive ways. The explicit biological component had dropped from the discussion, but prowar analyses of German transgressions invariably blamed German culture, which was said to emphasize militarism, unquestioned allegiance to the higher power of the state, and disdain for conventional morality. In the hands of such prowar proponents as Princeton's Gauss, German culture was both singular and unalterable, serving as the ultimate author of characteristic acts of a people.

Boasians, many of whom had emotional and intellectual ties to Germany, found the conclusion that German crimes stemmed from a unified German culture to be an oversimplification of the complexity of German thought and feeling. They also objected to the implication of numerous prowar arguments that consecrated the United States as the embodiment of the universal values of truth and morality. To counter such arguments, Boas insisted that culture signified that different peoples had ways of life that were unique to them and which possessed their own integrity. Americans, he warned in a 1916 letter to the *New York Times*, were mistaken in their assertion that the world would be better off if the people of the world would "bestow upon themselves the benefactions of our regime." The American claim that "our solution is the only democratic and the ideal one" contradicted "the fundamental idea that nations have distinctive individualities, which are expressed in their modes of life, thought, and feeling." Treating cultures as expressing the values of distinct people, not universal claims to truth and morality, Boas noted that all cultures functioned with regard to particular circumstances. The best approach, Boas concluded, was to allow Germans, Austrians, and Russians to solve their problems in their own ways. Cultures were by no means totally unrelated to one another (diffusion was, after all, a crucial component of construction of cultures), but the distinctive nature of the interaction between practices and circumstances required an awareness of the limitations of Wilsonian claims that the United States should and could export its values.[69]

Boasian versions of culture as unique solutions to particular contingencies held the possibility for a relativism in which cultures were so particular that they could be evaluated only by their own members, who thoroughly imbibed their criteria. Their own cosmopolitanism made it unlikely that the Boas circle would adopt that position in the immediate postwar years. Boas himself rejected the tribalism of "One-Hundred-Percent Americanism," ending his letter to the *Times* with a statement of hyphenation. His loyalty, he maintained, was divided between his political allegiance to the United States and the German ideals of his youth. Indeed, the failure of hyphenation and cosmopolitanism to prevail during the war led a number of Boasians to investigate how cultures gave way under stress and failed to live upon their own values. They were especially attuned to the inability of the value of individualism in the United States to resist the war pressure for conformity. That drive for conformity had made Boas's position at Columbia tenuous during the war years. His colleague Goldenweiser was fired, and Boas depended upon Elsie Clews Parsons's subvention to pay his secretary.

Boas's use of the culture concept to make sense of the effect of war on American culture appeared in two articles in the *Dial* in which he taxed the United States with losing the advantages of cosmopolitanism through the conservatism of its ruling class. Proposing self-reflexivity as an antidote, he located few ways in which Americans encouraged or rewarded it.[70] Yet Boas was aware of how fragile a tool self-reflexivity was. His own profession had failed to engage in it during the war. In a letter to the *Nation* in 1919, Boas condemned those anthropologists whom he claimed spied for the United States while working in Mexico. The charges became a heated issue and earned Boas censure from the American Anthropological Association for allegedly unjustly criticizing President Wilson and disdaining the principles of American democracy. For his part, Edward Sapir measured health of societies in the immediate postwar era less by its opportunities for reflexivity than by its authenticity. Sapir's standard revolved around whether culture meshed individual needs and social expectations. Such a standard allowed him great purchase on the ways personality hinged on the impersonal values of the group, but it also ran the risk of circumscribing the sorts of things authentic people did and hardening culture into a finished product.[71]

The war gave a boost to institutional economics, at least in the short run. Veblenian interpretation did a better job of explaining how the economy functioned during the war and its immediate aftermath than did more mainstream economic discourses. Nor was Veblen particularly surprised or daunted by the postwar political turmoil. The usually pessimistic Veblen even entertained hopes of transformation in 1919, glimpsing in the particular conjuncture a realistic chance to overturn the rule of the leisure class. Veblen had long postulated that machine discipline would end metaphysical illusions and prompt all those with interests in manipulation of material to agitate for a society in which industry suppressed the fraud and force of business. The weaknesses of ruling cliques after the war was one sign that such changes were possible. So too were the strikes of 1919 and the Bolshevik and German revolutions, despite Veblen's disagreement with some of the ideological preferences involved. The moment closed, of course, but Veblen did not fully close up the chances for revolution. Much of his work in the 1920s was devoted to explaining the tendencies toward stagnation in an economy in which metaphysical mystification authorized the fatal control of business over industry, a condition that made plausible the prospect for an engineers' soviet as a source of change. Other institutionalists, such as John Commons and Veblen's student Wesley Mitchell, turned their attention to reform efforts, correcting the inevitable misfirings of capitalist economies with such welfare measures as unemployment insurance and old-age pensions and moving to codify Veblen's work on business cycles, respectively. Postwar institutionalists continued to reject the naturalism of classical economics, but their work began to drift toward detailing the regularities in production and distribution that made convention something akin to a foundation.[72]

The understanding of the unconscious in the postwar years dampened the creativity and multiplicity that was ascribed to it before the war. The ability of depth psychology to explain shell shock, the paralysis of soldiers who had suffered no organic damage, increased its scientific prestige in the immediate postwar years and intensified efforts to map the nonconscious mind. Those efforts yielded less the respect for its ultimate untamed quality than its operation in accordance to discoverable laws. Freud and other schools of psychoanalysis had never denied the lawlike behavior of the unconscious, yet his emphasis on day residue in the interpretation of dreams and on the serendipitous attachments of the unconscious that could be revealed only through free association gave his work its multiplicity. Postwar analysts, stirred by professional desires to cure and by a new respect for the savagery of the unconscious that the war had revealed, turned their attention to codifying the basis of personality. Freud himself had never abandoned his ambition to formulate a unified theory of human psychology. In the postwar years, he began to solidify his theories of mental geography. In American therapeutics, the many truths of the prewar years began to take on a more mechanical cast, with the self determined by fairly standard-issue sexual desire.[73]

For John Dewey, the war proved fodder for reevaluation. Without ever publicly conceding the justice of Bourne's criticism, Dewey moved in retrospect to register more clearly the unprofitable aspects of the war. As Robert Westbrook has noted, the war did not shake Dewey's pragmatism. "One could regard the war as a failed experiment without seeing it as a failure of experimentalism." Despite his shoddy treatment of Bourne (he refused to serve on any editorial boards that Bourne served on, virtually ensuring the latter's dismissal), Dewey gradually accepted the justice of Bourne's criticism of "war technique" and his own failure to make support for the war conditional on specific plans to achieve true democratic aims rather than on high-flown rhetoric.[74] In reevaluating his position, Dewey in effect reaffirmed his prewar understanding of multiplicity. The false unities of evolutionary progress did not, Dewey maintained, cancel the search for the ways in which many truths could be forged together in a common endeavor.

Multiplicity, then, survived the war as a crucial part of American cultural life. The contribution of the great explosion of multiplicity in the early twentieth century had been profound. The combined efforts of men and women in fields ranging from anthropology to psychology had weakened notions that a single principle could make sense of all relevant phenomena. The upshot of the first two decades was that understanding contingency on its own terms was as important, if not more so, than applying a universal law. In so doing, twentieth-century multiplicity revealed the ways in which nineteenth-century syntheses could produce reductionism. Pluralists in the early twentieth century demonstrated the limitations of such staples of nineteenth-century unity as evolutionary progress, prescribed morality, the aesthetics of uplift, the neat harmonies of classical economics, and the whole, autonomous self. In the new century, fewer intellectuals hewed to such positions, and those who did were constrained to reformulate them.

Adams's fear that once the false unity of nineteenth-century thought fell by the wayside, twentieth-century multiplicity would lead to chaos did not come to pass. It did not because the antifoundationalism of twentieth-century multiplicity did not preclude efforts to create new, more meaningful syntheses. The rejection of singular principles did not foster among most pluralists an embrace of pure chance. The world that they discerned was not one that was so fluid and ephemeral that no general patterns could be discerned. For only a few was the world a world of particulars alone. Like William James, other twentieth-century pluralists aimed to find ways to acknowledge the claims of both the one and the many. Dewey, Veblen, Boas, and other related investigators took as their project a way to meld flux and determinants, to establish ways to understand the breadth of this world without relying upon given foundations or explanations that claimed to explain everything. The point, as they understood it, was to learn to make the world in which we live.

At times in the years after 1920, men and women have understood the legacy of early-twentieth-century multiplicity to favor a full attack on universals, on determinations, and on hierarchies, regarding such things as detrimental to human understanding and well-being. A sign of the success of multiplicity in American life is the degree to which educated men and women habitually respond to overarching schemes and unifying theories by maintaining that "things are complicated." There is, of course, good reason to hold such a position. Much of the death and oppression of the twentieth century was the handiwork of those who believed in the singularity of the truths they supposedly possessed. Nazism, Stalinism, and religious funda-mentalism have shared, whatever their great differences, a commitment to absolute truth and the use of power to enforce it. That we are deeply suspi-cious of those who would chop reality to conform to theory is the great legacy of the pluralists of the early twentieth century. Yet we might do well to recall that some forms of unity serve us well. Few people go around without any generalizations. A sense of unity allows us to recognize that apparently un-like things are connected or that some hierarchies, such as those that rank ending injustice as more important than the flavor of our toothpaste, are valuable, even necessary. Early-twentieth-century multiplicity captured the limitations of previous unities but hardly provided definitive answers to the questions of which patterns were persistent or when totalizing and abstrac-tion were required. Perhaps the greatest legacy of early-twentieth-century multiplicity is the recognition that it left us no choice but to negotiate anew the interplay of the one and the many.

Notes

1. Lisa Ann Szefel, "The Creation of an American Poetic Community," 1890–1920 (PhD diss., Rochester: University of Rochester, 2004), dissects the accessibility of the New Poetry, 172–275. Of particular note is the way in which the war created fissures in the community, directed in large measure at German sympathizer George Sylvester Viereck, who had been a leading force behind the Poetry Society of America.

2. Roosevelt's war views can be found in Theodore Roosevelt, *The Americanism of Theodore Roosevelt: Selections from His Writings and Speeches,* compiled by Hermann Hagedorn (New York: Houghton Mifflin, 1923), and *America and the World War* (New York: Charles Scribner's Sons, 1915). Roosevelt's consistent attack on multi-plicity is documented in David Traxel, *Crusader Nation: The United States in Peace and the Great War, 1898–1920* (New York: Alfred A. Knopf, 2006); and John Milton Cooper, *The Warrior and the Priest: Woodrow Wilson and Theodore Roosevelt* (Cam-bridge, MA: Belknap Press of Harvard University Press, 1983). The irony of the last is that it is not entirely clear who was the warrior and who was the priest.

3. Charles Forcey, *The Crossroads of Liberalism: Croly, Weyl, Lippmann, and the Progressive Era, 1900–1925* (New York: Oxford University Press, 1961); Norman Gordon Levin, *Woodrow Wilson and World Politics: America's Response to War and Rev-

olution (New York: Oxford University Press, 1968); William Appleman Williams, *The Contours of American History* (Chicago: Quadrangle Books, 1966).

4. Croly, quoted in Forcey, *Crossroads of Liberalism*, 223.

5. George F. Kennan, *American Diplomacy, 1900–1951* (Chicago: University of Chicago Press, 1951). Arthur Link comes to Wilson's defense in *Wilson the Diplomatist* (Baltimore: Johns Hopkins University Press, 1957). Wilson's absolute and rigid moralism and his trust in the universal workings of history became the object of derision in the years that followed the war, most notably in Sigmund Freud and William C. Bullitt, *Thomas Woodrow Wilson, Twenty-eighth President of the United States; A Psychological Study* (Boston, MA: Houghton Mifflin, [1931] 1967). Stuart Rochester, *American Liberal Disillusionment* (University Park: Pennsylvania State University Press, 1976), 134–44, points to Bullitt as a key example of a liberal whose great dreams burst in the aftermath of the war.

6. Gauss, quoted in Susan Hegeman, *Patterns for America: Modernism and the Concept of Culture* (Princeton, NJ: Princeton University Press, 1999), 52–53.

7. Arthur O. Lovejoy, letter to the editor, *New Republic* 10 (February 17, 1917), 75.

8. Arthur Lovejoy, letter to the editor, *Nation* (April 4, 1918), 402; Carol S. Gruber, *Mars and Minerva: World War I and the Uses of the Higher Learning in America* (Baton Rouge: Louisiana State University Press, 1975), 170–73.

9. C. Roland Marchand's, *The American Peace Movement and Social Reform, 1898–1918* (Princeton, NJ: Princeton University Press, 1972) remains the authoritative source on pacifism and peace movements before the war.

10. John Dewey, "Conscience and Compulsion," *New Republic* 11 (July 1, 1917), 298.

11. John Dewey, "Force and Coercion," *International Journal of Ethics* (April 1916), 359–67.

12. George Herbert Mead, *The Conscientious Objector* (New York: National Security League, 1917), 5–6.

13. Ibid., 9.

14. George Herbert Mead, "War Issue to U.S. Forced by Kaiser," *Chicago Herald*, August 2, 1917.

15. George Herbert Mead, "America's Ideals and the War," *Chicago Herald*, August 2, 1917.

16. Terrance MacMullan, "On War as Waste: Jane Addams's Pragmatic Pacifism," *Journal of Speculative Philosophy* 15, no. 2 (2001); Jane Addams, "The Revolt against War," *Survey* (July 17, 1915), 355–59, and *Peace and Bread in Time of War* (Boston, MA: Hall, 1922).

17. Felix Adler, *The World Crisis and Its Meaning* (New York: D. Appleton, 1915), 120–30.

18. Gruber, *Mars and Minerva*, 47–51.

19. Veblen's late-arrival reversal of conventional wisdom echoes in its challenge his contention that invention is the mother of necessity, in which he cited how

invented machines created pressures to use them. See Thorstein Veblen, *The Instinct of Workmanship and the State of the Industrial Arts* (New Brunswick, NJ: Transaction Publishers, [1914] 1990), 316.

20. For Veblen's view of the war and peace, see Thorstein Veblen, *Imperial Germany and the Industrial Revolution* (New York and London: Macmillan, 1915), and *An Inquiry into the Nature of Peace and the Terms of Its Perpetuation* (New York and London: Macmillan, 1917). An insightful analysis of the particular nature of Veblen's position can be found in Christopher Capozzola, "Thorstein Veblen and the Politics of War, 1914–1920," *International Journal of Politics, Culture and Society* 13, no. 2 (1999): 255–72. Veblen's wife is quoted in Sylvia Bartley, "Intellect Surveilled: Thorstein Veblen and the Organs of State Security," Second Conference of the International Thorstein Veblen Association, Carleton College, Northfield, Minnesota, 1996, http://elegant-technology.com/TVbarSI.html.

21. Veblen, *Inquiry into the Nature of Peace*. See also Capozzola, "Thorstein Veblen and the Politics of War."

22. George Herbert Mead, "Review of *The Nature of Peace and the Terms of Its Perpetuation* by Thorsten Veblen," *Journal of Political Economy* 26 (1918): 752–62. Quotations are from pages 760 and 761.

23. John Dewey, *Germany Philosophy and Politics* (New York: Henry Holt, 1915), 164.

24. Robert B. Westbrook, *John Dewey and American Democracy* (Ithaca, NY: Cornell University Press, 1991), 198–220.

25. David Kennedy, *Over Here: The First World War and American Society* (New York: Oxford University Press, 1980), 49–53, 90–92. Kennedy's brief for Dewey and other reluctant prowar progressives is aimed at the cult of Randolph Bourne that arose in the 1960s and against such arguments as Stuart I. Rochester, *American Liberal Disillusionment in the Wake of World War I* (University Park: Pennsylvania State University Press, 1976), which indicts liberals for naive idealism. Kennedy's defense of Dewey is fairly laconic and has drawn a vigorous dissent from Robert Westbrook, Dewey's most thorough biographer. A recent return to the issue that believes Dewey had the better of the argument is James Livingston, "War and the Intellectuals: Bourne, Dewey, and the Fate of Pragmatism," *Journal of the Gilded Age and Progressive Era* 2, no. 4 (October 2003), http://www.historycooperative.org/journals/jga/2.4/livingston.html.

26. Lippmann, quoted in Kennedy, *Over Here: The First World War and American Society*, 39–40.

27. David Levering Lewis, *W. E. B. DuBois*, vol. 1, *Biography of a Race, 1868–1919* (New York: Henry Holt, 1993), 501–77.

28. Particularly valuable recent treatments of Bourne include Casey Blake, *Beloved Community: The Cultural Criticism of Randolph Bourne, Van Wyck Brooks, Waldo Frank and Lewis Mumford* (Chapel Hill: University of North Carolina Press, 1990); and Leslie Vaughan, *Randolph Bourne and the Politics of Cultural Radicalism* (Lawrence: University Press of Kansas, 1997).

29. Randolph Bourne, "American Use for German Ideals," *New Republic* 4 (September 4, 1915), 117–19.

30. Randolph Bourne, "Below the Battle," in *War and the Intellectuals: Essays by Randolph S. Bourne, 1915–1919*, edited by Carl Resek (New York: Harper Torchbooks, 1964), 20. Laski's criticism was made in Harold Laski, "The Liberalism of Randolph Bourne," *Freeman* (May 19, 1920), 237.

31. Randolph Bourne, "The Collapse of American Strategy," in *War and the Intellectuals: Essays by Randolph S. Bourne, 1915–1919*, edited by Carl Resek (New York: Harper Torchbooks, 1964), 22–35.

32. Randolph Bourne, "War and the Intellectuals," in *War and the Intellectuals: Essays by Randolph S. Bourne, 1915–1919*, edited by Carl Resek (New York: Harper Torchbooks, 1964), 9–10.

33. Bourne, "War and the Intellectuals," 8–9.

34. Randolph Bourne, "Twilight of the Idols," in *War and the Intellectuals: Essays by Randolph S. Bourne, 1915–1919*, edited by Carl Resek (New York: Harper Torchbooks, 1964), 57.

35. Ibid., 54.

36. Ibid., 61.

37. Randolph Bourne, "A War Diary," in *War and the Intellectuals: Essays by Randolph S. Bourne, 1915–1919*, edited by Carl Resek (New York: Harper Torchbooks, 1964), 43.

38. "For Freedom and Democracy," *North American Review* 206 (March 30, 1917): 482–88. Eldon Eisenach, *The Lost Promise of Progressivism* (Lawrence: University Press of Kansas, 1994), 225–65, is the most thorough argument about the ideological and cultural links between the war effort and one strain of progressivism.

39. Cited in "'I Didn't Raise My Boy to Be a Soldier': Singing against the War," History Matters, http://historymatters.gmu.edu/d/4942.

40. See Nancy Cott, *The Grounding of Modern Feminism* (New Haven, CT: Yale University Press, 1987), 242–67; Frances H. Early, *A World without War: How U.S. Feminists and Pacifists Resisted World War I* (Syracuse, NY: Syracuse University Press, 2004); and Erika Kuhlman, *Petticoats and White Feathers: Gender Conformity, Race, the Progressive Peace Movement, and the Debate over War, 1895–1919* (Westport, CT: Greenwood, 1997).

41. George Creel, *Rebel at Large: Recollections of Fifty Crowded Years* (New York: G. P. Putnam's Sons, 1947); Jennifer D. Keene, *Doughboys, the Great War, and the Remaking of America* (Baltimore: Johns Hopkins University Press, 2001), 62–81; Kennedy, *Over Here: The First World War and American Society*, 45–92; Traxel, *Crusader Nation*, 304–33.

42. Christopher Capozzola, "The Only Badge Needed Is Your Patriotic Fervor: Vigilance, Coercion, and the Law in World War I America," *Journal of American History* 88, no. 4 (March 2002): 1358–64.

43. In addition to Kennedy and Traxel, see Thomas Fleming, *The Illusion of Victory: America in World War I* (New York: Basic Books, 2003), 93–136. Bishop William

Quayle, as reported in "Moral Flabbiness in Peace Talk," *Literary Digest* 19 (October 1918): 28–29, cited in History Matters, http://historymatters.gmu.edu/d/4972/.

44. E. A. Schwartz, "The Lynching of Robert Prager, the United Mine Workers, and the Problems of Patriotism in 1918," *Journal of the Illinois State Historical Society*, Winter 2003, http://www.findarticles.com/p/articles/mi_qa3945/is_200301/ai_n 9170046.

45. See Gary Gerstle, *American Crucible: Race and Nation in the Twentieth Century* (Princeton, NJ: Princeton University Press, 2002), especially 14–121; and David W. Noble, *The Progressive Mind, 1890–1917* (New York: Rand McNally, 1970), 152–72, for a discussion of Roosevelt's racial thought. Roosevelt's speech is found in Theodore Roosevelt, *The Americanism of Theodore Roosevelt: Selections from His Writings and Speeches*, compiled by Hermann Hagedorn (Boston, MA: Houghton Mifflin, 1932), 384.

46. Roger Daniels, *Guarding the Golden Door: American Immigration Policy and Immigrants since 1882* (New York: Hill and Wang, 2004), and John Higham, *Strangers in the Land: Patterns of American Nativism, 1860–1925* (New York: Atheneum, 1963), 210–50, tell the story of wartime ethnic conflict.

47. John Hope Franklin and Alfred A. Moss Jr., *From Slavery to Freedom: A History of Negro Americans*, 6th ed. (New York: Alfred A. Knopf, 1988), 310–23, offers an overview. Henri Florette, *Bitter Victory: A History of Black Soldiers in World War I* (Garden City, NY: Doubleday, 1970), details African-American experience in the armed struggle. William M. Tuttle Jr., *Race Riot: Chicago in the Red Summer of 1919* (New York: Atheneum, 1970), and Robert Haynes, *A Night of Violence: The Houston Riot of 1917* (Baton Rouge: Louisiana State University Press, 1976), tell the story of specific riots.

48. Kennedy, *Over Here*, 73, 263–64; and Paul Buhle and Nicole Schulman, *Wobblies! A Graphic History of the Industrial Workers of the World*, ed. Paul Buhle (London and New York: Verso, 2005). For a discussion of labor relations in general, see Joseph A. McCartin, *Labor's Great War: The Struggle for Industrial Democracy and the Origins of Modern American Labor Relations, 1912–1921* (Chapel Hill: University of North Carolina Press, 1997).

49. The most thorough survey of the moral policing during the war is Nancy K. Bristow, *Making Men Moral: Social Engineering during the Great War* (New York: New York University Press, 1996).

50. Stuart Sherman, "The Naturalism of Mr. Dreiser," *Nation* (December 2, 1915): 648, 650; H. L. Mencken, *A Book of Prefaces* (New York: Alfred A. Knopf, 1917); Stuart Sherman, "Beautifying American Literature," *Nation* 29 (November 1917), 594; Henry May, *The End of American Innocence* (New York: Oxford University Press, [1959] 1970), 391; Joan Shelley Rubin, *The Making of Middlebrow Culture* (Chapel Hill: University of North Carolina Press, 1992), 42–61.

51. Allan Stockdale, quoted in Scott Nearing, *The Making of a Radical: A Political Autobiography* (Harborside, ME: Social Science Institute, 1972), 100.

52. Cattell's position, antagonistic as it was to the war effort, was actually widely

held among enthusiasts for the war in mid-1917. As David Kennedy demonstrates, a number of prowar congressmen were flabbergasted that the Wilson administration was seriously contemplating providing men to fight alongside the Allies in Europe. For a different view of the Cattell–Butler affair, see Michael Sokal, "James McKeen Cattell, Columbia University, and the Ironies of Academic Freedom, 1891–1917," New York Academy of Sciences, http://www.nyas.org/events/eventDetail.asp ?eventID=130&date=4/28/2004%206:00:00%20PM.

53. Gruber, Mars and Minerva, 116–60, 207–10.

54. Ibid., 163–212; Ellen Nore, Charles Beard: An Intellectual Biography (Carbondale: Southern Illinois University Press, 1983), 70–96; and Robert C. Cottrell, Roger Nash Baldwin and the American Civil Liberties Union (New York: Columbia University Press, 2000).

55. Henry Cabot Lodge, Speech of August 12, 1919, http://www.firstworldwar .com/source/lodge_leagueofnations.htm. Discussions of the meaning of the treaty fight may be found in Traxel, 339–49; Lloyd E. Ambrosius, Woodrow Wilson and the American Diplomatic Tradition: The Treaty Fight in Perspective (New York: Cambridge University Press, 1985); and Thomas Andrew Bailey, Woodrow Wilson and the Lost Peace (Chicago: Quadrangle Books, 1963). Kristofer Allerfeldt, Beyond the Huddled Masses: American Immigration and the Treaty of Versailles (London: I. B. Tauris, 2006), addresses the domestic worries prompted by the treaty.

56. Daniels, Coming to America, 265–86; Higham, Strangers, 234–324; Gerstle, American Crucible, 14–128.

57. Paul S. Boyer, Purity in Print: The Vice-Society Movement and Book Censorship in America (New York: Charles Scribner's, 1968), is a general history. Paul Vanderham, James Joyce and Censorship: The Trials of Ulysses (New York: New York University Press, 1998), explores the Joyce case in particular. Kevin White, Sexual Liberation or Sexual License? The American Revolt against Victorianism (Chicago: Ivan R. Dee, 2000), and Rochelle Gurstein, The Repeal of Reticence: A History of America's Cultural and Legal Struggles over Free Speech, Obscenity, Sexual Liberation, and Modern Art (New York: Hill and Wang, 1996), offer a counter to traditional views of liberation from constraints as progress.

58. See Robert Sklar, Movie-Made America: A Cultural History of American Movies (New York: Vintage, 1975), 67–85, and Andrea Friedman, Prurient Interests: Gender, Democracy, and Obscenity in New York City, 1909–1945 (New York: Columbia University Press, 2000), chapter 2, for discussions of postwar film censorship.

59. Theodore Draper, The Roots of American Communism (New York: Viking Press, 1957), 1–281, details the struggles of the movement during the period covered in this book.

60. Susan Curtis, A Consuming Faith: The Social Gospel and Modern American Culture (Baltimore: Johns Hopkins University Press, 1991), 185–227; and George Marsden, Fundamentalism and American Culture (Oxford University Press, 2006), 141–63.

61. J. Gresham Machen, "The Church in the War," address at Princeton Seminary, May 6, 1919, published in the Presbyterian (May 29, 1919), 10–18, and "Liber-

alism or Christianity," *Princeton Theological Review* 20 (1922): 93–117. The first was a response to Harry Fosdick's "The Trenches and the Church at Home," *Atlantic Monthly* (January 1919), 22–33, in which Fosdick blamed the loss of belief on the superstitions of orthodox and fundamentalist dogma. Darryl G. Hart, "When Is a Fundamentalist a Modernist?"; J. Gresham Machen, "Cultural Modernism, and Conservative Protestantism," *Journal of the American Academy of Religion* (Fall 1997), 605–33; and Hart, *Defending the Faith: J. Gresham Machen and the Crisis of Conservative Protestantism in Modern America* (Baltimore: Johns Hopkins University Press, 1994).

62. Henry May, *The End of American Innocence* is indispensable. See also Christine Stansell, *American Moderns: Bohemian New York and the Creation of a New Century* (New York: Metropolitan, 2000); Steven Biel, *Independent Intellectuals in the United States, 1910–1945* (New York: New York University Press, 1992); and Casey Blake, *Beloved Community: The Cultural Criticism of Randolph Bourne, Van Wyck Brooks, Waldo Frank and Lewis Mumford* (Chapel Hill: University of North Carolina Press, 1990), as well as memoirs of Floyd Dell, Max Eastman, and Mabel Dodge Luhan.

63. Carl L. Becker, *The United States: An Experiment in Democracy* (New York: Harper and Brothers, 1920), 296–331.

64. James Branch Cabell, *Jurgen: A Comedy of Justice* (New York: McBride, 1919). On Cabell and his milieu, see Louis Rubin, *No Place on Earth; Ellen Glasgow, James Branch Cabell, and Richmond-in-Virginia* (Austin: University of Texas Press, 1959).

65. Sherwood Anderson, *Winesburg, Ohio* (New York: B. W. Huebsch, 1919), quotation from pages 4 and 5.

66. Albion Small, "Fifty Years of Sociology in the United States," *American Journal of Sociology* 21 (1916): 860–61; and Small, "Technique as an Approach to Science," *AJS* 27 (1922): 646–51, quoted in Robert C. Bannister, *Sociology and Scientism: The American Quest for Objectivity, 1880–1940* (Chapel Hill: University of North Carolina Press, 1987), 61, 62.

67. Bannister, *Sociology and Scientism*, and Mark Smith, *Social Science in the Crucible: The American Debate over Objectivity and Purpose, 1918–1941* (Durham, NC: Duke University Press, 1994), discuss the development of the rise of a science of particulars.

68. Smith, *Social Science*, 23–48.

69. Boas, letter to the editor, *New York Times*, January 8, 1916, quoted in Susan Hegeman, *Patterns for America: Modernism and the Concept of Culture* (Princeton, NJ: Princeton University Press, 1999), 53.

70. Franz Boas, "The Mental Attitude of the Educated Classes," *Dial* (September 5, 1918), 145–48, and "Nationalism," *Dial* (March 8, 1919), 23–37.

71. Hegeman, *Patterns for America*, 81–157.

72. For Veblen's postwar career, see Joseph Dorfman, *Thorstein Veblen and His America* (New York: Viking, 1934); Douglas Dowd, *Thorstein Veblen* (New York: New York University Press, 1964), 85–135; and John Wenzler, "Transcendental Economics: The Quest to Harmonize Economic and Moral Law in Nineteenth-Century American Social Thought" (PhD diss., Rochester: University of Rochester, 1998),

459–536. Commons and his legacy are detailed in Karen McCally, "'A Bundle of Rights': The Commons School and American Social Policy, 1905–1945," (PhD diss., Rochester: University of Rochester, 2001).

73. Nathan E. Hale Jr., *The Rise and Crisis of Psychoanalysis in the United States: Freud and the Americans, 1917–1985* (New York: Oxford University Press, 1995), 3–184.

74. Westbrook, *John Dewey and American Democracy*, 231.

Chronology

1900   Republican William McKinley handily defeats William Jennings Bryan in a rematch of 1896, with the central issue American imperialism. The Associated Press is established, leading to charges of an information trust. Theodore Roosevelt expounds his mix of racial thought and masculine strength in *The Strenuous Life*. Josiah Royce publishes *The World and the Individual*. New York court acquits actress Olga Nethersole of obscenity charges brought by the New York Society for the Suppression of Vice for her role in the play *Sapho*, much to the delight of feminist and socialite supporters. Sigmund Freud's *Interpretation of Dreams* explores the complexities of the unconscious self. Max Planck discovers "black box" laws. Theodore Dreiser's *Sister Carrie* published.

1901   Financier J. P. Morgan incorporates U.S. Steel. President William McKinley assassinated in Buffalo, elevating Theodore Roosevelt to the presidency and opening the way for national progressivism. Marconi conducts transatlantic radio transmission. Frank Norris's naturalistic *Octopus* published. The twelve-volume *Jewish Encyclopedia* begun.

1902   American war against the Philippines ends with an estimated 250,000 Filipino deaths. American debut of Claude Debussy's *Prélude à l'après-midi d'un faune*. Jane Addams publishes her *Democracy and Social Ethics*, outlining her pragmatist-inflected sense of the good. Scott Joplin composes "The Entertainer." Hutchins Hapgood inspects Jewish life on the Lower East Side of New York in *Spirit of the Ghetto*. Alfred Stieglitz establishes Photo-Secession, an invitation-only group of photographers eager to establish a distinctive photographic aesthetic. Charles Horton Cooley lays out his version of the social self in *Human Nature and Social Organization*. William James issues *Varieties of Religious Experience*.

1903   W. E. B. Du Bois publishes his famed *Souls of Black Folk*. Jack London's account of despair, *People of the Abyss*, is published. Henry James's *Ambassadors*, an intricate exploration of consciousness straining to understand pleasure, is published. Tenor Enrico Caruso makes his American debut, as do actor John Barrymore and musical entertainer George M. Cohan. Wright Brothers fly in Kill Devil Hill near Kittyhawk, North Carolina. Edwin Porter's *The Great Train Robbery* establishes the aesthetic possibilities of movies.

1904   Theodore Roosevelt elected president. The Supreme Court by a 5–4 vote dissolves the Northern Securities rail holding company as a violation of antitrust laws. Helen Keller graduates from Radcliffe. New York subway opens. World Congresses convene in conjunction with the St. Louis World's Fair, with physicist Ernest Rutherford and sociologist Max Weber among the participants. New Humanist Paul Elmer More publishes the first of his *Shelbourne Essays*. Ida Tarbell issues *History of the Standard Oil Company*.

1905   Einstein's *annus mirabilis*, featuring six path-breaking papers, among which are the theory of special relativity, the light quantum hypothesis, and the relationship of inertia and energy content. Edith Wharton writes *House of Mirth*. Efforts to arrest the actors of *Mrs. Warren's Profession* prompts playwright George Bernard Shaw to coin term "Comstockery" as synonym for prudery. *Lochner v. New York* establishes limits on the ability of government to regulate working hours and wages. Founding of the Niagara Movement to end segregation and discrimination against black people. Algernon Crapsey heresy trial by Episcopalian Church leaders. The *New York Review*, the organ of Catholic modernism founded by theologians and philosophers associated with St. Joseph's seminary in Yonkers, New York, lasted until 1907. Pittsburgh nickelodeon ushers in "nickel madness," establishing movies as a premier art and entertainment form. Industrial Workers of the World formed as alternative to the craft-union reformism of the American Federation of Labor.

1906   Upton Sinclair publishes *The Jungle*, a story of immigrant family in industrial Chicago. Earthquake virtually destroys San Francisco. Architect Stanford White assassinated. First Victrola manufactured, facilitating new forms of music consumption. Congress passes the Hepburn Act, regulating railroads, and Pure Food and Drug Acts, extending notions of promotion of the general welfare and modifying reach of private property. Elsie Clews Parsons publishes *The Family*. Atlanta race riot.

1907   Bank panic and depression spread through the economy. Henry James returns from England and writes *American Scene*. William James publishes *Pragmatism: A New Name for Some Old Ways of Thinking*. Jack London's apocalyptic tale of revolution and repression, *The Iron Heel*, appears. Albert Michelson wins Nobel Prize in science. Walter Rauschenbusch writes *Christianity and the Social Crisis*, establishing intellectual and theological basis for the Social Gospel. H. L. Mencken writes *The Philosophy of Friedrich Nietzsche*.

1908:   Japanese immigration prohibited. William Howard Taft elected president. Manufacture of automobiles passes the 50,000 mark. African American boxer Jack Johnson wins heavyweight championship. "The Eight"—group of realist painters, including John Sloan, Robert Henri, and George Luks—exhibit in New York in challenge to the National Academy of Design. *Muller v. Oregon*, featuring the "Brandeis brief" detailing the effects of working conditions, holds that laws regulating the wages and hours of women are constitutional. Dixieland Jazz Band organized in New Orleans. Arthur Bentley publishes *Process of Government*, an extended argument for the shifting alliances of groups as the basis for political dynamics. D. W. Griffith becomes a director at American Biograph, where he would direct over four hundred films.

1909   Model T begins mass production. Van Wyck Brooks publishes *Wine of the Puritans*. Ezra Pound publishes *Personae* and *Exultations*. Gertrude Stein publishes *Three Lives*. Gertie the Dinosaur, first animated cartoon, appears. First colored motion pictures made and exhibited. National Association for the Advancement of Colored

People established. Robert Millikan's oil-drop experiment demonstrates that electric charges are quanta, not continuous. Sigmund Freud and Carl Jung lecture at Clark University in Worcester, Massachusetts, on psychoanalysis. William James responds to critics of pragmatism in *Meaning of Truth*. "Uprising of the 20,000," the strike of New York City garment workers, lasts four months.

1910   Bombing at anti-union *Los Angeles Times* results in conviction of labor leaders James and Joseph McNamara. Congress passes the Mann Act in response to moral panic about white slavery. Haley's comet passes by earth without the dire consequences predicted. Jane Addams publishes *Twenty Years at Hull House*, her account of her work and its purposes. Charles William Eliot's *Harvard Classics*, consisting of fifty volumes of selections, detailed what Eliot thought educated people needed to know. Film censorship takes hold; SF board bans thirty-two releases. The Vatican insists that all priests take an oath against modernism when they are ordained.

1911   Supreme Court dissolves Standard Oil and American Tobacco monopolies. The Triangle Shirtwaist Fire results in death of 146 when exit doors are locked . The *Masses* is relaunched under the editorship of Max Eastman. Theodore Dreiser returns to print with *Jennie Gerhardt*. Irving Berlin recognizes a trend with "Alexander's Ragtime Band." George Santayana identifies the old cultural assumptions in talk in Berkeley, California, "The Genteel Tradition in American Philosophy." Charles Ives begins work on *Piano Sonata No. 2, Concord, Mass., 1840–1860*, which he fundamentally completes by 1915. Joel Spingarn strikes a blow for amoral criticism in *New Criticism*. Franz Boas stakes out the case for cultural multiplicity in *The Mind of Primitive Man*.

1912   Harriet Monroe helps initiate the new poetry with *Poetry, a Magazine of Verse*, published in Chicago, Illinois. Massachusetts establishes minimum wage for women and children. Juliette Low establishes Girl Scouts on model of Baden-Powell's Girl Guides. Jim Thorpe declared the "greatest athlete in the world" for Olympic triumphs. "World's Largest Metaphor" sinks in the Atlantic. James Weldon Johnson publishes *Autobiography of an Ex-Colored Man*. Theodore Dreiser publishes *The Financier*. Lawrence strike of clothing workers, under the auspices of the IWW, testifies to continued class conflict. "Progressive election" between Democrat Woodrow Wilson, Republican William Howard Taft, Progressive Theodore Roosevelt, and Socialist Eugene Debs establishes the saliency of reform among the American people. John Ryan established Catholic position on social reform with *Living Wage*. Walter Weyl argues for a flexible approach to reform that combines mixed economy, a recognition of the persistence of small property owners, and the virtues of consumerism, in *New Democracy*. Thorstein Veblen's *Instinct of Workmanship* published. Mack Sennett establishes Keystone Studios.

1913   Webb-Kenyon Act prohibits the interstate shipment of liquor. Poetry renaissance continues with Robert Frost's *Boy's Will* and Vachel Lindsay's *General Booth Enters into Heaven*. William Marion Reedy establishes the *Mirror* in St. Louis. Willa Cather publishes *O Pioneers*; Ellen Glasgow does the same with *Virginia*. Charlie Chaplin begins his illustrious movie career. Henri Bergson visits the United States to great acclaim. Charles Beard's *Economic Interpretation of the Constitution* causes great consternation with its contention that the signers of the Constitution were motivated by economic interests. Alice Paul forms National Woman's Party. Stravinsky's *Rite of Spring* performed in Paris. George Herriman's *Krazy Kat* appears for the first time. The Paterson silk strike and related pageant at Madison Square Garden, organized by Greenwich Village radicals, draws national attention. The Armory Show introduces Americans to European modern art.

1914   The Great War begins in Europe (July 28–August 26). President Wilson sends Marines to Vera Cruz after arrest of U.S. sailors. First income tax paid. Ford establishes five-dollar minimum for eight-hour day and establishes moving assembly line. The New Republic, "less to inform or entertain its readers than to start little insurrections in the realm of their convictions," begins publication. Margaret Anderson founds *The Little Review*. Intellectual arguments for different flavors of progressivism are on display in Louis Brandeis's *Other People's Money* and Herbert Croly's *Progressive Democracy*. *Tender Buttons: Objects, Food, Rooms* by Gertrude Stein and Amy Lowell's *Sword Blades and Other Poems* published, opening new directions in nonrealist literature. Margaret Sanger initiates birth control movement, publishes *Family Limitation* pamphlet. Walter Lippmann publishes *Drift and Mastery*, which takes the absence of firm foundation as the condition in which politics are to be conducted. Black dance-band leader Jim Reese Europe gives March 11 jazz concert at Carnegie Hall. W. C. Handy hates to see the evening sun go down, in what is considered the premier example of classic blues, "The St. Louis Blues."

1915   The sinking of the Lusitania spurs new wave of outrage at German U-boat warfare. Secretary of state William Jennings Bryan leaves cabinet in disagreement with Wilson's handling of the affair. Van Wyck Brooks publishes *America's Coming-of-Age*; Theodore Dreiser creates a sensation with *The 'Genius.'* D. W. Griffith's *Birth of a Nation* engenders strong protest for its racism and earns great praise for its craftsmanship. T. S. Eliot publishes "The Love Song of J. Alfred Prufrock." Charlotte Perkins Gilman publishes *Herland*. Thorstein Veblen details the clash between business and industrial impulses in *Theory of Business Enterprise*.

1916   Louis Brandeis becomes the first Jew to serve on the United States Supreme Court. D. W. Griffith mounts epic *Intolerance* as riposte to critics. Einstein publishes general theory of relativity, which deals with the effects of acceleration on the shape of space and the flow of time. Susan Glaspell's feminist classic, *Trifles*, is staged by the leading little theater, the Provincetown Players. Jessie Taft's *The Woman Movement from the Point of View of Social Consciousness* details how emulation results in female acceptance of subordination. Jeanette Rankin of Montana becomes the first woman elected to the House of Representatives. Randolph Bourne's "Trans-National America" argues for a form of cultural pluralism, rejecting campaigns against "hyphenation."

1917   The United States declares war on the Central Powers on April 6. Committee on Public Information established to inform and shape public opinion. Espionage Act passed, augmented in 1918 by the Sedition Act, which made it illegal to criticize the government. East St. Louis race riot. Phelps Dodge Corporation deports over 1,000 suspected radicals and labor organizers from Bisbee, Arizona. Bolsheviks seize power in Russia. H. L. Mencken publishes his *Book of Prefaces*.

1918   President Wilson lays out his "Fourteen Points of Peace." The First World War ends. Willa Cather publishes *My Antonia*. *The Education of Henry Adams* appears posthumously. W. I. Thomas and Florian Znaniecki publish their landmark study of cultural contact, *The Polish Peasant in Europe and America*. Mary Follett takes on American individualism in *The New State*.

1919   Versailles Treaty signed. Eighteenth Amendment prohibiting alcohol ratified. Chicago Race riot. Haitian revolt against U.S. occupation. Largest strike wave in American history, with over four million workers involved in industrial action. John Reed's account of the Bolshevik Revolution, *Ten Days That Shook the World*, published, as was James Cabell's *Jürgen* and Sherwood Anderson's *Winesburg, Ohio*. Yiddish Art Theatre found by Maurice Schwartz. D. W. Griffith produces a film, *Broken Blossoms*, that details the love of a Chinese man for a poor and neglected English girl played by Lillian Gish. Alice Hamilton, long-time campaigner against industrial toxins, becomes first woman professor at Harvard in the industrial hygiene program. Einstein's general theory of relativity confirmed by a British team's observations of the near-total eclipse of the sun on May 29. Heightened racial violence plagues the nation.

1920   Nineteenth Amendment extending suffrage to women ratified. Bombing on Wall Street sparks "red scare" crackdowns. Warren G. Harding elected president, returning nation to "normalcy." Chicago "Black Sox" throw the World Series. Sinclair Lewis publishes *Main Street*; F. Scott Fitzgerald, *This Side of Paradise*. Eugene Debs, Prisoner 9653, runs for president from Atlanta jail cell.

~

Bibliographic Essay

General discussions of American life in the early twentieth century abound. John Whiteclay Chambers, *The Tyranny of Change: America in the Progressive Era, 1900–1917* (New York: St. Martin's Press, 1980) reviews politics and society. Steven J. Diner, *A Very Different Age: Americans of the Progressive Era* (New York: Hill and Wang, 1998) is a thorough social history. Michael E. McGerr, *A Fierce Discontent: The Rise and Fall of the Progressive Movement in America, 1870–1920* (New York: Free Press, 2003), links progressive reform to the growing social chasms, seeing it as an effort to tame both top and bottom. Nell Painter, *Standing at Armageddon: The United States, 1877–1919* (New York: W. W. Norton, 1987) traces reform impulses, class conflicts, and racial and gender clashes. Mark Sullivan, *Our Times: America at the Birth of the Twentieth Century* (New York: Scribner's, [1926] 1996) is chock-full of telling incidents and smart observations about everyday life. David Traxel, *Crusader Nation: The United States in Peace and the Great War, 1898–1920* (New York: Alfred A. Knopf, 2006), concentrates on the role of unity thought on foreign policy and domestic reform.

Investigation of cultural and intellectual life begins with the indispensable Henry May, *The End of American Innocence: A Study of the First Years of Our Own Time, 1912–1917* (New York: Knopf, 1959; reissued Columbia, 1992). Two subsequent insightful, provocative, and quite divergent accounts of the links between cultural change and social life are T. J. Jackson Lears, *No Place of Grace: Antimodernism and the Transformation of American Culture, 1880–1920* (New York: Pantheon, 1981), and James Livingston, *Pragmatism*

283

and the Political Economy of Cultural Revolution, 1850–1940 (Chapel Hill: University of North Carolina Press, 1994). James Kloppenberg, *Uncertain Victory: Social Democracy and Progressivism in European and American Thought, 1870–1920* (New York: Oxford University Press, 1986) details the ways the United States joined in the transatlantic effort to find via media between Marxism and economic liberalism. Morton Gabriel White, *Social Thought in America: The Revolt against Formalism* (Boston, MA: Beacon Press, 1957), examines how William James, John Dewey, Thorstein Veblen, and Oliver Wendell Holmes strengthened the antifoundational strain in American culture. Peter Conn, *The Divided Mind: Ideology and Imagination in America, 1898–1917* (New York: Cambridge University Press, 1983), and George Cotkin, *Reluctant Modernism: American Thought and Culture, 1880–1900* (New York: Twayne, 1992), explore the ways in which change and stasis coexisted in the late nineteenth and early twentieth centuries. Stephen Kern, *The Culture of Time and Space, 1880–1918* (Cambridge, MA: Harvard University Press, 1983), and William R. Everdell, *The First Moderns: Profiles in the Origins of Twentieth-Century Thought* (Chicago: University of Chicago Press, 1997), expertly put cultural transformation in transatlantic perspective. Edward Wagenknecht, *American Profile, 1900–1909* (Amherst: University of Massachusetts Press, 1982), is a delightful memoir that covers a broad swathe of thought and culture.

Greenwich Village was the site of much intellectual and cultural rebellion in the early twentieth century and has attracted much commentary. Worthwhile studies of efforts to link radical politics and aesthetic departure include Rick Beard and Leslie Cohen Berlowitz, eds., *Greenwich Village: Culture and Counterculture* (New Brunswick, NJ: Rutgers University Press, 1993); Martin Green, *New York 1913: The Armory Show and the Paterson Strike Pageant* (New York: Charles Scribner's Sons, 1988); Daniel Joseph Singal, ed., *Modernist Culture in America* (Belmont, CA: Wadsworth, 1991); Christine Stansell, *American Moderns: Bohemian New York and the Creation of a New Century* (New York: Metropolitan, 2000); Edward Abrahams, *The Lyrical Left: Randolph Bourne, Alfred Stieglitz, and the Origins of Cultural Radicalism in America* (Charlottesville: University Press of Virginia, 1986); Leslie Fishbein, *Rebels in Bohemia: The Radicals of the Masses* (Chapel Hill: University of North Carolina Press, 1982); and Steven Watson, *Strange Bedfellows* (New York: Abbeville Press, 1991). Bohemianism as an international phenomenon is covered in David Weir, *Anarchy and Culture: The Aesthetic Politics of Modernism* (Amherst: University of Massachusetts Press, 1997); and Elizabeth Wilson, *Bohemians: The Glamorous Outcasts* (New Brunswick, NJ: Rutgers University Press, 2000). Modernism as an aesthetic and philosophical entity is the province of Andreas Huyssen, *After the Great Divide: Modernism, Mass*

Culture, Postmodernism (Bloomington and Indianapolis: Indiana University Press, 1986); Anat Matar, *Modernism and the Language of Philosophy* (London: Routledge, 2006); and Thomas Strychacz, *Modernism, Mass Culture, and Professionalism* (New York: Cambridge University Press, 1993).

Early-twentieth-century physics is covered in P. C. W. Davies, *About Time: Einstein's Unfinished Revolution* (New York: Simon and Schuster, 1995); John R. Gribbin, *Annus Mirabilis: 1905, Albert Einstein, and the Theory of Relativity* (New York: Chamberlain Bros., 2005); Jean Eisenstaedt, *The Curious History of Relativity: How Einstein's Theory of Gravity Was Lost and Found Again* (Princeton, NJ: Princeton University Press, 2006); O. B. Hardison Jr., *Disappearing through the Skylight: Culture and Technology in the Twentieth Century* (New York: Penguin Books, 1989); Etienne Klein and Marc Lachièze-Rey, *The Quest for Unity: The Adventure of Physics* (New York: Oxford University Press, 1999); Richard Panek, *The Invisible Century: Einstein, Freud, and the Search for Hidden Universes* (New York: Viking, 2004); and Theodore Porter, "The Death of the Object: Fin-de-Siècle Philosophy of Physics," in *Modernist Impulses in the Social Sciences*, edited by Dorothy Ross (Baltimore: Johns Hopkins University Press, 1994), 128–51. Porter has done important work in the history of statistics. See particularly *The Rise of Statistical Thinking, 1820–1900* (Princeton, NJ: Princeton University Press, 1986). Darwinism and its impact on science and culture is a well-covered subject. Of particular relevance to the development of multiplicity is Cynthia Russett, *Darwin in America: The Intellectual Response, 1865–1912* (San Francisco, CA: W. H. Freeman, 1976); and Daniel J. Wilson, *Science, Community and the Transformation of American Philosophy, 1860–1930* (Chicago: University of Chicago Press, 1990).

Studies of pragmatism have abounded in recent years. In addition to the Kloppenberg and Livingston volumes cited above, readers will profit from Andrew Feffer, *The Chicago Pragmatists and American Progressivism* (Ithaca, NY: Cornell University Press, 1993); James Hoopes, *Consciousness in New England: From Puritanism and Ideas to Psychoanalysis and Semiotic* (Baltimore: Johns Hopkins University Press, 1989); Paul Jay, *Contingency Blues: The Search for Foundations in American Criticism* (Madison: University of Wisconsin Press, 1997); Hans Joas, *Pragmatism and Social Theory* (Chicago: University of Chicago Press, 1993); David Marcell, *Progress and Pragmatism: James, Dewey, Beard and the American Idea of Progress* (Westport, CT: Greenwood, 1972); Louis Menand, *The Metaphysical Club: A Story of Ideas in America* (New York: Farrar, Straus and Giroux, 2001); C. J. Misak, *Truth, Politics, Morality: Pragmatism and Deliberation* (New York: Routledge, 2000); Morton White, *Pragmatism and the American Mind: Essays and Reviews in Philosophy and Intellectual History* (New York: Oxford University Press, 1973); and Robert B. Westbrook, *Democratic Hope: Pragmatism and the Politics of Truth* (Ithaca, NY: Cornell University Press, 2005). John P. Diggins, *The Promise of Pragmatism: Modernism and the Crisis of Knowledge and Authority* (Chicago: University of Chicago Press, 1994), is a not entirely convincing dissent from recent celebrations. Exemplary studies of individual pragmatists include Robert B. Westbrook, *John Dewey and American Democracy* (Ithaca, NY: Cornell University Press, 1991); Neil Coughlan, *Young John Dewey: An Essay in American Intellectual History* (Chicago: University of Chicago Press, 1975); George Cotkin, *William James, Public Philosopher* (Baltimore: Johns Hopkins University Press, 1990); Howard M. Feinstein, *Becoming William James* (Ithaca, NY: Cornell University Press, 1984); Robert D. Richardson, *William James: In the Maelstrom of American Modernism: A Biography* (Boston, MA: Houghton Mifflin, 2006); Joseph Brent, *Charles Sanders Peirce: A Life* (Bloomington: Indiana University Press, 1998); Mitchell Aboulafia, *The Mediating Self: Mead, Sartre, and Self-Determination* (New Haven, CT: Yale University Press, 1986); Gary A. Cook, *George Herbert Mead: The Making of a Social Pragmatist* (Urbana and Chicago: University of Illinois Press, 1993); Ruth Leys, "Mead's Voices: Imitation as Foundation; or, the Struggle against Mimesis," in *Modernist Impulses in the Social Sciences*, ed. Dorothy Ross (Baltimore: Johns Hopkins University Press, 1994), 210–35; and Hans Joas, *G. H. Mead, a Contemporary Re-Examination of His Thought* (Cambridge: Polity Press, 1985).

Pragmatism was not the only American philosophy of multiplicity. See Jeffrey S. Brown, "Vitalism and the Modernist Search for Meaning: Subjectivity, Social Order, and the Philosophy of Life in the Progressive Era" (PhD diss., University of Rochester, 2001); Gillis Harp, *Positivist Republic: Auguste Comte and the Reconstruction of American Liberalism, 1865–1920* (University Park: Pennsylvania State University Press, 1995); and Jennifer Ratner-Rosenhagen, "'Neither Rock nor Refuge': American Encounters with Nietzsche and the Search for Foundations" (PhD diss., Brandeis University, 2003).

Among worthwhile treatments of multiplicity in religion are R. Scott Appleby, *"Church and Age Unite!" The Modernist Impulse in American Catholicism* (Notre Dame, IN: University of Notre Dame Press, 1992); Jay P. Dolan, *The American Catholic Experience: A History from Colonial Times to the Present* (Notre Dame and London: University of Notre Dame Press, 1992); John T. McGreevy, *Catholicism and American Freedom: A History* (New York: W. W. Norton, 2003); Mark Noll, *Between Faith and Criticism: Evangelicals, Scholarship, and the Bible in America* (San Francisco: Harper and Row/San Francisco, 1986); Susan Curtis, *A Consuming Faith: The Social Gospel and Modern Amer-*

ican Culture (Baltimore: Johns Hopkins University Press, 1991); David Danbom, *The World of Hope: Progressives and the Struggle for an Ethical Public Life* (Philadelphia: Temple University Press, 1987); George Marsden, *Fundamentalism and American Culture* (Oxford University Press, 2006); and Ferenc Morton Szasz, *The Divided Mind of Protestant America, 1880–1930* (Tuscaloosa: University of Alabama Press, 1982). Dewey's ethics are explicated in Abraham Edel, *Ethical Theory and Social Change: The Evolution of John Dewey's Ethics, 1908–1932* (New Brunswick, NJ: Transaction, 2001). Sexual morality is dissected in Paul S. Boyer, *Purity in Print: The Vice-Society Movement and Book Censorship in America* (New York: Charles Scribner's, 1968); John D'Emilio and Estelle B. Freedman, *Intimate Matters: A History of Sexuality in America* (New York: Harper and Row, 1988); and Kevin White, *Sexual Liberation or Sexual License? The American Revolt against Victorianism* (Chicago: Ivan R. Dee, 2000).

The literature on artistic practice is immense. Readers would do well to start with Lawrence Levine, *Highbrow/Lowbrow: The Emergence of Cultural Hierarchy in America* (Cambridge, MA: Harvard University Press, 1988). On comics, Ian Gordon, *Comic Strips and Consumer Culture, 1890–1945* (Washington, DC: Smithsonian Institution Press, 1998), and Jerry Robinson, *The Comics: An Illustrated History of Comic Strip Art* (New York: Putnam, 1974), are excellent places to begin. Patrick McDonnell, Karen O'Connell, and Georgia Riley de Havenon provide trenchant commentary and extraordinary illustrations in *Krazy Kat: The Comic Art of George Herriman* (New York: Harry N. Abrams, 1986).

Music in the first twenty years of the twentieth century is a particularly rich field for discerning the contours of multiplicity. Charles Ives has attracted much attention. Frank Rossiter, *Charles Ives and His America* (New York: Liveright, 1975), and J. Peter Burkholder, ed., *Charles Ives and His World* (Princeton, NJ: Princeton University Press, 1996), are superb starting places. That latter has a number of noteworthy essays that link Ives's politics, life in insurance, and music. Larry Starr and Christopher Alan Waterman, *American Popular Music from Minstrelsy to MTV* (New York: Oxford University Press, 2003) is an excellent starting point for the history and practice of American popular music. Susan Curtis, *Dancing to a Black Man's Tune: A Life of Scott Joplin* (Columbia: University of Missouri Press, 2004), tells the story of the leading practitioner of ragtime. William J. Schafer and Johannes Riedel, *The Art of Ragtime: Form and Meaning of an Original Black American Art* (Baton Rouge: Louisiana State University Press, 1973), explore the meaning of the form. The blues have had numerous treatments. Two classical and dissimilar accounts are Albert Murray, *Stomping the Blues* (New York:

Da Capo Press, 2000), and Alan Lomax, *The Land Where the Blues Began* (New York: Pantheon Books, 1993).

The premier popular form, and in many ways the characteristic art of the twentieth century, the movies, can be investigated in Robert Sklar, *Movie-Made America: A Cultural History of American Movies* (New York: Vintage, 1975), and in the Scribner's series *History of the American Cinema*. Relevant volumes are Charles Musser, *The Emergence of Cinema: The American Screen to 1907*, Eileen Bowser, *The Transformation of the Cinema, 1907–1915*, and Richard Kozarski, *An Evening's Entertainment: The Age of the Silent Feature Picture, 1915–1927*. A superb history of silent film is Kevin Brownlow, *The Parade's Gone By* (New York: Ballantine Books, 1969). See also Miriam Hansen, *Babel and Babylon: Spectatorship in American Silent Film* (Cambridge, MA: Harvard University Press, 1991). Charlie Chaplin has been the subject of David Robinson, *Chaplin, His Life and Art* (New York: McGraw-Hill, 1985), and Charles Maland, *Chaplin and American Culture: The Evolution of a Star Image* (Princeton, NJ: Princeton University Press, 1989). David Wark Griffith receives his due in Tom Gunning, *D. W. Griffith and the Origins of American Narrative Film* (Urbana: University of Illinois Press, 1991); Richard Schickel, *D. W. Griffith: An American Life* (New York: Simon and Schuster, 1983); and Scott Simmon, *The Films of D. W. Griffith* (Cambridge: Cambridge University Press, 1993).

Explorations of the vast literature on American writing would do well to begin with the relevant essays in two recent examinations, both edited by Emory Elliott: *The Columbia Literary History of the United States* (New York: Columbia University Press, 1988), and *The Columbia History of the American Novel* (New York: Columbia University Press, 1991). The novel is the focus of Maxwell Geismar's *Last of the Provincials, 1915–1925* (Boston, MA: Houghton Mifflin, 1947), and *American Moderns, from Rebellion to Conformity* (New York: Hill and Wang, 1958); David L. Minter, *A Cultural History of the American Novel: Henry James to William Faulkner* (Cambridge: Cambridge University Press, 1994); Jay Martin, *Harvests of Change: American Literature, 1865–1914* (Englewood Cliffs, NJ: Prentice-Hall, 1967); and Malcolm Bradbury, *The Modern American Novel* (Oxford: Oxford University Press, 1983). The complicated Theodore Dreiser is explored, inspected, and dissected in Rachel Bowlby, *Just Looking: Consumer Culture in Dreiser, Gissing, and Zola* (New York: Methuen, 1985), Clare Virginia Eby, *Dreiser and Veblen, Saboteurs of the Status Quo* (Columbia: University of Missouri Press, 1998); Richard R. Lingeman, *Theodore Dreiser: An American Journey* (New York: John Wiley and Sons, 1993); Jerome Loving, *The Last Titan: A Life of Theodore Dreiser* (Berkeley: University of California Press, 2005); and Ellen

Moers, *Two Dreisers* (New York: Viking Press, 1969). Walter Benn Michaels, *The Gold Standard and the Logic of Naturalism: American Literature at the Turn of the Century* (Berkeley: University of California Press, 1987), is a particularly provocative interpretation of naturalism. On Gertrude Stein, see James R. Mellow, *Charmed Circle: Gertrude Stein and Company* (New York: Avon, 1975), and Steven Meyer, *Irresistible Dictation: Gertrude Stein and the Correlations of Writing and Science* (Stanford, CA: Stanford University Press, 2001). J. David Hoeveler, *The New Humanism: A Critique of Modern America, 1900–1940* (Charlottesville: University Press of Virginia, 1977), and Milton Hindus, *Irving Babbitt, Literature and the Democratic Culture* (New Brunswick, NJ: Transaction Books) address the efforts of the New Humanists to sustain the constant division in humans between animality and spirituality against what they saw as a flood of multiplicity.

Modern painting and sculpture gets its due from Matthew Baigell, *A Concise History of American Painting and Sculpture* (Boulder, CO: Westview, 1996), Richard Brettell, *Modern Art, 1851–1929: Capitalism and Representation* (Oxford: Oxford University Press, 1999); Lloyd Goodrich, *Pioneers of Modern Art in America: The Decade of the Armory Show* (New York: Frederick A. Praeger, 1963); and Robert Hughes, *The Shock of the New* (New York: Alfred A. Knopf, 1991), and *American Visions: The Epic History of Art in America* (New York: Alfred A. Knopf, 1997). Special investigations include Milton Brown, *The Story of the Armory Show* (New York: Abbeville Press, 1988); Rebecca Zurier, *Picturing the City: Urban Vision and the Ashcan School* (Berkeley: University of California Press, 2006); Richard Whelan, *Alfred Stieglitz: A Biography* (Boston, MA: Little, Brown, 1995).

Among the valuable discussions of the conceptions of the self in the early twentieth century are Mitchell Aboulafia, *The Mediating Self: Mead, Sartre, and Self-Determination* (New Haven, CT: Yale University Press, 1986); the essays in David Bakhurst and Christine Sypnowich, eds., *The Social Self* (London: Sage, 1995); Roy F. Baumeister, "How the Self Became a Problem: A Psychological Review of Historical Research," *Journal of Personality and Social Psychology* 52 (January 1987): 163–76; Ian Burkitt, *Social Selves: Theories of the Social Formation of Personality* (London: Sage, 1991); Philip Cushman, *Constructing the Self, Constructing America* (New York: Addison-Wesley, 1995); John P. Hewitt, *Dilemmas of the American Self* (Philadelphia: Temple University Press, 1989); John O'Donnell, *The Origins of Behaviorism: American Psychology, 1870–1920* (New York: New York University Press, 1985); and Dorothy Ross, *G. Stanley Hall: The Psychologist as Prophet* (Chicago: University of Chicago Press, 1972). Jeffrey Sklansky, *The Soul's Economy: Market Society and Selfhood in American Thought, 1829–1920* (Chapel Hill: University of North Carolina Press, 2002), is a provocative challenge to social psychology and its implications.

Depth psychology in the United States is the subject of John Burnham, *Paths into American Culture: Psychology, Medicine, and Morals* (Philadelphia: Temple University Press, 1988); Eric Caplan, *Mind Games: American Culture and the Birth of Psychotherapy* (Berkeley: University of California Press, 1998); Nathan G. Hale, *The Beginnings of Psychoanalysis in the United States, 1876–1917* (New York: Oxford University Press, 1971), and *The Rise and Crisis of Psychoanalysis in United States: Freud and the Americans, 1917–1985* (New York: Oxford University Press, 1995); Saul Rosenzweig, *Freud, Jung, and Hall the King-maker: The Historic Expedition to America (1909), with G. Stanley Hall as Host and William James as Guest* (St. Louis, MO: Rana House, 1992); and Eli Zaretsky, *Secrets of the Soul: A Social and Cultural History of Psychoanalysis* (New York: Alfred A. Knopf, 2004). Jung's place is not as extensively studied as Freud's, but Eugene Taylor, "Jung before Freud, Not Freud before Jung: The Reception of Jung's Work in American Psychoanalytic Circles between 1904 and 1909," *Journal of Analytical Psychology* 43 (January 1998): 97–114, gives helpful clues.

Nancy Cott, *The Grounding of Modern Feminism* (New Haven, CT: Yale University Press, 1987), is indispensable to an understanding of the movement in the early twentieth century. Studies of the conceptualization of gender are Rosalind Rosenberg, *Beyond Separate Spheres: Intellectual Roots of Modern Feminism* (New Haven, CT: Yale University Press, 1982), and Cynthia Eagle Russett, *Sexual Science: The Victorian Construction of Womanhood* (Cambridge, MA: Harvard University Press, 1989). James Livingston places feminism at the heart of modern reconstruction of personality in *Pragmatism, Feminism, and Democracy: Rethinking the Politics of American History* (New York: Routledge, 2001). Among the highlights in the literature on early-twentieth-century gender relations are Martha Banta, *Imaging American Women: Idea and Ideals in Cultural History* (New York: Columbia University Press, 1987), and Gail Bederman, *Manliness & Civilization: A Cultural History of Gender and Race in the United States, 1880–1917* (Chicago: University of Chicago Press, 1996). Ellen F. Fitzpatrick, *Endless Crusade: Women Social Scientists and Progressive Reform* (New York: Oxford University Press, 1990), David M Kennedy, *Birth Control in America; the Career of Margaret Sanger* (New Haven, CT: Yale University Press, 1970), and Beryl Satter, *Each Mind a Kingdom: American Women, Sexual Purity, and the New Thought Movement, 1875–1920* (Berkeley: University of California Press, 1999), are just a few of the perceptive works on the multiplicity of women's activities in the first decade of the twentieth century.

Social science has attracted a number of first-rate scholars. Dorothy Ross, *The Origins of American Social Science* (New York: Cambridge University Press, 1991), is the standard survey. Essays in her edited volume, *Modernist Impulses in the Human Sciences, 1870–1930* (Baltimore: Johns Hopkins University Press, 1994) and Donald Levine, *Visions of the Sociological Tradition* (Chicago: University of Chicago Press), provide international context. Particularly valuable investigations include Robert Bannister, *Sociology and Scientism: The American Quest for Objectivity, 1880–1940* (Chapel Hill: University of North Carolina Press, 1987); Mary Jo Deegan, *Jane Addams and the Men of the Chicago School, 1892–1918* (New Brunswick, NJ: Transaction Books, 1986); William Fine, *Progressive Evolutionism and American Sociology, 1890–1920* (Ann Arbor: University of Michigan Research Press, 1976); Mary O. Furner, *Advocacy and Objectivity: A Crisis in the Professionalization of American Social Science, 1865–1905* (Lexington: University Press of Kentucky, 1975); Charles Page, *Class and American Sociology from Ward to Ross* (New York: Dial Press, 1940); Jean B. Quandt, *From the Small Town to the Great Community: The Social Thought of Progressive Intellectuals* (New Brunswick, NJ: Rutgers University Press, 1970); Dennis Smith, *The Chicago School: A Liberal Critique of Capitalism* (New York: St. Martin's, 1988); Mark Smith, *Social Science in the Crucible: The American Debate over Objectivity and Purpose, 1918–1941* (Durham, NC: Duke University Press, 1994); and R. Jackson Wilson, *In Quest of Community: Social Philosophy in the United States, 1860–1920* (New York: John Wiley, 1968). Paul Kress, *Social Science and the Idea of Process: The Ambiguous Legacy of Arthur F. Bentley* (Urbana: University of Illinois Press, 1970), is a worthwhile examination of a major concept of a thinker often unacknowledged in traditional accounts.

Herbert Blumer, ed., *An Appraisal of Thomas and Znaniecki's* The Polish Peasant in Europe and America (New York: Social Science Research Council, 1939) and Eli Zaretsky, "Editor's Introduction," W. I. Thomas and Florian Znaniecki, *The Polish Peasant in Europe and America* (Urbana: University of Illinois Press, 1984), take measure of the most intellectually important case study of social life of the period.

Those interested in political economy will profit from Joseph Dorfman, *Thorstein Veblen and His America* (New York: Viking, 1934); James Livingston, "The Social Analysis of Economic History and Theory: Conjectures on Late Nineteenth-Century American Development," *American Historical Review* 92, no. 1 (1987): 69–95; Karen McCally, "'A Bundle of Rights': The Commons School and American Social Policy, 1905–1945" (PhD diss., University of Rochester, 2001); and John Wenzler, "Transcendental Economics: The Quest to Harmonize Economic and Moral Law in Nineteenth-Century American Social Thought" (PhD diss., University of Rochester, 1998).

Race in American thought is summarized in Lee D. Baker, *From Savage to Negro: Anthropology and the Construction of Race, 1896–1954* (Berkeley and Los Angeles: University of California Press, 1998); Franz Boas, *Race and Democratic Society* (New York: J. J. Augustin, 1945); George M. Fredrickson, *The Black Image in the White Mind: The Debate on Afro-American Character and Destiny, 1817–1914* (New York: Harper and Row, 1971); Thomas F. Gossett, *Race: The History of an Idea in America* (New York: Oxford University Press, 1997); Matthew Pratt Guterl, *The Color of Race in America, 1900–1940* (Cambridge, MA: Harvard University Press, 2001); and Matthew Frye Jacobson, *Whiteness of a Different Color: European Immigrants and the Alchemy of Race* (Cambridge, MA: Harvard University Press, 1998). Ivan Hannaford, *Race: The History of an Idea in the West* (Baltimore: Johns Hopkins University Press, 1996), takes a broad perspective and is especially valuable. George W. Stocking, *Race, Culture, and Evolution: Essays in the History of Anthropology* (New York: Free Press, 1968), lays out the contributions of Franz Boas, as do Regna Darnell, *And Along Came Boas: Continuity and Revolution in Americanist Anthropology* (Amsterdam: John Benjamins, 1998); Michael A. Elliott, *The Culture Concept: Writing and Difference in the Age of Realism*, Critical American Studies Series (Minneapolis: University of Minnesota Press, 2002); Susan Hegeman, *Patterns for America: Modernism and the Concept of Culture* (Princeton, NJ: Princeton University Press, 1999), 35–57; and Vernon J. Williams Jr., *Rethinking Race: Franz Boas and His Contemporaries* (Lexington: University Press of Kentucky, 1996). Adam Kuper, *Culture: The Anthropologists' Account* (Cambridge, MA: Harvard University Press, 1999) and Walter Benn Michaels, *Our America: Nativism, Modernism, and Pluralism* (Durham, NC: Duke University Press, 1995), point to the limitations of the culture concept.

W. E. B. Du Bois is the subject of David Levering Lewis, *W. E. B. Du Bois: Biography of a Race, 1868–1919* (New York: Henry Holt, 1993) and Arnold Rampersand, *The Art and Imagination of W. E. B. Du Bois* (New York: Schocken, 1990). Wilson Jeremiah Moses, *The Golden Age of Black Nationalism, 1850–1925* (New York and London: Oxford University Press, 1988), and Kwame Anthony Appiah, *In My Father's House: Africa in the Philosophy of Culture* (New York and London: Oxford University Press, 1993), 28–46 criticize Du Bois's views as confused; Thomas Holt dissents in his essay "W. E. B. DuBois's Archaeology of Race: Rereading 'The Conservation of Races,'" in Michael B. Katz and Thomas J. Sugrue, eds., *W. E. B. DuBois, Race, and the City: "The Philadelphia Negro" and Its Legacy* (Philadelphia: University of Pennsylvania Press, 1998), 61–76.

The practice of history in the early twentieth century is the focus of Ellen Fitzpatrick, *History's Memory: Writing America's Past, 1880–1980* (Cambridge, MA: Harvard University Press, 2002); John Higham, *History: Professional Scholarship in America* (Baltimore: Johns Hopkins University Press, 1989); and Ellen Nore, *Charles A. Beard: An Intellectual Biography* (Carbondale: Southern Illinois University Press, 1983). Peter Novick, *That Noble Dream: The Objectivity Question and the American Historical Profession* (Cambridge and New York: Cambridge University Press, 1988), is especially acute on the contributions of Charles Beard and Carl Becker.

In addition to works cited above, that endlessly debated, never-settled phenomenon, progressivism, may be approached from Nancy Cohen, *The Reconstruction of American Liberalism, 1865–1914* (Chapel Hill: University of North Carolina Press, 2002); Eldon Eisenach, *The Lost Promise of Progressivism* (Lawrence: University Press of Kansas, 1994); Leon Fink, *Progressive Intellectuals and the Dilemmas of Democratic Commitment* (Cambridge, MA: Harvard University Press, 1997); Charles Forcey, *The Crossroads of Liberalism: Croly, Weyl, Lippmann, and the Progressive Era, 1900–1925* (New York: Oxford University Press, 1961); Barbara Fried, *The Progressive Assault on Laissez-Faire: Robert Hale and the First Law and Economics Movement* (Cambridge, MA: Harvard University Press, 1998); Richard Hofstadter, *The Age of Reform from Bryan to F.D.R.* (New York: Vintage Books, 1962); Robert D. Johnston, *The Radical Middle Class: Populist Democracy and the Question of Capitalism in Progressivism Era Portland* (Princeton, NJ: Princeton University Press, 2003); Elizabeth Sanders, *Roots of Reform: Farmers, Workers, and the American State, 187–1917* (Chicago: University of Chicago Press, 1999); and Martin Sklar, *The Corporate Reconstruction of American Capitalism: The Market, the Law, and Politics* (New York: Cambridge University Press, 1988). For the working-class component, see Shelton Stromquist, *Reinventing "The People": The Progressive Movement, the Class Problem, and the Origins of Modern Liberalism* (Urbana: University of Illinois Press, 2006). Two superb efforts to place progressivism in international context are Daniel T. Rodgers, *Atlantic Crossings: Social Politics in a Progressive Age* (Cambridge, MA: Belknap Press of Harvard University Press, 1998), and Marc Stears, *Progressives, Pluralists, and the Problems of the State: Ideologies of Reform in the United States and Britain, 1909–1926* (Oxford: Oxford University Press, 2002). Kevin Mattson is particularly sharp on new notions of democracy: Kevin Mattson, *Creating a Democratic Public: The Struggle for Urban Participatory Democracy during the Progressive Era* (University Park: Pennsylvania State University Press, 1998).

David Kennedy, *Over Here: The First World War and American Society* (New York: Oxford University Press, 1980), is the definitive work on the subject. Nancy K. Bristow brings to light the efforts at moral and sexual reform during the war in *Making Men Moral: Social Engineering during the Great War* (New York: New York University Press, 1996). Carol S. Gruber handles the effect of the war on the Academy in *Mars and Minerva: World War I and the Uses of the Higher Learning in America* (Baton Rouge: Louisiana State University Press, 1975). C. Roland Marchand, *The American Peace Movement and Social Reform, 1898–1918* (Princeton, NJ: Princeton University Press, 1972), remains the authoritative source on pacifism and peace movements before the war. See also Robert David Johnson, *The Peace Progressives and American Foreign Relations* (Cambridge, MA: Harvard University Press, 1995). Christopher Capozzola, "Thorstein Veblen and the Politics of War, 1914–1920," *International Journal of Politics, Culture and Society* 13, no. 2 (1999): 255–72, recounts a complicated position toward the war. His "The Only Badge Needed Is Your Patriotic Fervor: Vigilance, Coercion, and the Law in World War I America," *Journal of American History*, March 2002, 1358–64, is a fresh look at the arguments for regulation and coercion of the population during the war. Historians have generally talked about the effects of the war on thought as fostering disillusionment. Stuart I. Rochester, *American Liberal Disillusionment in the Wake of World War I* (University Park: Pennsylvania State University Press, 1976), and Stanley Coben, *Rebellion against Victorianism: The Impetus for Cultural Change in 1920s America* (New York: Oxford University Press, 1991), are valuable examples of such interpretations. No similar work has been undertaken for high culture, social thought, or the social sciences.

Clive Bush, *Halfway to Revolution: Investigation and Crisis in the Work of Henry Adams, William James and Gertrude Stein* (New Haven, CT: Yale University Press, 1991), 1; Olaf Hansen, *Aesthetic Individualism and Practical Intellect: American Allegory in Emerson, Thoreau, Adams, and James* (Princeton, NJ: Princeton University Press, 1990); and R. P Blackmur, *Henry Adams* (New York: Harcourt Brace Jovanovich, 1980), explore Adams's attitudes toward multiplicity.

Index

Morton, Jelly Roll, 75
movies, 86, 91; aesthetic potential of, 96; anarchy in, 93; Charlie Chaplin and, 93–95; comedies, 93; criticisms of, 92–93; Griffith, D.W. and, 96, 99; popularity of, 92; review boards and, 253–254; working-class and, 92–94; *See also* cinema
Mrs. Warren's Profession (Shaw), 110
Musketeers of Pig Alley, The, (Griffith), 96
multiplicity, 3, 11, 217, 239n; Henry Adams and, 4, 265; aesthetic, 79; Sherwood Anderson and, 259–60; anthropology and, 178; the arts and, 28, 32–33 108–109, 114, 118–119; as attempt to account for contingency, 7; beauty and, 74, 79, 119; Arthur Bentley and, 195–196; Franz Boas and, 178–179; Randolph Bourne and, 184–185, 233, 238, 242–243; Catholicism and, 53, 56; cinema and, 30, 32; context of, 9; critics of, 64, 225, 243, *See also* cultural conservatives; culture and, 186, 190, 226–227; cultural crisis, and, 11; defined 3–4, 6, 11; democracy and, 215; development of, 9; John Dewey and, 42–44, 62–64, 233, 265; difference from postmodernism, 10; Theodore Dreiser and, 249; ethnicity and, 185, 253; facets of, 6; feminists and, 156, 162; Sigmund Freud and, 151, 264; Germany and, 229; history and, 199; Horace Kallen and, 184; Walter Lippmann and, 6; legacies of, 266; literature and, 259–60; George Herbert Mead and, 142, 236; morality and, 59, 61–64, 215, 248 music and 91; Friedrich Nietzsche and, 112; Charles S. Peirce and, 39; physics and, 25–27; politics and, 196, 198; post-war period and, 245,

257, 261, 265; pragmatism and, 47, 241; progressivism and, 7, 209–210, 212, 216; precursors of, 7; in public discourse, 48; race and, 180, 186, 246, 253; religion and, 49–50, 53, 54n, 55–56, 255; sexuality and, 150, 249; social sciences and, 172–173, 178, 261; social self and, 132, 137, 141, 143–144, 147, 153–154, 156, 160, 163; social thought and, 191; sociology and, 38; of time and space, 28, 30, 33, 35; truth and, 10, 36, 38, 40–41, 47; Thorstein Veblen and, 190; World War I and, 225–227, 233–234, 248, 250
Mundelein, Cardinal George, 55
Murray, Albert, 102
music; African-American, 88; blues, 101–102; of Charles Ives, 91; ragtime, 88, 89n, 90, 101; Tin Pan Alley, 88
Mutt and Jeff (Fisher), 29
Mutual Film Corp. v. Industrial Commission of Ohio, 253

Nation, The, 3, 11, 84, 249, 263; on physics, 27
National Academy of Design, 114
National Association for the Advancement of Colored People, 99, 110, 186, 187n
National Board of Review, 99
National Civil Liberties Bureau, 251
National Trade Union League of America, 238
Nazism, 266
Nearing, Scott, 250
"Negro, The," (Du Bois), 189
neoscholasticism, 56
Nethersole, Olga, 110
neurosis, 147, 151–152
neutrality, 228
New Criticism (Spingarn), 110

pluralism, 6, 10, 173, 194, 265;
Randolph Bourne on, 184; Horace
Kallen on, 184; immigrants and, 183;
legacies of, 266; race and, 177;
World War I and, 226, 233, 234,
238. *See also* multiplicity
Poe, Edgar Allan, 83
Poincare, Henri, 26–27
*Polish Peasant in Europe and America,
The,* (Thomas and Znaniecki),
191–195
political economy, 171, 201, 203, 213
Pope Leo, 55
populism, 212
Porter, Edward, 31
positivism, 37
post-impressionism, 33, 100, 109, 116;
Armory Show and, 118; criticism of,
118; cubism and, 116; fauvism and,
116
post-war period; culture and, 253, 263;
economics, 263; literature and,
257–260; morality and, 253;
multiplicity in 253–266; immigrants
and, 253, 262; pessimism and, 257;
psychology and, 264–265; religion,
255–257; social sciences and,
260–263
Pound, Ezra, 75, 227
Prager, Robert, 245–246
pragmatism, 2, 8, 11, 239n, 240; Jane
Addams and, 49, 232; appeal of, 48;
controversy surrounding, 46;
correspondence theory and, 41;
criticisms of, 45–46, 48; definition
of, 38; of John Dewey, 38, 41–49,
62–64; influence of, 49; of William
James, 39–40; of George Herbert
Mead, 140–148, 231–232; morality
and, 63; multiplicity and, 47, 63,
241; of Charles S. Peirce, 39;
progressivism and, 49; psychology
and, 43; Josiah Royce's reaction to,

44; on truth, 41, 43; World War I
and, 48, 64, 226, 229, 231–232, 234,
238, 241
Pragmatism (James), 40
Pratt, James, 36; criticisms of
pragmatism, 45; and verification
problem, 46
preparedness programs, 230, 248
Presbyterian Review, 52
Prince, Morton, 147
Princeton University, 19
Principles of Psychology (James), 132
*Process of Government: A Study of Social
Pressures* (Bentley), 195–198
progress 2, 3, 9, 55–57, 62, 114, 116,
151, 153, 188
Progressive Farmers and Householders'
Union of America, 247
Progressive Party, 208, 244
progressives. *See* progressivism
progressivism, 7, *210*; characteristics of,
208; democracy and, 215–216;
government ownership and, 212;
historiography of, 208–209; on labor,
214; motives of progressives, 209;
multiplicity and, 209, 211; populist
influence on, 212; Progressive Party
and, 208; property rights and, 212,
214; reform and, 208, 245; social
property and, 212; socialism and,
209–10; Walter Weyl and, 211;
Wilsonian, 252; World War I and,
234, 243
prohibition, 208, 245
proletarianization, 129
property rights; John Commons on,
214; corporate property and, 212,
214; Walter Lippmann on, 211;
redefinition of, 211; social property
and, 212, 213; Walter Weyl on, 211
Protestantism; heresy trials and, 52;
liberal, 51, 255–256. *See also* religion
Provincetown Players, 75, 105

~

About the Author

Daniel H. Borus is associate professor of history at the University of Rochester. He is the author of *Writing Realism: Howells, James, and Norris in the Mass Market* and the editor of *These United States: Portraits of America in the 1920s* and *Looking Backward*.